GENTLEMEN'S ALLIANCE CROSS

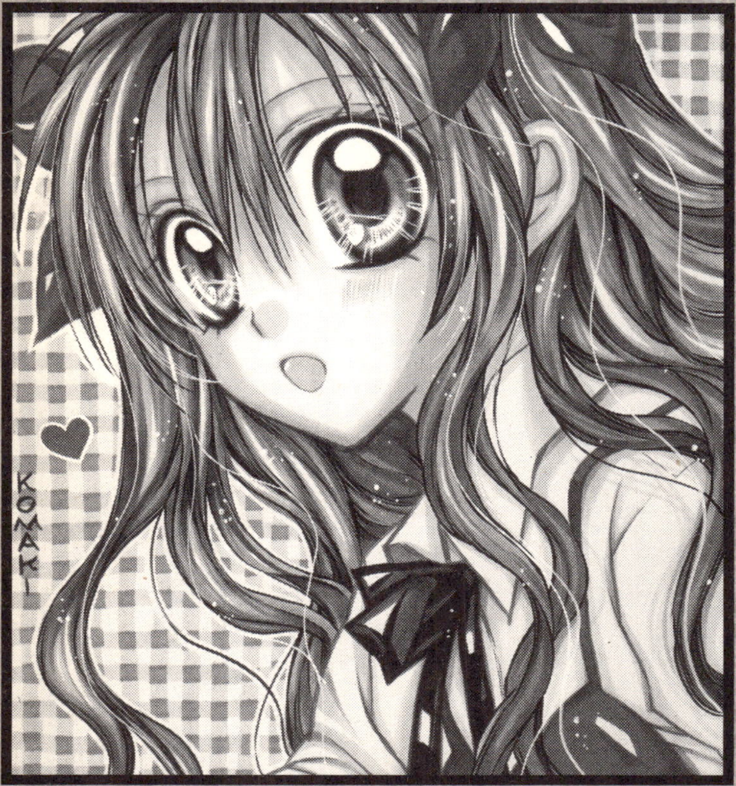
KOMAKI

Story & Art by
Arina Tanemura

Vol. 8

CONTENTS

Chapter 33: On a Night Like This, I Think of You, Closer than Being Next to Me 3

Chapter 34: A Sorrowful Memory 51

Chapter 35: The Dancer and the Golden Etude 85

Bonus Stories:
The Love Labyrinth 119
Together with Okorimakuri-kun! 1 136
Together with Okorimakuri-kun! 2 142
Shojo Eve: Eve's Applework 24 Hours 147

Notes on the Text 181

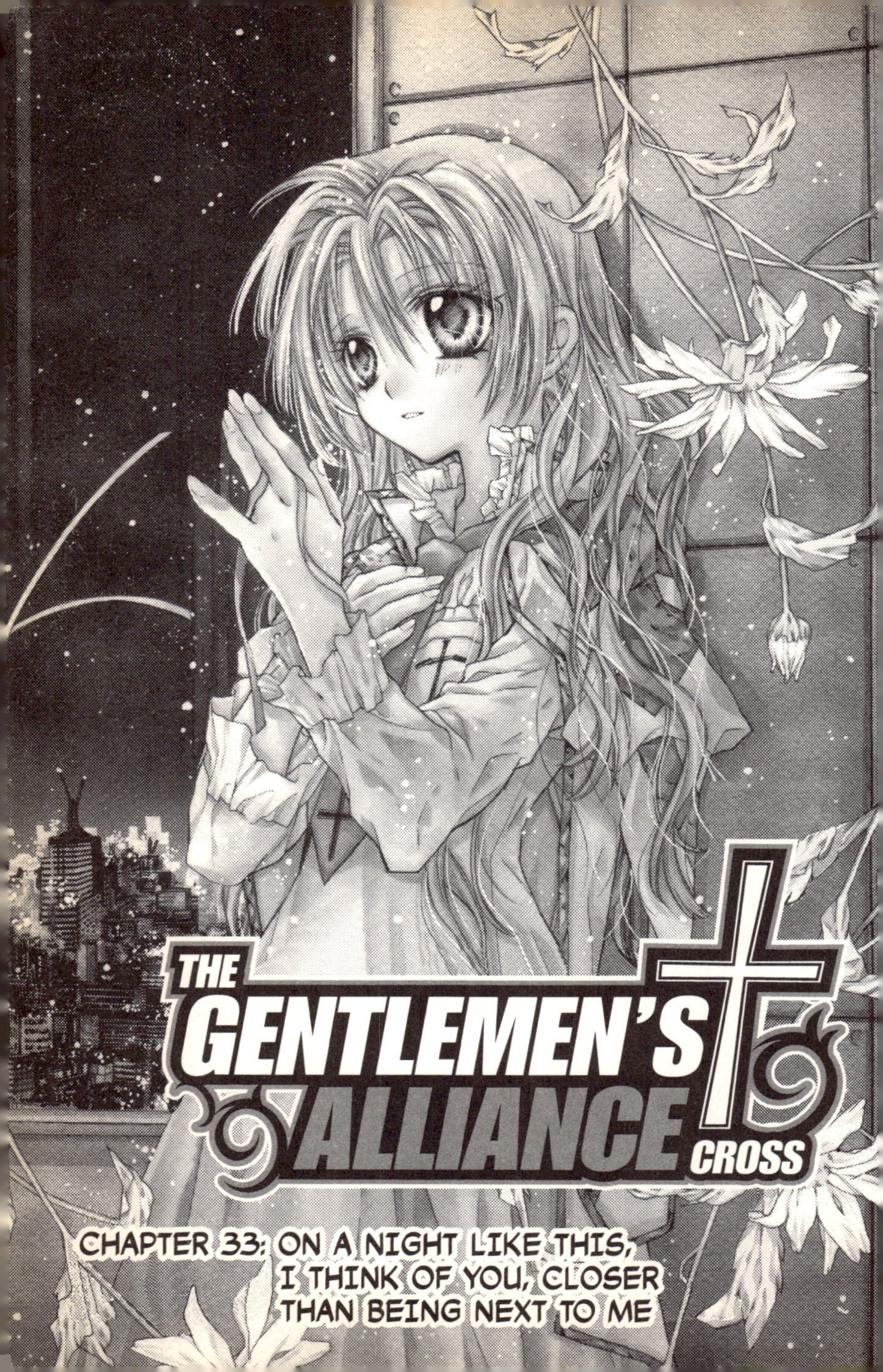
THE GENTLEMEN'S ALLIANCE CROSS
CHAPTER 33: ON A NIGHT LIKE THIS, I THINK OF YOU, CLOSER THAN BEING NEXT TO ME

CHARACTER INTRODUCTIONS

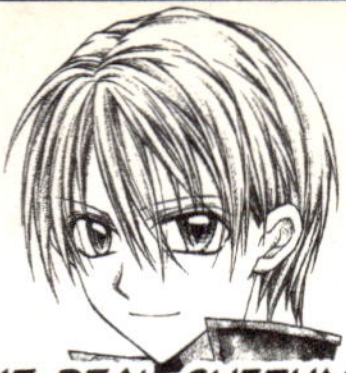

(Younger Twin)

THE REAL SHIZUMASA

An illness prevents him from attending school. He helped Haine mend her yanki ways.

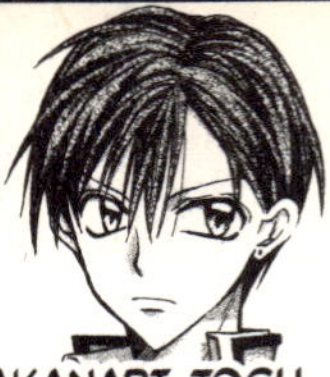

(Elder Twin)

TAKANARI TOGU

Student Council President

The double. Referred to as "the Emperor" and is the highest authority in school. Wrote Haine's favorite picture book.

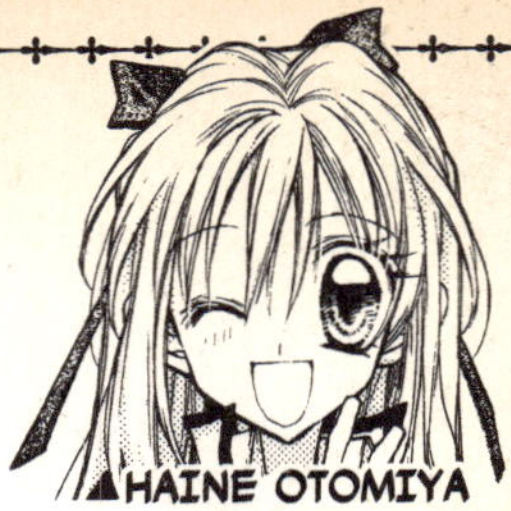

HAINE OTOMIYA

Bodyguard & General Affairs

A cheerful girl who is in love with Shizumasa-sama. Former juvenile delinquent. Adopted into the Otomiya family in fourth grade.

MAGURI TSUJIMIYA

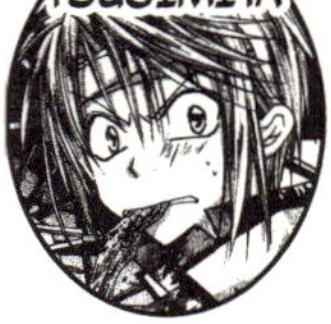

Vice President

Childhood friends with Maora, and now they've become lovers.♥

MAORA

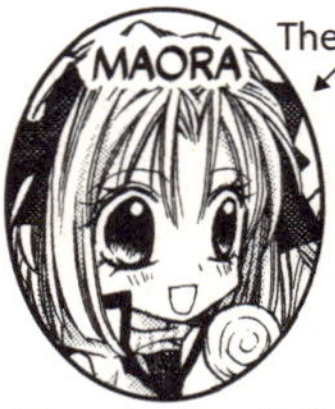

Planning Events & Accounting

Childhood friend of Maguri.

The Same Person!!

POSTMAN

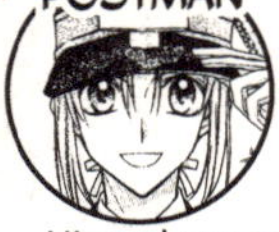

His real name is Ichinomiya Yoshitaka. A very cute boy!!

USHIO AMAMIYA

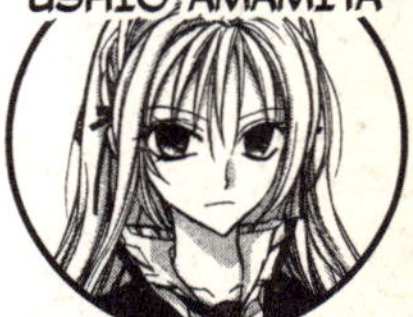

Clerk

Haine's friend. Haine is dearer to her than anyone.

THE GENTLEMEN'S ALLIANCE CROSS

Haine Otomiya is a former juvenile delinquent who attends Imperial Academy. One day, she is appointed the rank of "Platinum" as Emperor Shizumasa Togu's girlfriend. Now having found out that there are two Emperors, Haine's heart sways between Shizumasa and Takanari.

Haine and the student council members are now in their second year of high school, and they head out to the mountains for freshmen orientation. Haine ends up sharing a room with Takanari, and is shaken when Takanari tells her, "Tonight I'll make you mine." She tries to avoid him, but she can't help kissing him when he's asleep!

Haine pretends that she mistook him for Shizumasa, and the two end up in an awkward situation... But after Takanari comes to her rescue at the bottom of the cliff, Haine confesses that she loves him.

Meanwhile, Haine finds out that Ushio, whom she thought hated men, was fooling around with many boys at school. But Ushio wants to be the most important person to Haine. Haine returns the Emperor's ribbon—the sign she's broken up with him—and goes to Ushio...

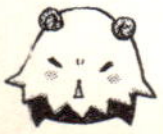

STORY THUS FAR

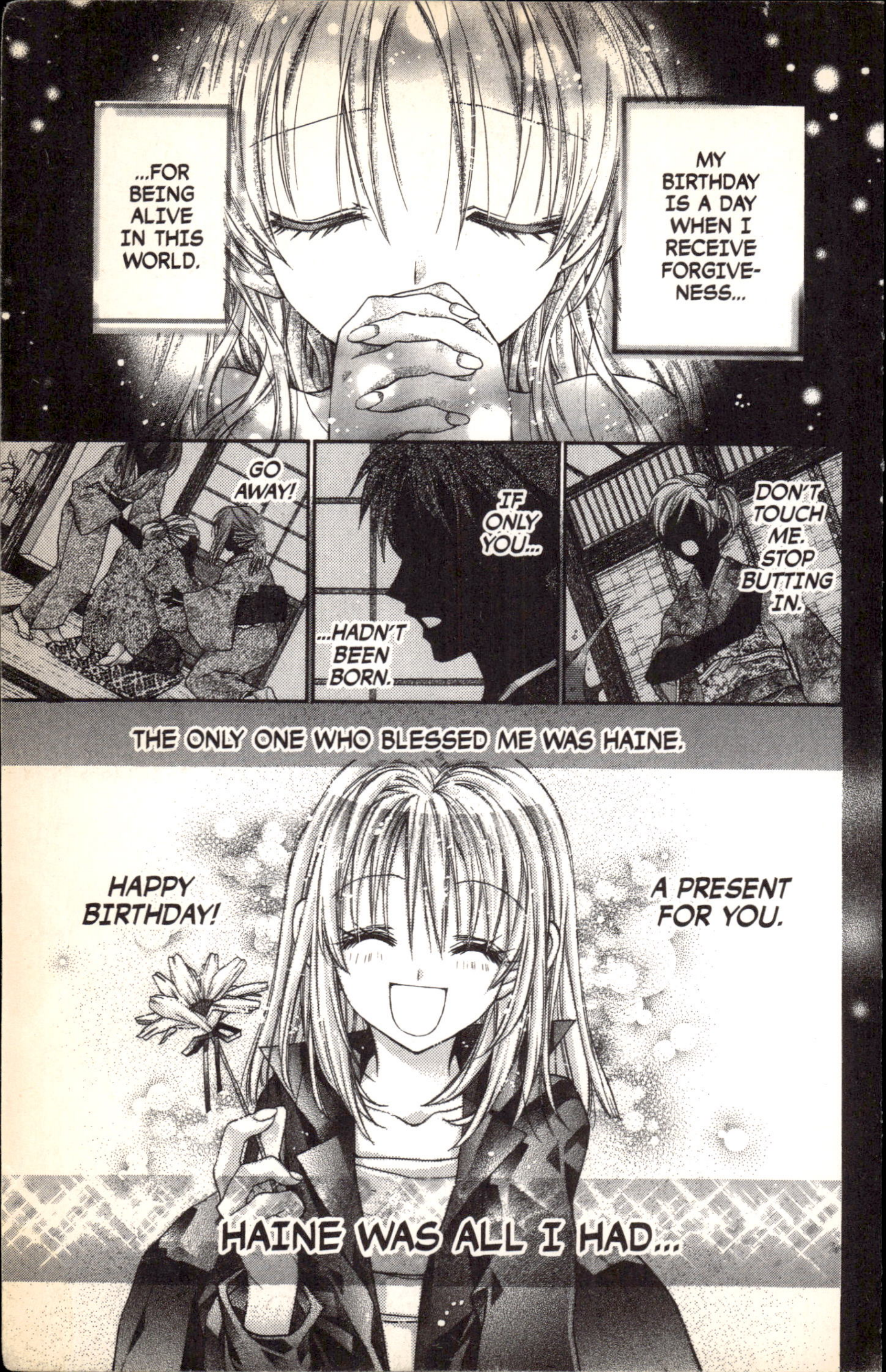
MY BIRTHDAY IS A DAY WHEN I RECEIVE FORGIVENESS...
...FOR BEING ALIVE IN THIS WORLD.
DON'T TOUCH ME. STOP BUTTING IN.
IF ONLY YOU...
...HADN'T BEEN BORN.
GO AWAY!
THE ONLY ONE WHO BLESSED ME WAS HAINE.
A PRESENT FOR YOU.
HAPPY BIRTHDAY!
HAINE WAS ALL I HAD...

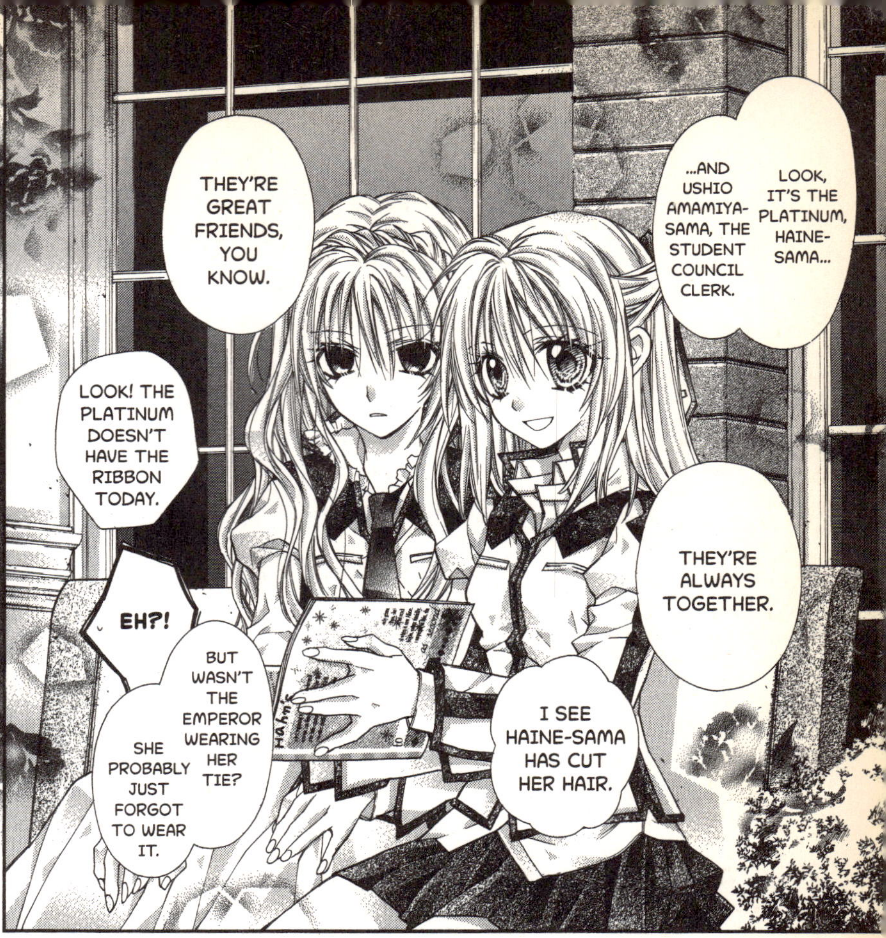
LOOK, IT'S THE PLATINUM, HAINE-SAMA...
...AND USHIO AMAMIYA-SAMA, THE STUDENT COUNCIL CLERK.
THEY'RE GREAT FRIENDS, YOU KNOW.
THEY'RE ALWAYS TOGETHER.
LOOK! THE PLATINUM DOESN'T HAVE THE RIBBON TODAY.
I SEE HAINE-SAMA HAS CUT HER HAIR.
EH?!
BUT WASN'T THE EMPEROR WEARING HER TIE?
SHE PROBABLY JUST FORGOT TO WEAR IT.

Chapter 33: On a Night Like This, I Think of You, Closer than Being Next to Me

Lead-in
I've always, always loved you...

☆ Spoilers. I'm giving away the story.

Ah, the chapter title page... (What about it?) I had planned to draw Haine and Ushio on all chapter title pages during the Ushio arc, but the illustration for this chapter is a little different. It's supposed to be an image of "Ushio by herself, but she's not lonely because she can feel Haine and Maora nearby." I really like how Ushio isn't wearing the school uniform. It's draped on top of her.

I had some trouble drawing the "forest"—Ushio's mental world. Ushio gives me the feeling that she's not even looking at the real Haine. Then I realized that the time inside Ushio had completely stopped. Well, she stopped it. I guess she doesn't want to grow up. And that's why I wrote "The Love Labyrinth" (which you'll find in this volume). Although it's over, I don't think she'll be able to change immediately. (It's Ushio, after all.) She'll start moving ahead slowly. By the way, I've never been popular with boys, but for some reason I'm really popular with girls, so I can understand how Haine feels a lot. You really need a lot of energy for friendship!

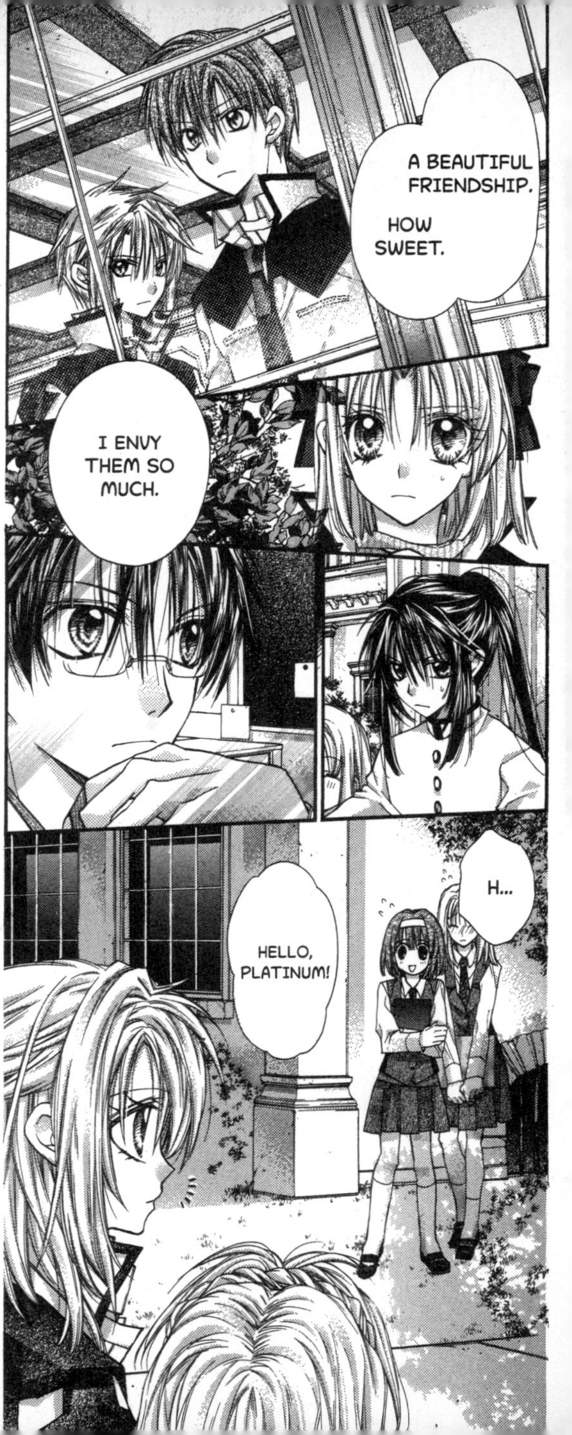
A BEAUTIFUL FRIENDSHIP.
HOW SWEET.
I ENVY THEM SO MUCH.
H...
HELLO, PLATINUM!

Hello ✿

Hello! I'm Arina Tanemura! I bring you *The Gentleman's Alliance †* volume 8 with Komaki-chan on the cover!

Of all the manga series I have created, the longest has been seven volumes, so "eight" is a very moving number for me. Wonderful!!

The series has just celebrated its third anniversary in the magazine, and it's still continuing to break the record of my longest running series!!

Well then, here begins the end of the Ushio arc and the start of the Haine arc...♪

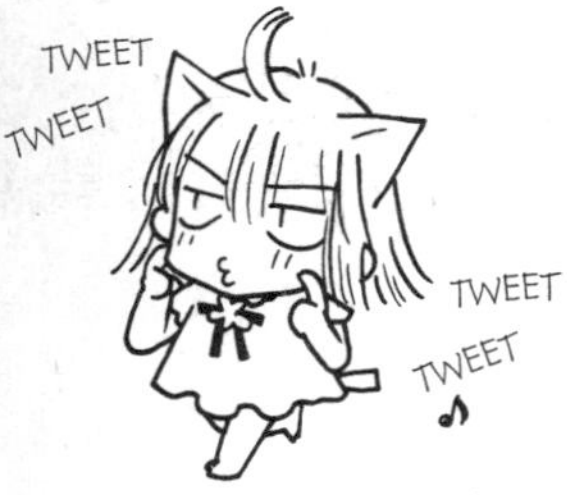
TWEET
TWEET
TWEET
TWEET ♪

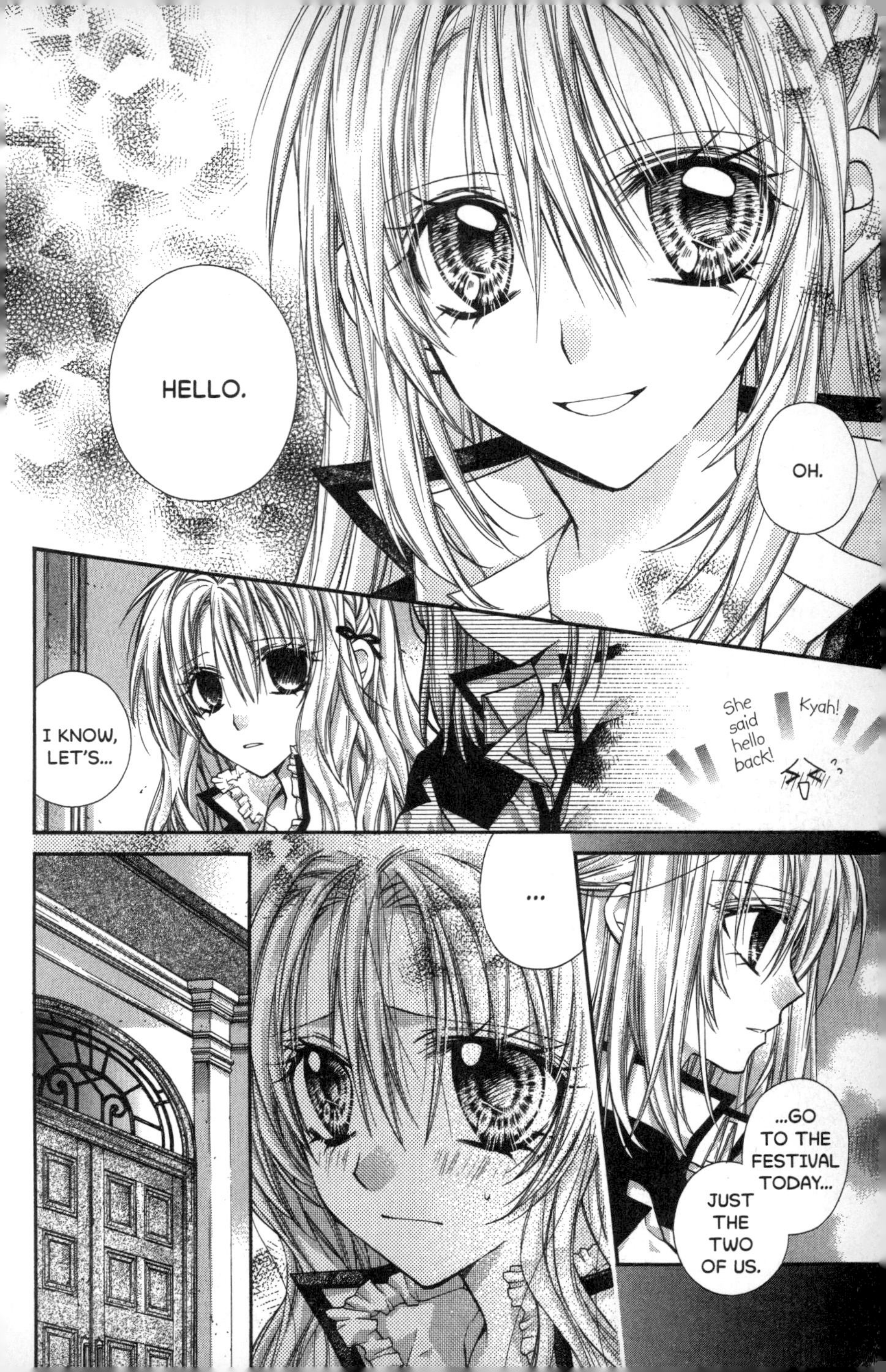
OH.
HELLO.
Kyah!
She said hello back!
I KNOW, LET'S...
...GO TO THE FESTIVAL TODAY...
JUST THE TWO OF US.
...

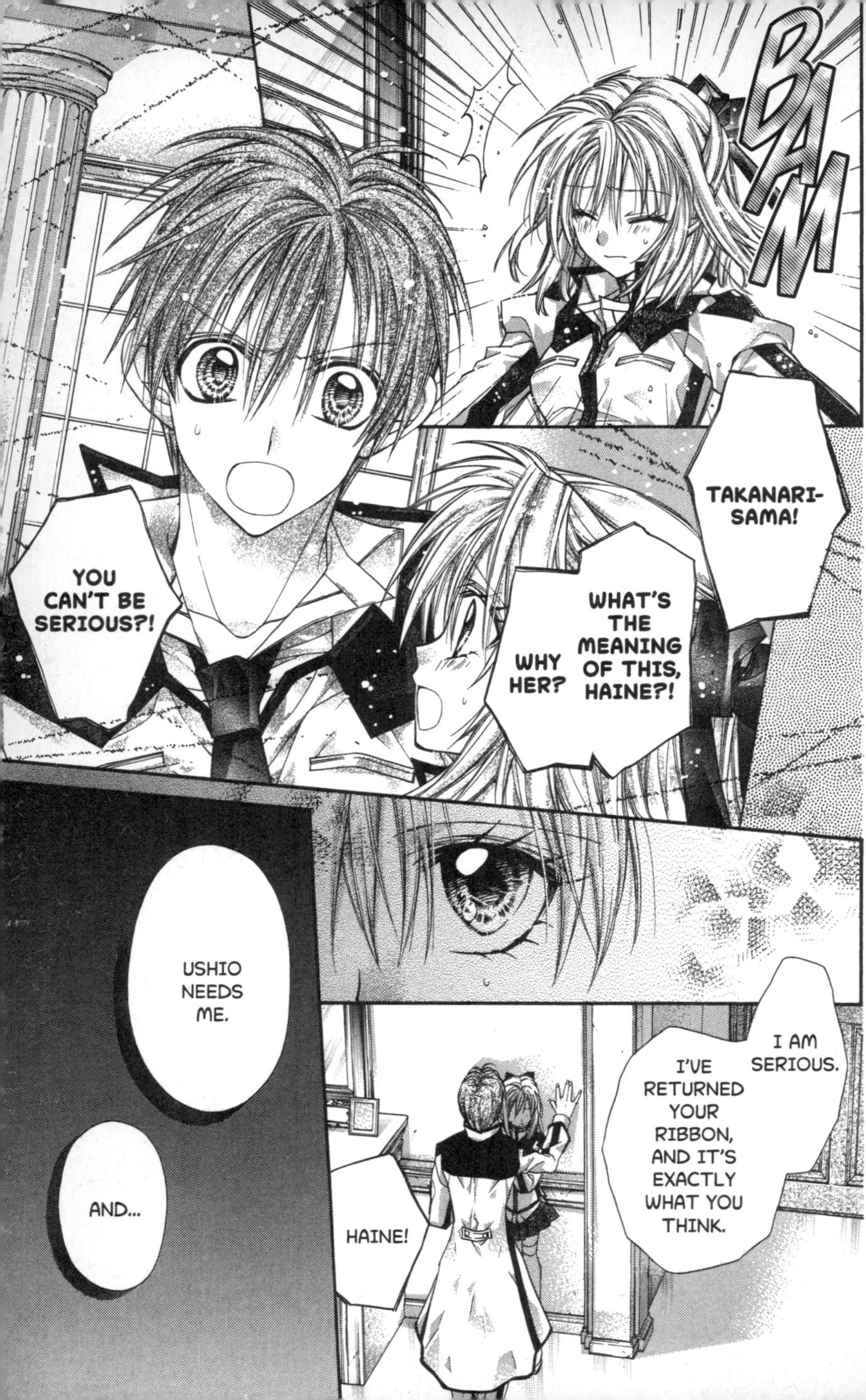
BAM
TAKANARI-SAMA!
WHAT'S THE MEANING OF THIS, HAINE?!
WHY HER?
YOU CAN'T BE SERIOUS?!
I AM SERIOUS.
I'VE RETURNED YOUR RIBBON, AND IT'S EXACTLY WHAT YOU THINK.
HAINE!
USHIO NEEDS ME.
AND...

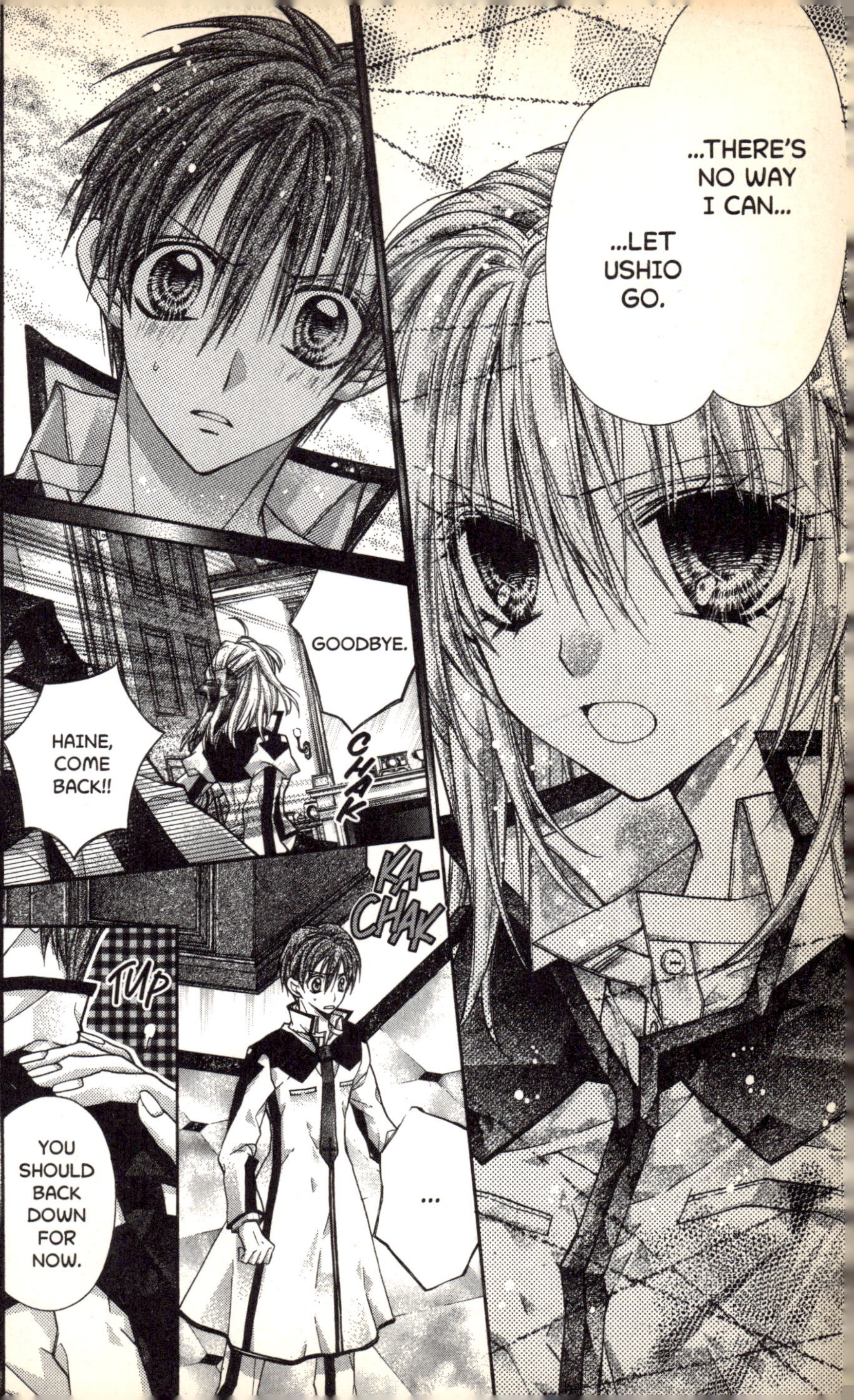
...THERE'S NO WAY I CAN...
...LET USHIO GO.
GOODBYE.
CHAK
HAINE, COME BACK!!
KA-CHAK
TUP
...
YOU SHOULD BACK DOWN FOR NOW.

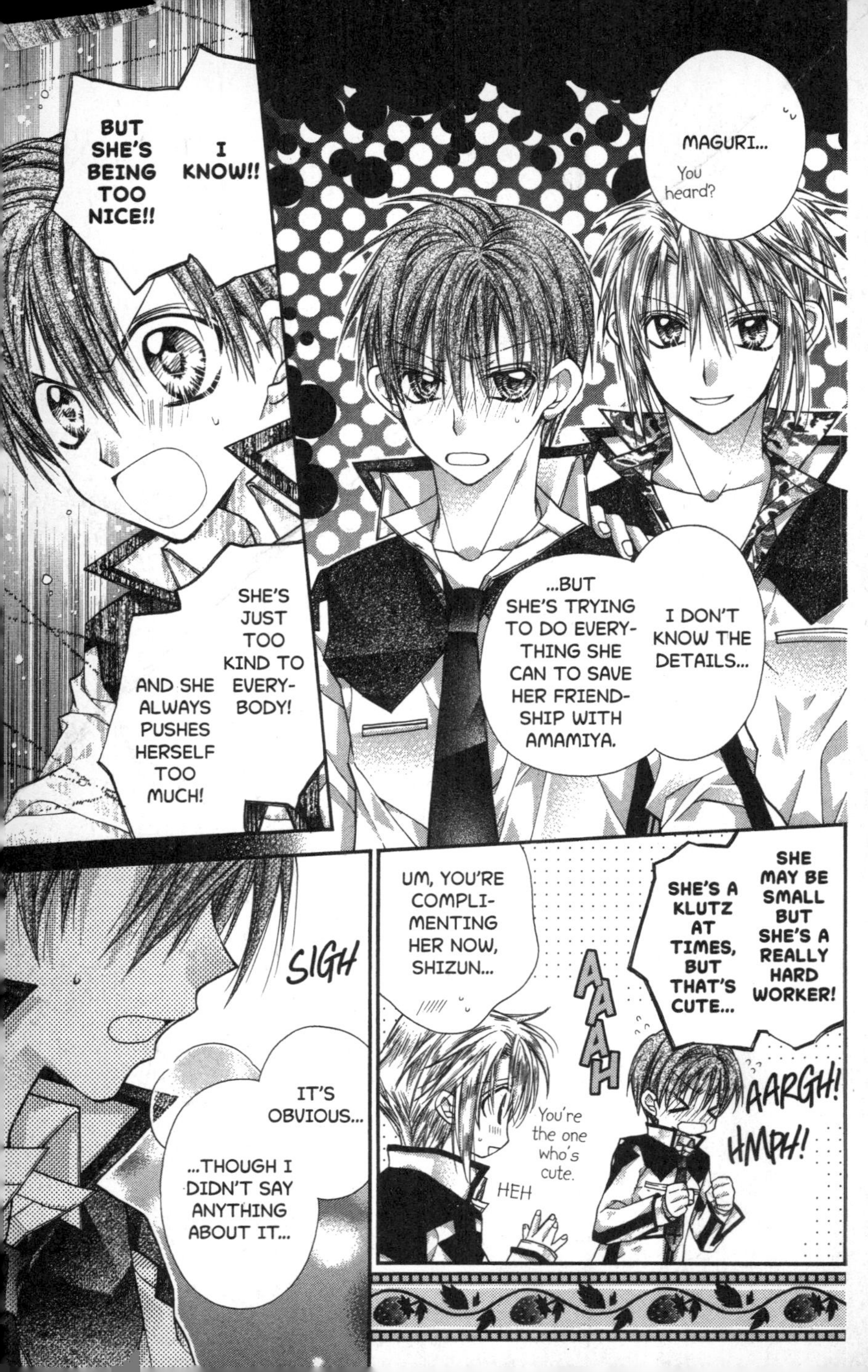
MAGURI... You heard?
I DON'T KNOW THE DETAILS...
...BUT SHE'S TRYING TO DO EVERYTHING SHE CAN TO SAVE HER FRIENDSHIP WITH AMAMIYA.
I KNOW!!
BUT SHE'S BEING TOO NICE!!
SHE'S JUST TOO KIND TO EVERYBODY!
AND SHE ALWAYS PUSHES HERSELF TOO MUCH!
SHE MAY BE SMALL BUT SHE'S A REALLY HARD WORKER!
SHE'S A KLUTZ AT TIMES, BUT THAT'S CUTE...
UM, YOU'RE COMPLIMENTING HER NOW, SHIZUN...
AAAAH
AARGH!
HMPH!
You're the one who's cute.
HEH
SIGH
IT'S OBVIOUS...
...THOUGH I DIDN'T SAY ANYTHING ABOUT IT...

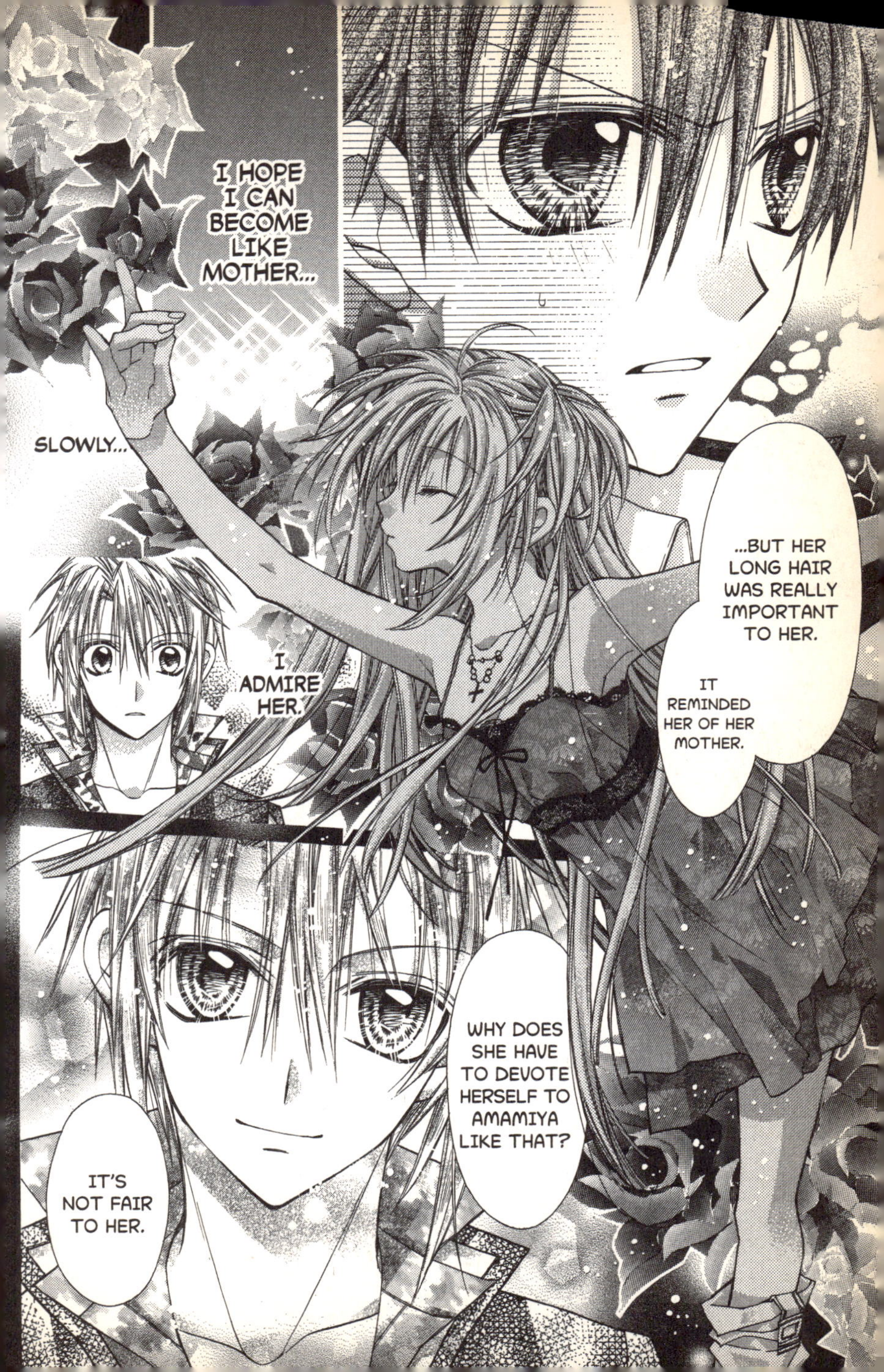
...BUT HER LONG HAIR WAS REALLY IMPORTANT TO HER.
IT REMINDED HER OF HER MOTHER.
I HOPE I CAN BECOME LIKE MOTHER...
SLOWLY...
I ADMIRE HER.
WHY DOES SHE HAVE TO DEVOTE HERSELF TO AMAMIYA LIKE THAT?
IT'S NOT FAIR TO HER.

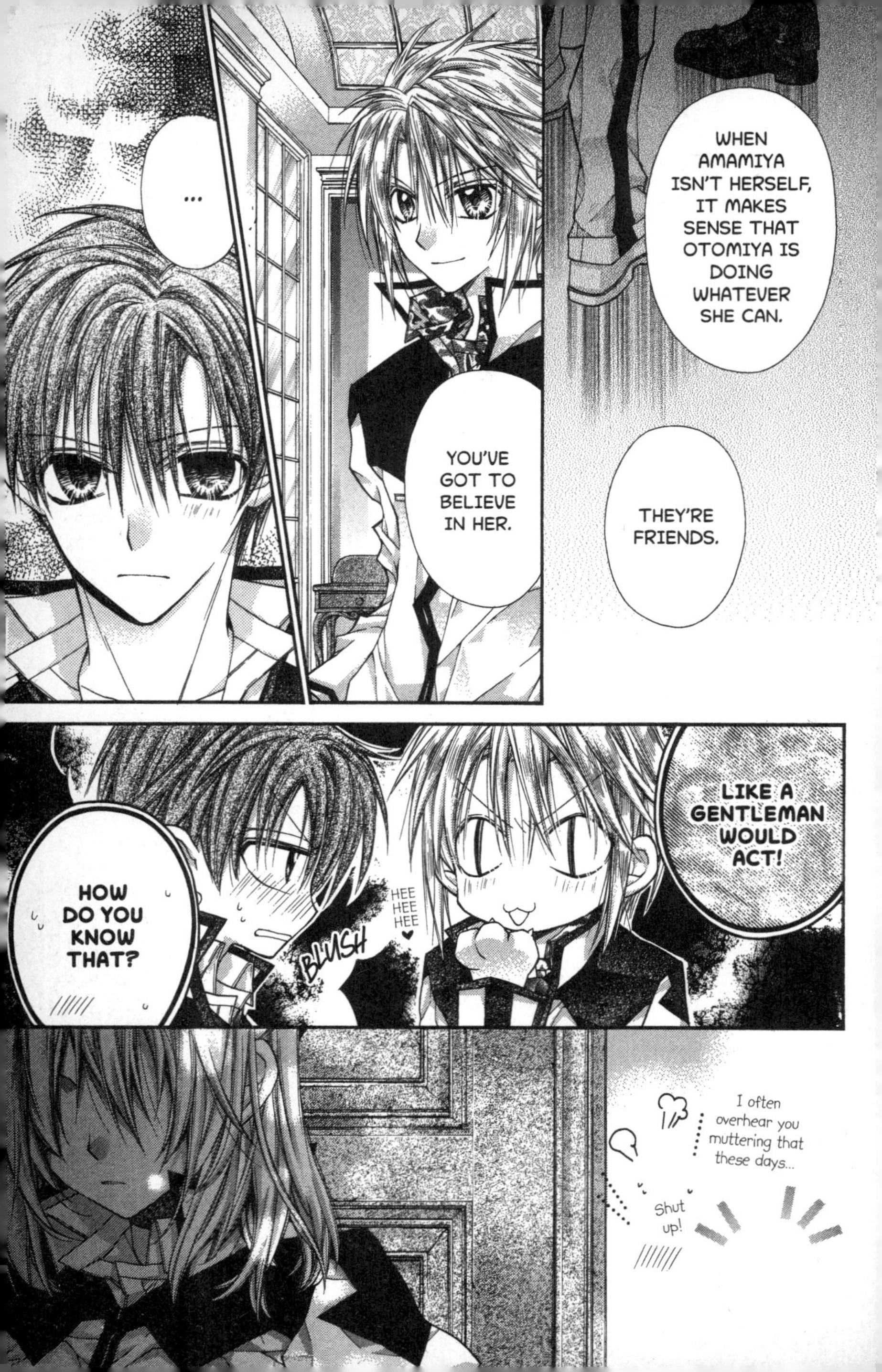
WHEN AMAMIYA ISN'T HERSELF, IT MAKES SENSE THAT OTOMIYA IS DOING WHATEVER SHE CAN.
THEY'RE FRIENDS.
YOU'VE GOT TO BELIEVE IN HER.
...
LIKE A GENTLEMAN WOULD ACT!
HEE HEE HEE
BLUSH
HOW DO YOU KNOW THAT?
I often overhear you muttering that these days...
Shut up!

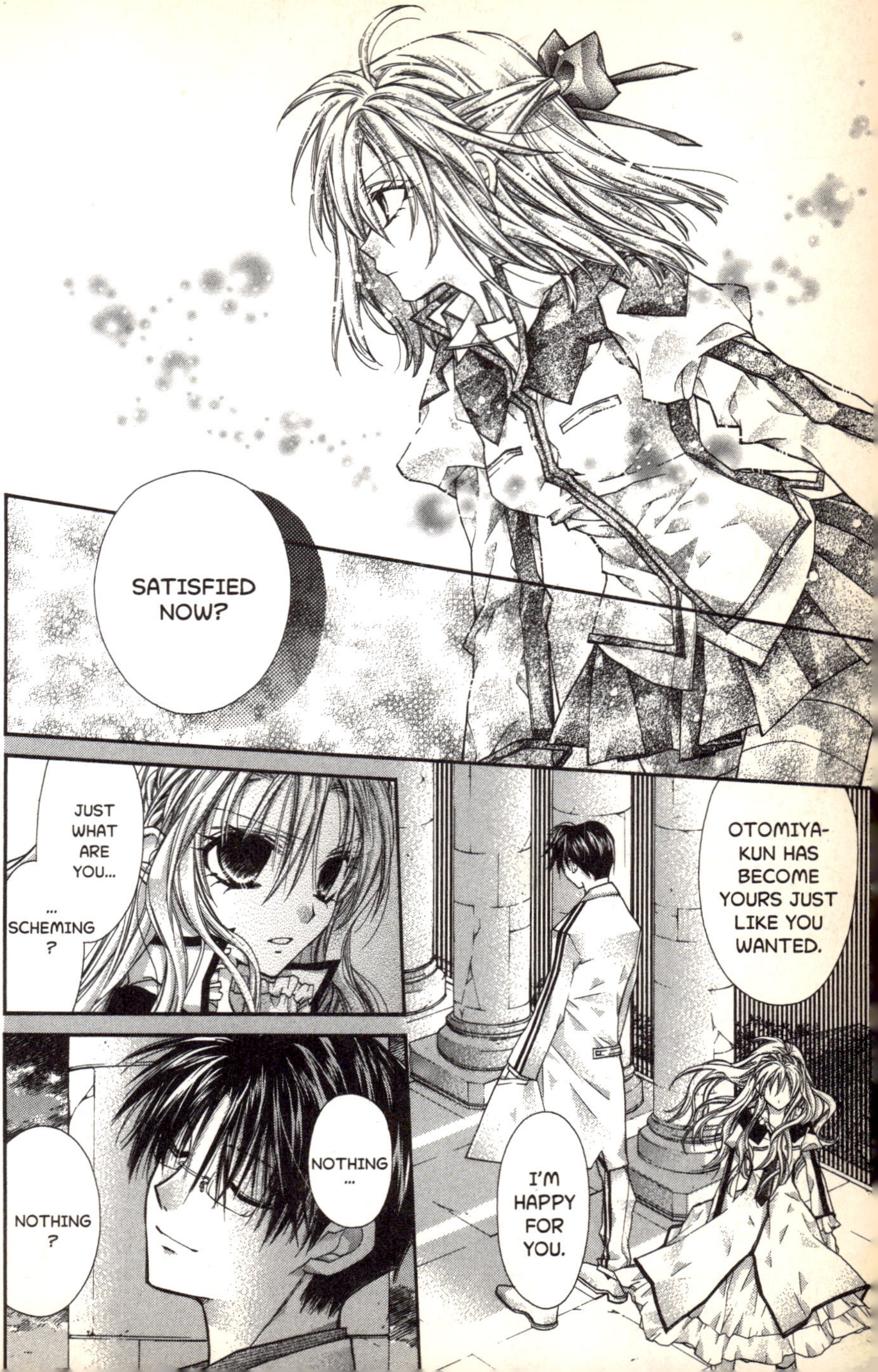
SATISFIED NOW?
OTOMIYA-KUN HAS BECOME YOURS JUST LIKE YOU WANTED.
I'M HAPPY FOR YOU.
JUST WHAT ARE YOU... ...SCHEMING?
NOTHING...
NOTHING?

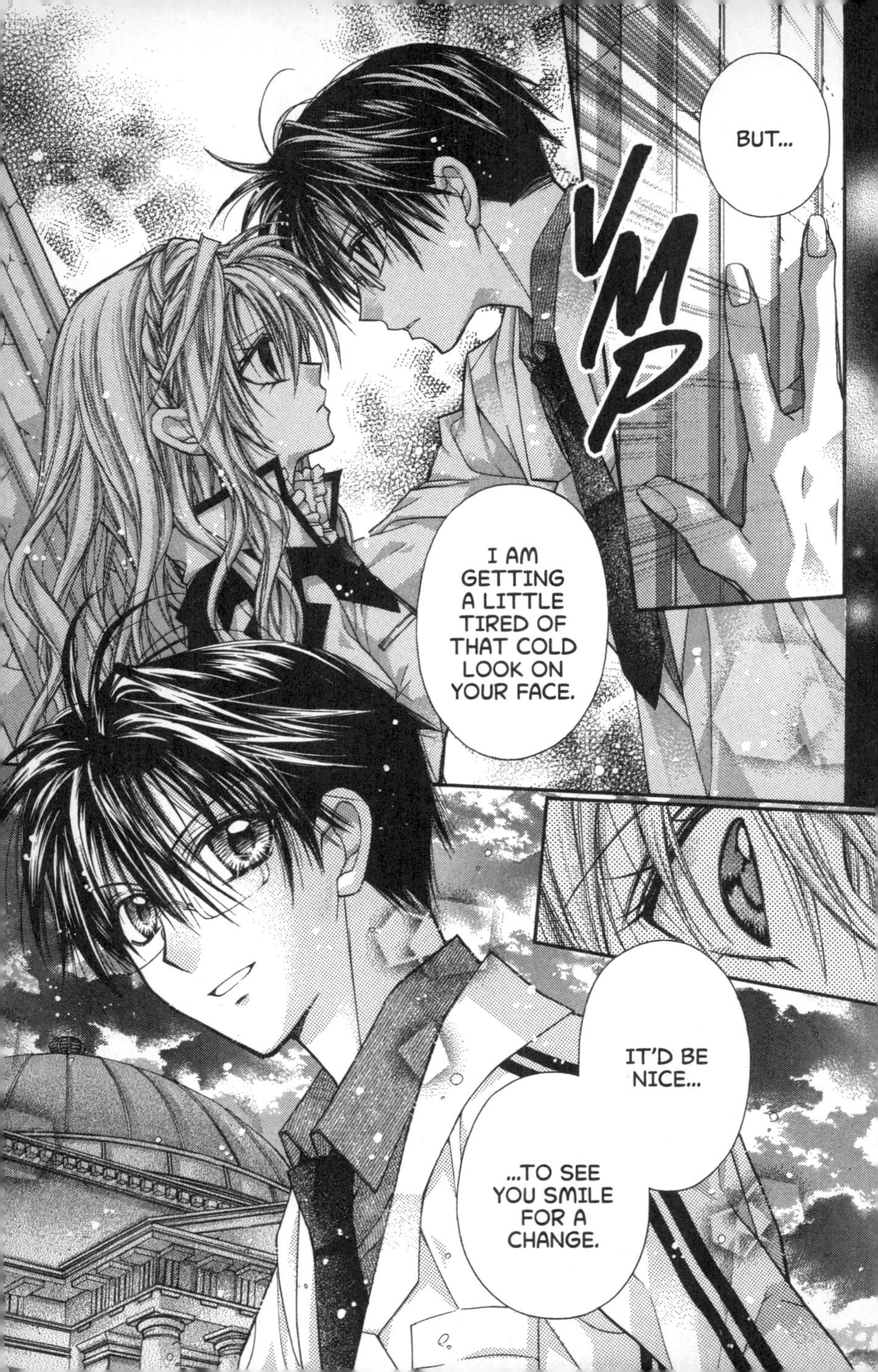
BUT...
VMP
I AM GETTING A LITTLE TIRED OF THAT COLD LOOK ON YOUR FACE.
IT'D BE NICE...
...TO SEE YOU SMILE FOR A CHANGE.

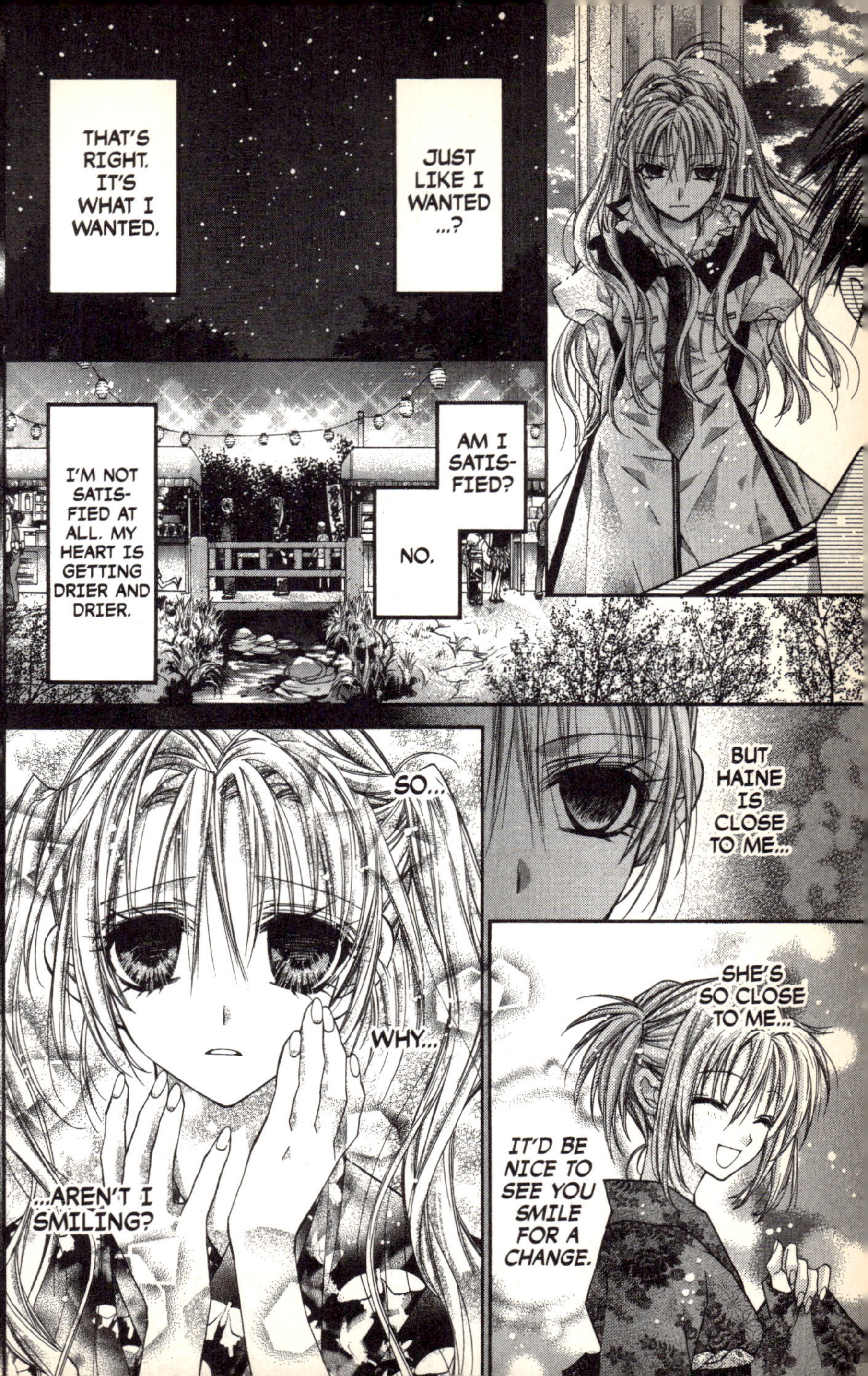
JUST LIKE I WANTED ...?
THAT'S RIGHT. IT'S WHAT I WANTED.
AM I SATIS-FIED?
NO.
I'M NOT SATIS-FIED AT ALL. MY HEART IS GETTING DRIER AND DRIER.
BUT HAINE IS CLOSE TO ME...
SHE'S SO CLOSE TO ME...
IT'D BE NICE TO SEE YOU SMILE FOR A CHANGE.
SO...
WHY...
...AREN'T I SMILING?

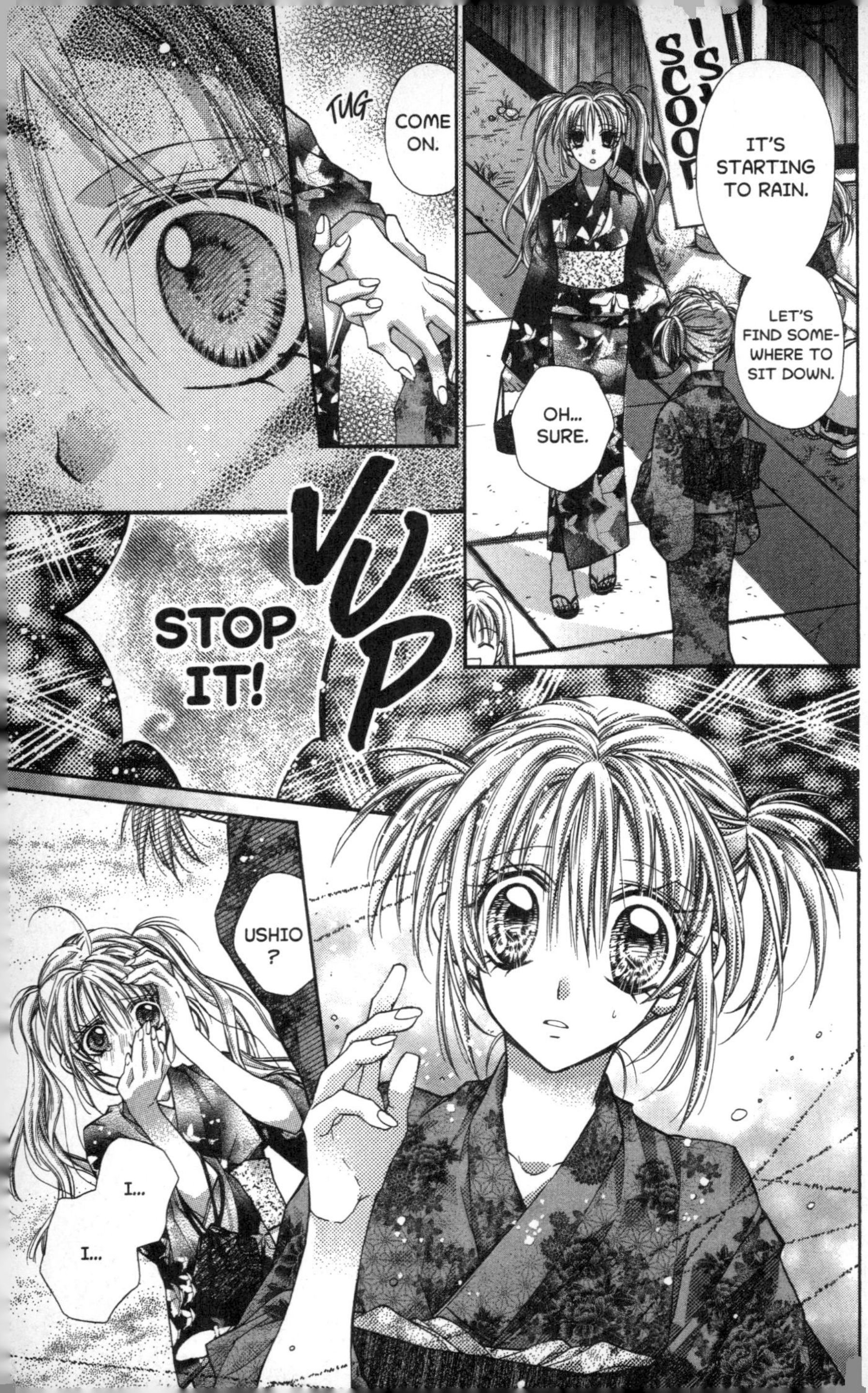
IT'S STARTING TO RAIN.
LET'S FIND SOME-WHERE TO SIT DOWN.
OH... SURE.
TUG
COME ON.
VUP
STOP IT!
USHIO?
I...
I...

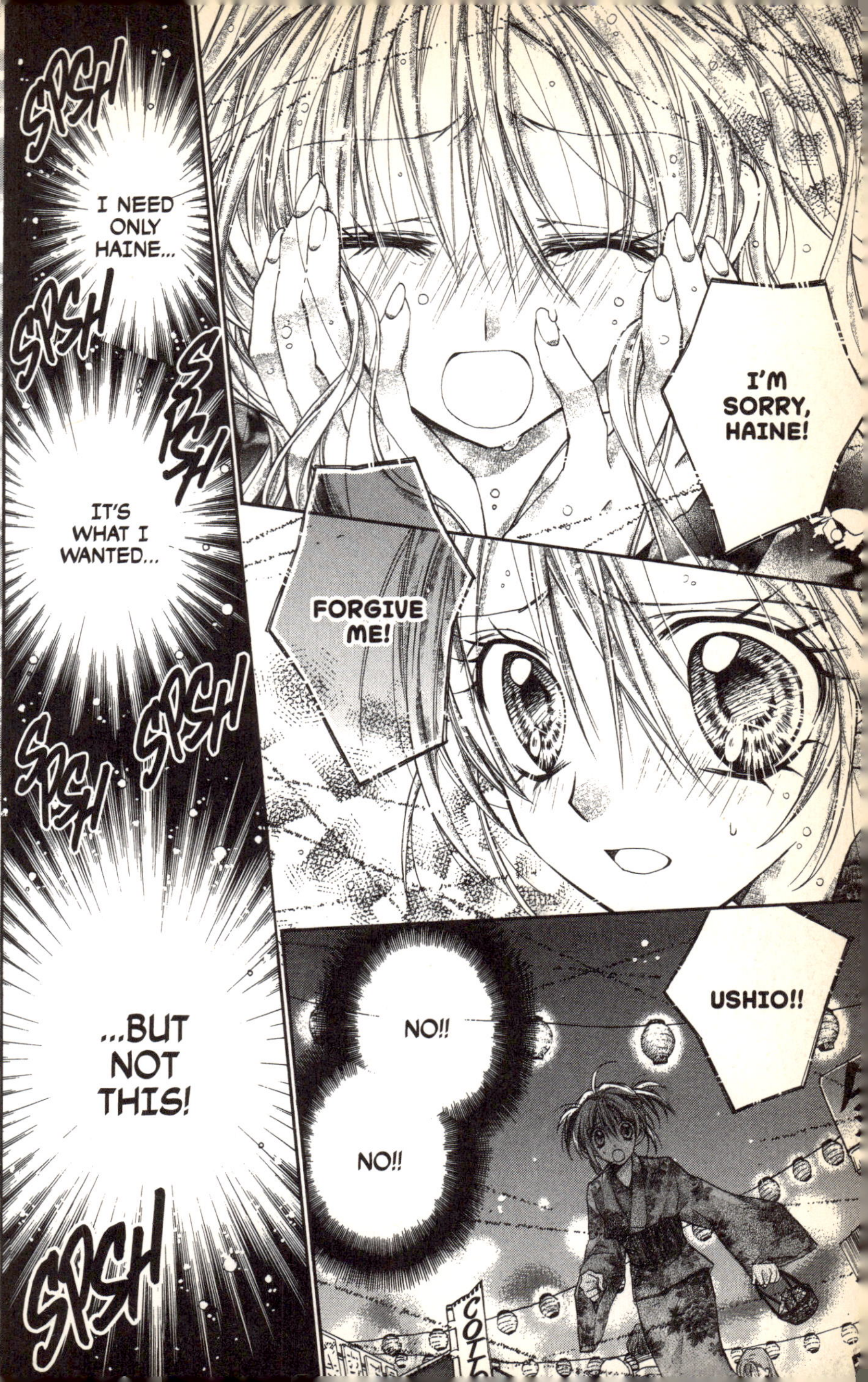
I'M SORRY, HAINE!
FORGIVE ME!
USHIO!!
NO!!
NO!!
SPSH
I NEED ONLY HAINE...
SPSH
SPSH
IT'S WHAT I WANTED...
SPSH
SPSH
...BUT NOT THIS!
SPSH

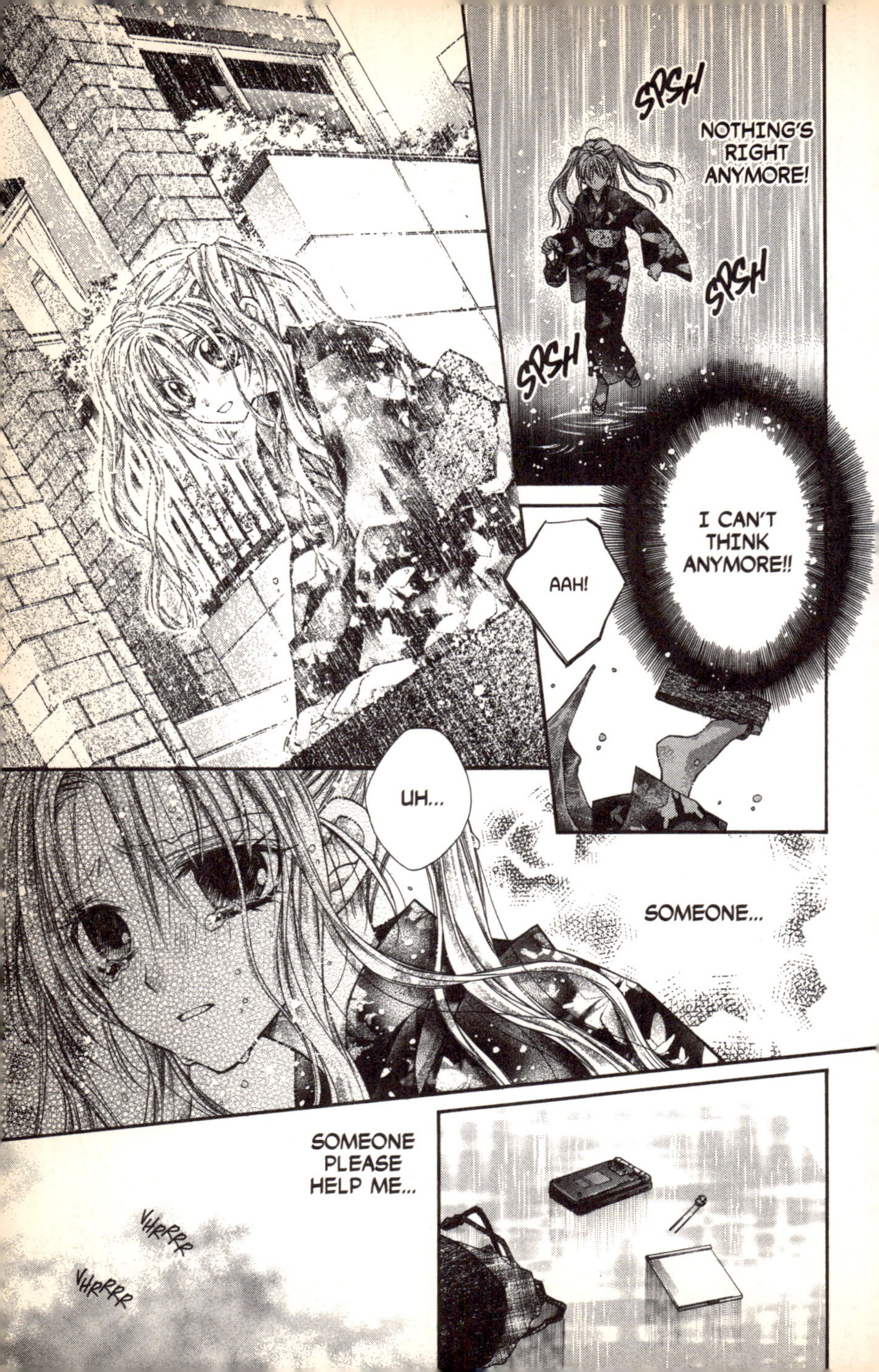
SPSH
NOTHING'S RIGHT ANYMORE!
SPSH
SPSH
I CAN'T THINK ANYMORE!!
AAH!
UH...
SOMEONE...
SOMEONE PLEASE HELP ME...
VHRRR
VHRRR

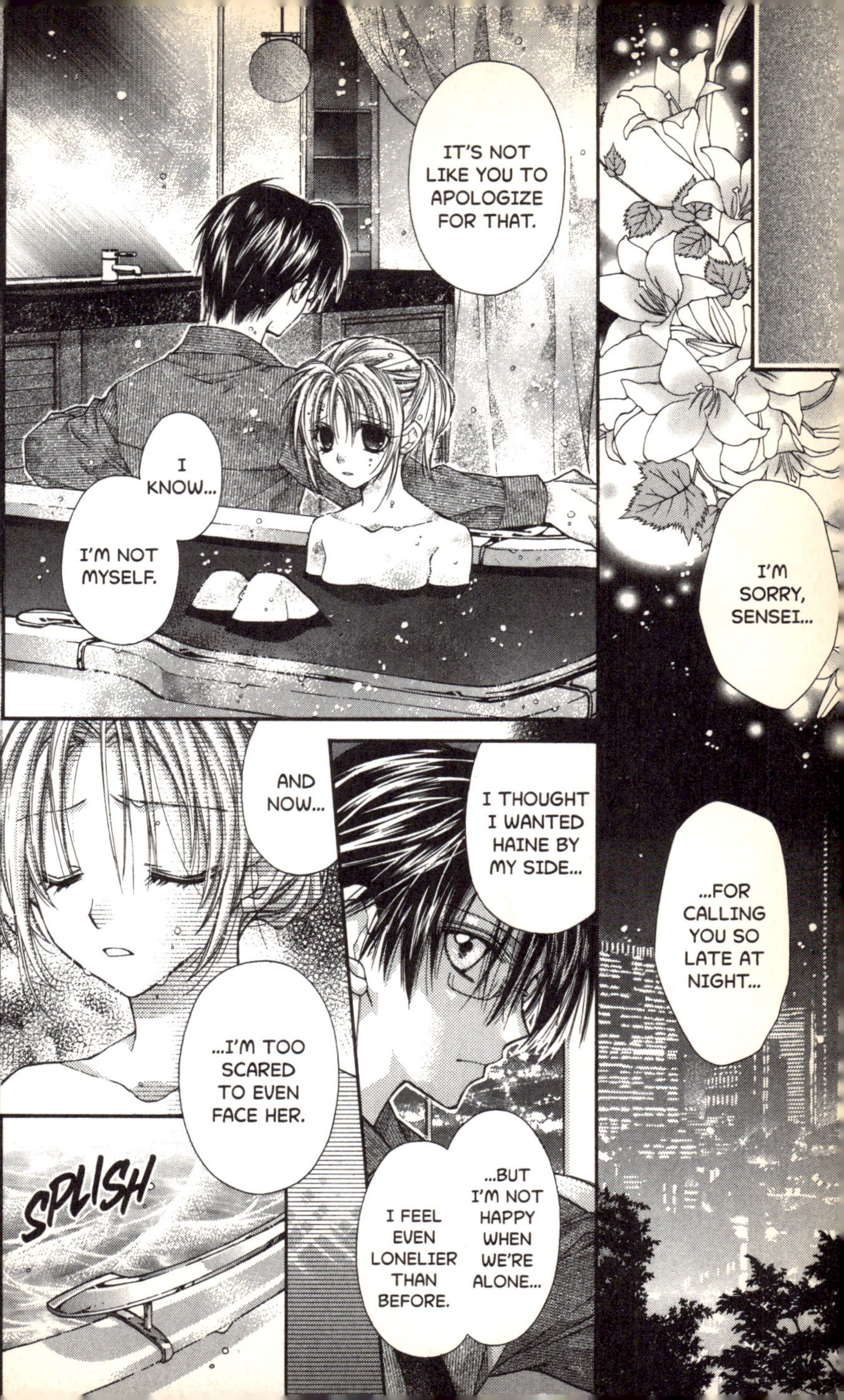
I'M SORRY, SENSEI...
...FOR CALLING YOU SO LATE AT NIGHT...
IT'S NOT LIKE YOU TO APOLOGIZE FOR THAT.
I KNOW...
I'M NOT MYSELF.
I THOUGHT I WANTED HAINE BY MY SIDE...
...BUT I'M NOT HAPPY WHEN WE'RE ALONE...
I FEEL EVEN LONELIER THAN BEFORE.
AND NOW...
...I'M TOO SCARED TO EVEN FACE HER.
SPLISH

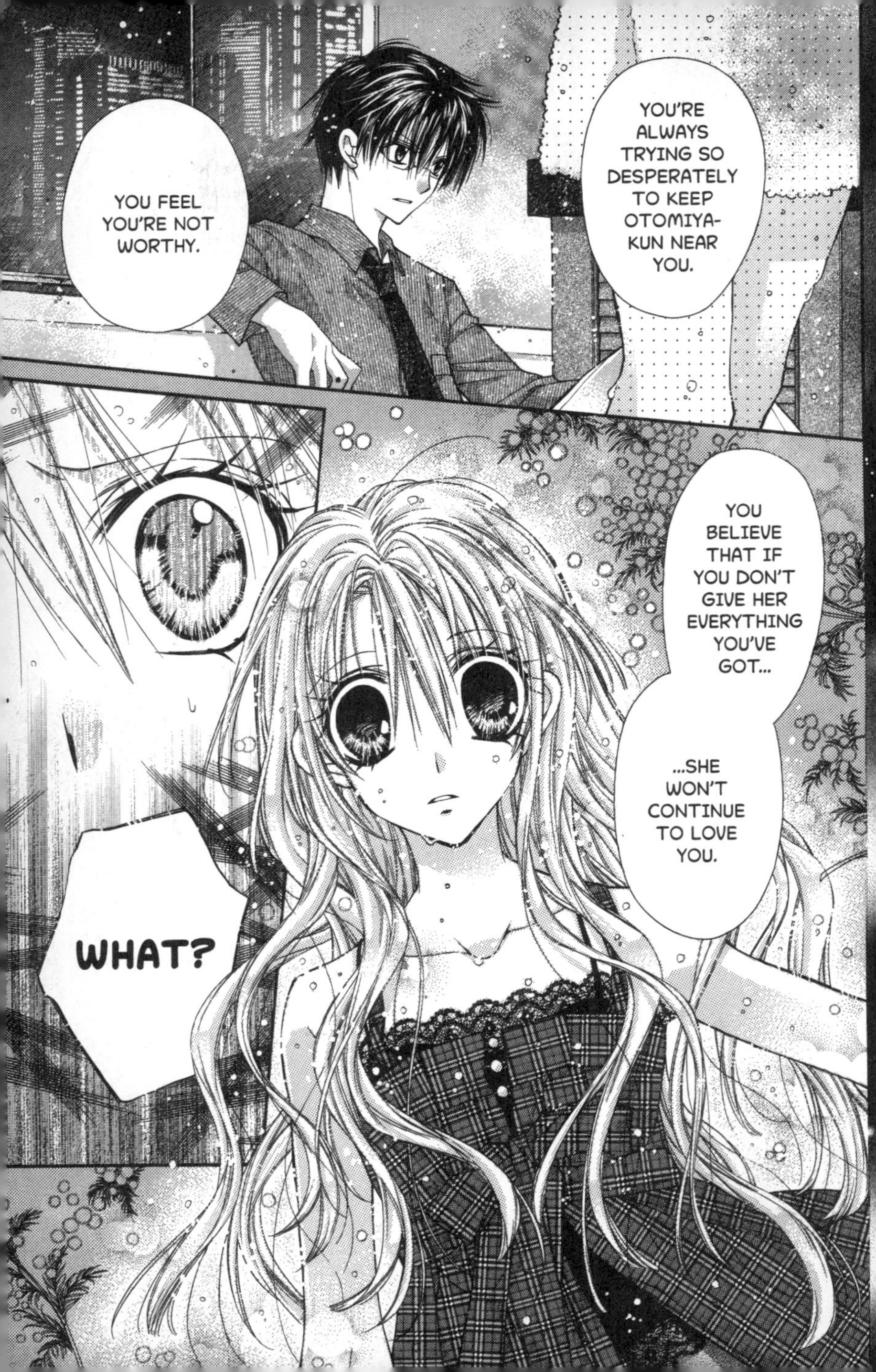
YOU'RE ALWAYS TRYING SO DESPERATELY TO KEEP OTOMIYA-KUN NEAR YOU.
YOU FEEL YOU'RE NOT WORTHY.
YOU BELIEVE THAT IF YOU DON'T GIVE HER EVERYTHING YOU'VE GOT...
...SHE WON'T CONTINUE TO LOVE YOU.
WHAT?

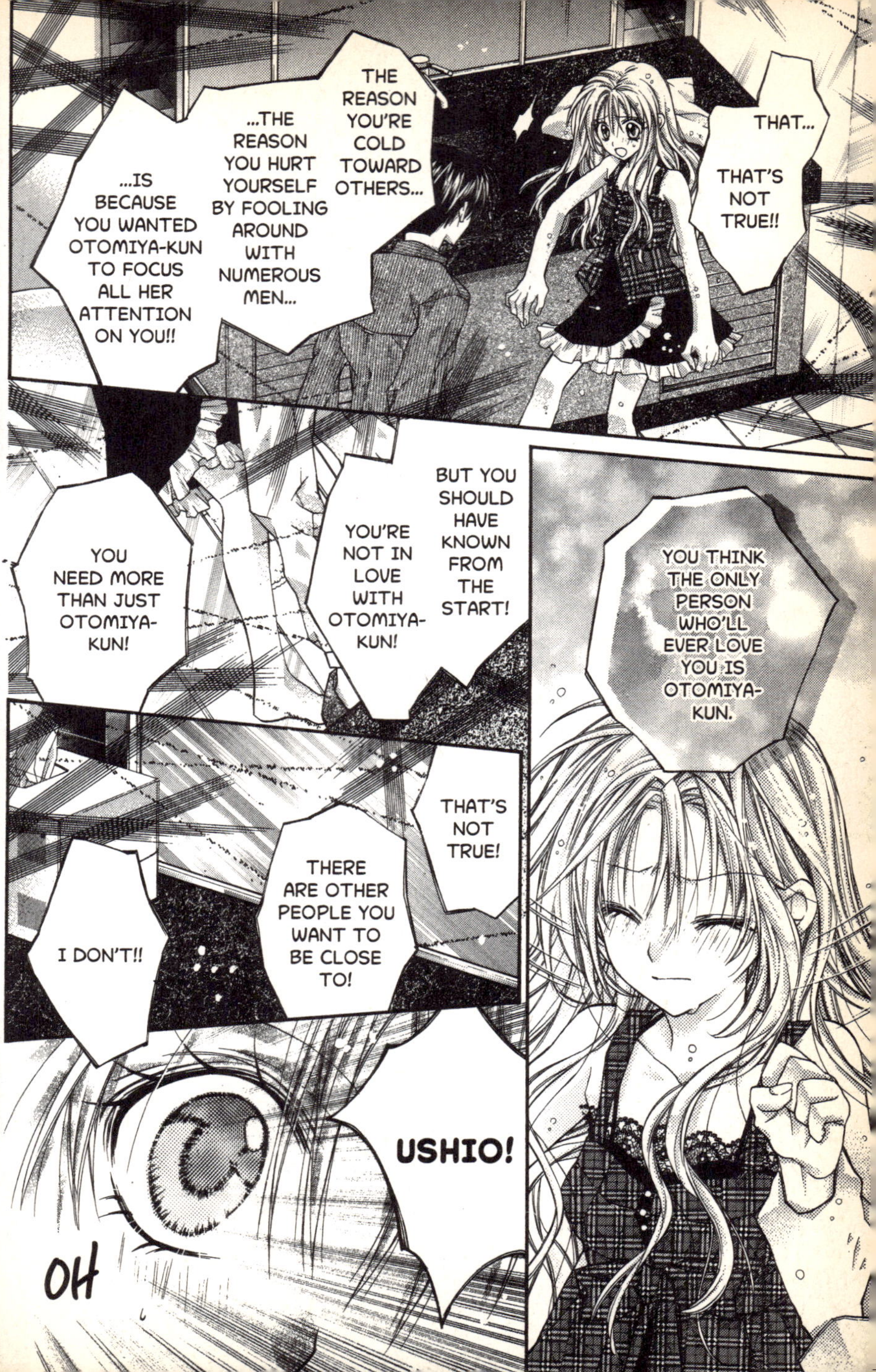
THAT...
THAT'S NOT TRUE!!
THE REASON YOU'RE COLD TOWARD OTHERS...
...THE REASON YOU HURT YOURSELF BY FOOLING AROUND WITH NUMEROUS MEN...
...IS BECAUSE YOU WANTED OTOMIYA-KUN TO FOCUS ALL HER ATTENTION ON YOU!!
YOU THINK THE ONLY PERSON WHO'LL EVER LOVE YOU IS OTOMIYA-KUN.
BUT YOU SHOULD HAVE KNOWN FROM THE START!
YOU'RE NOT IN LOVE WITH OTOMIYA-KUN!
YOU NEED MORE THAN JUST OTOMIYA-KUN!
THAT'S NOT TRUE!
THERE ARE OTHER PEOPLE YOU WANT TO BE CLOSE TO!
I DON'T!!
USHIO!
OH

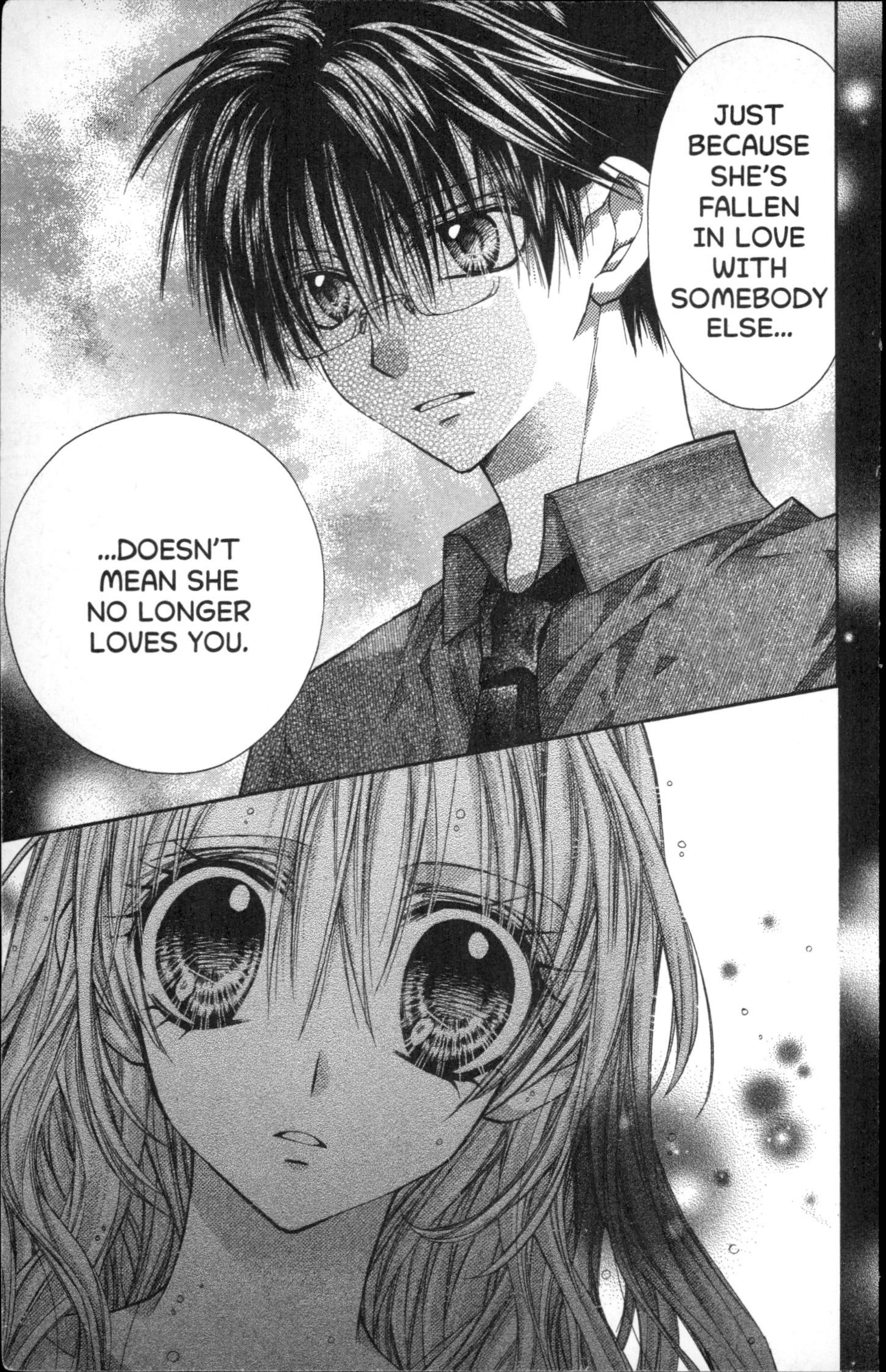
JUST BECAUSE SHE'S FALLEN IN LOVE WITH SOMEBODY ELSE...
...DOESN'T MEAN SHE NO LONGER LOVES YOU.

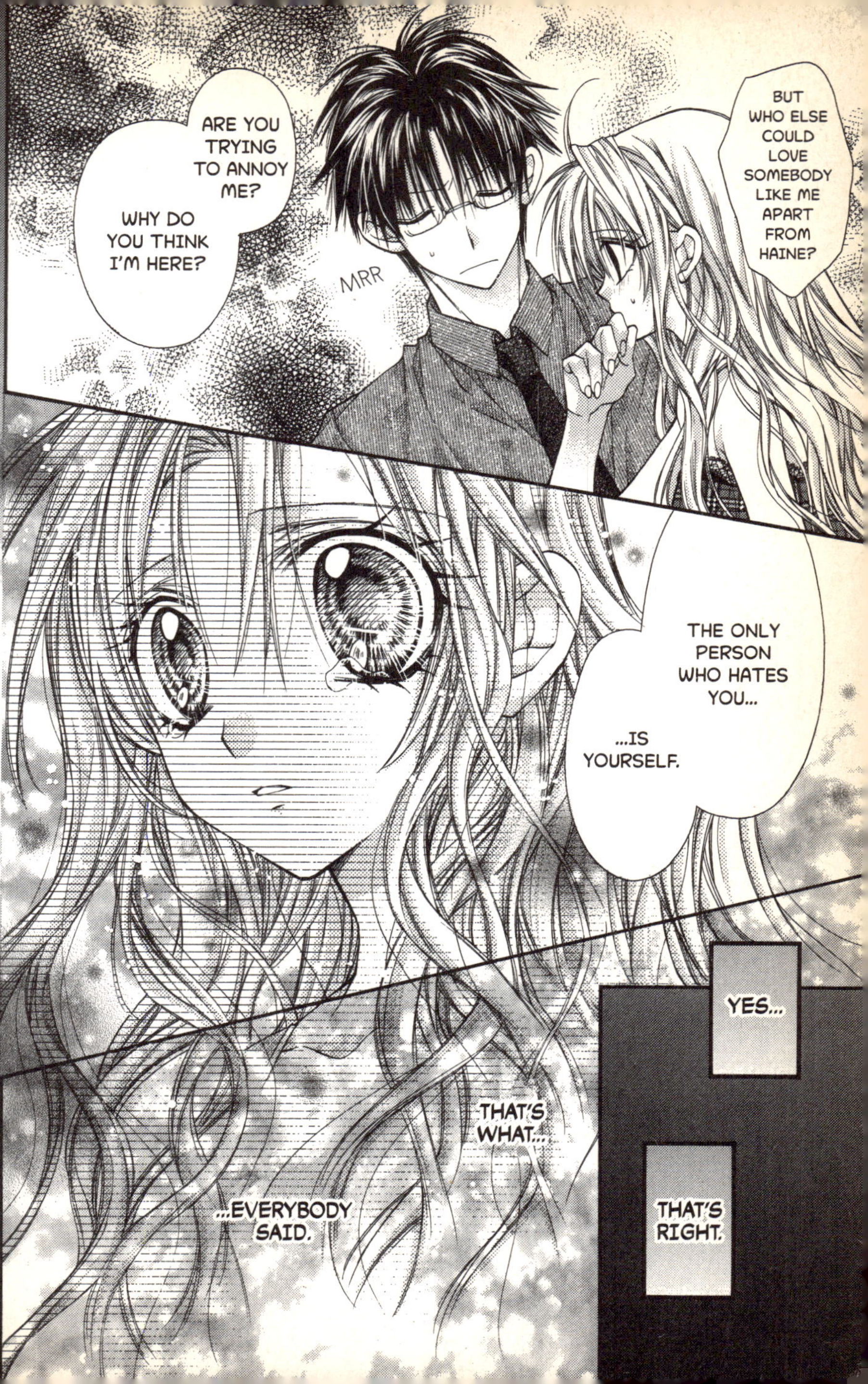
BUT WHO ELSE COULD LOVE SOMEBODY LIKE ME APART FROM HAINE?
MRR
ARE YOU TRYING TO ANNOY ME?
WHY DO YOU THINK I'M HERE?
THE ONLY PERSON WHO HATES YOU...
...IS YOURSELF.
YES...
THAT'S RIGHT.
THAT'S WHAT...
...EVERYBODY SAID.

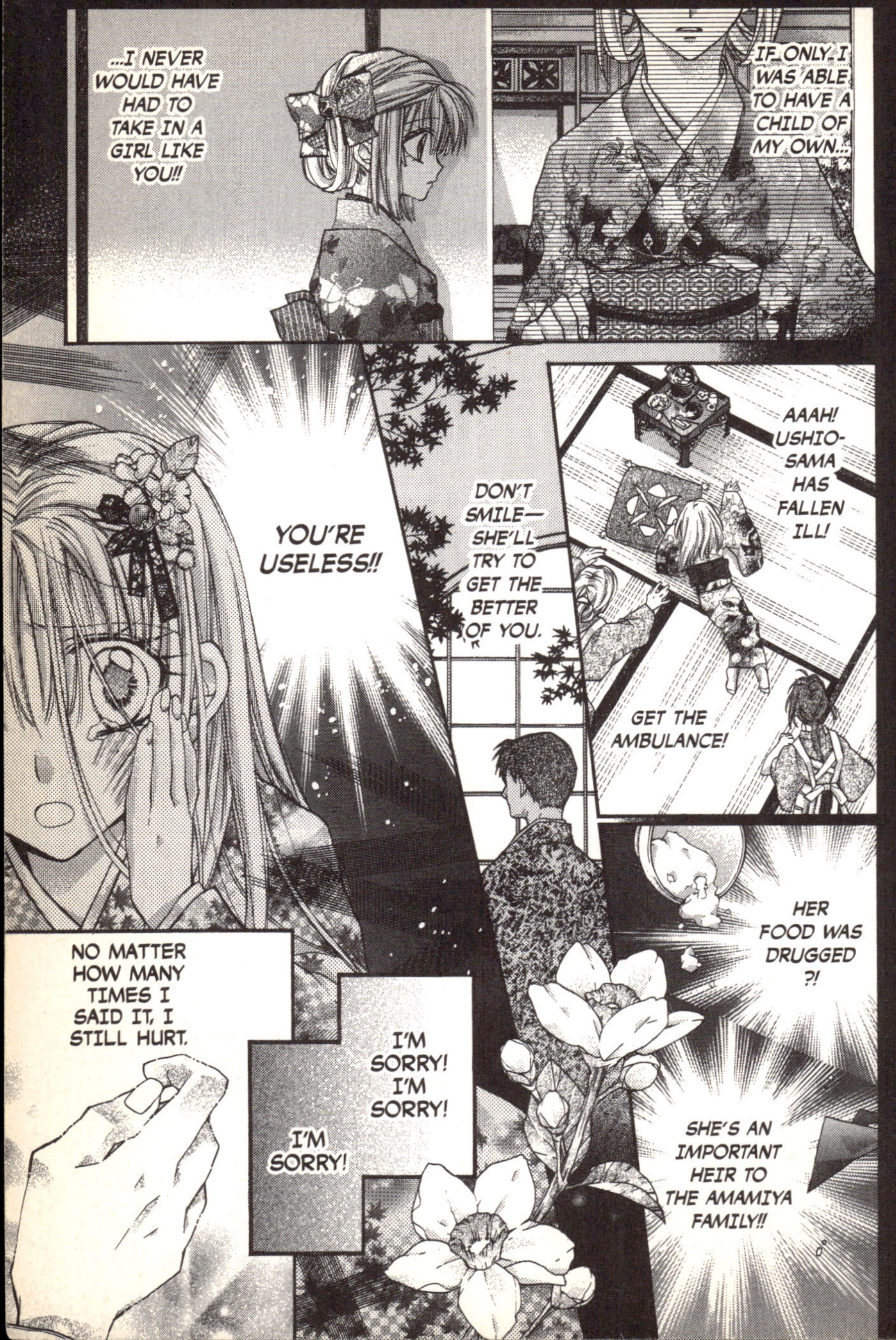
IF ONLY I WAS ABLE TO HAVE A CHILD OF MY OWN...
...I NEVER WOULD HAVE HAD TO TAKE IN A GIRL LIKE YOU!!
AAAH! USHIO-SAMA HAS FALLEN ILL!
GET THE AMBULANCE!
DON'T SMILE— SHE'LL TRY TO GET THE BETTER OF YOU.
YOU'RE USELESS!!
HER FOOD WAS DRUGGED ?!
SHE'S AN IMPORTANT HEIR TO THE AMAMIYA FAMILY!!
I'M SORRY! I'M SORRY!
I'M SORRY!
NO MATTER HOW MANY TIMES I SAID IT, I STILL HURT.

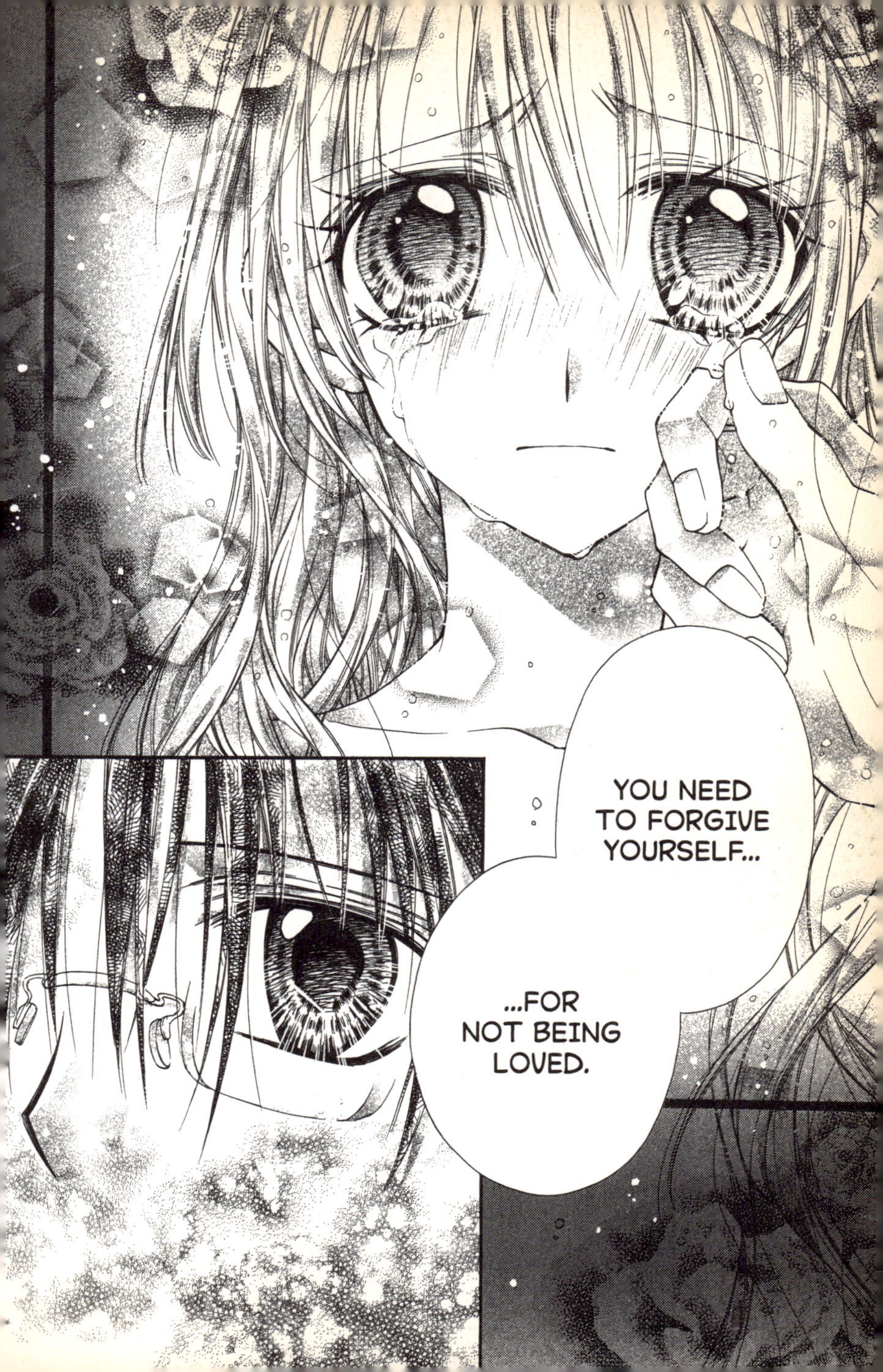
YOU NEED TO FORGIVE YOURSELF...
...FOR NOT BEING LOVED.

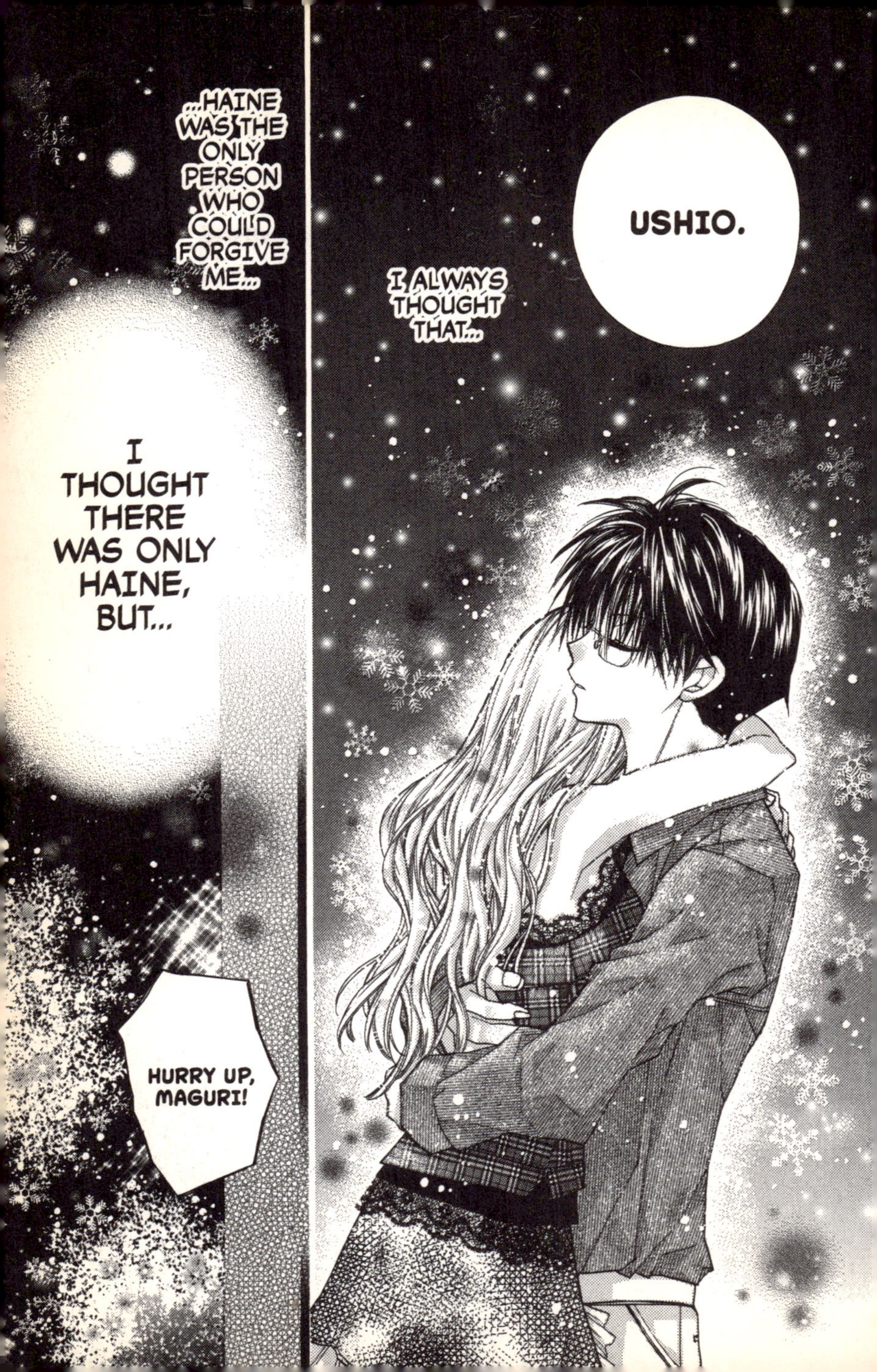
USHIO.
I ALWAYS THOUGHT THAT...
...HAINE WAS THE ONLY PERSON WHO COULD FORGIVE ME...
I THOUGHT THERE WAS ONLY HAINE, BUT...
HURRY UP, MAGURI!

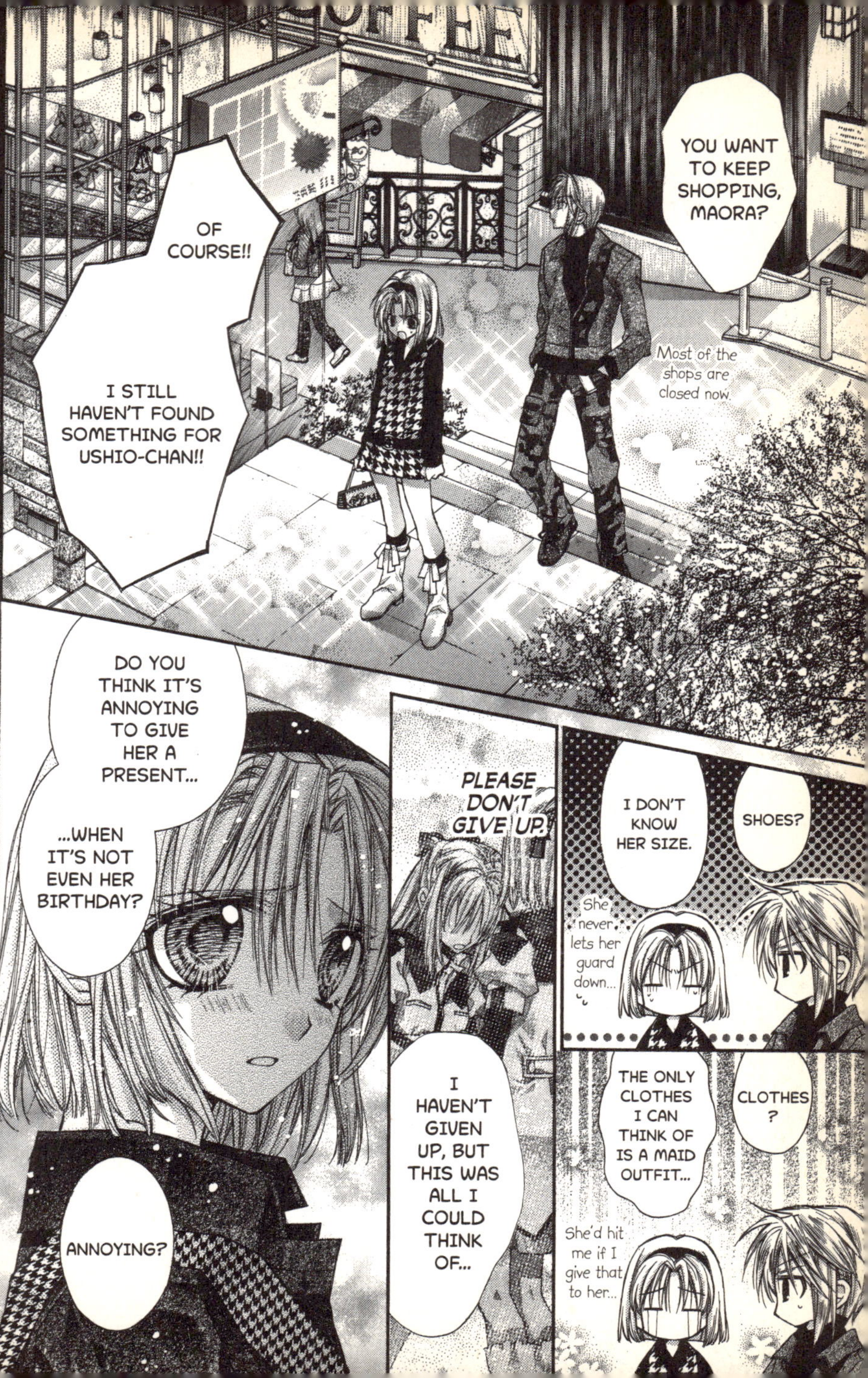
YOU WANT TO KEEP SHOPPING, MAORA?
Most of the shops are closed now.
OF COURSE!!
I STILL HAVEN'T FOUND SOMETHING FOR USHIO-CHAN!!
SHOES?
I DON'T KNOW HER SIZE.
She never lets her guard down...
CLOTHES?
THE ONLY CLOTHES I CAN THINK OF IS A MAID OUTFIT...
She'd hit me if I give that to her...
PLEASE DON'T GIVE UP.
I HAVEN'T GIVEN UP, BUT THIS WAS ALL I COULD THINK OF...
DO YOU THINK IT'S ANNOYING TO GIVE HER A PRESENT...
...WHEN IT'S NOT EVEN HER BIRTHDAY?
ANNOYING?

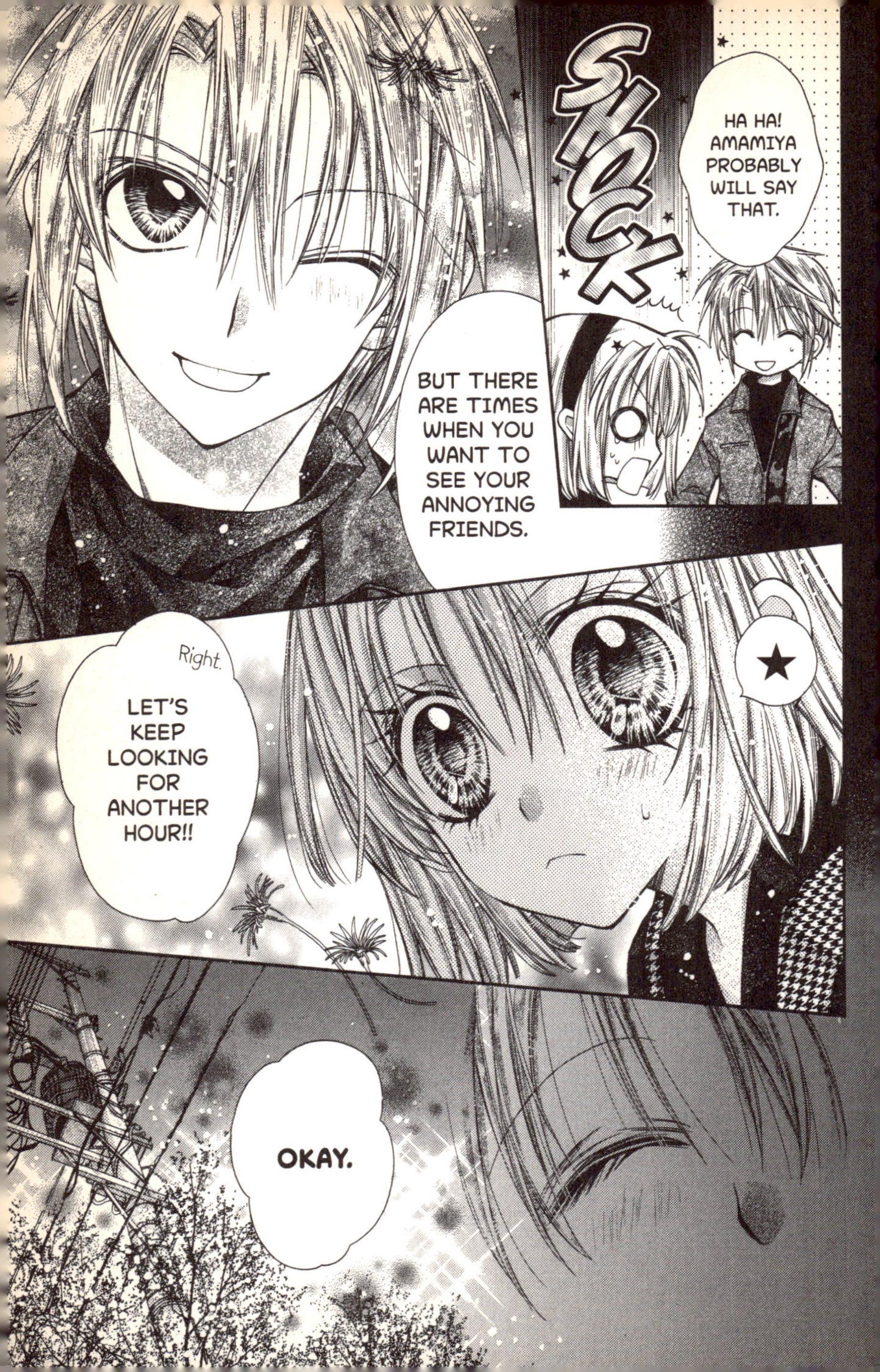
HA HA! AMAMIYA PROBABLY WILL SAY THAT.
SHOCK
BUT THERE ARE TIMES WHEN YOU WANT TO SEE YOUR ANNOYING FRIENDS.
★
Right.
LET'S KEEP LOOKING FOR ANOTHER HOUR!!
OKAY.

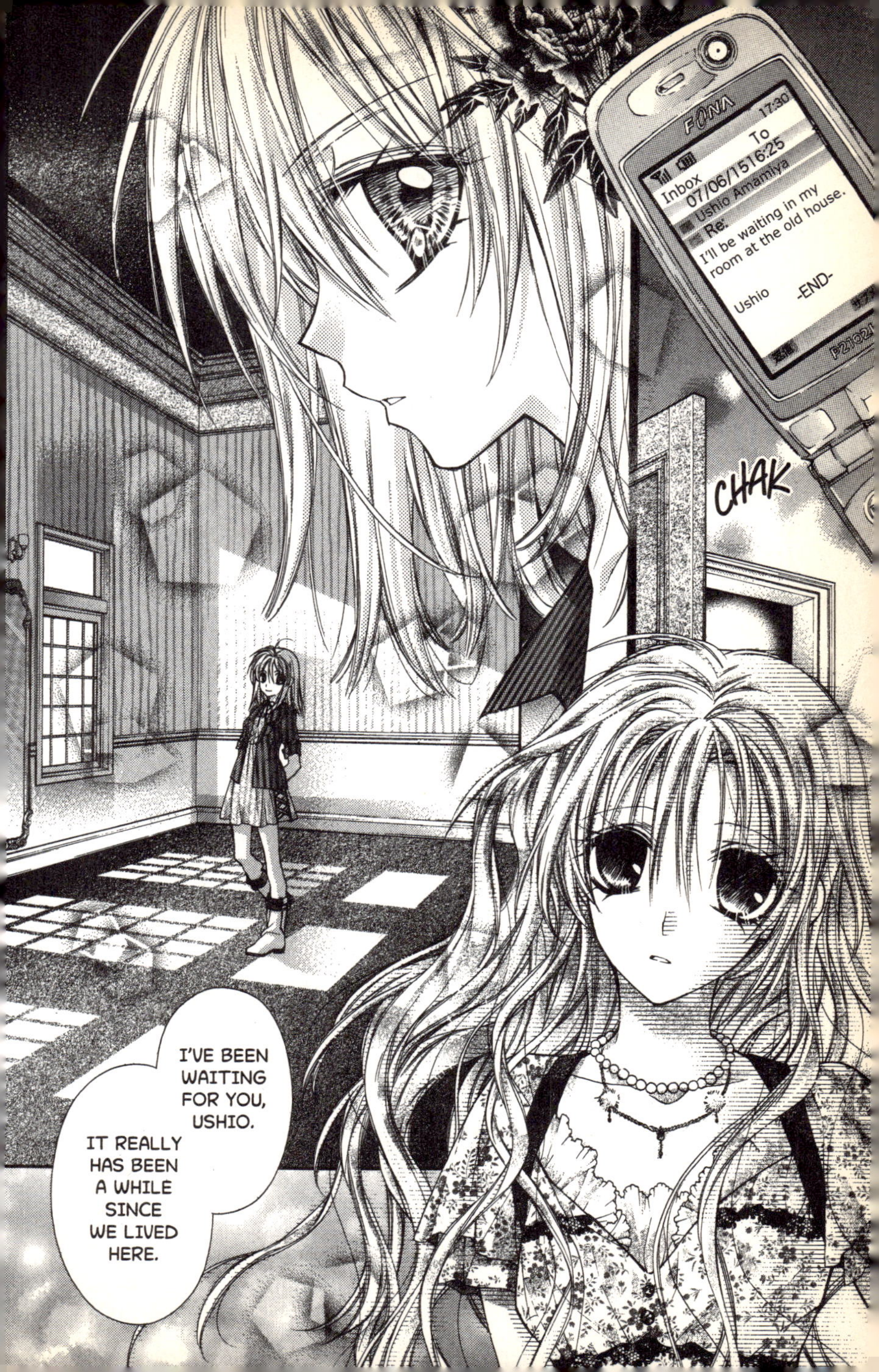
FONA
17:30
Inbox To
07/06/15 16:25
Ushio Amamiya
Re.
I'll be waiting in my room at the old house.
Ushio -END-
CHAK
I'VE BEEN WAITING FOR YOU, USHIO.
IT REALLY HAS BEEN A WHILE SINCE WE LIVED HERE.

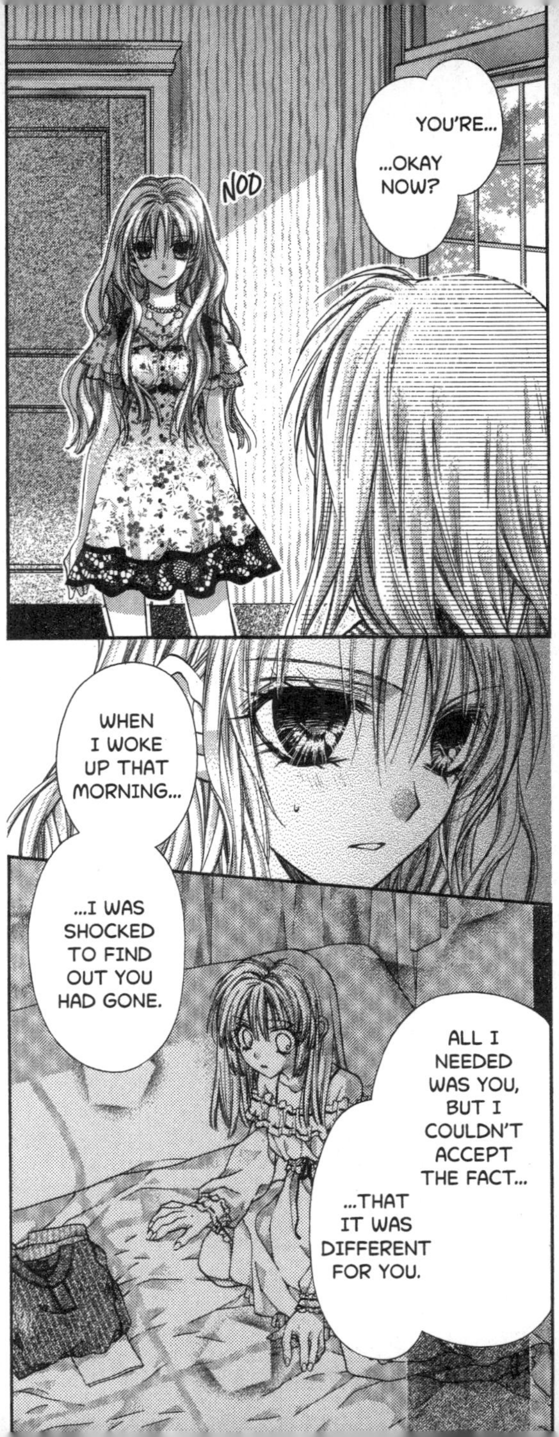
YOU'RE...
...OKAY NOW?
NOD
WHEN I WOKE UP THAT MORNING...
...I WAS SHOCKED TO FIND OUT YOU HAD GONE.
ALL I NEEDED WAS YOU, BUT I COULDN'T ACCEPT THE FACT...
...THAT IT WAS DIFFERENT FOR YOU.

Eve's ☆ Applework 24 Hours

※I may give away a part of the story. Please read this after you read the story.

I wrote this quickly when I really had no time, so there are a lot of parts I'm not really satisfied with... (Maybe I'll even do a sequel...)

I had a really cute classmate back in elementary school who didn't seem to have a lot of friends (but it's not that she didn't have any friends at all), and I remembered her being really happy when I went to play with her at her house. So the idea of this story is based on my thought, "I guess really cute girls are lonely." (By the way, I was the carefree, gagster type of person.)

My favorite character in the story is Eve.♪ I like her girlish, rather noisy attitude.

By the way, my favorite panel was "Are you sure you're okay in the head?"

A sequel, huh...

Maybe about Eve and Kashi-Kun when they start going out...

Dating and whatnot...

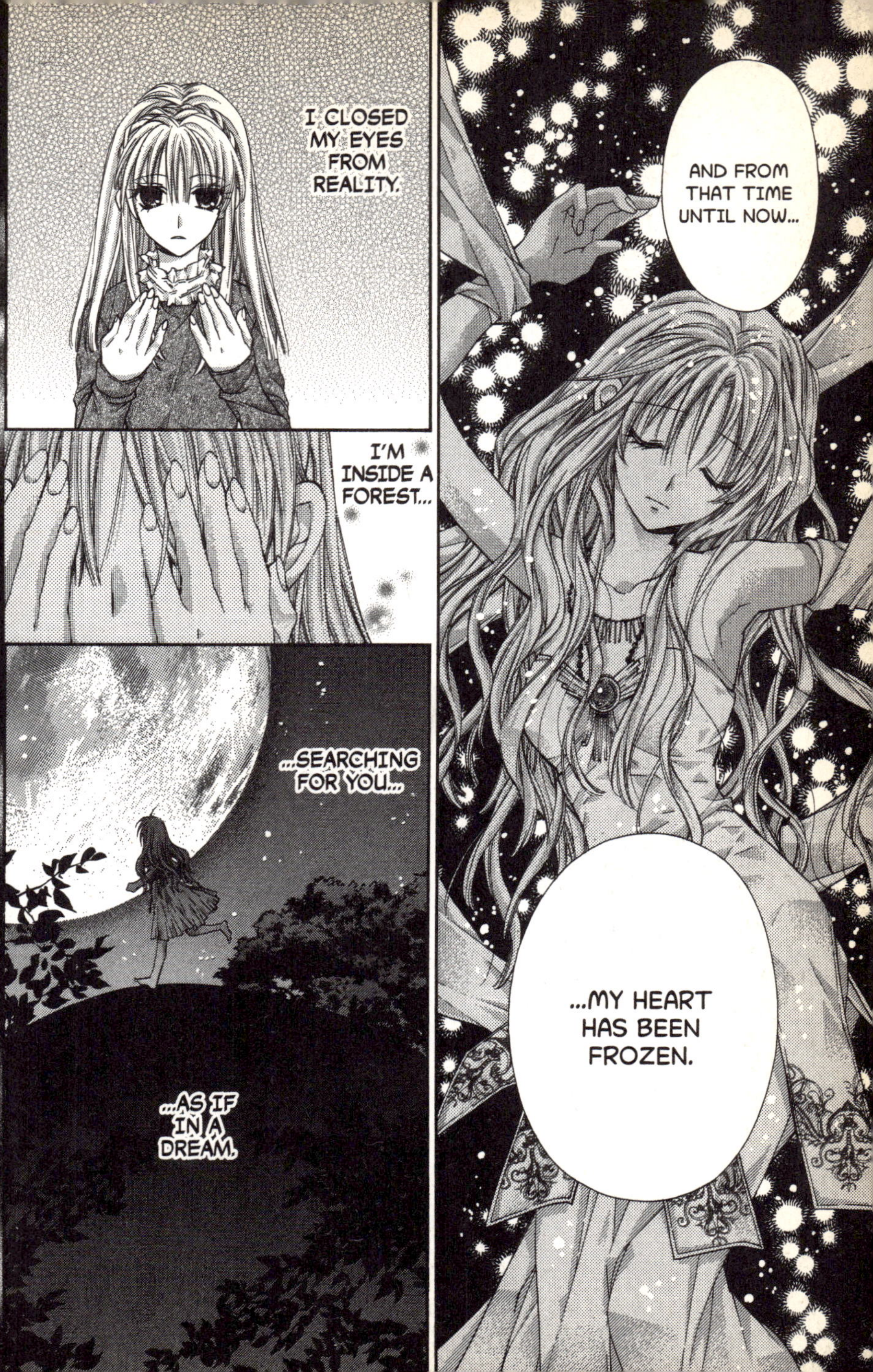
AND FROM THAT TIME UNTIL NOW...
...MY HEART HAS BEEN FROZEN.
I CLOSED MY EYES FROM REALITY.
I'M INSIDE A FOREST...
...SEARCHING FOR YOU...
...AS IF IN A DREAM.

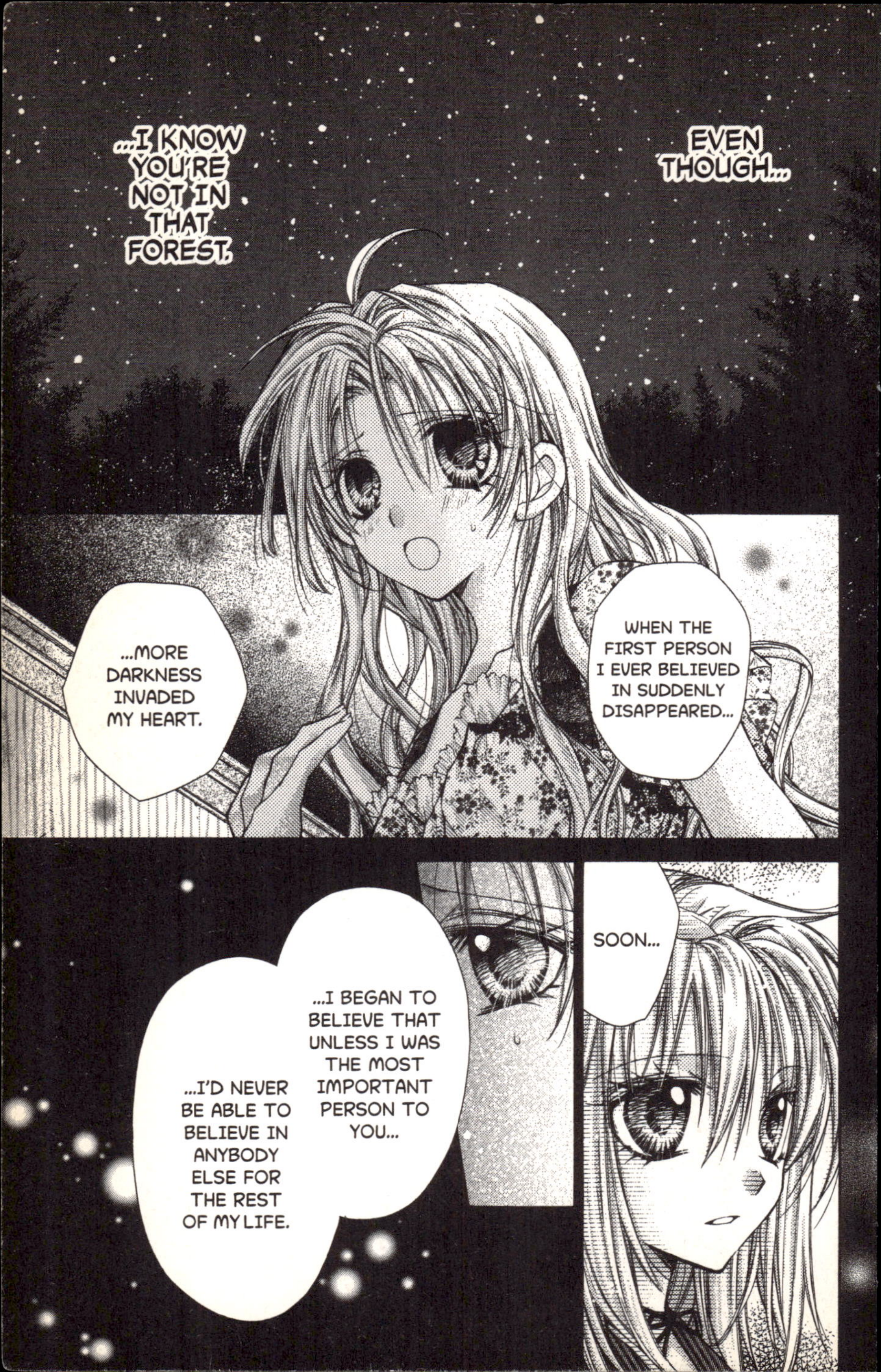
EVEN THOUGH...
...I KNOW YOU'RE NOT IN THAT FOREST.
WHEN THE FIRST PERSON I EVER BELIEVED IN SUDDENLY DISAPPEARED...
...MORE DARKNESS INVADED MY HEART.
SOON...
...I BEGAN TO BELIEVE THAT UNLESS I WAS THE MOST IMPORTANT PERSON TO YOU...
...I'D NEVER BE ABLE TO BELIEVE IN ANYBODY ELSE FOR THE REST OF MY LIFE.

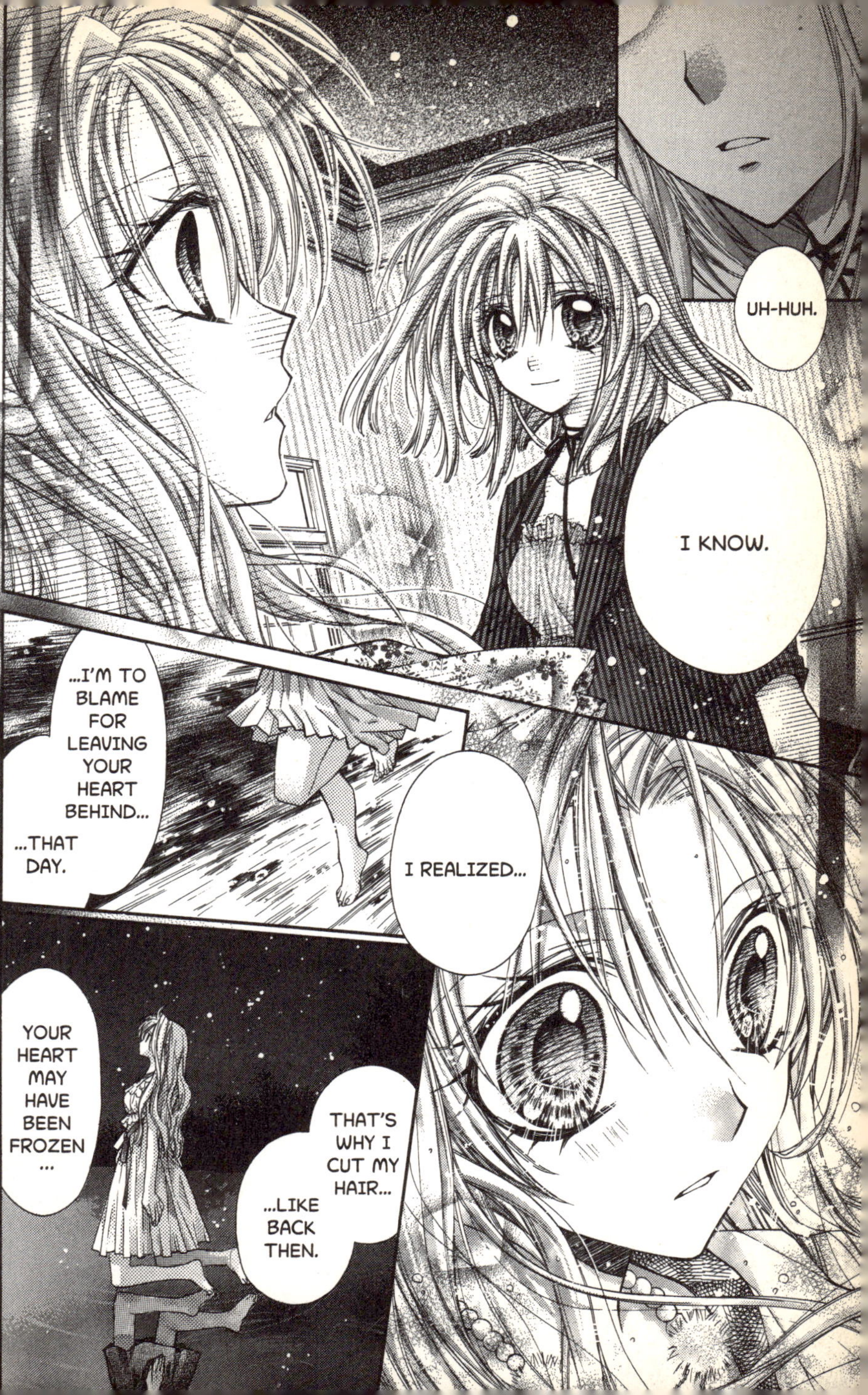
UH-HUH.
I KNOW.
I REALIZED...
...I'M TO BLAME FOR LEAVING YOUR HEART BEHIND...
...THAT DAY.
YOUR HEART MAY HAVE BEEN FROZEN...
THAT'S WHY I CUT MY HAIR...
...LIKE BACK THEN.

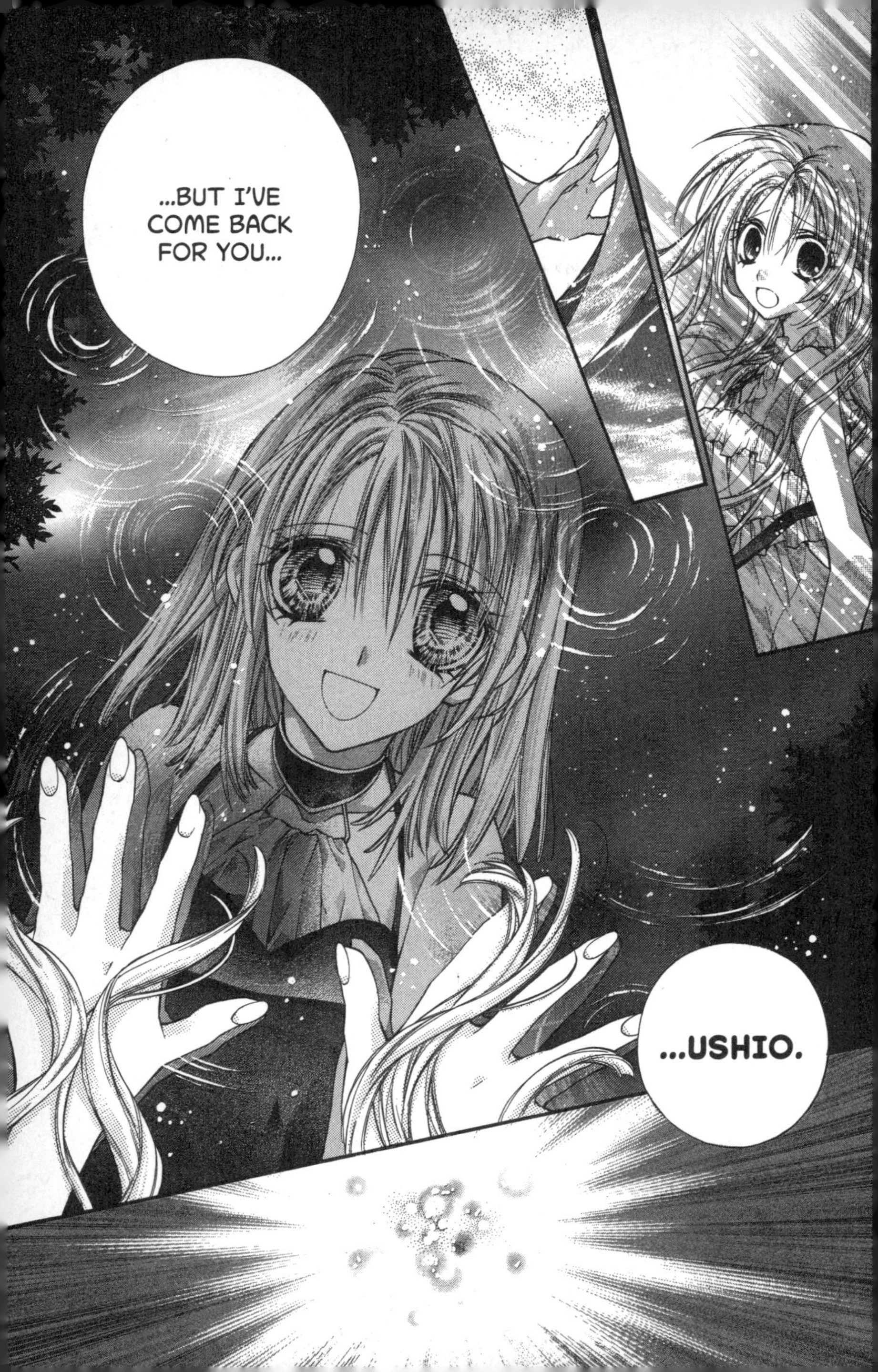
...BUT I'VE COME BACK FOR YOU...
...USHIO.

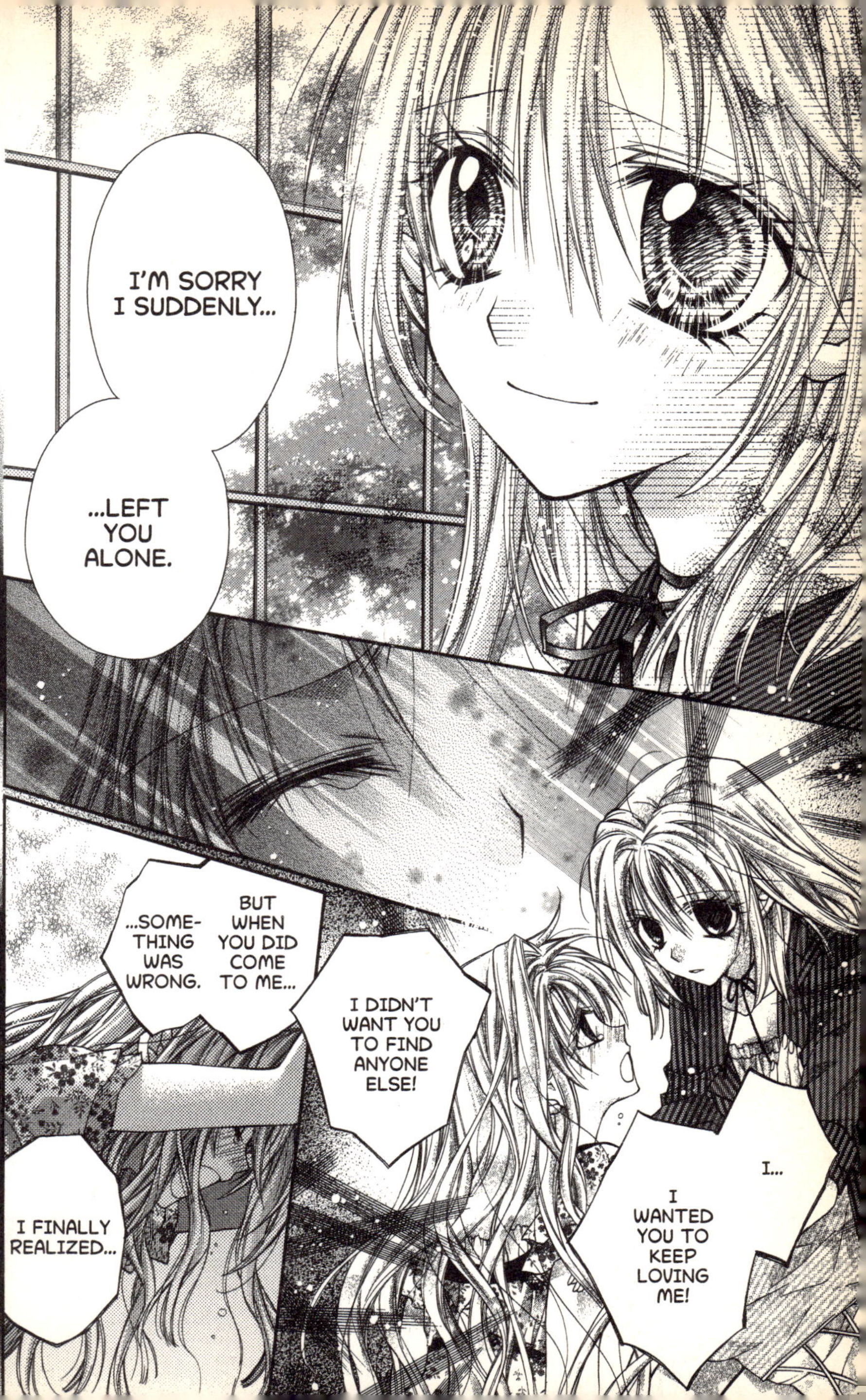
I'M SORRY I SUDDENLY...
...LEFT YOU ALONE.
BUT WHEN YOU DID COME TO ME...
...SOME-THING WAS WRONG.
I FINALLY REALIZED...
I DIDN'T WANT YOU TO FIND ANYONE ELSE!
I...
I WANTED YOU TO KEEP LOVING ME!

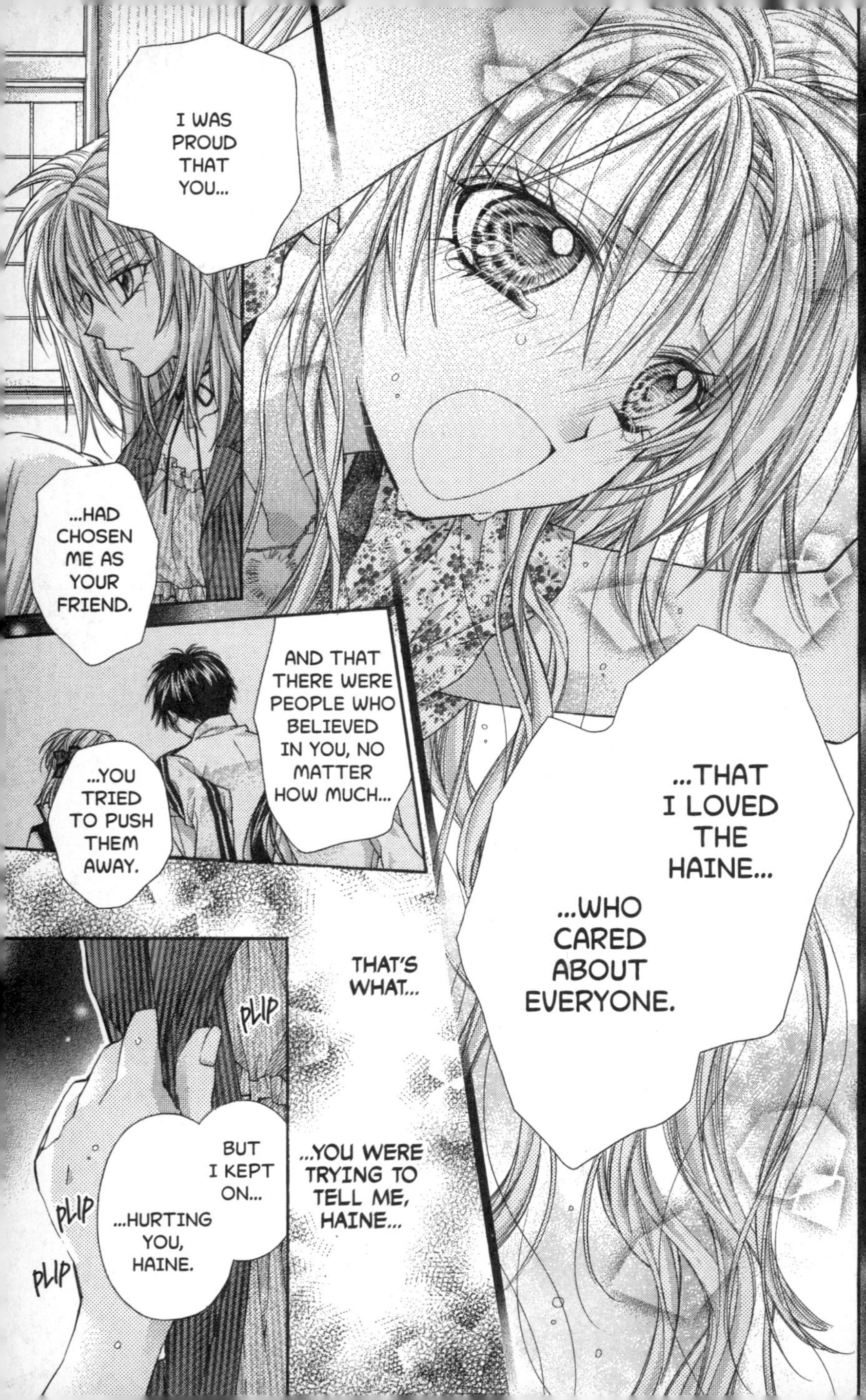
I WAS PROUD THAT YOU...
...HAD CHOSEN ME AS YOUR FRIEND.
AND THAT THERE WERE PEOPLE WHO BELIEVED IN YOU, NO MATTER HOW MUCH...
...YOU TRIED TO PUSH THEM AWAY.
...THAT I LOVED THE HAINE...
...WHO CARED ABOUT EVERYONE.
THAT'S WHAT...
...YOU WERE TRYING TO TELL ME, HAINE...
PLIP
BUT I KEPT ON...
...HURTING YOU, HAINE.
PLIP
PLIP

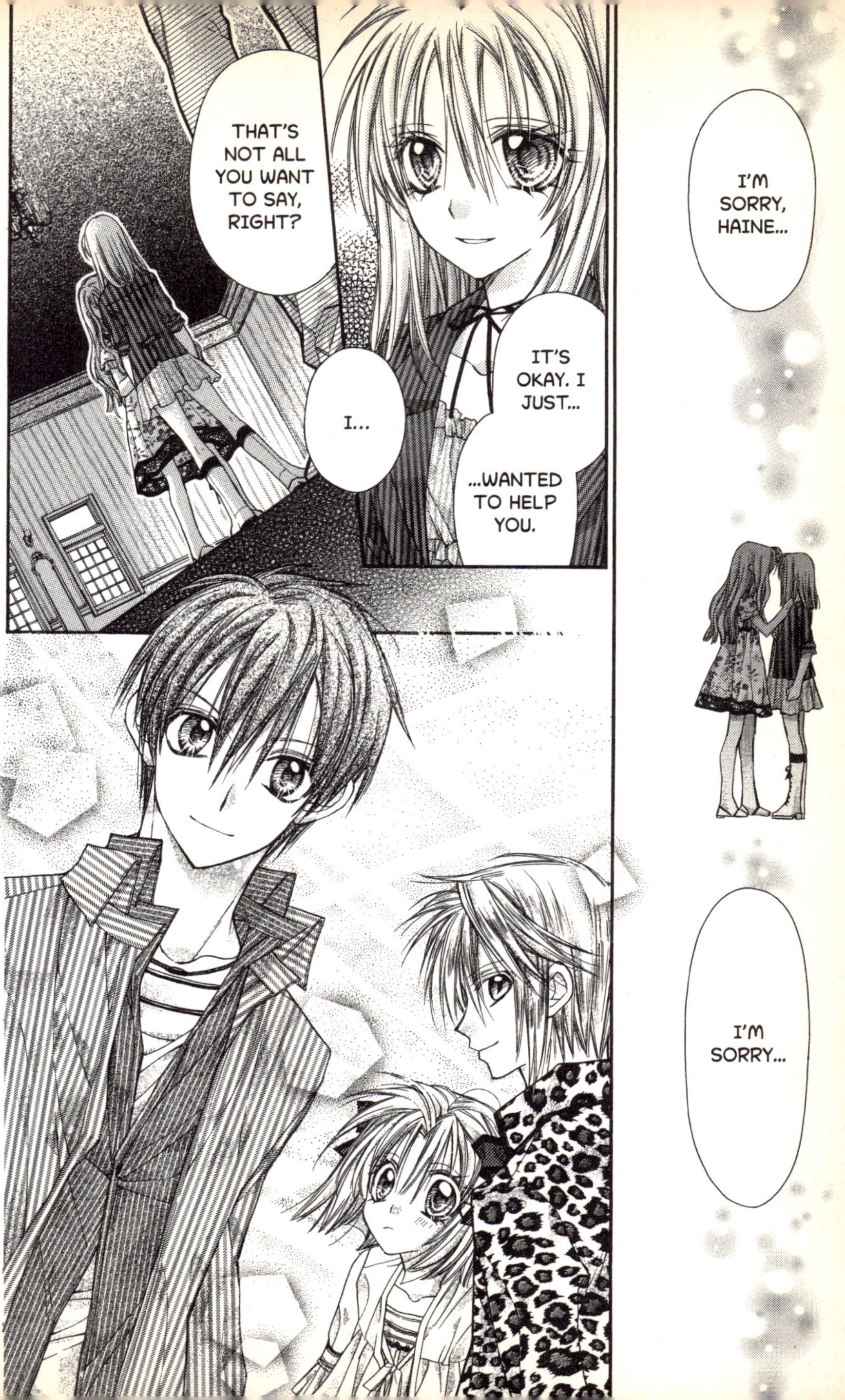
I'M SORRY, HAINE...
I'M SORRY...
IT'S OKAY. I JUST...
...WANTED TO HELP YOU.
THAT'S NOT ALL YOU WANT TO SAY, RIGHT?
I...

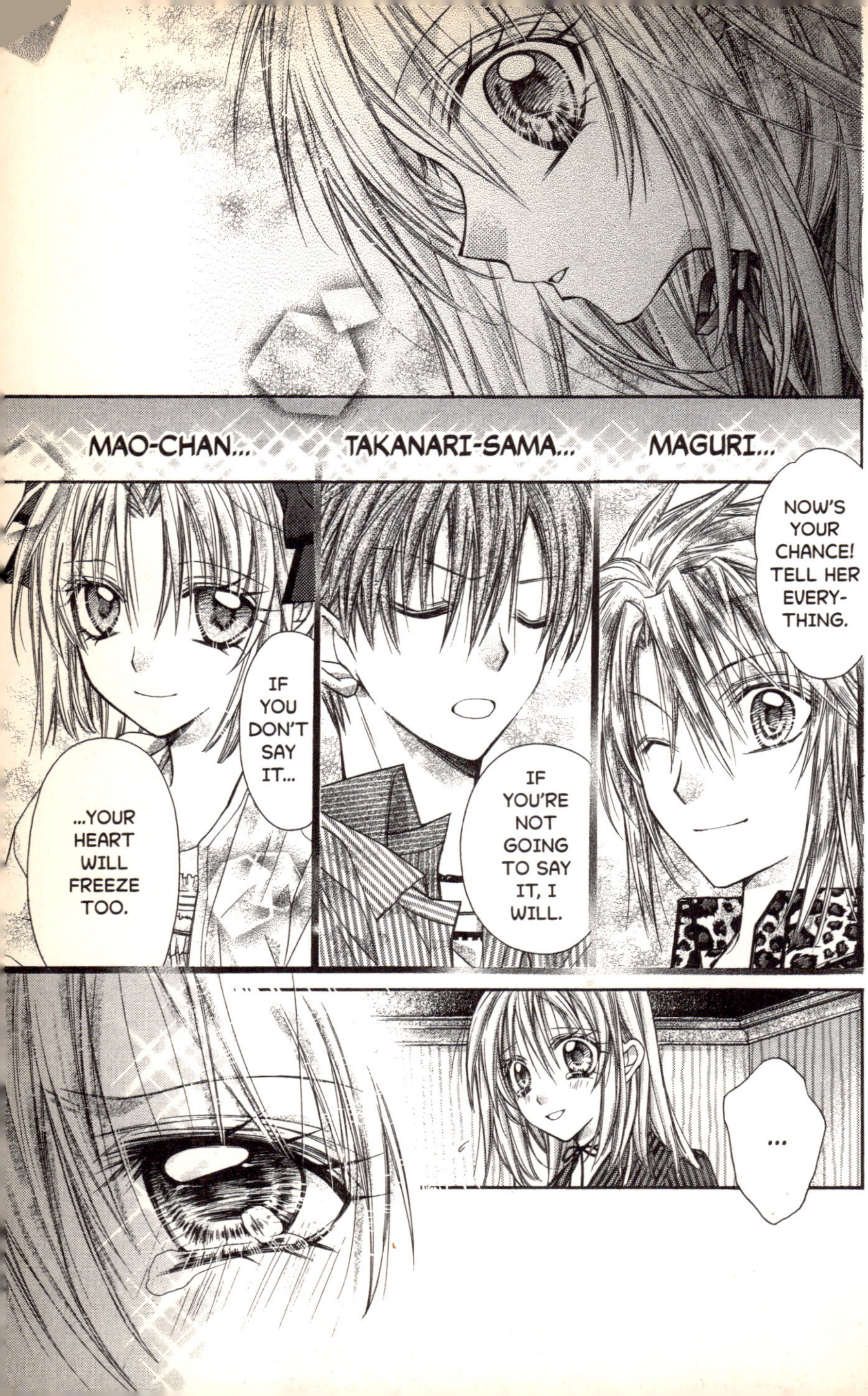
MAGURI...
NOW'S YOUR CHANCE! TELL HER EVERY-THING.
TAKANARI-SAMA...
IF YOU'RE NOT GOING TO SAY IT, I WILL.
MAO-CHAN...
IF YOU DON'T SAY IT...
...YOUR HEART WILL FREEZE TOO.
...

YOU LIAR!
YOU SAID I WAS THE ONLY PERSON YOU NEEDED!
YOU SAID YOU NEEDED ONLY ME...
YOU LIED TO ME, USHIO...

BUT...
...I...
I WANTED YOU TO BE HAPPY, USHIO!
THAT'S WHY—
I'M SORRY.
I'M SORRY, HAINE.

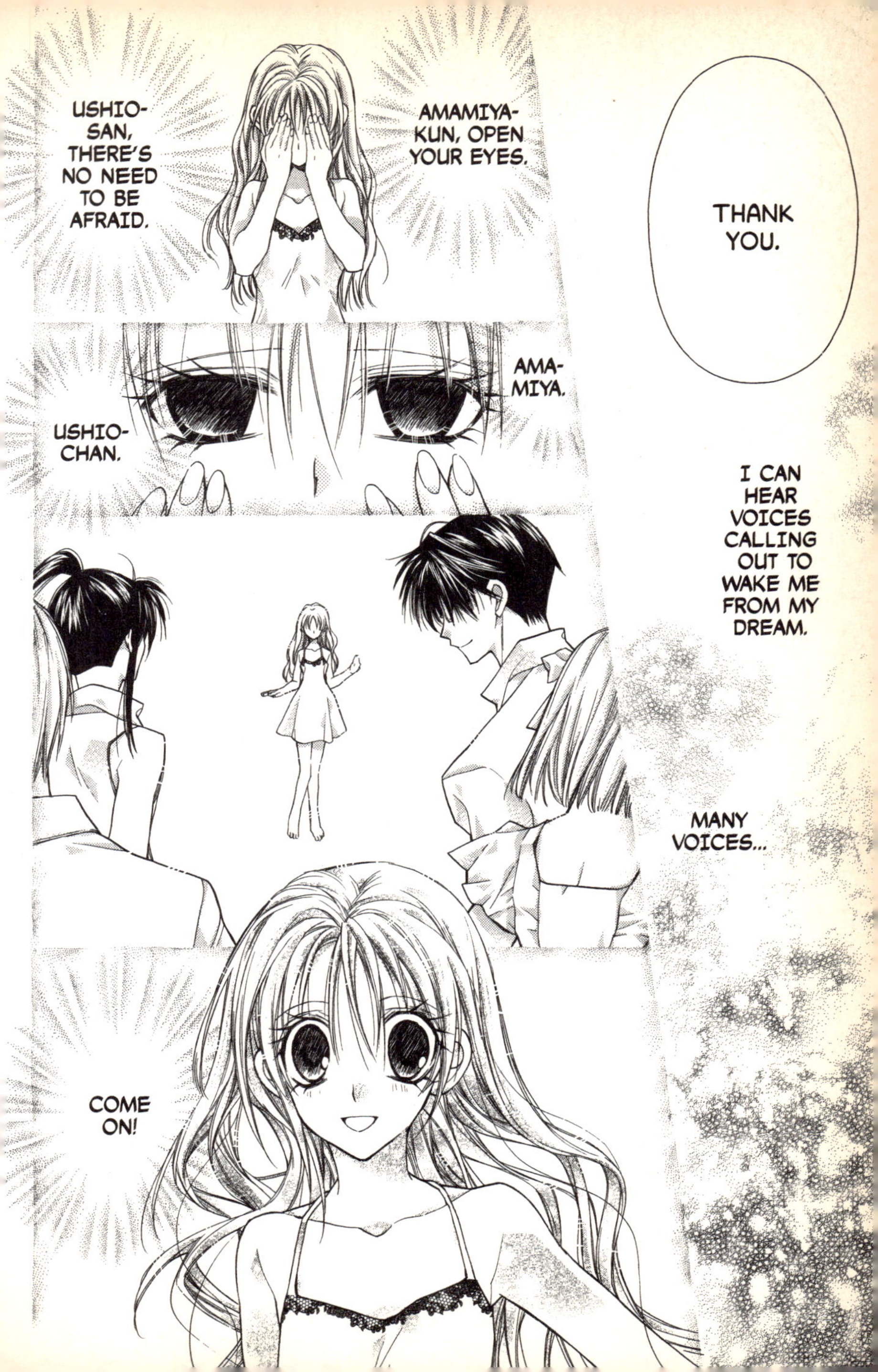
THANK YOU.
I CAN HEAR VOICES CALLING OUT TO WAKE ME FROM MY DREAM.
MANY VOICES...
AMAMIYA-KUN, OPEN YOUR EYES.
USHIO-SAN, THERE'S NO NEED TO BE AFRAID.
AMA-MIYA.
USHIO-CHAN.
COME ON!

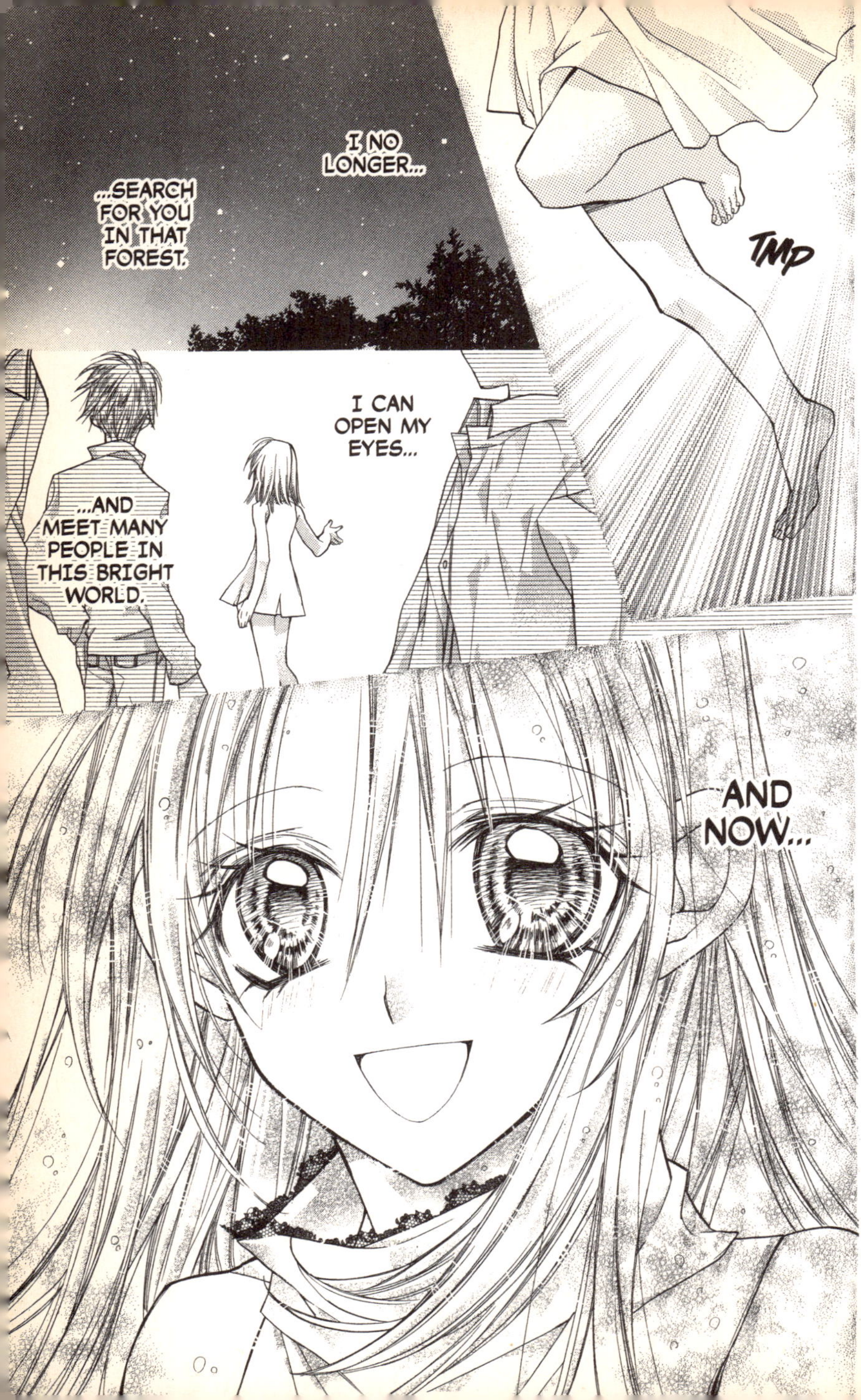
TMP
I NO LONGER...
...SEARCH FOR YOU IN THAT FOREST.
I CAN OPEN MY EYES...
...AND MEET MANY PEOPLE IN THIS BRIGHT WORLD.
AND NOW...

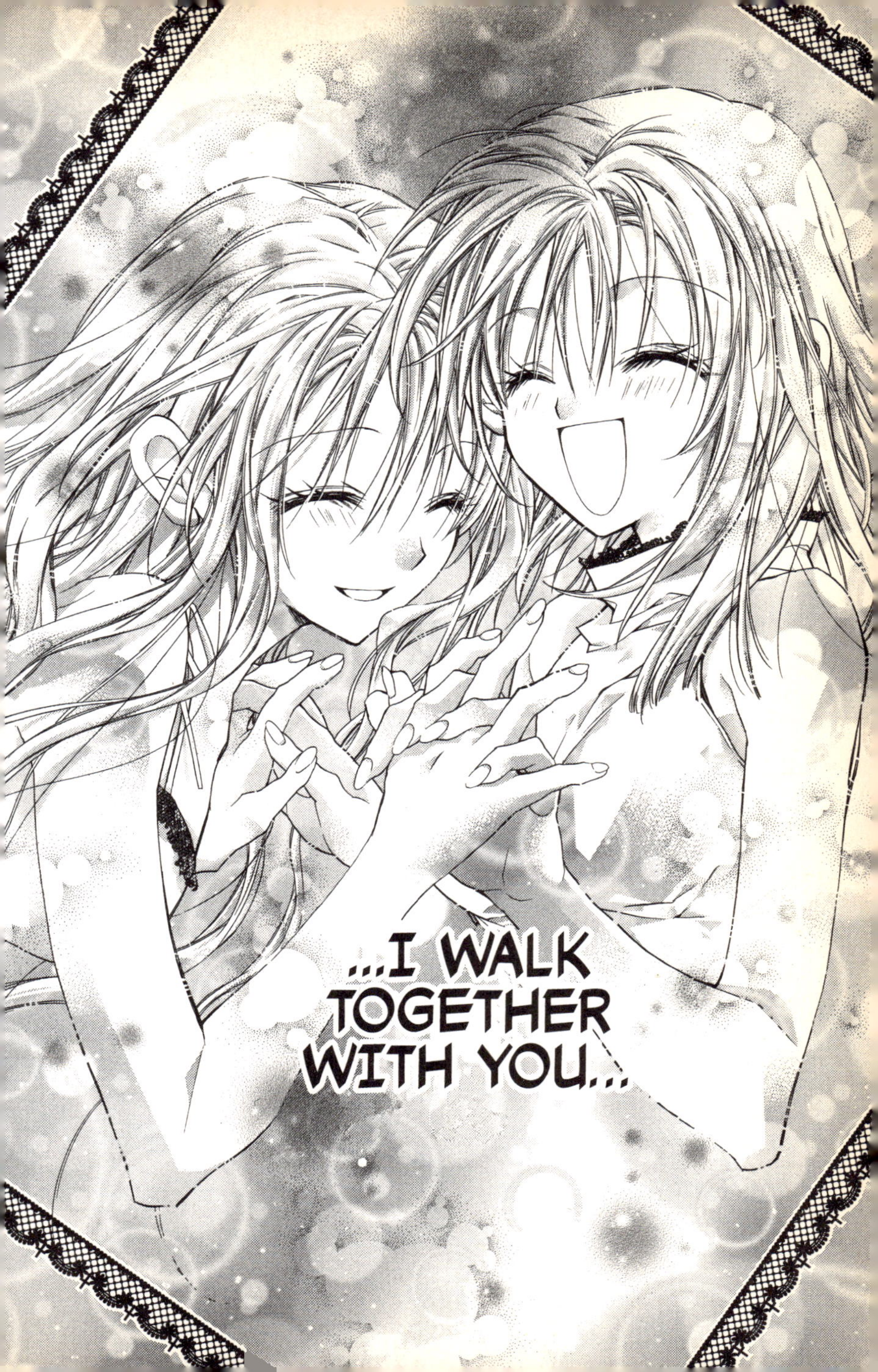
...I WALK TOGETHER WITH YOU...

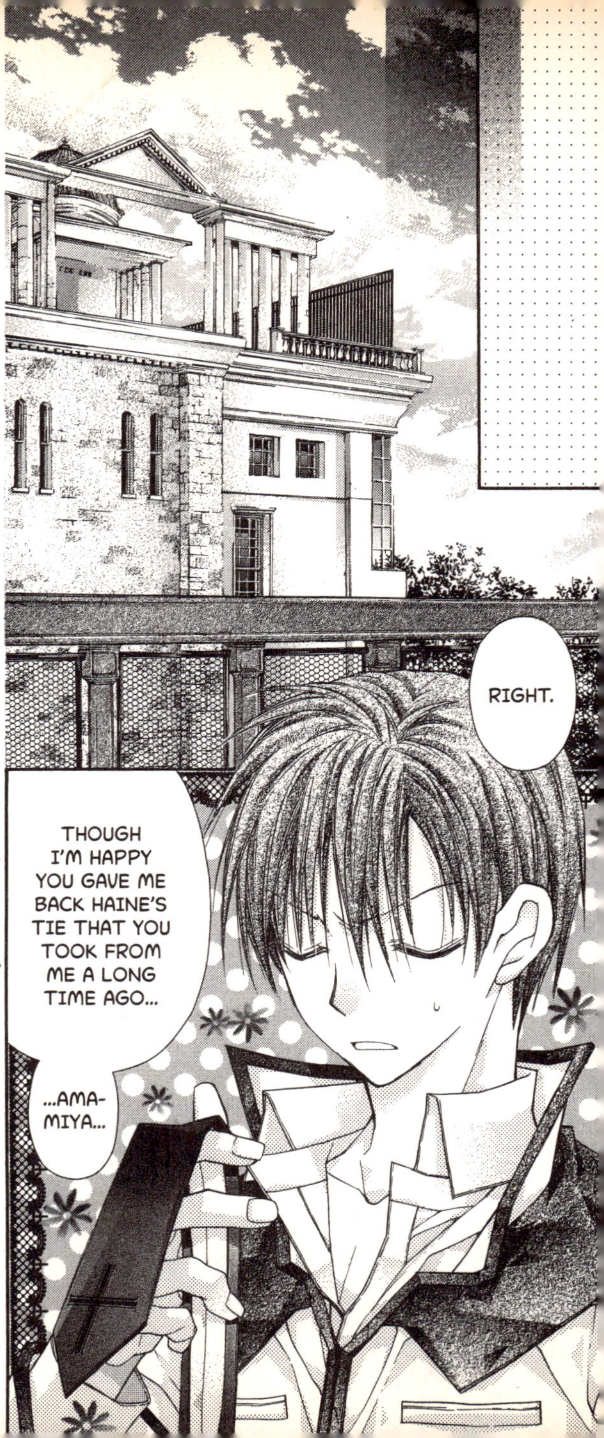
RIGHT.
THOUGH I'M HAPPY YOU GAVE ME BACK HAINE'S TIE THAT YOU TOOK FROM ME A LONG TIME AGO...
...AMA-MIYA...

Komaki Kamiya

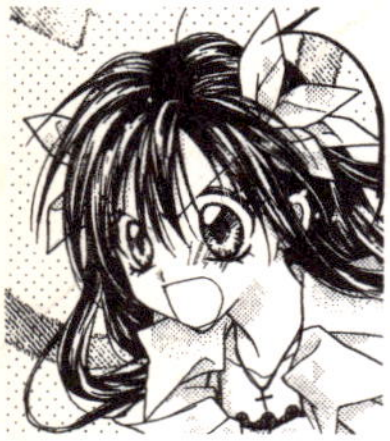

Birthday: June 12
Blood Type: A

She's Haine's younger sister and Tachibana's older sister. She started going out with Kusame due to a huge confusion. After a while they were both mutually in love. She dotes on her older sister. She talks in a rather haughty manner. She's a hard worker who is the Middle School Student Council President.

Comments

I never thought she would become this popular... But I really like her as well, so I guess it's understandable? The ribbon on her head is gradually getting bigger and bigger... (It was the same for Takuto in *Full Moon* too. Maybe I've got the tendency to do things like this?)

By the way, her order of priority is first Haine, then Kusame. Her older sister is everything to her.

She's always been fond of Haine, but because of their mother's condition, she's had to act like a grown-up. Haine is very important to her as someone she can rely on...

WHAT'S WITH THE SUDDEN CHANGE OF HEART?! IT'S CREEPING ME OUT!!
URGH!
Hm.
USHIO'S TIE
TAKANARI'S RIBBON
HAINE GAVE ME THE ONE SHE HAD BEEN WEARING.
GIVE IT BACK TO ME IF YOU DON'T WANT IT.
Am I the same as Amamiya to you, Haine?!
No, I like everyone.
Peacefully!! Equally!!
I HEARD YOU DUMPED ALL YOUR BOY-FRIENDS.
YUKKIE WAS CRYING.
YEAH...
TMP TMP TMP
I WON'T GIVE UP!!
TMP TMP
I'M GOING TO START FROM SCRATCH TO BECOME YOUR TRUE LOVER, USHIO-SAN!
DO YOUR BEST.
DECLARATION!!

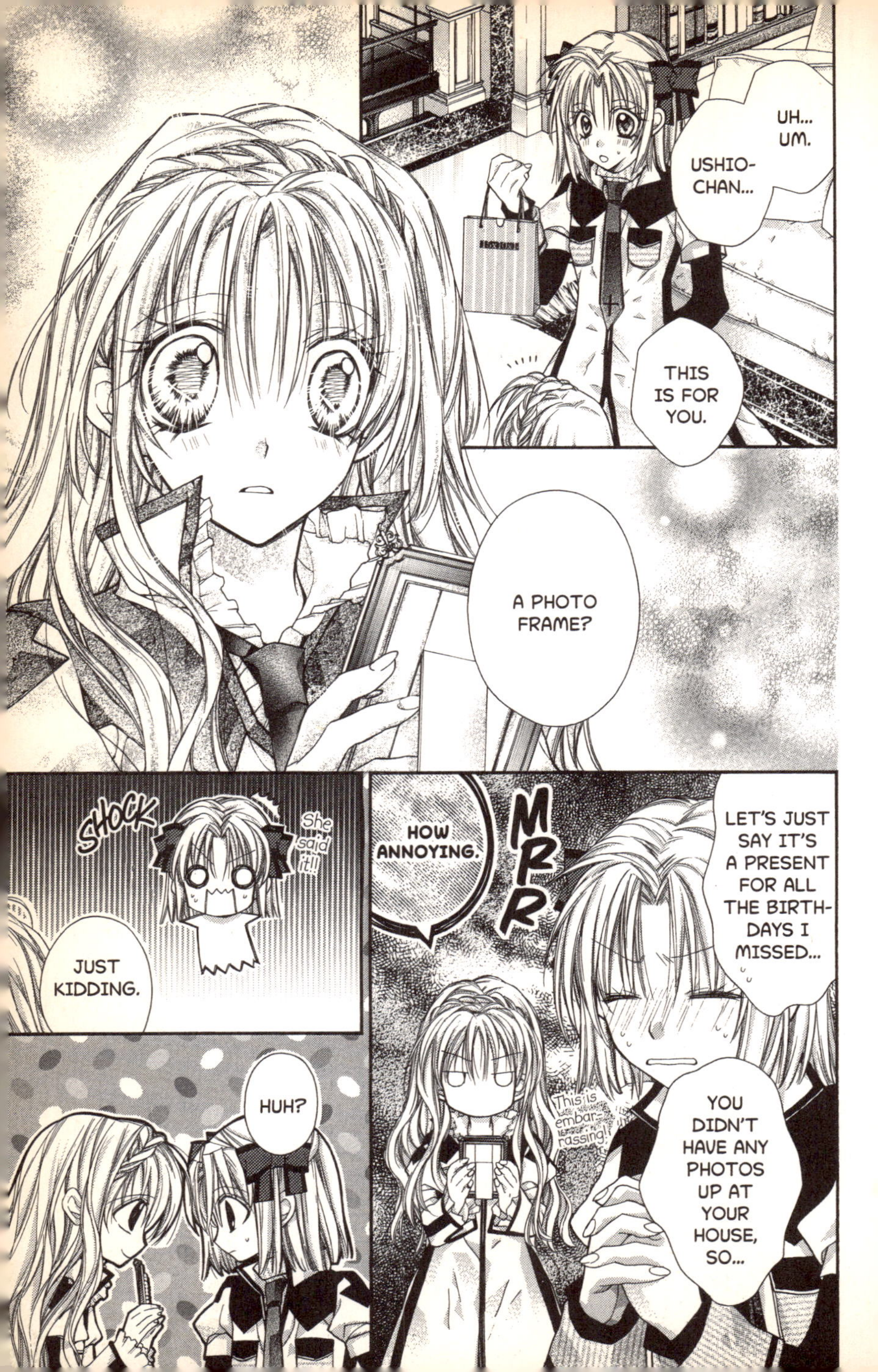
UH... UM.
USHIO-CHAN...
THIS IS FOR YOU.
A PHOTO FRAME?
LET'S JUST SAY IT'S A PRESENT FOR ALL THE BIRTH-DAYS I MISSED...
YOU DIDN'T HAVE ANY PHOTOS UP AT YOUR HOUSE, SO...
MRR
HOW ANNOYING.
This is embar-rassing!
SHOCK
She said it!!
JUST KIDDING.
HUH?

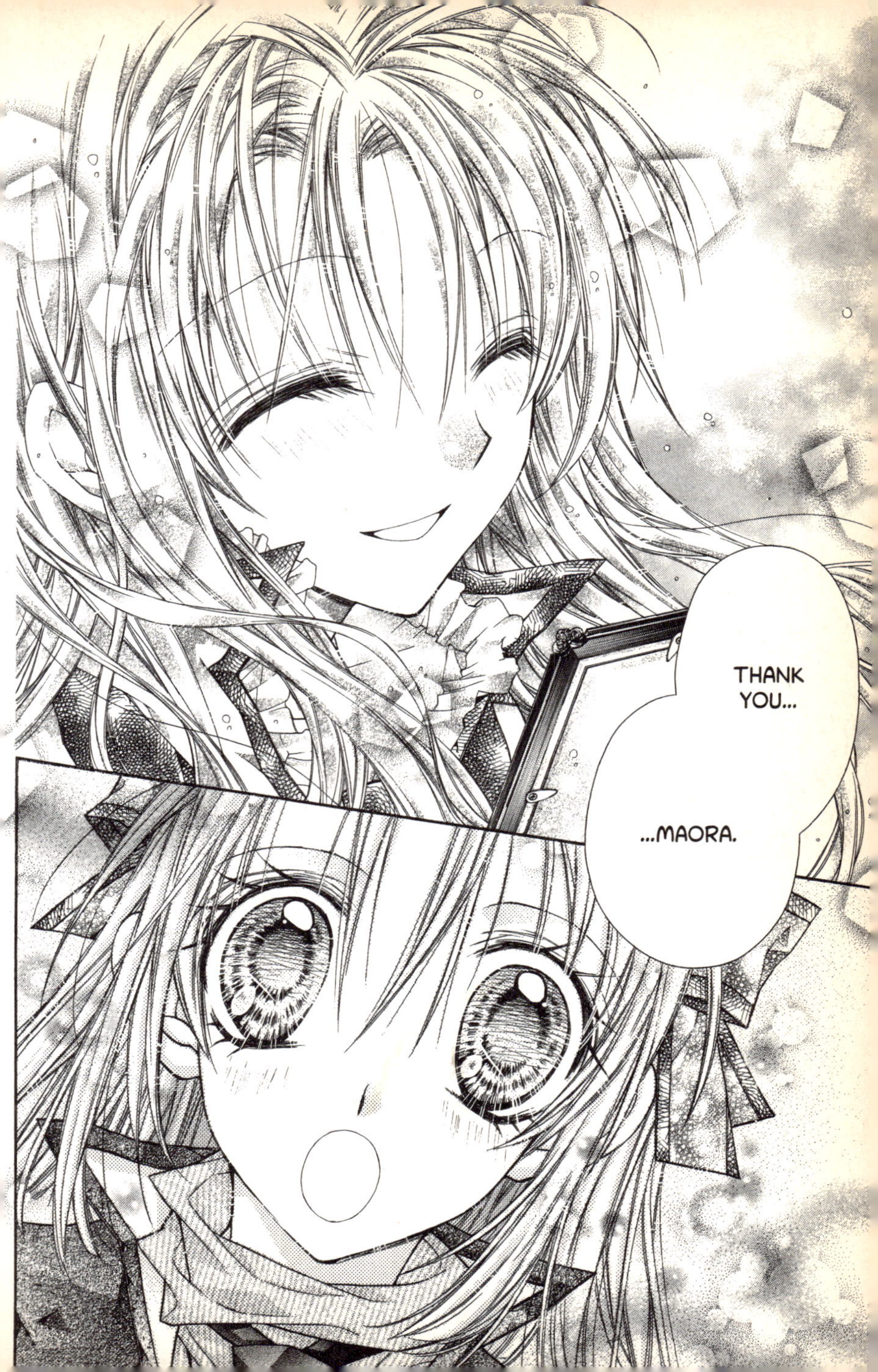
THANK YOU...
...MAORA.

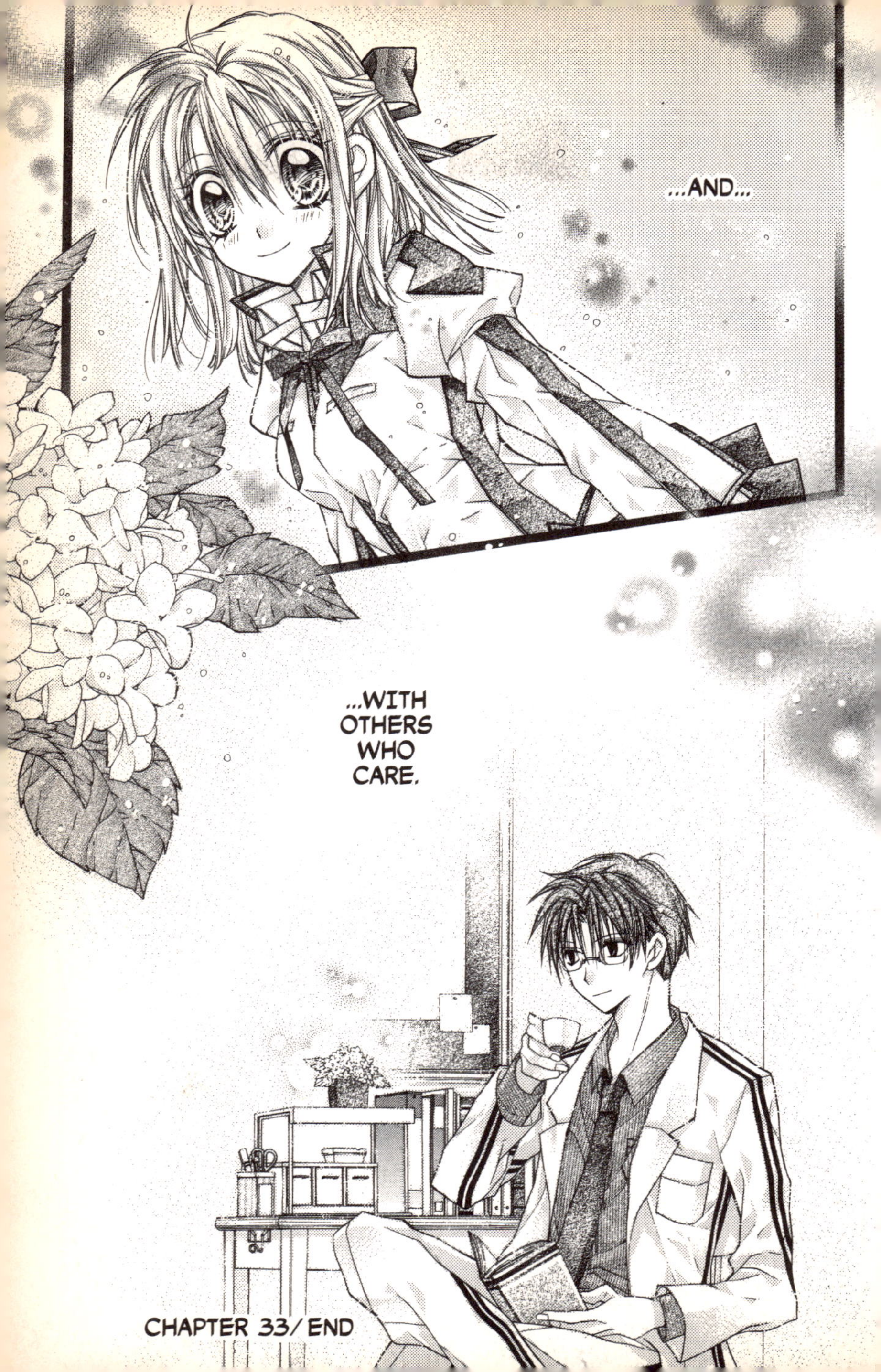
...AND...
...WITH OTHERS WHO CARE.
CHAPTER 33/ END

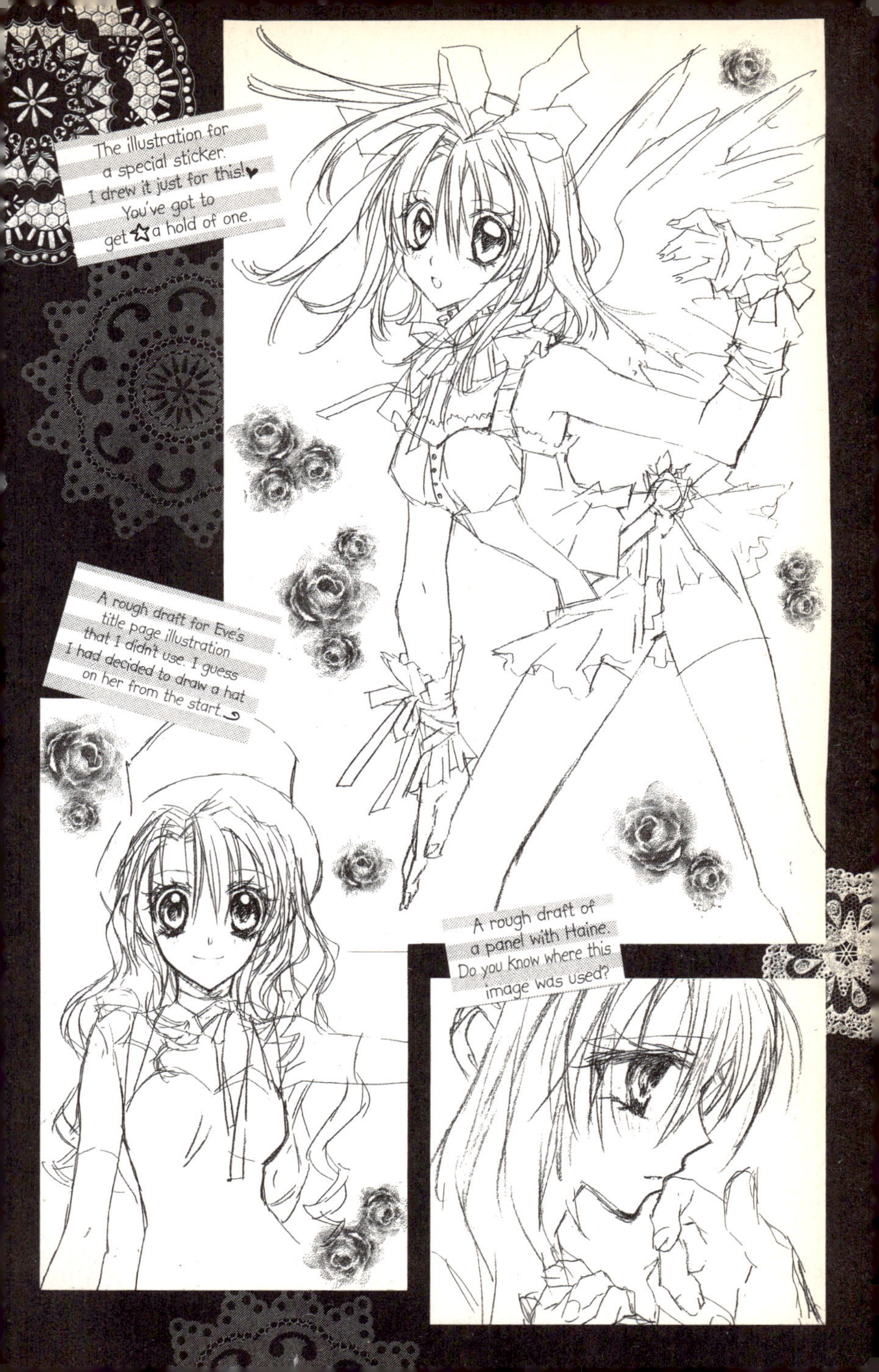
The illustration for a special sticker. I drew it just for this!♥ You've got to get ☆ a hold of one.
A rough draft for Eve's title page illustration that I didn't use. I guess I had decided to draw a hat on her from the start.
A rough draft of a panel with Haine. Do you know where this image was used?

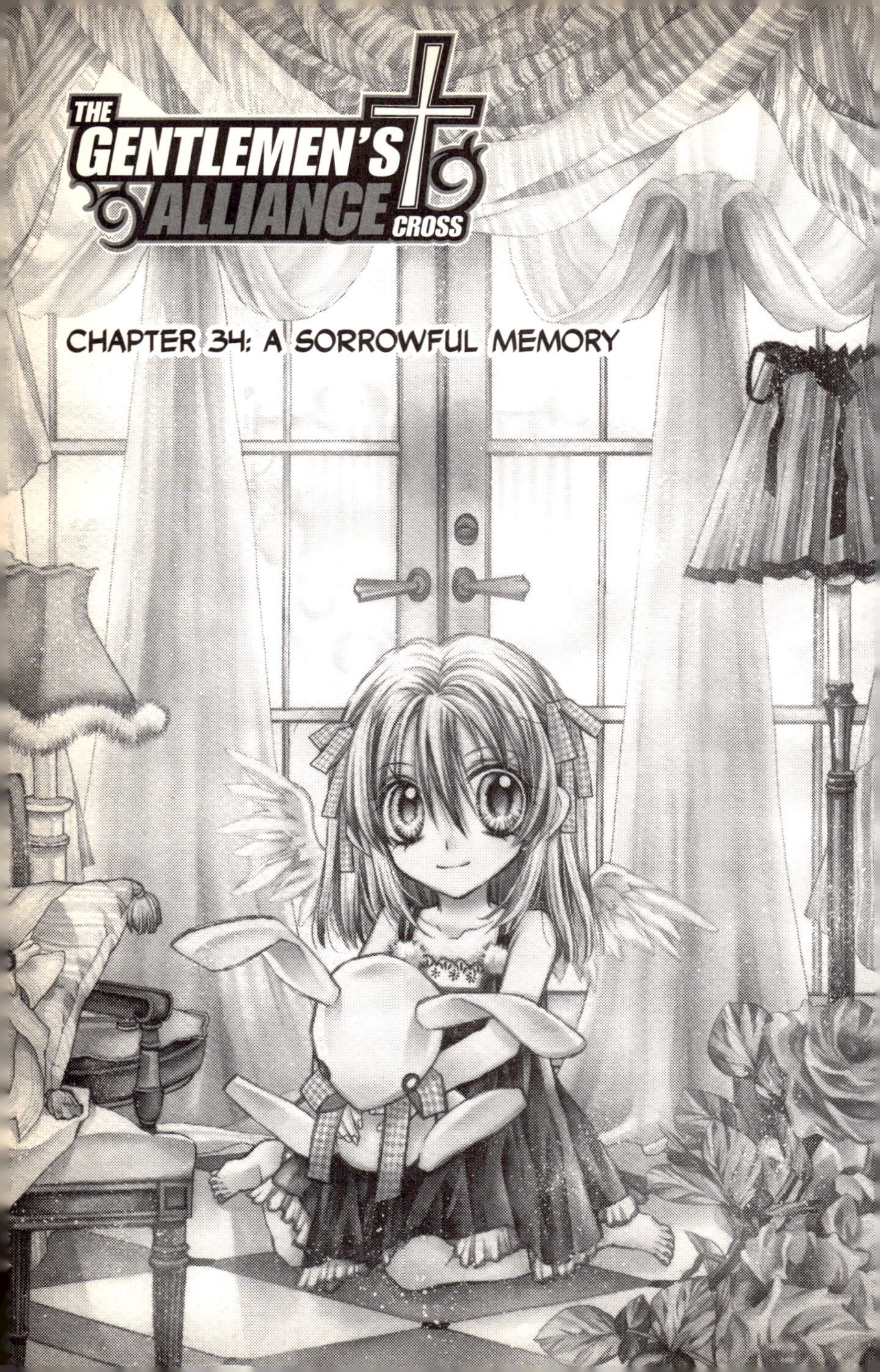
THE GENTLEMEN'S ALLIANCE CROSS
CHAPTER 34: A SORROWFUL MEMORY

This is the *name* (storyboard) for chapter 25 in volume 6. This is a typical *name* for me.

NAME

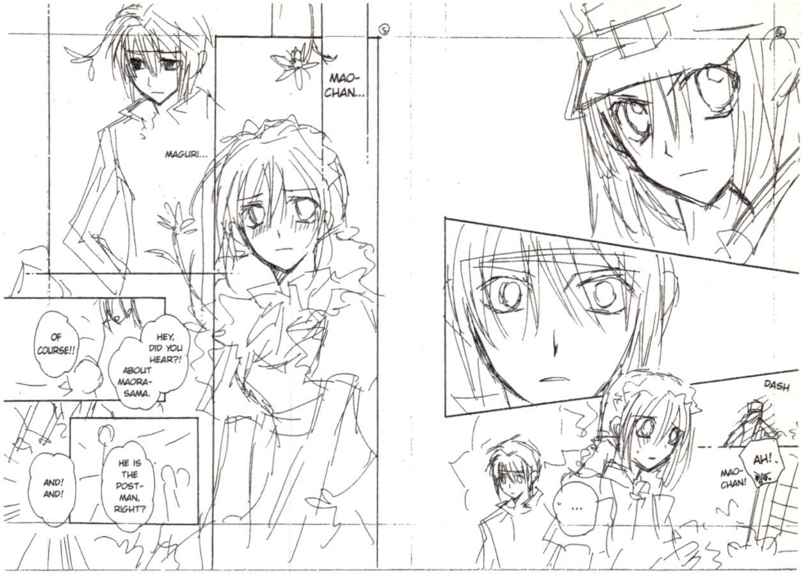
DASH
AH!
MAO-CHAN!
...
MAO-CHAN...
MAGURI...
HEY, DID YOU HEAR?!
ABOUT MAORA-SAMA.
OF COURSE!!
HE IS THE POST-MAN, RIGHT?
AND! AND!

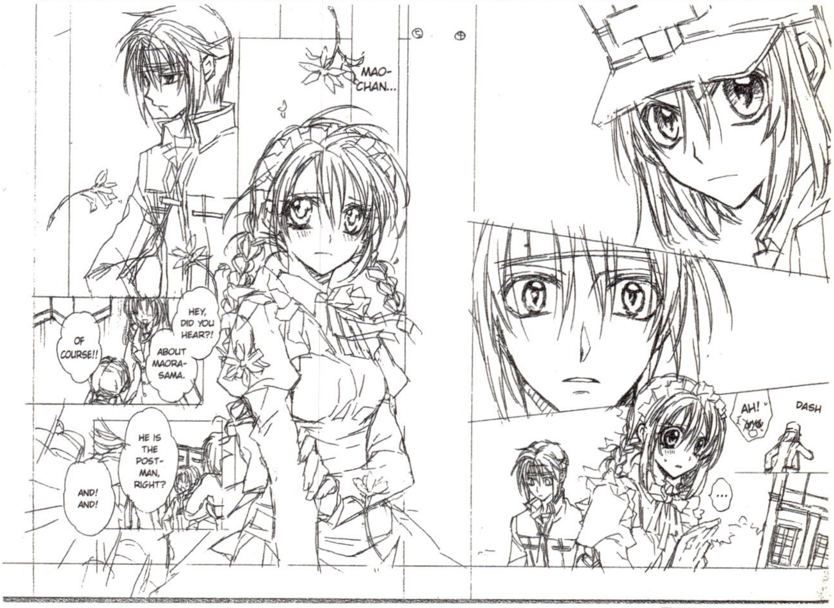
DASH
AH!
...
MAO-CHAN...
HEY, DID YOU HEAR?!
ABOUT MAORA-SAMA.
OF COURSE!!
HE IS THE POST-MAN, RIGHT?
AND! AND!

This is the rough draft. In the actual chapter, Mao-chan's expression on page 4, panel 1, is a little more held back, so please compare them.

ROUGH DRAFT

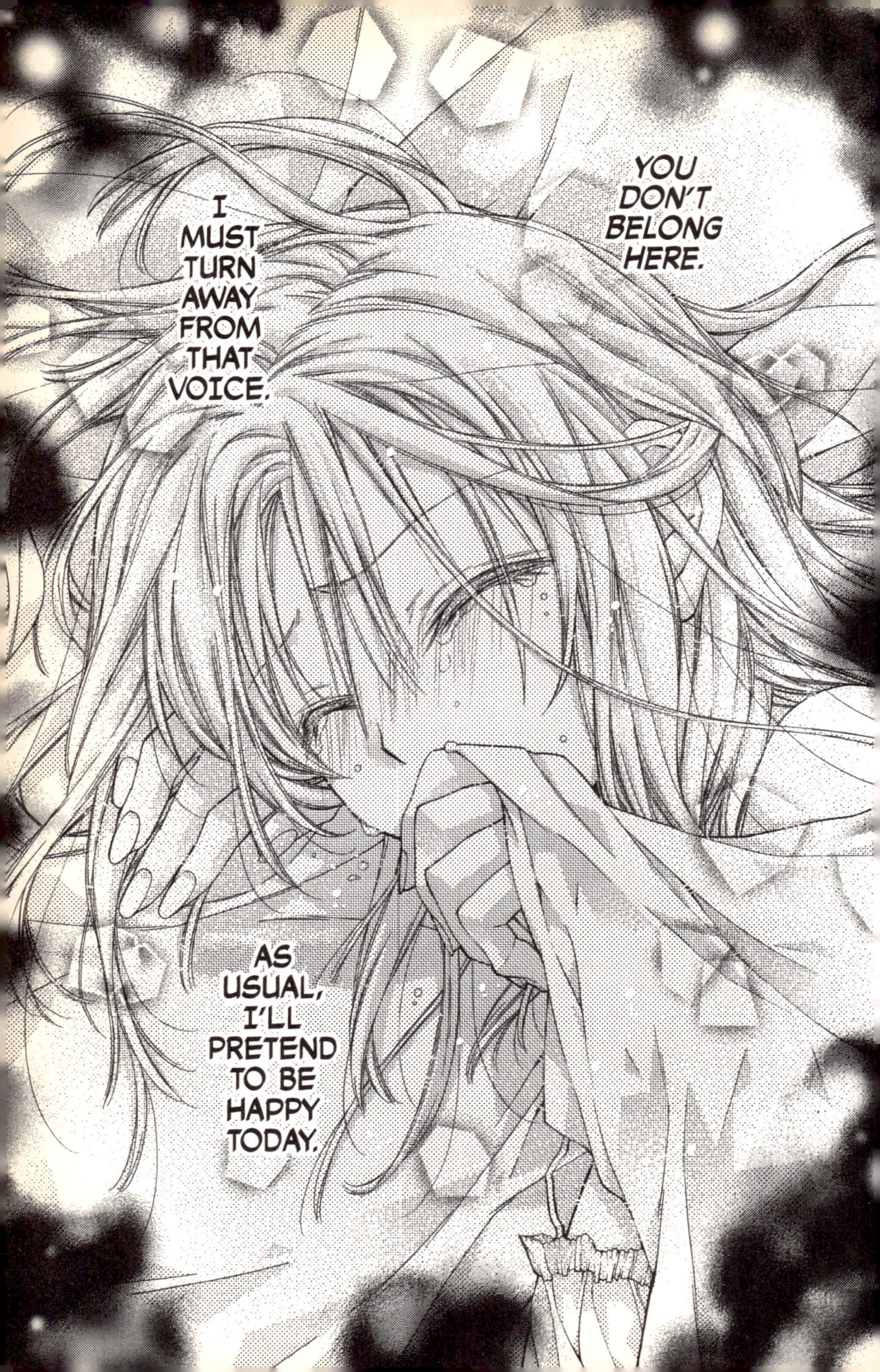
YOU DON'T BELONG HERE.
I MUST TURN AWAY FROM THAT VOICE.
AS USUAL, I'LL PRETEND TO BE HAPPY TODAY.

GOOD EVENING. ☆ I'M HAINE OTOMIYA.
SO.
MAO-CHAN! YOU AND MAGURI ...
HOW FAR HAVE YOU TWO ACTUALLY GONE?!
BHFF

Chapter 34: A Sorrowful Memory

※・I'm giving away the story.

Lead-in I'm Haine. Will you play with me?

Well then, here begins the long Haine arc! (It's slated to be six chapters in all.) I was happy to be able to draw the sensei whom I haven't been able to write about!! And, of course, the headmaster. (laugh) I had the "headmaster thing" in mind since the first chapter of the series. (That's why he's protecting the school.)

I feel so sorry for Maika-san... Haine was very precious to her for many reasons... The "Dark Mermaid" happened to be really popular. I'm sad I'm not able to use that name since the story will get serious! Kasuga is going to be a very important character so please be attentive. ♥

For the first time in the whole series, you get to see HaineKko take off her jacket. It's rather exciting. I want to draw her in color when I get the chance...

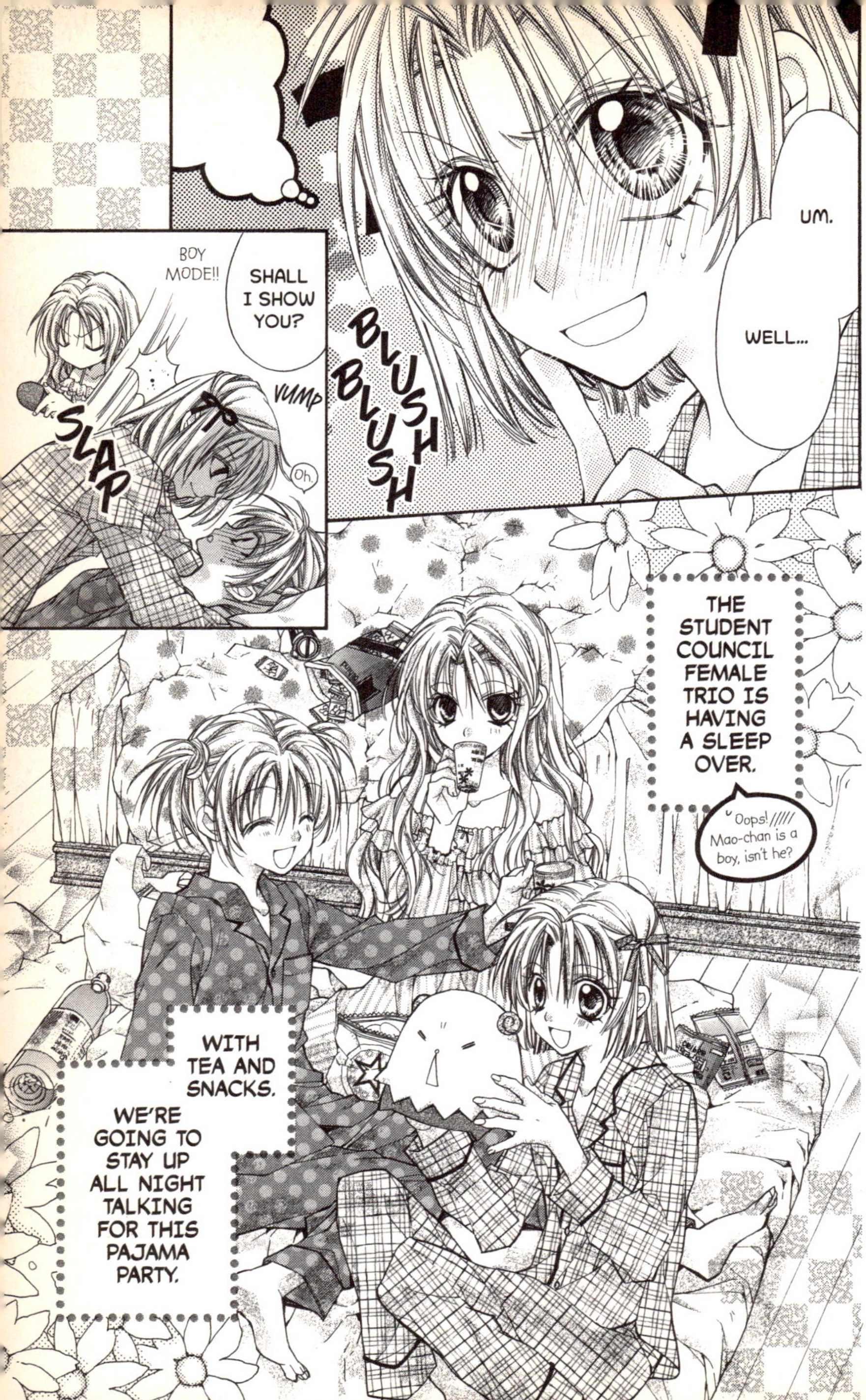
UM.
WELL...
BLUSH BLUSH
SHALL I SHOW YOU?
BOY MODE!!
VUMP
SLAP
Oh.
THE STUDENT COUNCIL FEMALE TRIO IS HAVING A SLEEP OVER.
Oops! ///// Mao-chan is a boy, isn't he?
WITH TEA AND SNACKS.
WE'RE GOING TO STAY UP ALL NIGHT TALKING FOR THIS PAJAMA PARTY.

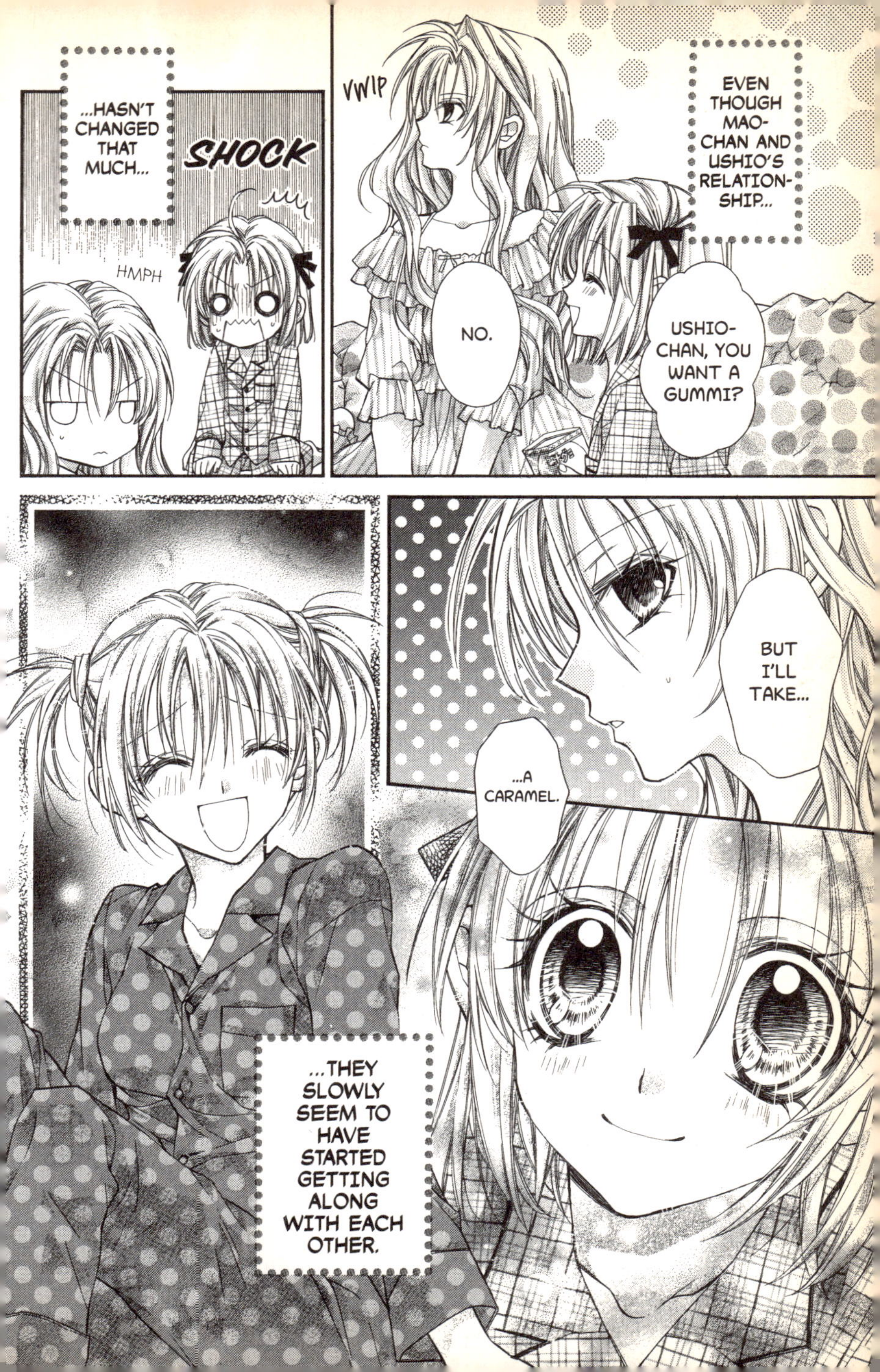
EVEN THOUGH MAO-CHAN AND USHIO'S RELATION-SHIP...
VWIP
USHIO-CHAN, YOU WANT A GUMMI?
NO.
...HASN'T CHANGED THAT MUCH...
SHOCK
HMPH
BUT I'LL TAKE...
...A CARAMEL.
...THEY SLOWLY SEEM TO HAVE STARTED GETTING ALONG WITH EACH OTHER.

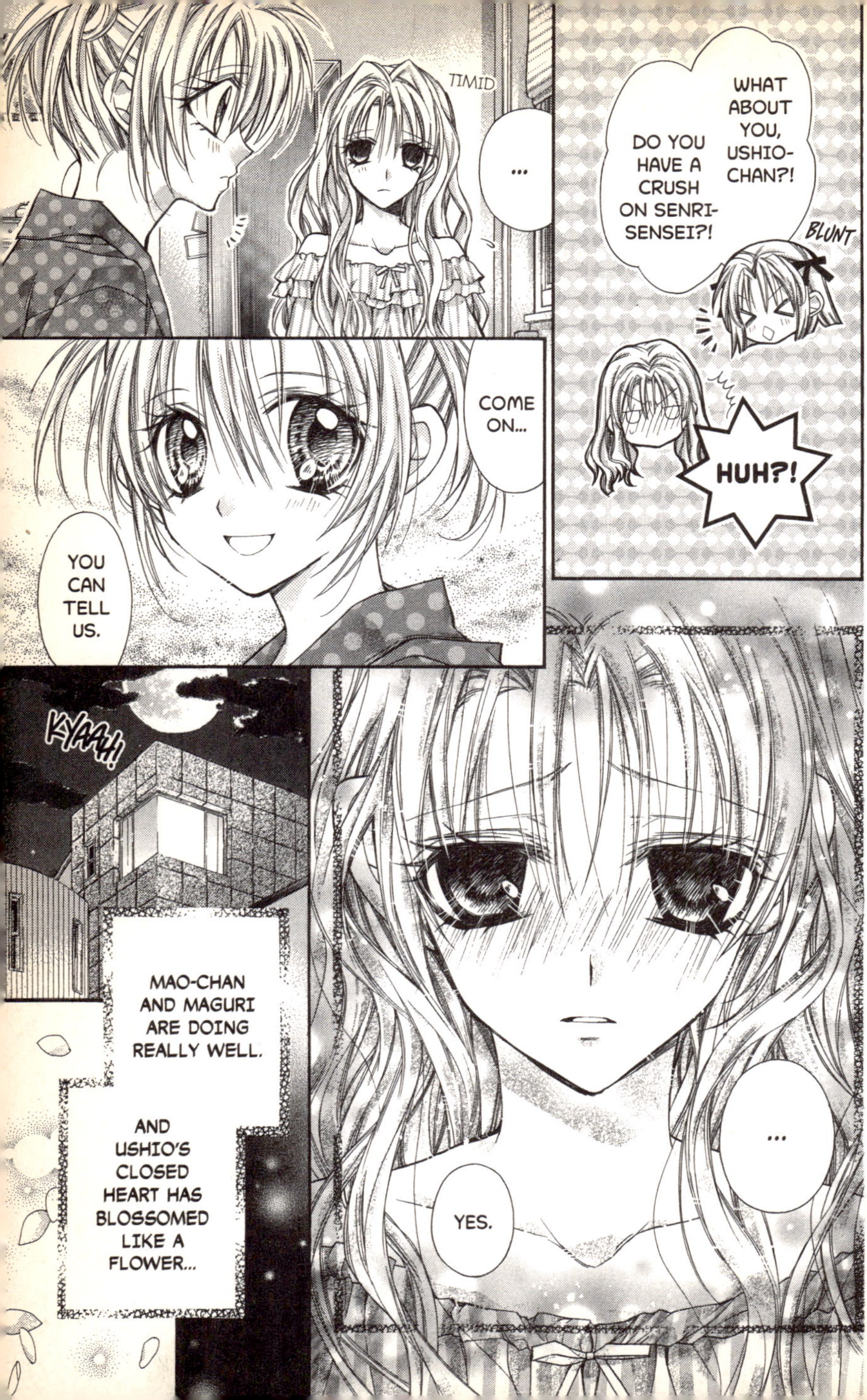
WHAT ABOUT YOU, USHIO-CHAN?!
DO YOU HAVE A CRUSH ON SENRI-SENSEI?!
BLUNT
HUH?!
TIMID
...
COME ON...
YOU CAN TELL US.
...
YES.
KYAAAH!
MAO-CHAN AND MAGURI ARE DOING REALLY WELL.
AND USHIO'S CLOSED HEART HAS BLOSSOMED LIKE A FLOWER...

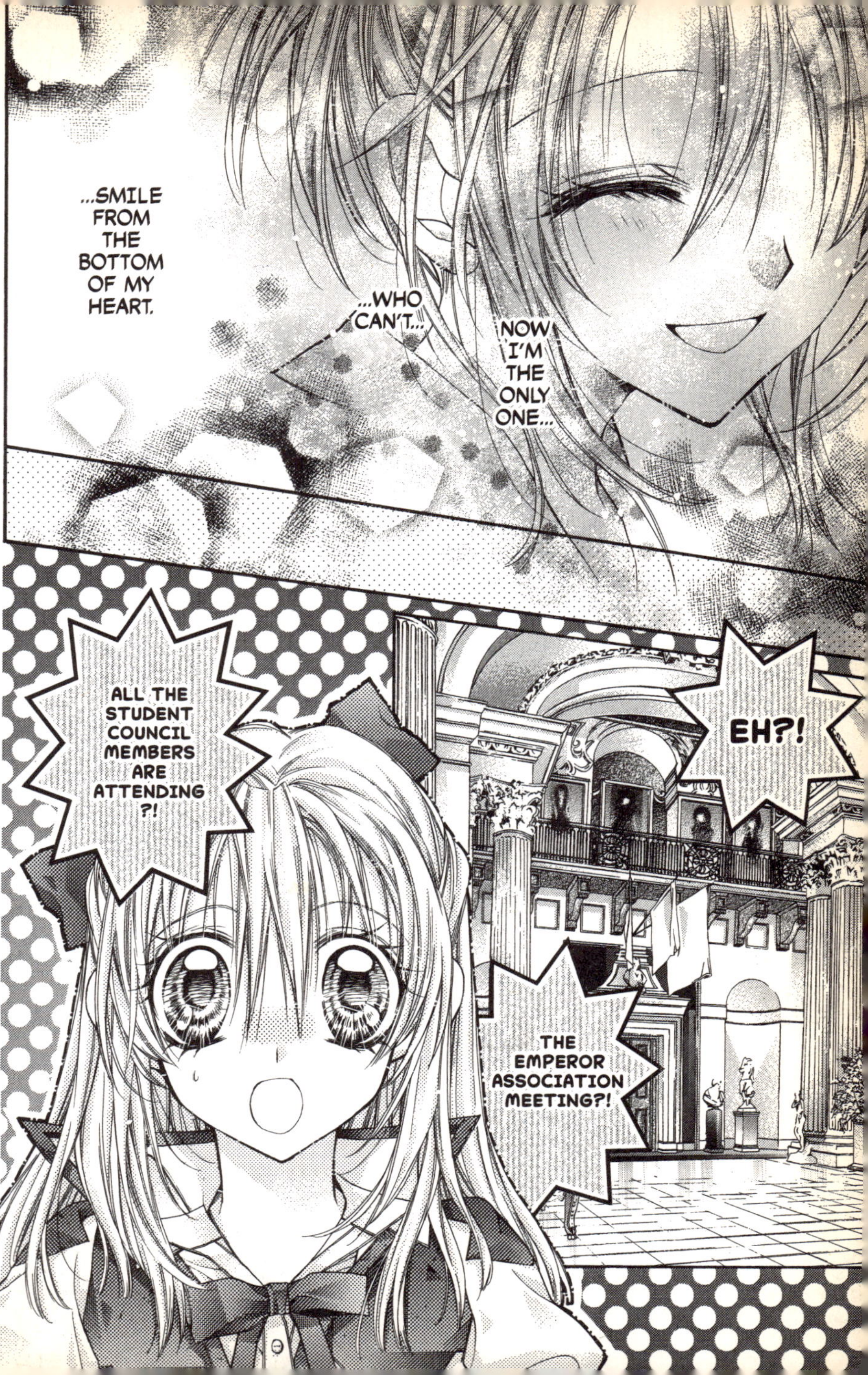
NOW I'M THE ONLY ONE...
...WHO CAN'T...
...SMILE FROM THE BOTTOM OF MY HEART.
EH?!
THE EMPEROR ASSOCIATION MEETING?!
ALL THE STUDENT COUNCIL MEMBERS ARE ATTENDING?!

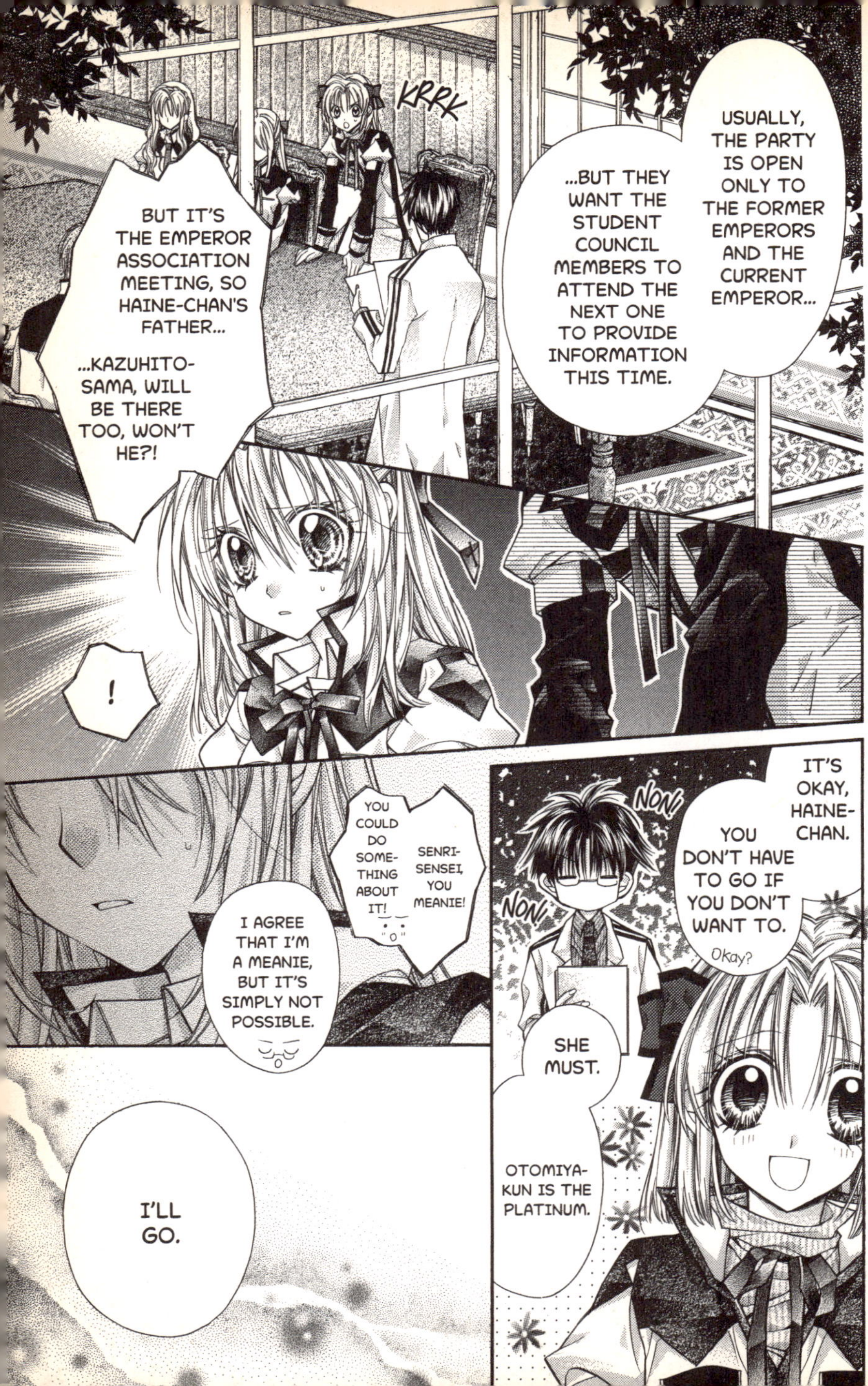
KRRK
USUALLY, THE PARTY IS OPEN ONLY TO THE FORMER EMPERORS AND THE CURRENT EMPEROR...
...BUT THEY WANT THE STUDENT COUNCIL MEMBERS TO ATTEND THE NEXT ONE TO PROVIDE INFORMATION THIS TIME.
BUT IT'S THE EMPEROR ASSOCIATION MEETING, SO HAINE-CHAN'S FATHER...
...KAZUHITO-SAMA, WILL BE THERE TOO, WON'T HE?!
!
IT'S OKAY, HAINE-CHAN.
YOU DON'T HAVE TO GO IF YOU DON'T WANT TO.
Okay?
NON!
NON!
SHE MUST.
OTOMIYA-KUN IS THE PLATINUM.
SENRI-SENSEI, YOU MEANIE!
YOU COULD DO SOMETHING ABOUT IT!
I AGREE THAT I'M A MEANIE, BUT IT'S SIMPLY NOT POSSIBLE.
I'LL GO.

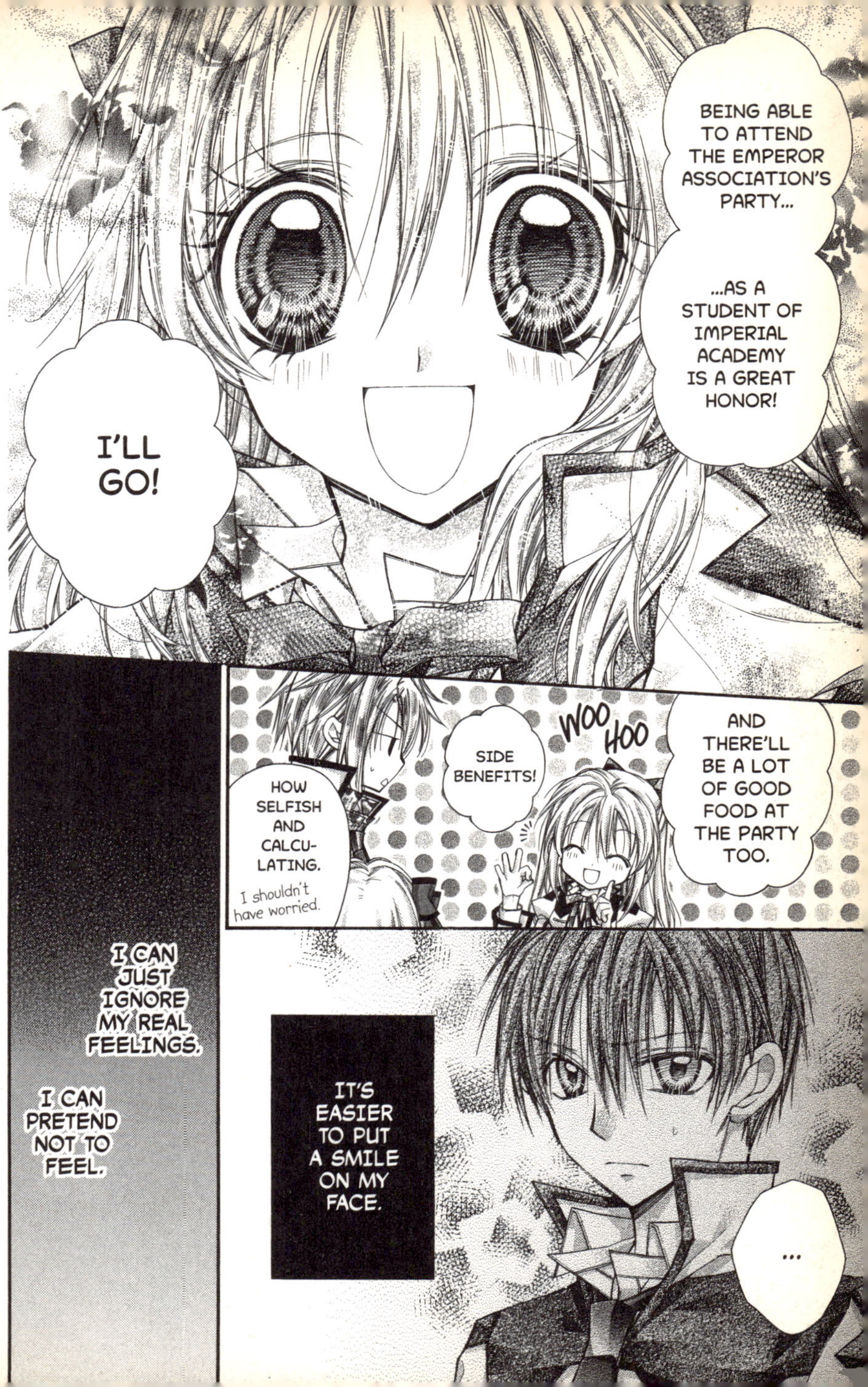
BEING ABLE TO ATTEND THE EMPEROR ASSOCIATION'S PARTY...
...AS A STUDENT OF IMPERIAL ACADEMY IS A GREAT HONOR!
I'LL GO!
AND THERE'LL BE A LOT OF GOOD FOOD AT THE PARTY TOO.
WOO HOO
SIDE BENEFITS!
HOW SELFISH AND CALCU-LATING.
I shouldn't have worried.
...
IT'S EASIER TO PUT A SMILE ON MY FACE.
I CAN JUST IGNORE MY REAL FEELINGS.
I CAN PRETEND NOT TO FEEL.

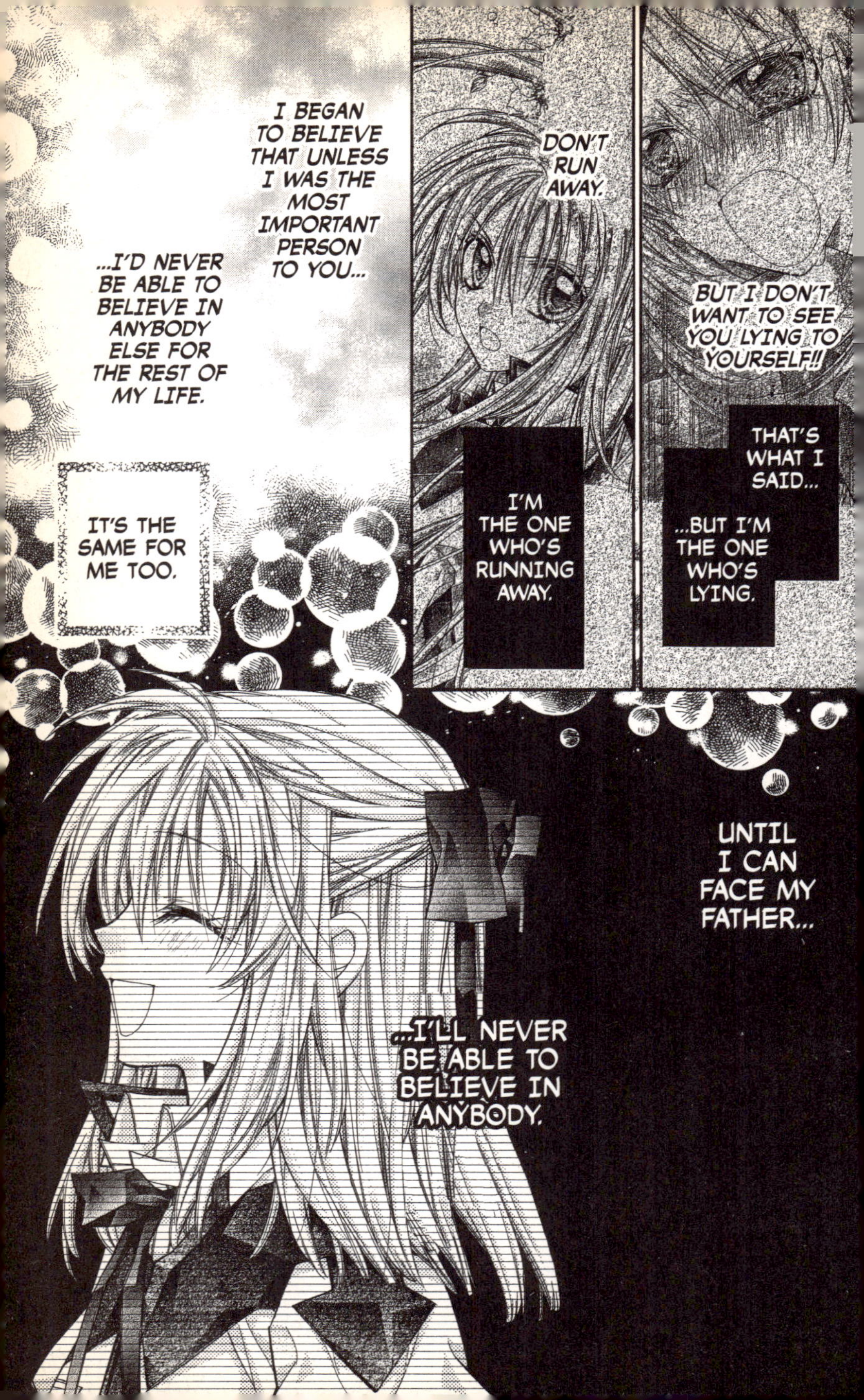
BUT I DON'T WANT TO SEE YOU LYING TO YOURSELF!!
THAT'S WHAT I SAID...
...BUT I'M THE ONE WHO'S LYING.
DON'T RUN AWAY.
I'M THE ONE WHO'S RUNNING AWAY.
I BEGAN TO BELIEVE THAT UNLESS I WAS THE MOST IMPORTANT PERSON TO YOU...
...I'D NEVER BE ABLE TO BELIEVE IN ANYBODY ELSE FOR THE REST OF MY LIFE.
IT'S THE SAME FOR ME TOO.
UNTIL I CAN FACE MY FATHER...
...I'LL NEVER BE ABLE TO BELIEVE IN ANYBODY.

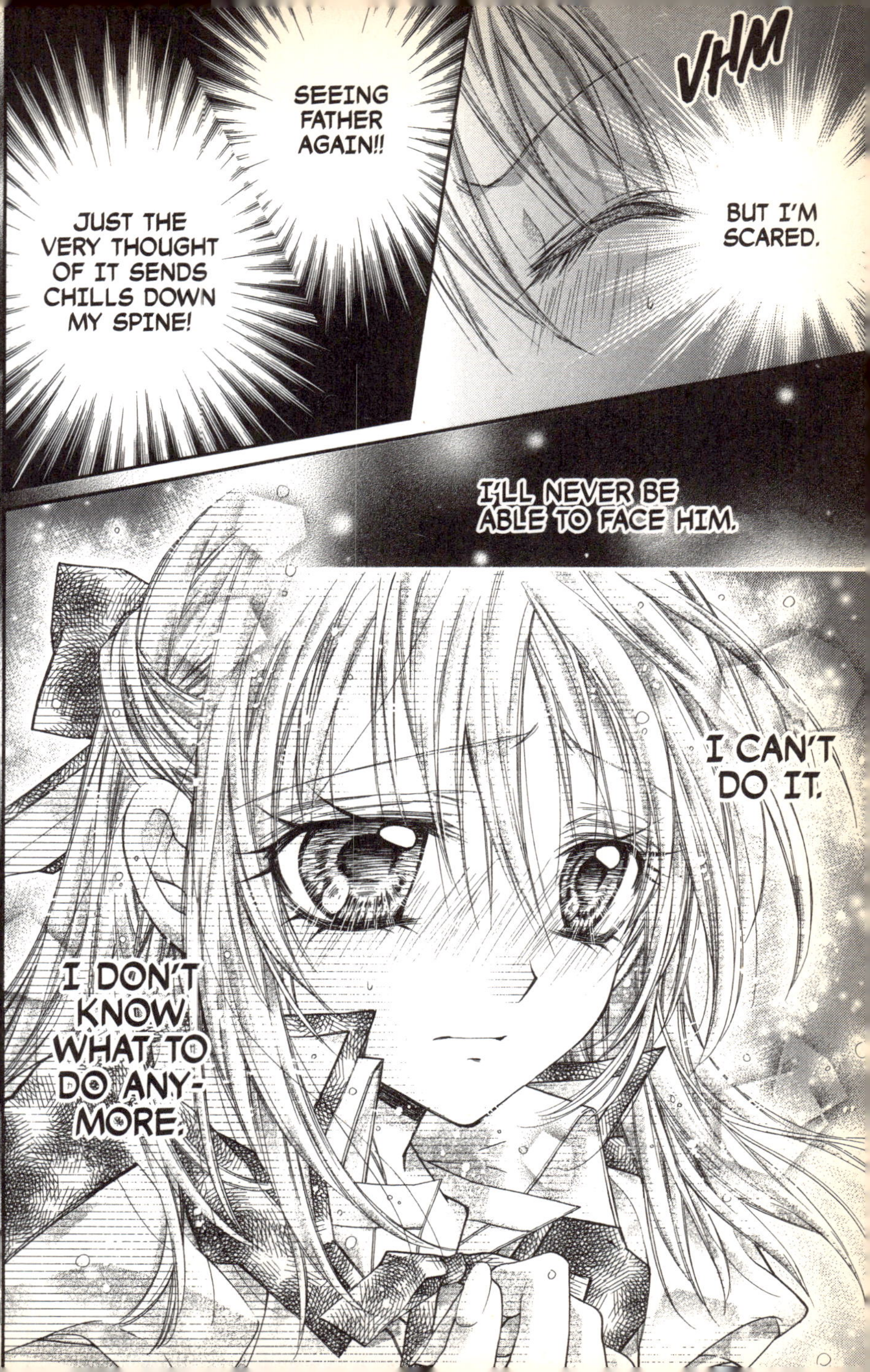
VHM
BUT I'M SCARED.
SEEING FATHER AGAIN!!
JUST THE VERY THOUGHT OF IT SENDS CHILLS DOWN MY SPINE!
I'LL NEVER BE ABLE TO FACE HIM.
I CAN'T DO IT.
I DON'T KNOW WHAT TO DO ANY-MORE.

※I'm giving away the story.

The Love Labyrinth

This is about the bonus story that features Ushio-chan as the main character.

There was a lot of response to this story for many reasons. I guess the story behind Ushio-chan's birth was quite shocking.

Those who have read the Ushio chapters in the main story may understand it, but the "mirror" referenced is the reflection in the water.

The mutual feeling between them isn't love, but a really strong kind of friendship. (That's why she can't find it anywhere...) ←That's why I called it "Labyrinth."

Ushio-chan seems to like older men. The young uncle (he doesn't appear in this) is her first love. I don't think she's interested in people her own age... Maguri is more like a pet to her.

Well, at the end of the bonus story, you'll see Ushio look off into the distance with a determined look on her face. That pretty much sums up the whole story. She has no interest in the current Haine, I think.

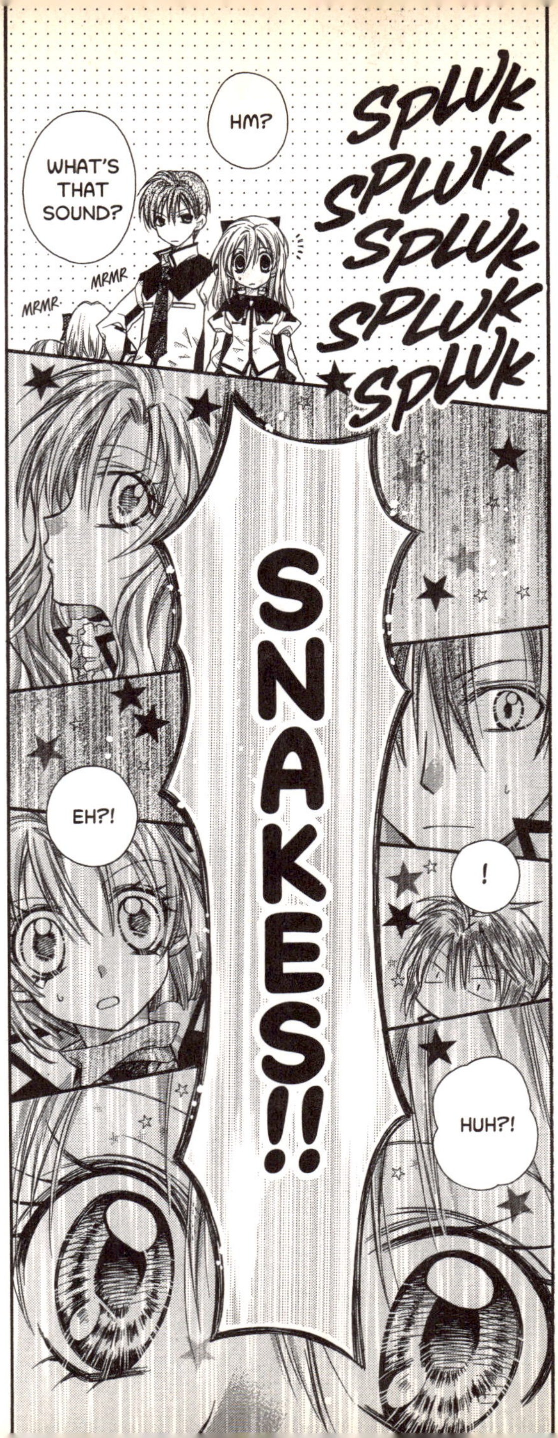
SPLUK SPLUK SPLUK SPLUK SPLUK
HM?
WHAT'S THAT SOUND?
MRMR
MRMR
SNAKES!!
!
HUH?!
EH?!

THEY'RE IN THE QUAD.
WHAT?! WHO IS IT?!
KYAH
RWAR
RWAR
HAINE OTOMIYA!!
COME THE HELL OUT!
KYAH
RWAR
DOOM
THEY'RE MY OLD YANKI GANG.

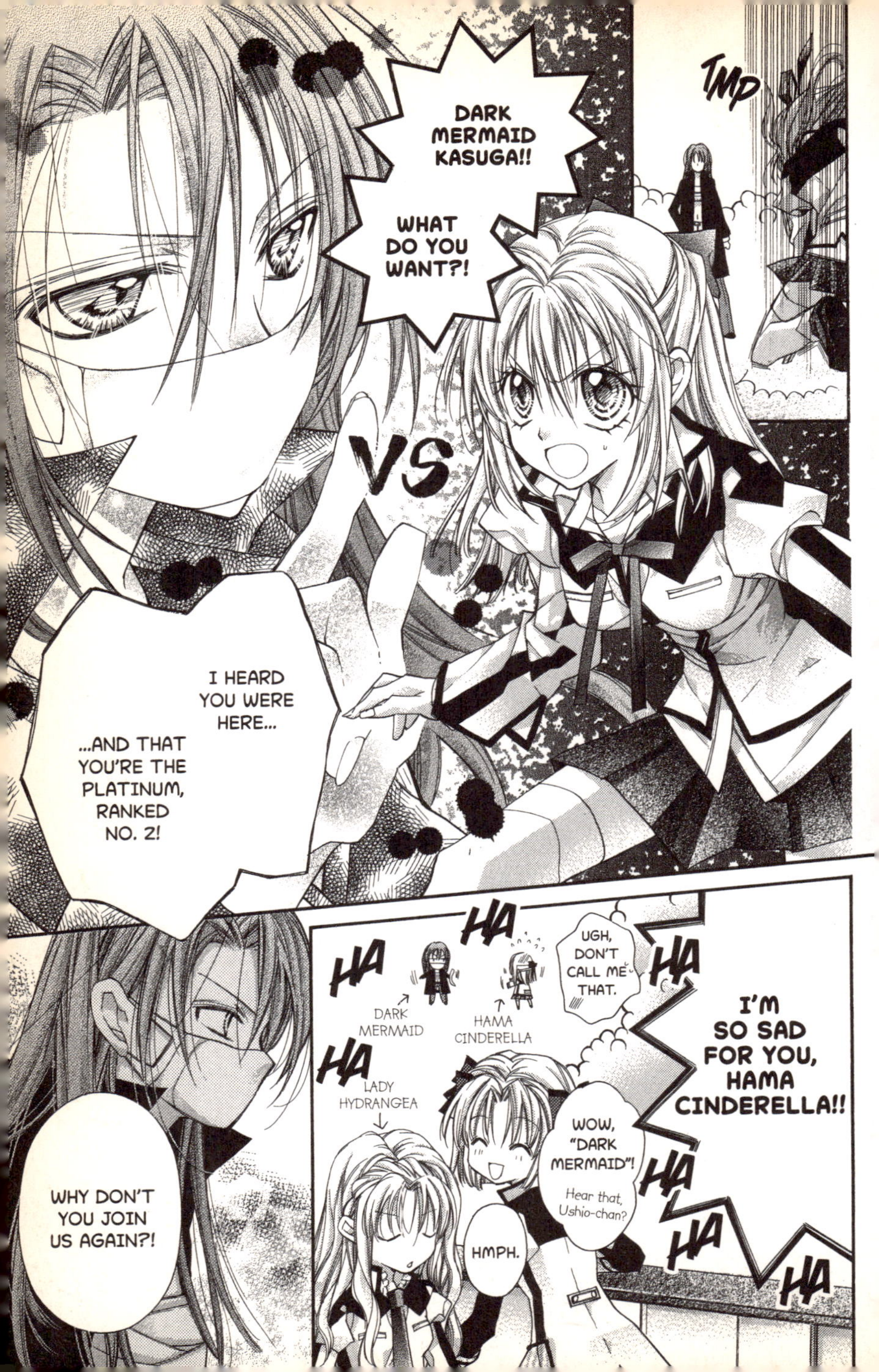
TMP
DARK MERMAID KASUGA!!
WHAT DO YOU WANT?!
VS
I HEARD YOU WERE HERE...
...AND THAT YOU'RE THE PLATINUM, RANKED NO. 2!
I'M SO SAD FOR YOU, HAMA CINDERELLA!!
HA
HA
HA
HA
HA
HA
HA
UGH, DON'T CALL ME THAT.
HAMA CINDERELLA
DARK MERMAID
LADY HYDRANGEA
WOW, "DARK MERMAID"!
Hear that, Ushio-chan?
HMPH.
WHY DON'T YOU JOIN US AGAIN?!

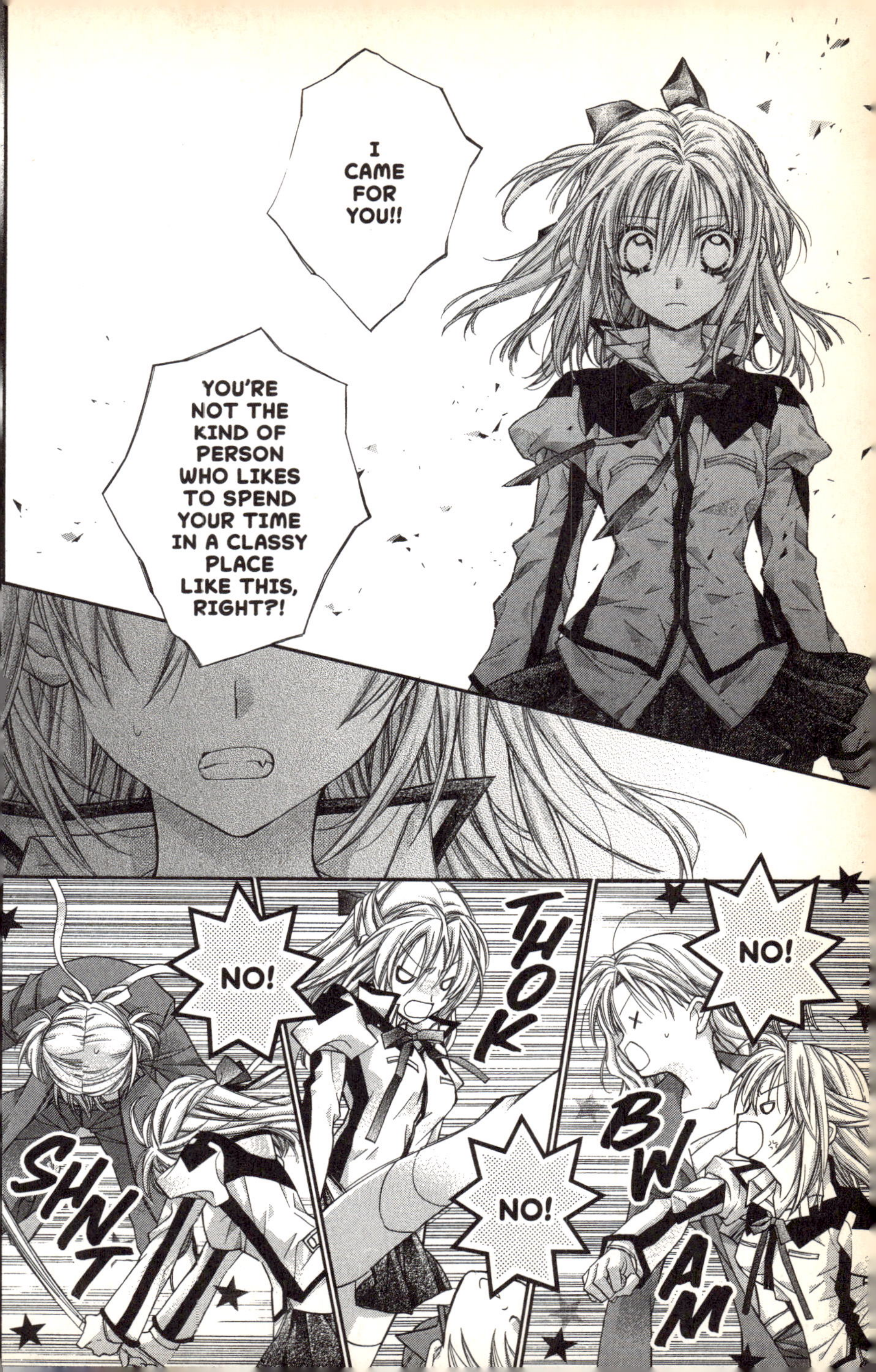
I CAME FOR YOU!!
YOU'RE NOT THE KIND OF PERSON WHO LIKES TO SPEND YOUR TIME IN A CLASSY PLACE LIKE THIS, RIGHT?!
NO!
BWAM
THOK
NO!
NO!
SHNT

KRAK KRAK
I'LL NEVER JOIN YOU AGAIN!
KRAK
I GIVE UP! I GIVE UP!
KRAK
KRAK KRAK
SEE YA!!
CATCH YOU LATER!
DON'T EVER COME BACK!!
STUPID STUPID IDIOTS!
NAH NAH NAH NAH NAH
NAH NAH NAH NAH NAH
HALT
GLINT
IT'S ALL RIGHT NOW, EVERY-BODY!!
GLINT
GLINT

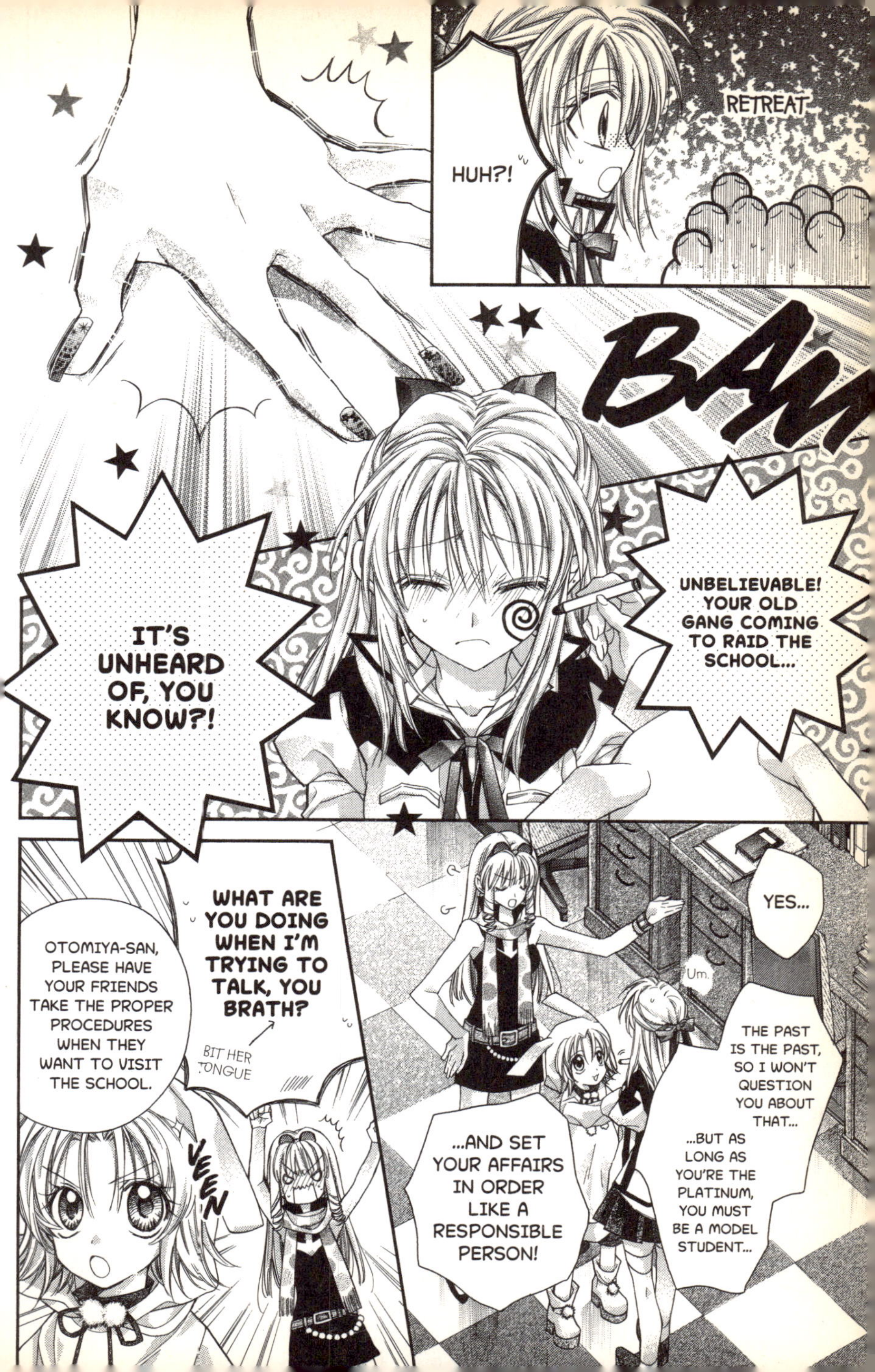

RETREAT
HUH?!
BAM
UNBELIEVABLE! YOUR OLD GANG COMING TO RAID THE SCHOOL...
IT'S UNHEARD OF, YOU KNOW?!
YES...
Um.
THE PAST IS THE PAST, SO I WON'T QUESTION YOU ABOUT THAT...
...BUT AS LONG AS YOU'RE THE PLATINUM, YOU MUST BE A MODEL STUDENT...
...AND SET YOUR AFFAIRS IN ORDER LIKE A RESPONSIBLE PERSON!
WHAT ARE YOU DOING WHEN I'M TRYING TO TALK, YOU BRATH?
BIT HER TONGUE
OTOMIYA-SAN, PLEASE HAVE YOUR FRIENDS TAKE THE PROPER PROCEDURES WHEN THEY WANT TO VISIT THE SCHOOL.
VEEN

Recent Events

✿ *Kamikaze Kaitou Jeanne Complete Collector's Edition*
I'm currently working on it!
(It will be published in Japan by October 2007. Six volumes total.)
Also, there's a newly drawn short essay at the end of the book, which is known as the "O-shi Chapters" at Shueisha!
I'm also going to write a 16-page bonus story to be included in the last volume.

✿ I attended an autograph session at Comic-Con in San Diego! It's a convention for all sorts of manga in the United States! (I've heard that Japanese manga artists who are fans of American comics attend it too...) It was at a very pretty place by the sea. I'd love to go again.

✿ I'm sorry this is so real-time, but a sheet of commemorative stickers will be given out as a present for the readers in the October and November editions of *Ribon* magazine to celebrate the third year and volume 8 of the series. It's going to be a lottery, but a sheet with 10 stickers with a very fancy mount board will be generously, generously, generously given out to 1000 people!!

This was all made possible by the really hard work of the designer, my supervisor, my former supervisor, the sales department, and many other people!!
I drew three illustrations from scratch specifically for this.

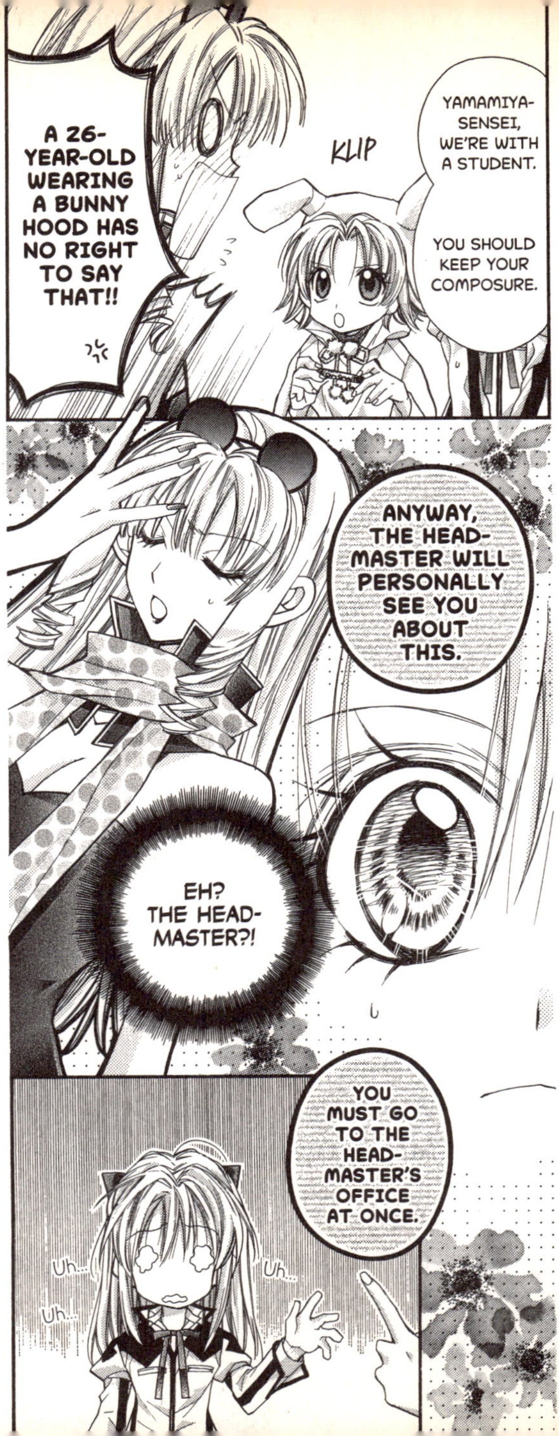
YAMAMIYA-SENSEI, WE'RE WITH A STUDENT.
YOU SHOULD KEEP YOUR COMPOSURE.
KLIP
A 26-YEAR-OLD WEARING A BUNNY HOOD HAS NO RIGHT TO SAY THAT!!
ANYWAY, THE HEAD-MASTER WILL PERSONALLY SEE YOU ABOUT THIS.
EH? THE HEAD-MASTER?!
YOU MUST GO TO THE HEAD-MASTER'S OFFICE AT ONCE.
Uh...
Uh...
Uh...

HEADMASTER
I NEVER THOUGHT IT WOULD GO THIS FAR...
I'm so ashamed.
WHAT DO I TELL TAKANARI-SAMA?
THE HEAD-MASTER...
...MUST BE A REALLY AMAZING PERSON. AFTER ALL, HE'S MIRUKO-SENSEI'S BOSS.
KNOK KNOK
COME IN.
EXCUSE ME.
CHAK

BOO !!!
YEEK!!
HUH?
HEAD-MASTER ?!
-san?!
THAT'S RIGHT.
HAVEN'T I MET YOU BEFORE...?
HAHA HA
I HEAR THAT A LOT.
I get the feeling that I see you at work all the time.
UM, I'M REALLY SORRY ABOUT BEFORE.
OH... DON'T WORRY ABOUT THAT. I DON'T MIND, ACTUALLY.
IT'S GOOD TO BE ENERGETIC. ♪
I knew it. There's his hat.

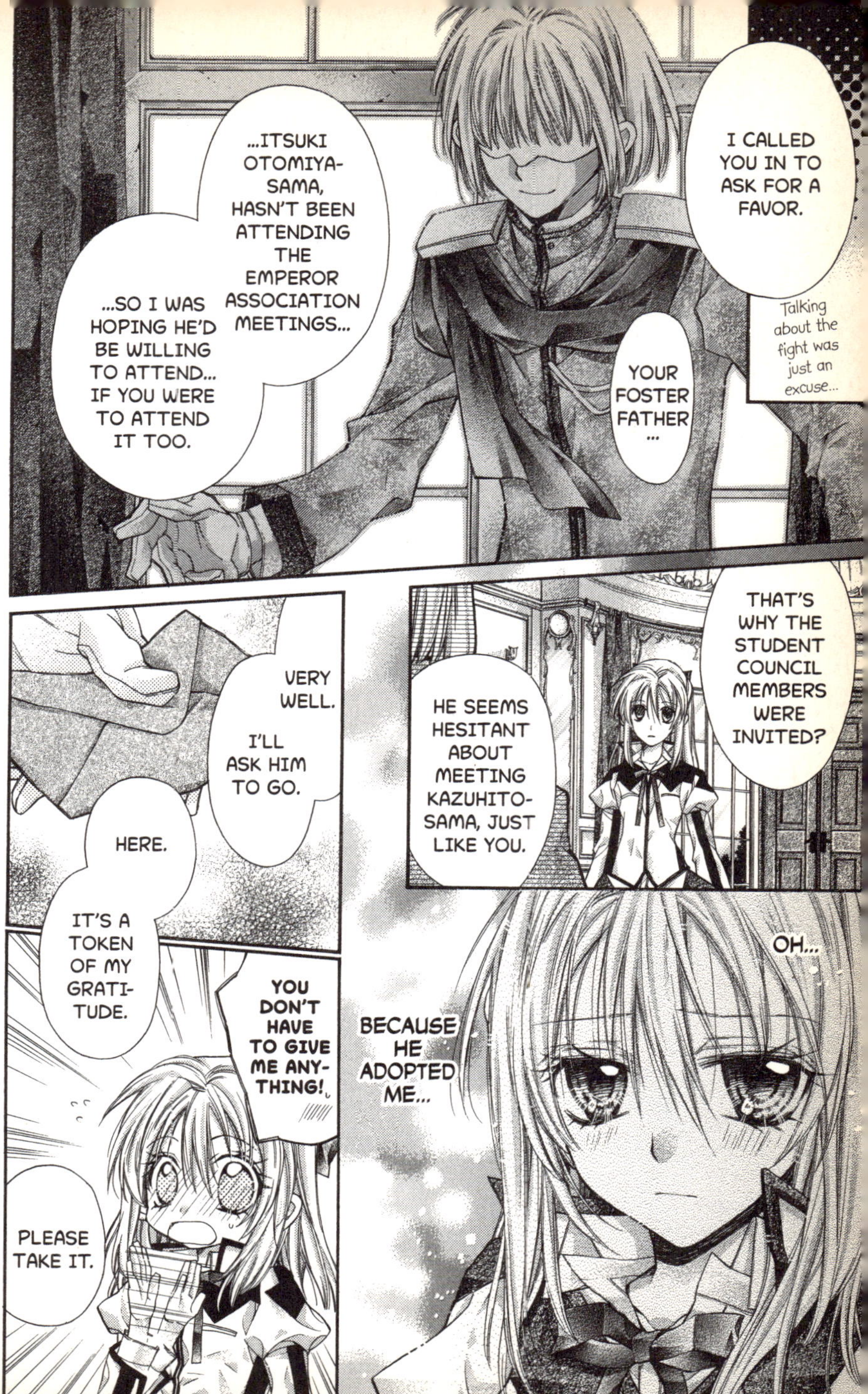
I CALLED YOU IN TO ASK FOR A FAVOR.
Talking about the fight was just an excuse...
YOUR FOSTER FATHER...
...ITSUKI OTOMIYA-SAMA, HASN'T BEEN ATTENDING THE EMPEROR ASSOCIATION MEETINGS...
...SO I WAS HOPING HE'D BE WILLING TO ATTEND... IF YOU WERE TO ATTEND IT TOO.
THAT'S WHY THE STUDENT COUNCIL MEMBERS WERE INVITED?
HE SEEMS HESITANT ABOUT MEETING KAZUHITO-SAMA, JUST LIKE YOU.
VERY WELL.
I'LL ASK HIM TO GO.
HERE.
IT'S A TOKEN OF MY GRATITUDE.
OH...
BECAUSE HE ADOPTED ME...
YOU DON'T HAVE TO GIVE ME ANYTHING!
PLEASE TAKE IT.

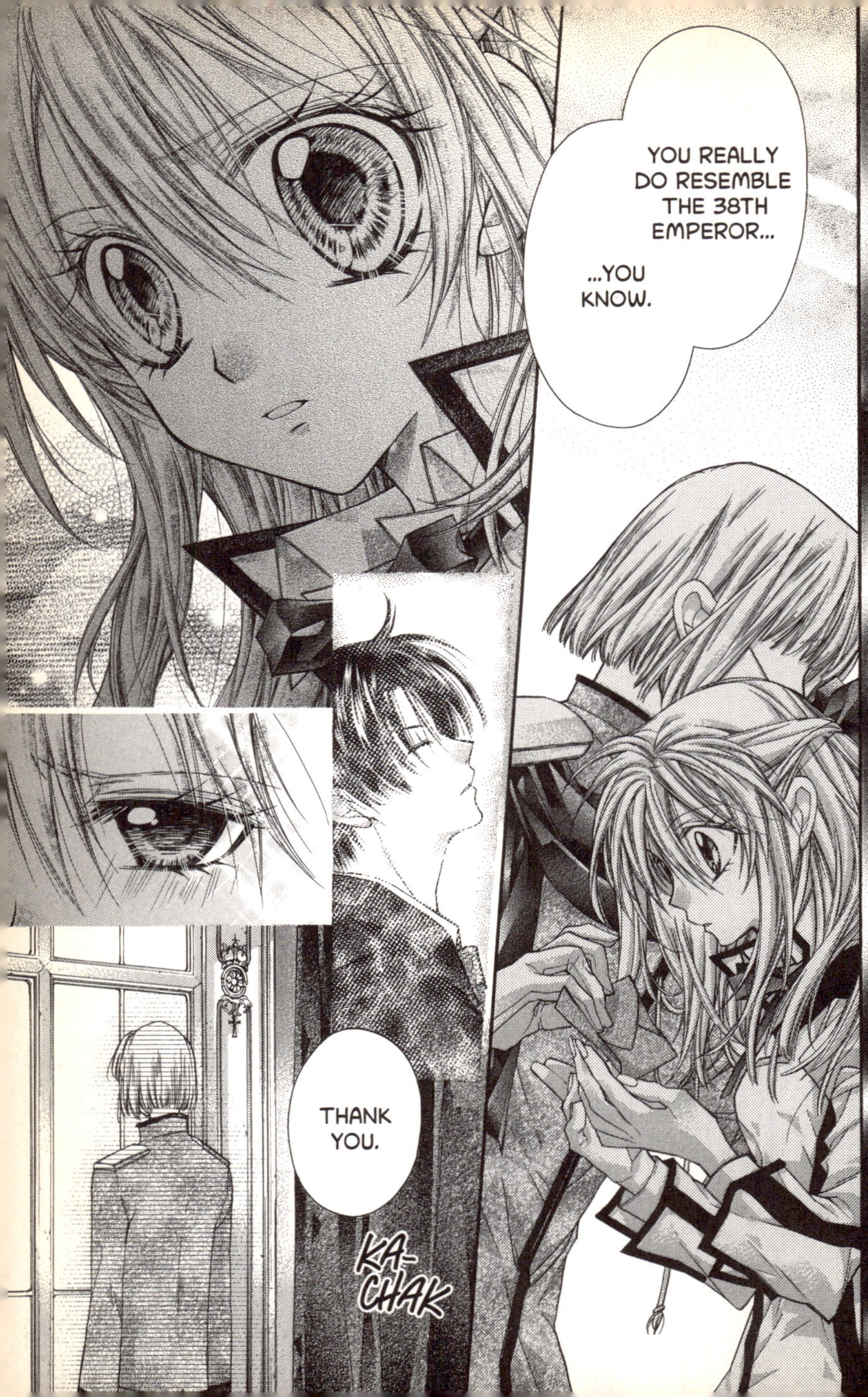
YOU REALLY DO RESEMBLE THE 38TH EMPEROR...
...YOU KNOW.
THANK YOU.
KA-CHAK

"HAINE"...
WHAT AN APPROPRIATE NAME.
HMM.
TMP
TMP
I COULDN'T GIVE IT BACK. WHAT IS THIS?
MONEY?
No Way.
IF IT'S MONEY, I HAVE TO GIVE IT BACK TO HIM!!
SHP
FLIP
AH!

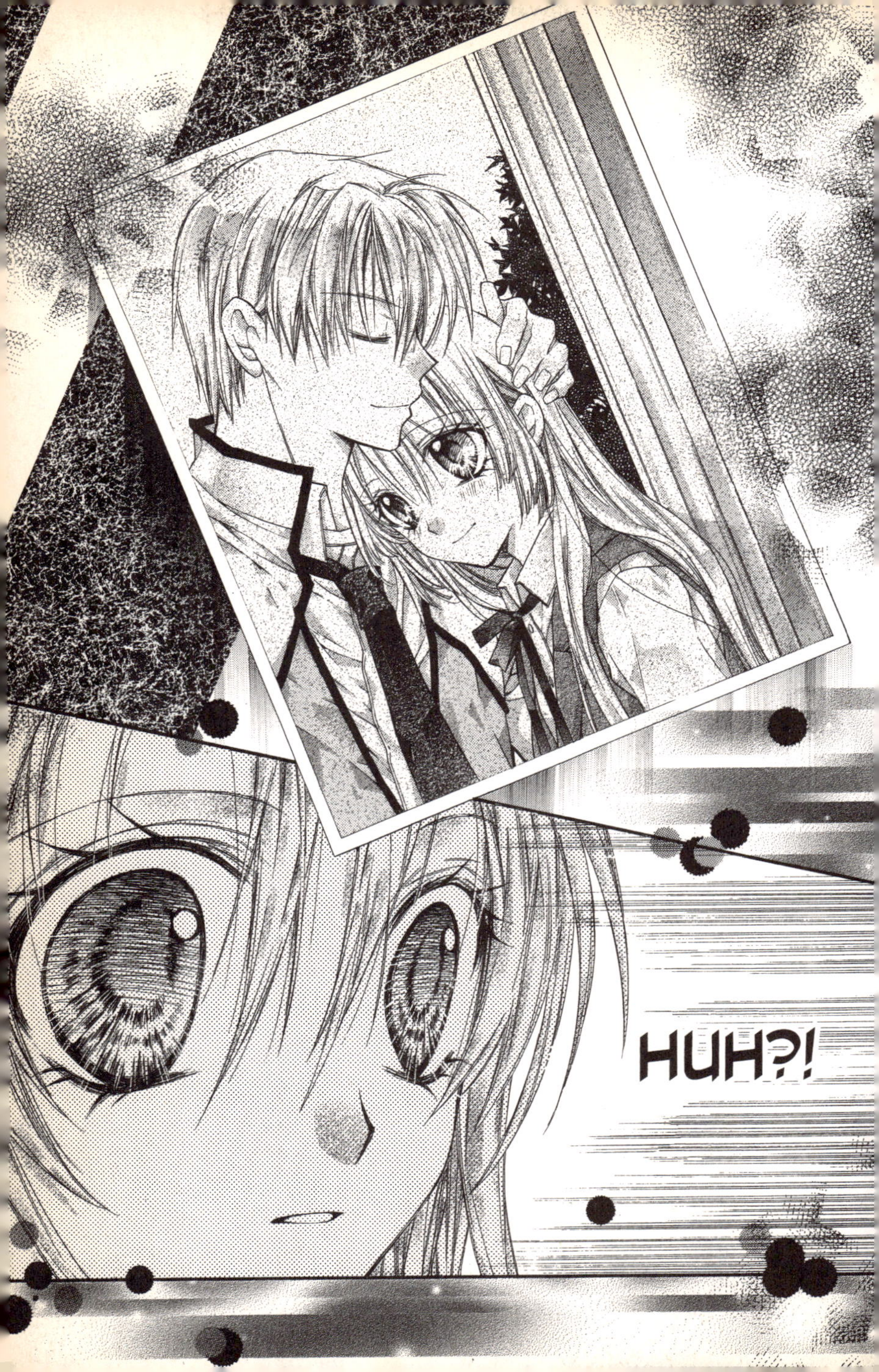
HUH?!

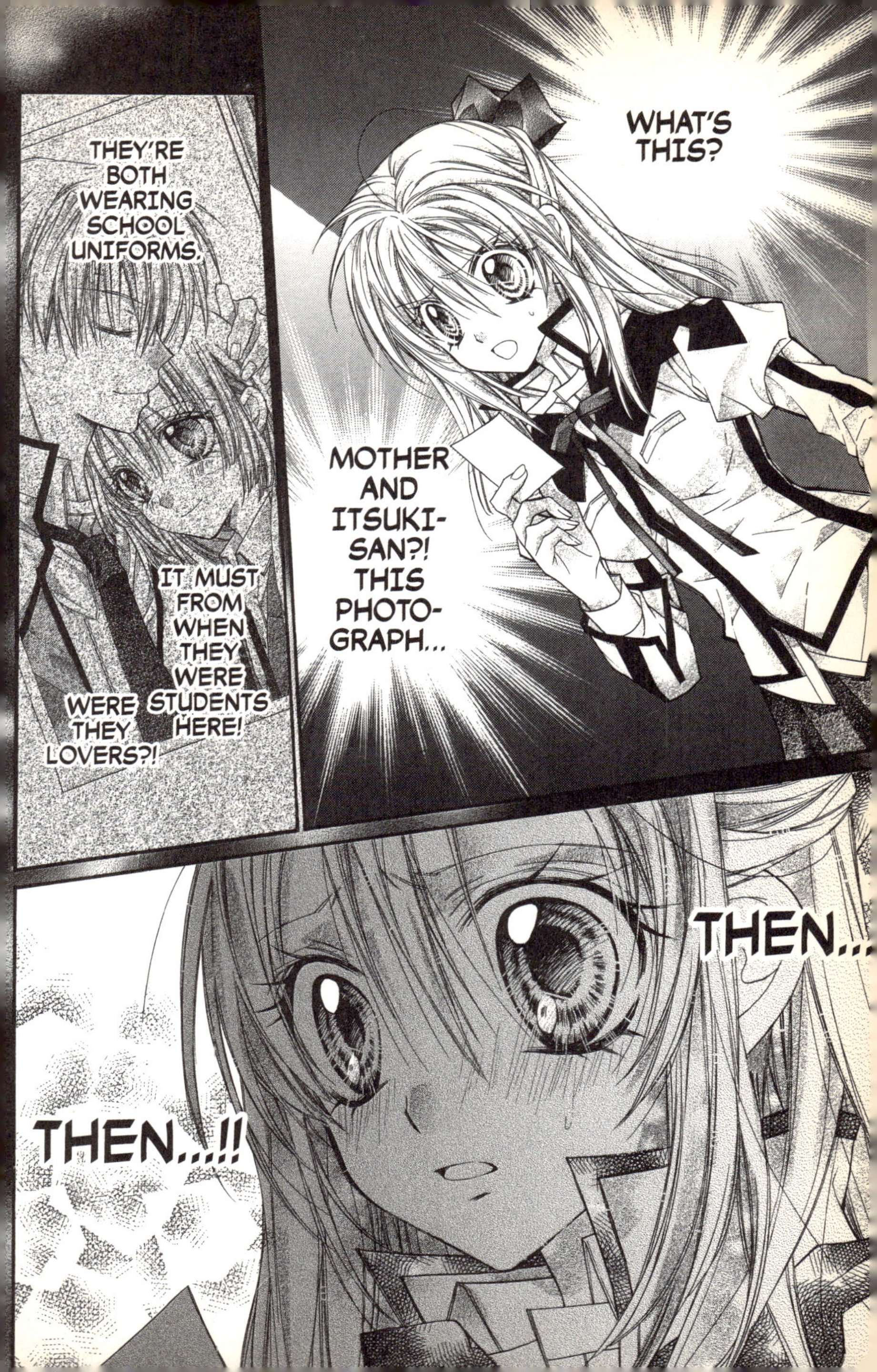
WHAT'S THIS?
MOTHER AND ITSUKI-SAN?! THIS PHOTOGRAPH...
THEY'RE BOTH WEARING SCHOOL UNIFORMS.
IT MUST FROM WHEN THEY WERE STUDENTS HERE!
WERE THEY LOVERS?!
THEN...
THEN...!!

Maika Kamiya

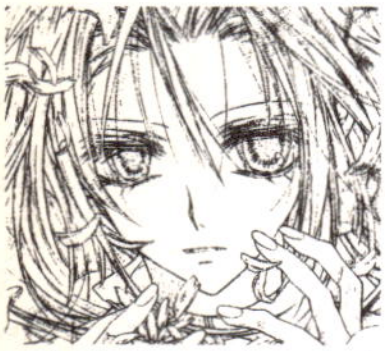

Birthday: March 15
Blood Type: O

Maika Rikyu was her maiden name. She's the mother of Haine, Komaki, and Tachibana. She's a kind, gentle person whom Haine adores. She has lost her memory and currently spends her days in a daze.

Comments

I worked really hard to give her a mysterious aura. She's a lot like Haine, and being too kind, she is unable to push people away. The reason why she has closed herself off from the world will become clear in the next volume, so please look forward to it!

I was happy to find out that she was in 9th place in the popularity vote.

To tell you the truth, I think she makes a "nice couple" with both of them... How sad...

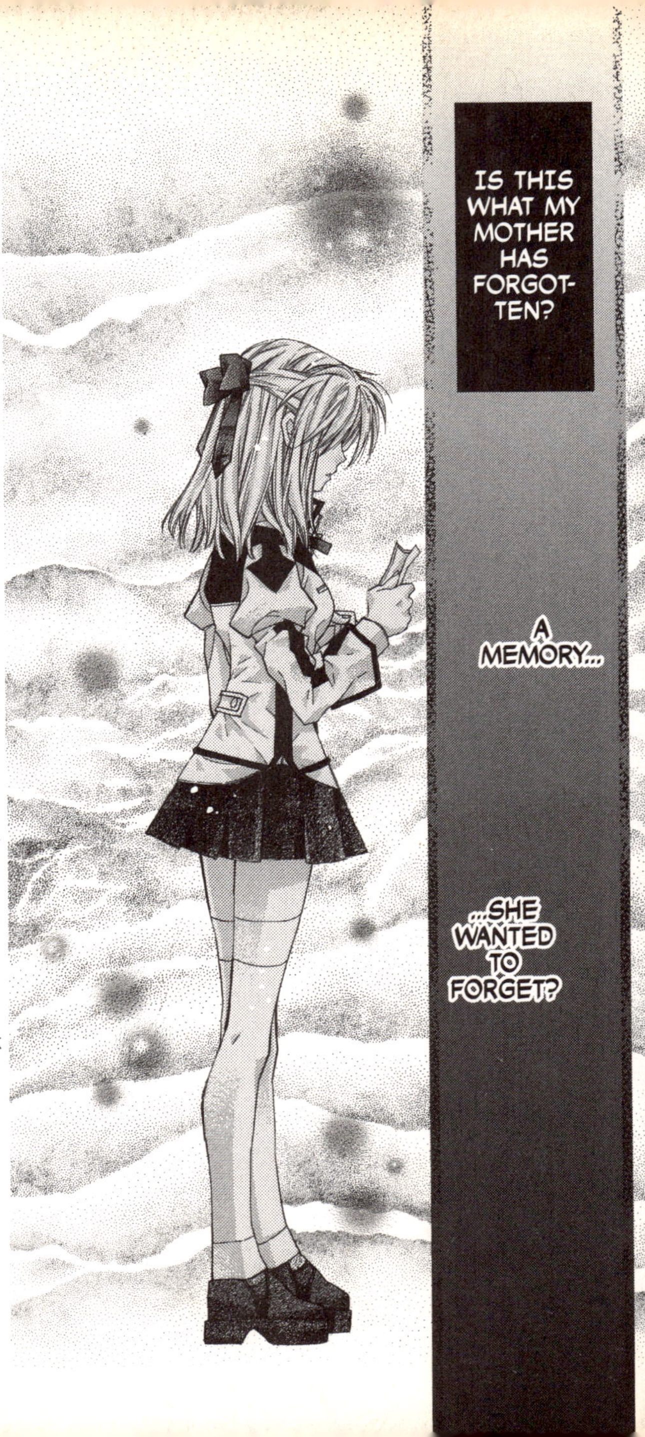
IS THIS WHAT MY MOTHER HAS FORGOTTEN?
A MEMORY...
...SHE WANTED TO FORGET?

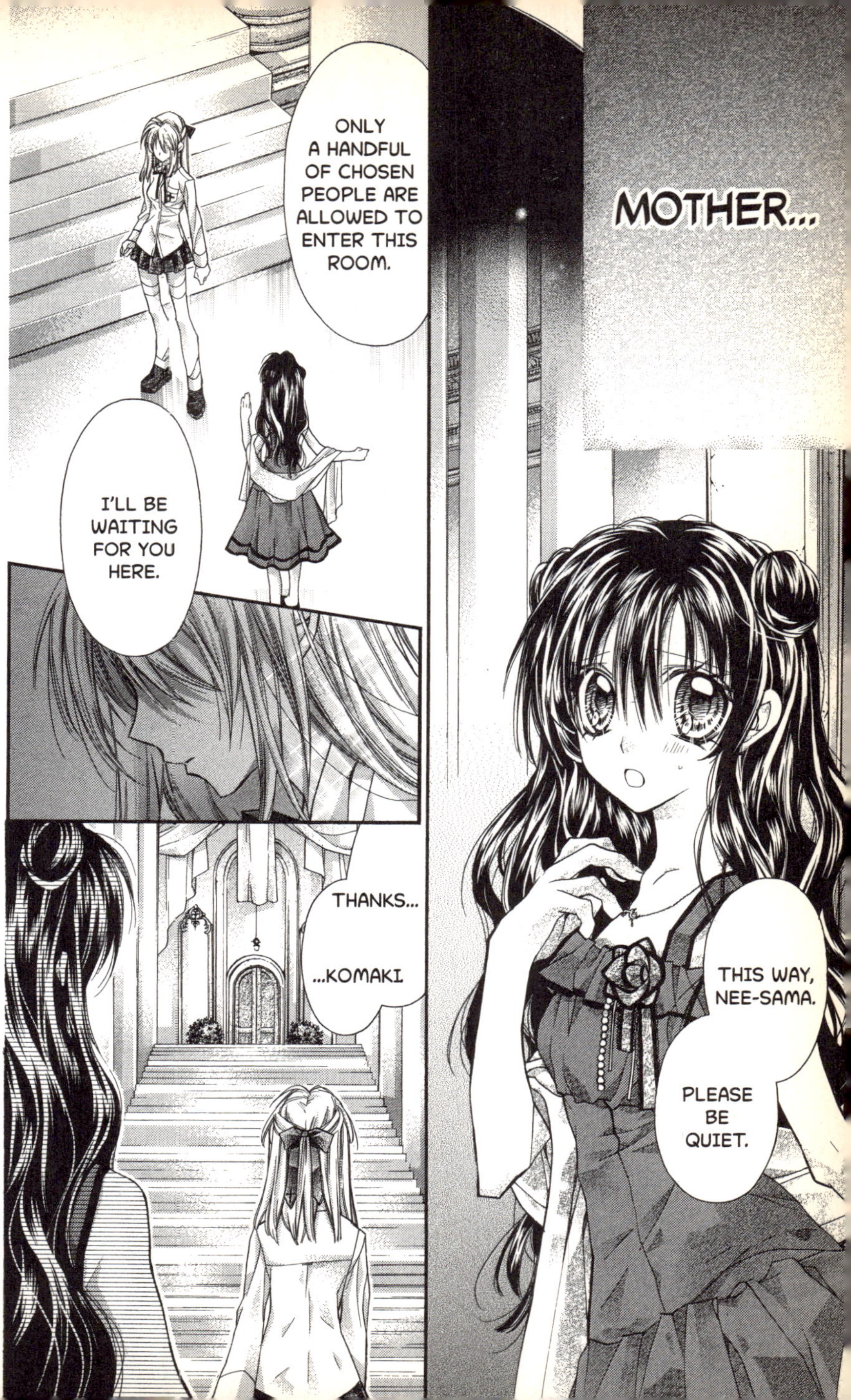
MOTHER...
THIS WAY, NEE-SAMA.
PLEASE BE QUIET.
ONLY A HANDFUL OF CHOSEN PEOPLE ARE ALLOWED TO ENTER THIS ROOM.
I'LL BE WAITING FOR YOU HERE.
THANKS...
...KOMAKI

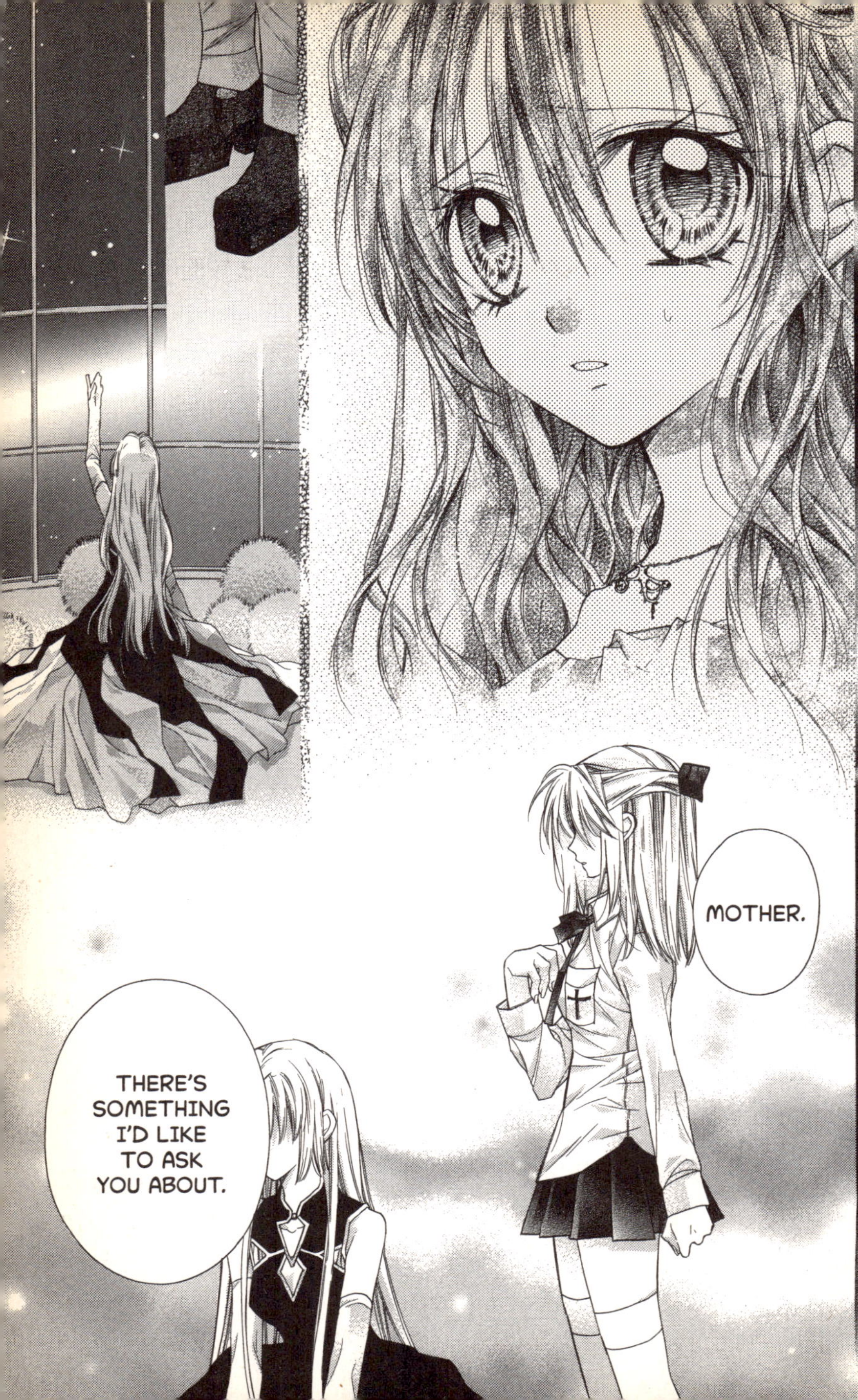
MOTHER.
THERE'S SOMETHING I'D LIKE TO ASK YOU ABOUT.

MOTHER.
STARE
MOTHER.
OH
MAIKA-SAMA.
MAIKA-SAMA.
MAIKA-SAMA.
IT'S A CUTE GIRL.
MAIKA-SAMA.

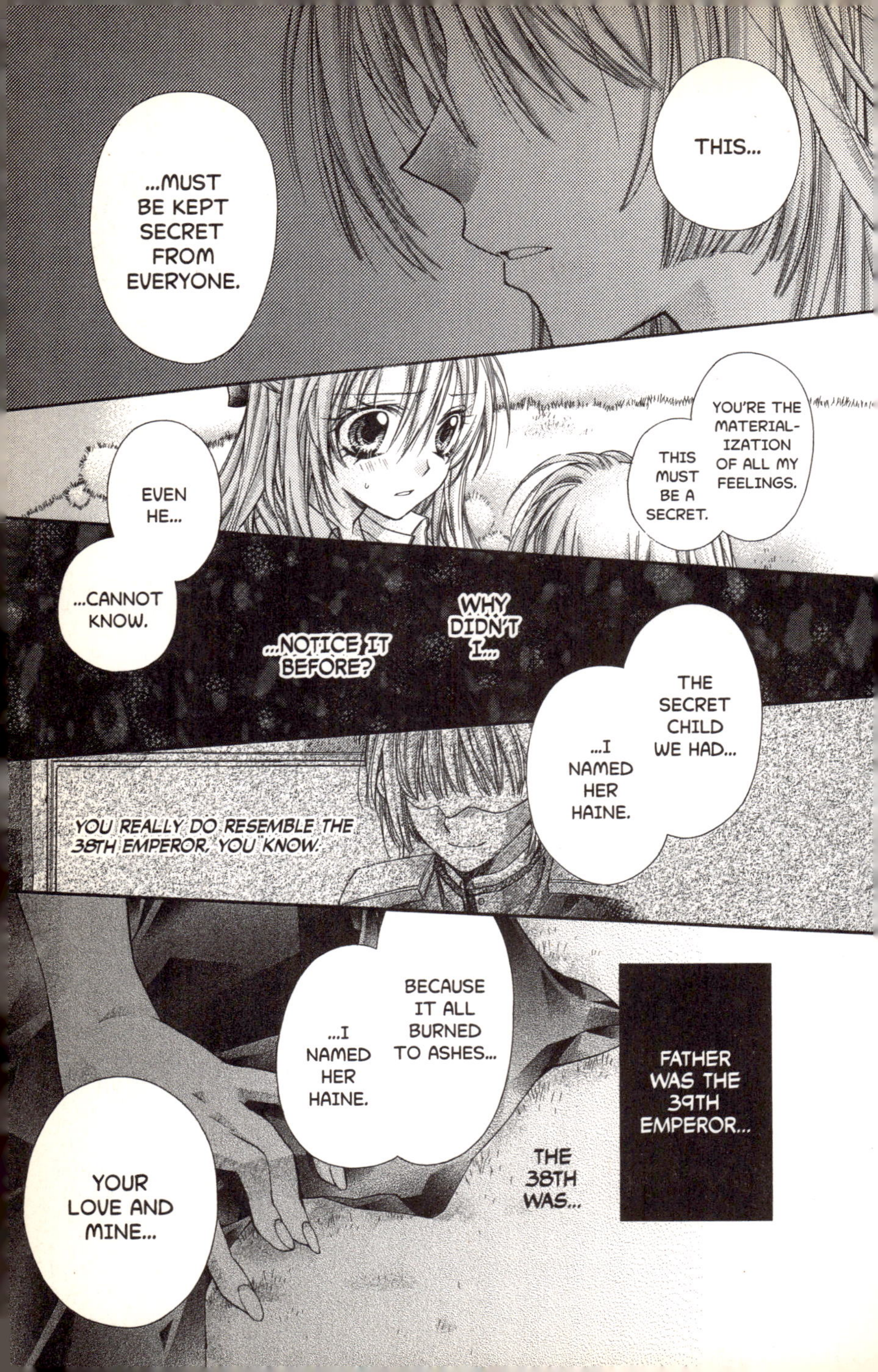
THIS...
...MUST BE KEPT SECRET FROM EVERYONE.
YOU'RE THE MATERIAL-IZATION OF ALL MY FEELINGS.
THIS MUST BE A SECRET.
EVEN HE...
...CANNOT KNOW.
WHY DIDN'T I...
...NOTICE IT BEFORE?
THE SECRET CHILD WE HAD...
...I NAMED HER HAINE.
YOU REALLY DO RESEMBLE THE 38TH EMPEROR, YOU KNOW.
FATHER WAS THE 39TH EMPEROR...
BECAUSE IT ALL BURNED TO ASHES...
...I NAMED HER HAINE.
THE 38TH WAS...
YOUR LOVE AND MINE...

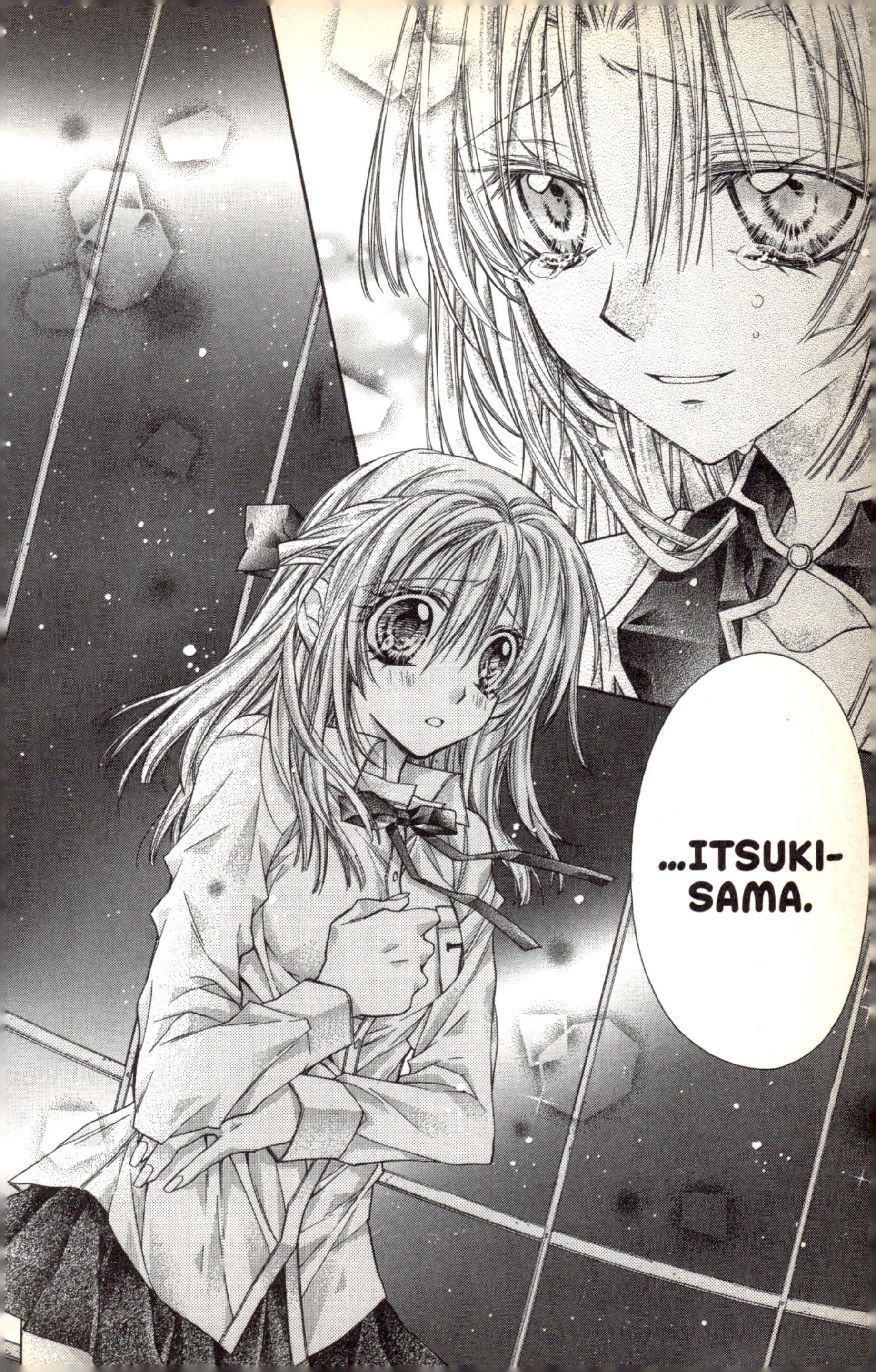
...ITSUKI-SAMA.

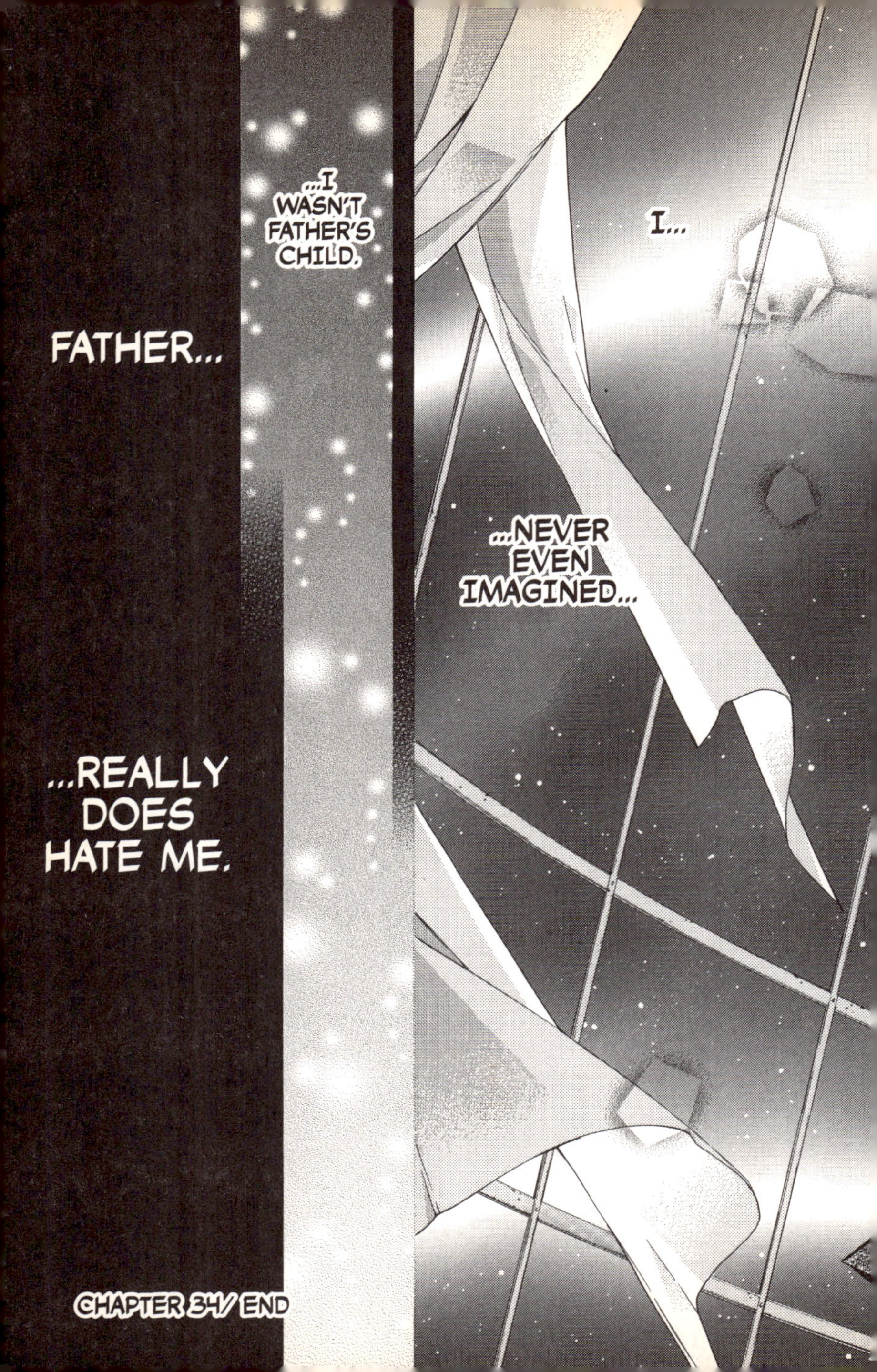
I...
...NEVER EVEN IMAGINED...
...I WASN'T FATHER'S CHILD.
FATHER...
...REALLY DOES HATE ME.
CHAPTER 34/ END

NAME

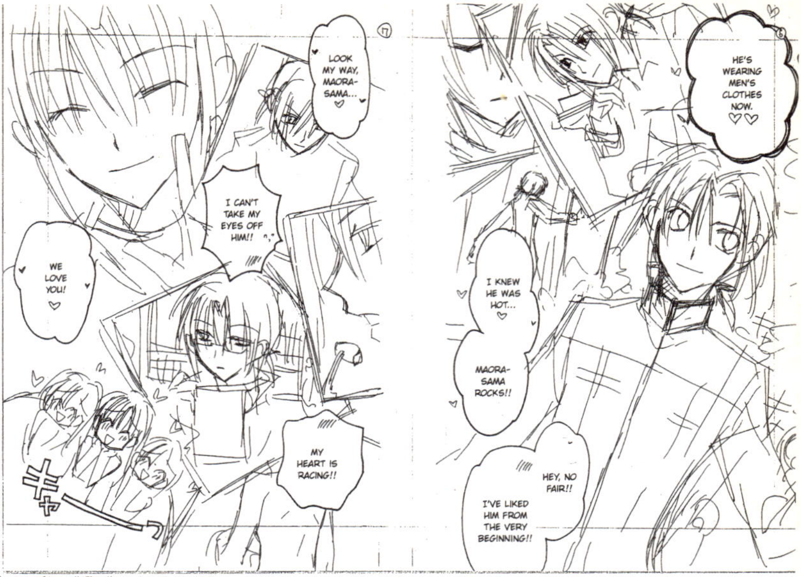
HE'S WEARING MEN'S CLOTHES NOW.
I KNEW HE WAS HOT...
MAORA-SAMA ROCKS!!
HEY, NO FAIR!!
I'VE LIKED HIM FROM THE VERY BEGINNING!!
LOOK MY WAY, MAORA-SAMA...
I CAN'T TAKE MY EYES OFF HIM!!
WE LOVE YOU!
MY HEART IS RACING!!

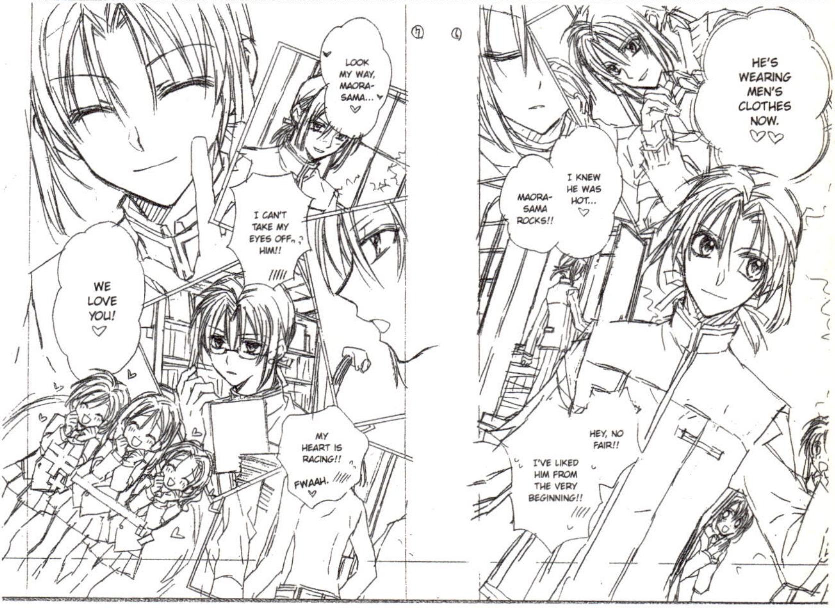
HE'S WEARING MEN'S CLOTHES NOW.
I KNEW HE WAS HOT...
MAORA-SAMA ROCKS!!
HEY, NO FAIR!!
I'VE LIKED HIM FROM THE VERY BEGINNING!!
LOOK MY WAY, MAORA-SAMA...
I CAN'T TAKE MY EYES OFF HIM!!
WE LOVE YOU!
MY HEART IS RACING!!
FWAAH.

ROUGH DRAFT

I drew the rough draft keeping the *name* in the final draft as well. This page was very popular with a lot of readers. Hurray!

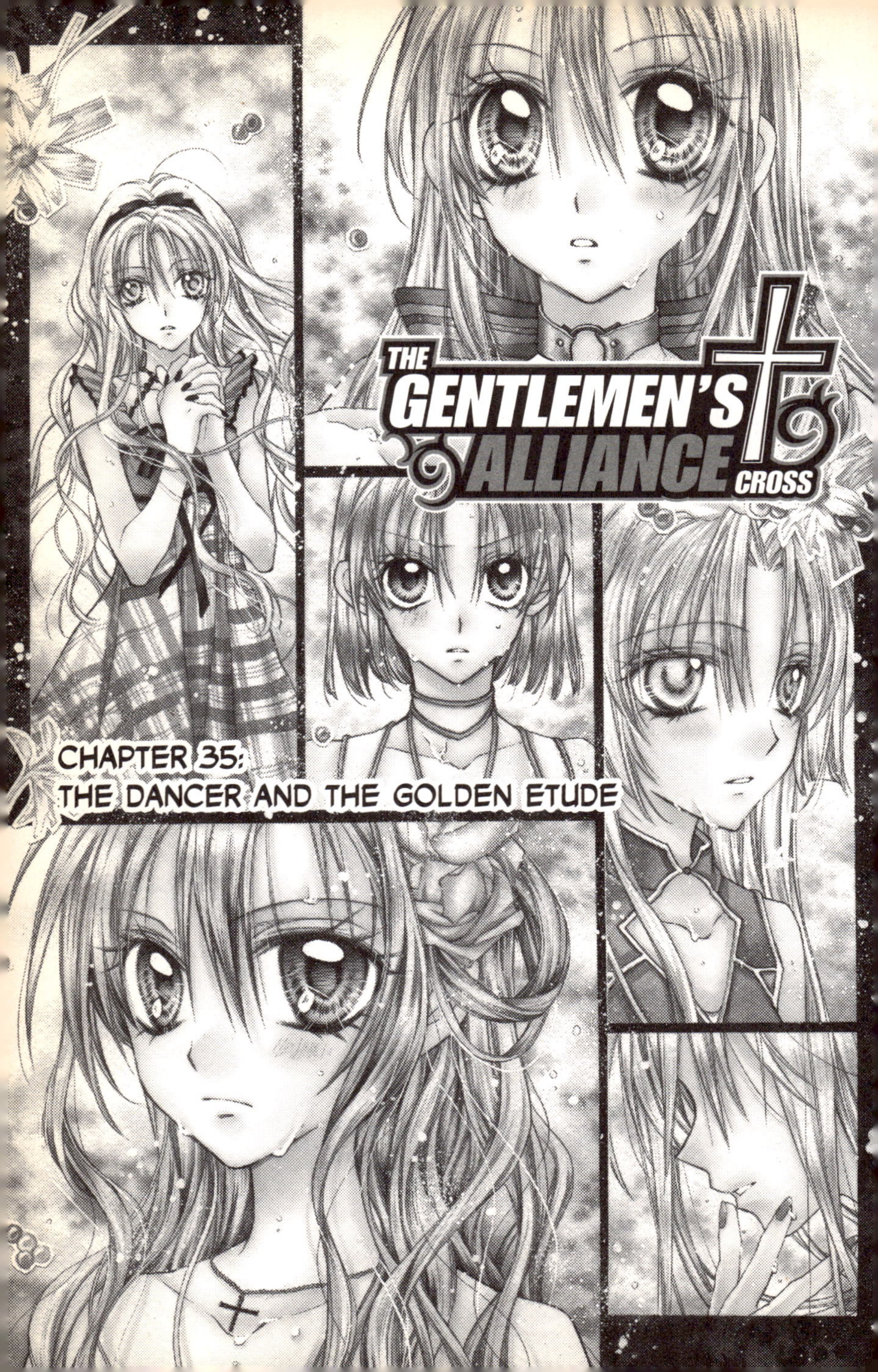
THE GENTLEMEN'S ALLIANCE CROSS
CHAPTER 35:
THE DANCER AND THE GOLDEN ETUDE

① How I created a page in chapter 33.

This is page 19 of chapter 33, the last of the Ushio arc. First, I jot the rough outline and fax it to my supervisor. (All the large changes are made here.)

② I write the plot (scenario).

Sen: "Ushio!!"
Senri calls Ushio by her name for the first time, and she comes to her senses. She is startled.

↓

Sen: "Just because she's fallen in love with somebody else doesn't mean she no longer loves you." Senri's face in close-up.
Ushio listens to him calmly. She finally realizes what she's been afraid of.

← ③ *Name* (Storyboard)

I write my plots out in detail, so it doesn't take me that long to draw the storyboard. Maybe it's about half a day for the plot, and one day for the storyboard? The fastest I've ever completed the plot and the storyboard was in three hours.
But my hand was aching in pain afterwards.

19
JUST BECAUSE SHE'S FALLEN IN LOVE WITH SOMEBODY ELSE...
...DOESN'T MEAN SHE NO LONGER LOVES YOU.

JUST BECAUSE SHE'S FALLEN IN LOVE WITH SOMEBODY ELSE...
...DOESN'T MEAN SHE NO LONGER LOVES YOU.

④ Rough draft →

Here's the rough draft. The minimum time it takes me is 30 minutes, and the maximum is about 5 hours. (Aaah!)(laugh) This...took me about an hour.

And the more time I take in doing it, the weirder the image ends up.

Aah...

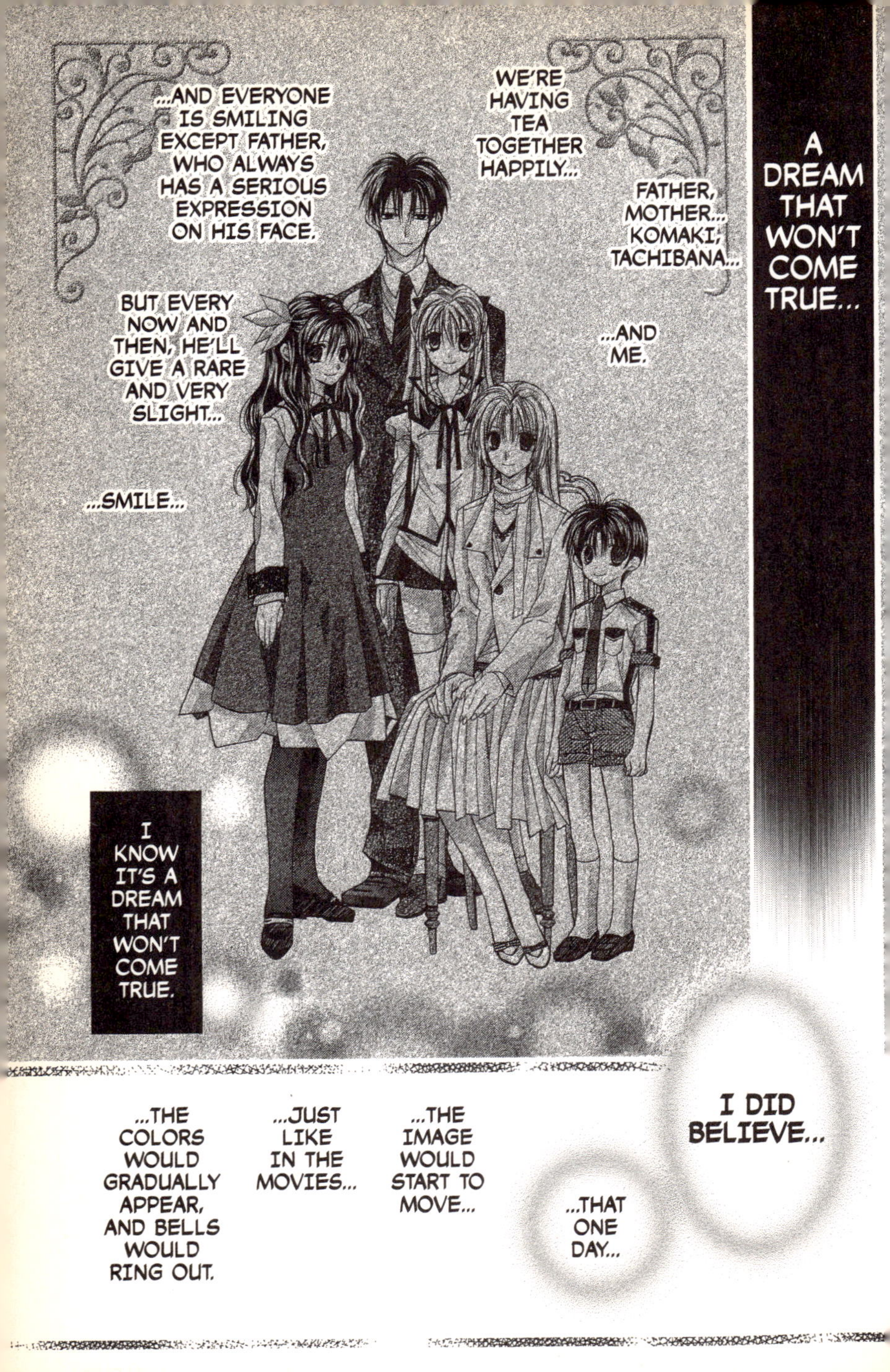
A DREAM THAT WON'T COME TRUE...
WE'RE HAVING TEA TOGETHER HAPPILY...
FATHER, MOTHER... KOMAKI, TACHIBANA...
...AND ME.
...AND EVERYONE IS SMILING EXCEPT FATHER, WHO ALWAYS HAS A SERIOUS EXPRESSION ON HIS FACE.
BUT EVERY NOW AND THEN, HE'LL GIVE A RARE AND VERY SLIGHT...
...SMILE...
I KNOW IT'S A DREAM THAT WON'T COME TRUE.
I DID BELIEVE...
...THAT ONE DAY...
...THE IMAGE WOULD START TO MOVE...
...JUST LIKE IN THE MOVIES...
...THE COLORS WOULD GRADUALLY APPEAR, AND BELLS WOULD RING OUT.

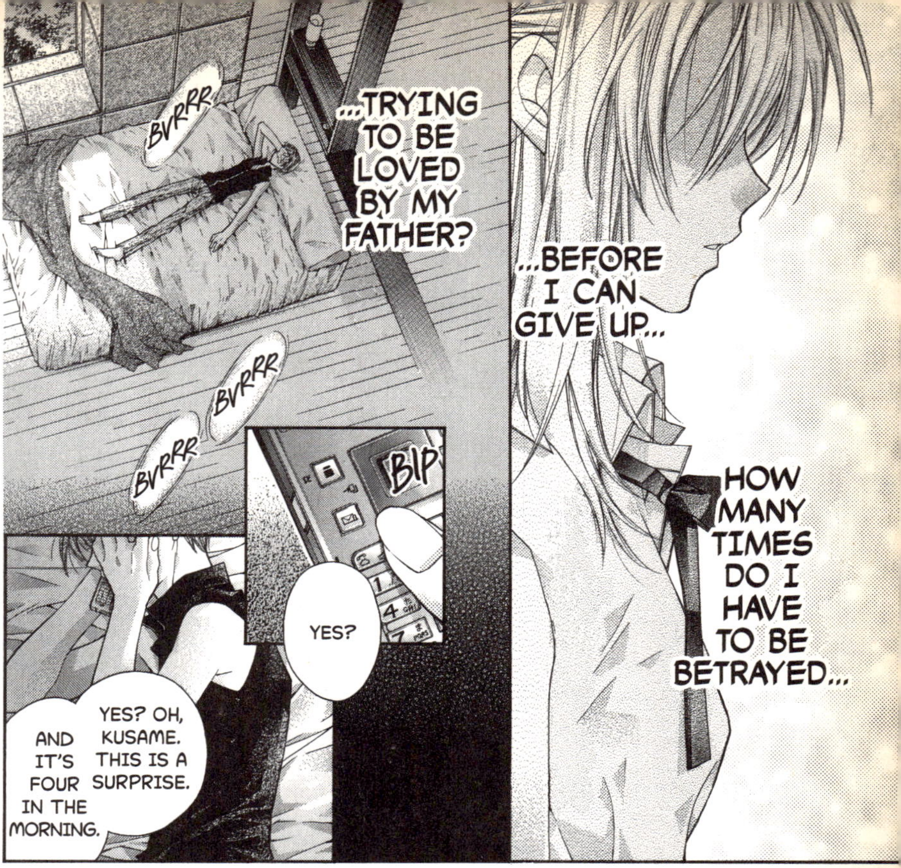
HOW MANY TIMES DO I HAVE TO BE BETRAYED...
...BEFORE I CAN GIVE UP...
...TRYING TO BE LOVED BY MY FATHER?
BVRRR
BVRRR
BVRRR
BIP
YES?
YES? OH, KUSAME. THIS IS A SURPRISE.
AND IT'S FOUR IN THE MORNING.

Chapter 35: The Dancer and the Golden Etude

※ I'm giving away the story.

Lead-in I want you to find the many shades of me.

For the chapter title page, Haine's face was the largest when I drew the *name*, but when I finished the rough draft, I liked how I had drawn Komaki's face, so her face ended up being the largest. It's the girl version of the chapter title page I drew for chapter 29. The person in the bottom right corner is Kasuga. (By the way, I took Komaki's and Kasuga's names from places in Aichi Prefecture, my birthplace. ♥)

I really like the first page of this chapter! It looks like a family photo...and I just love it since this really won't come true. Well then, I'm writing about the past. I love to write about the past! So this was really exciting for me. ♪ But! |||

There are chapters I can't write until the main story moves on, so I'm a little frustrated about not being able to write more...

I intend to move the story along slowly by adding stories of the past bit by bit. I was so moved when my fans noticed that Maika-san's cookies were floury. That's right. She got it from her mother. (laugh) ☆

It was love at first sight for Kazuhito-sama. Oh, the main character for this chapter actually happens to be Kazuhito. I was happy to realize he was easier to move around than I thought. Haine-chan got her characteristics from Itsuki-san, so there may have been people who noticed it beforehand... ← certain fans

↖ There was a chapter in volume 2 in which Haine's cookies were floury.

WHAT ?!
VMP
HAINE HAS DISAPPEARED ?!
TMP TMP TMP TMP
BAM
SHIZU-MASA!!
...?
WHAT'S WITH ALL THE NOISE?
JUST WAKE UP!!

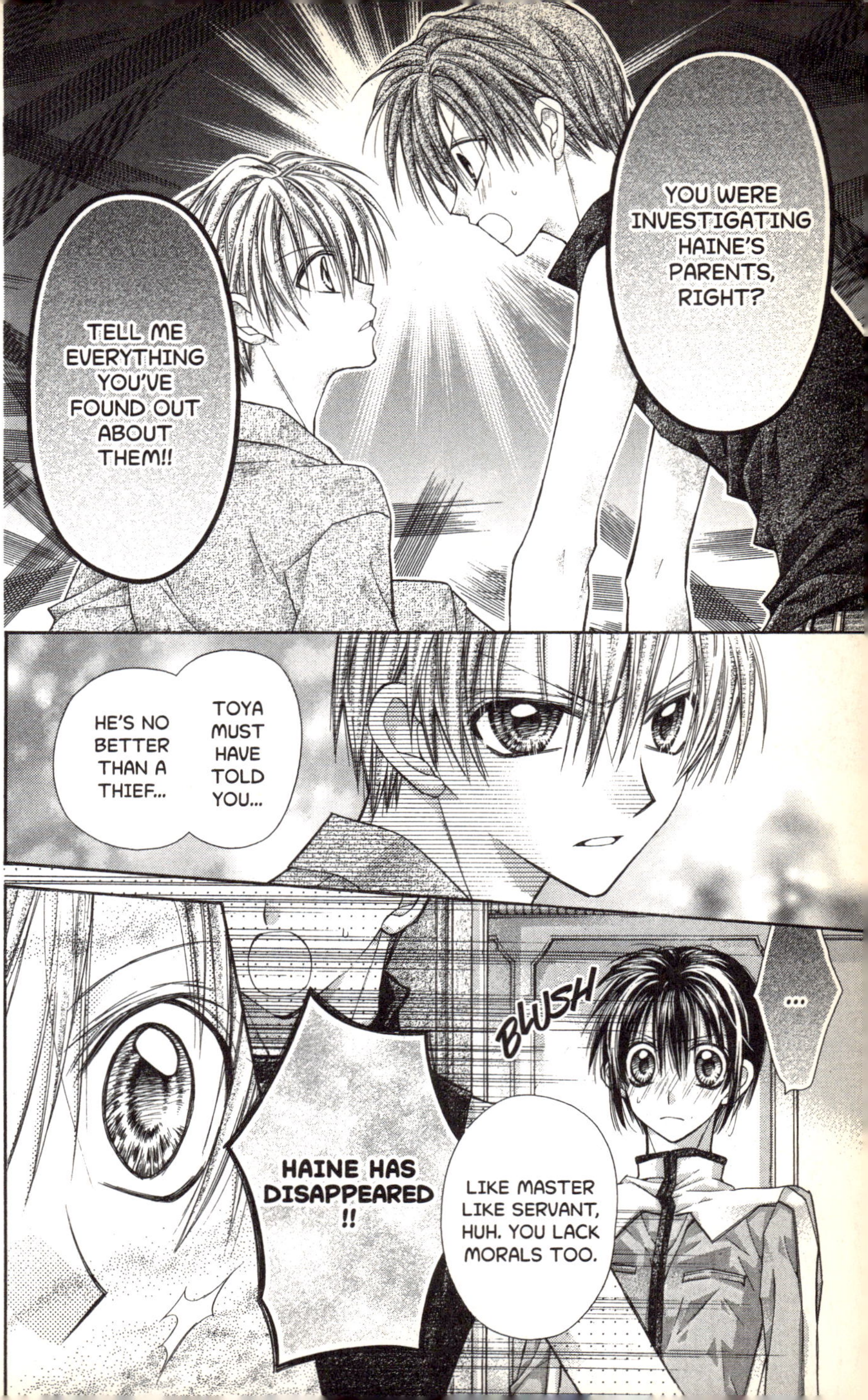
YOU WERE INVESTIGATING HAINE'S PARENTS, RIGHT?
TELL ME EVERYTHING YOU'VE FOUND OUT ABOUT THEM!!
TOYA MUST HAVE TOLD YOU...
HE'S NO BETTER THAN A THIEF...
...
BLUSH
LIKE MASTER LIKE SERVANT, HUH. YOU LACK MORALS TOO.
HAINE HAS DISAPPEARED!!

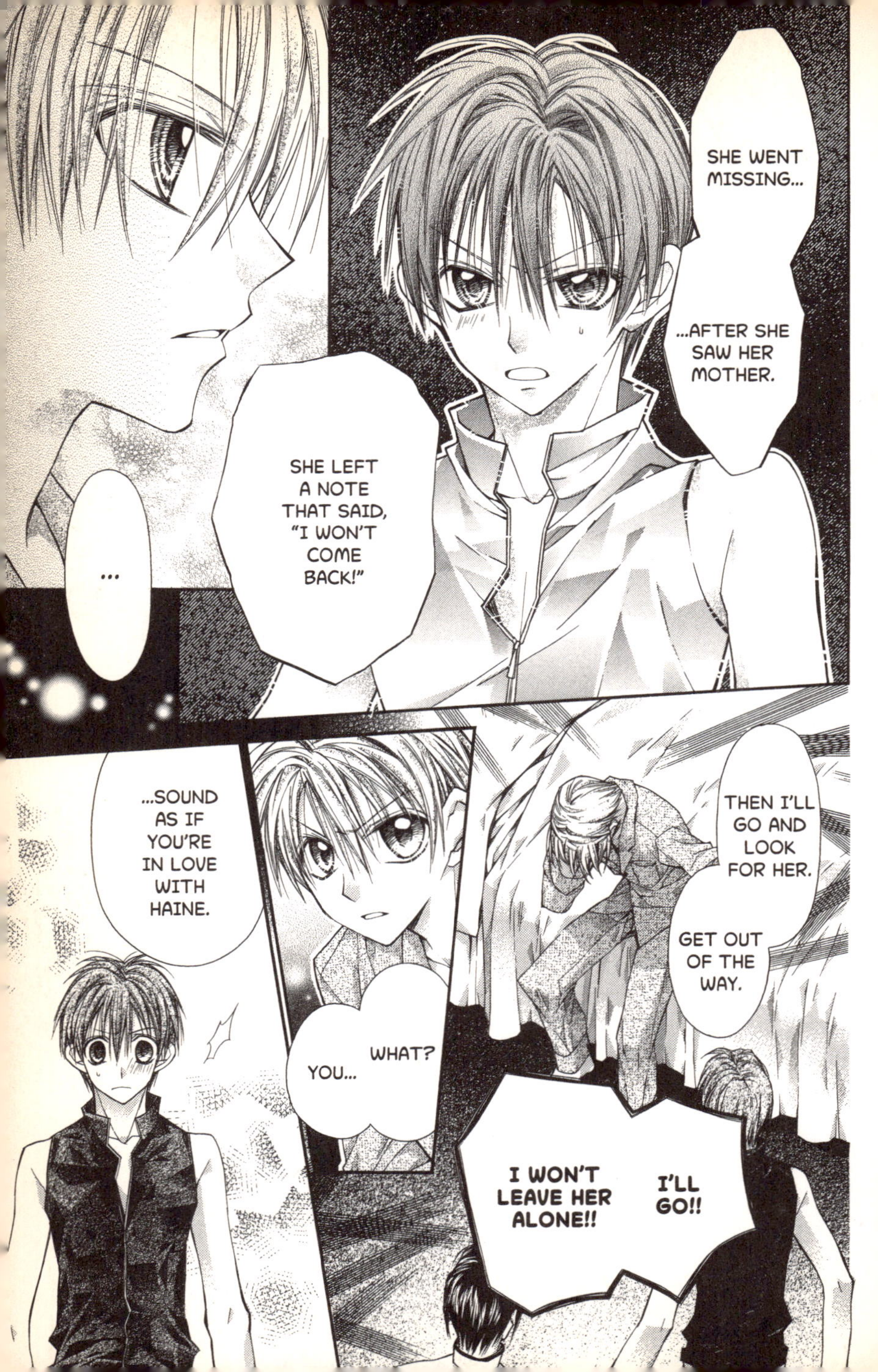
SHE WENT MISSING...
...AFTER SHE SAW HER MOTHER.
SHE LEFT A NOTE THAT SAID, "I WON'T COME BACK!"
...
THEN I'LL GO AND LOOK FOR HER.
GET OUT OF THE WAY.
I'LL GO!!
I WON'T LEAVE HER ALONE!!
WHAT?
YOU...
...SOUND AS IF YOU'RE IN LOVE WITH HAINE.

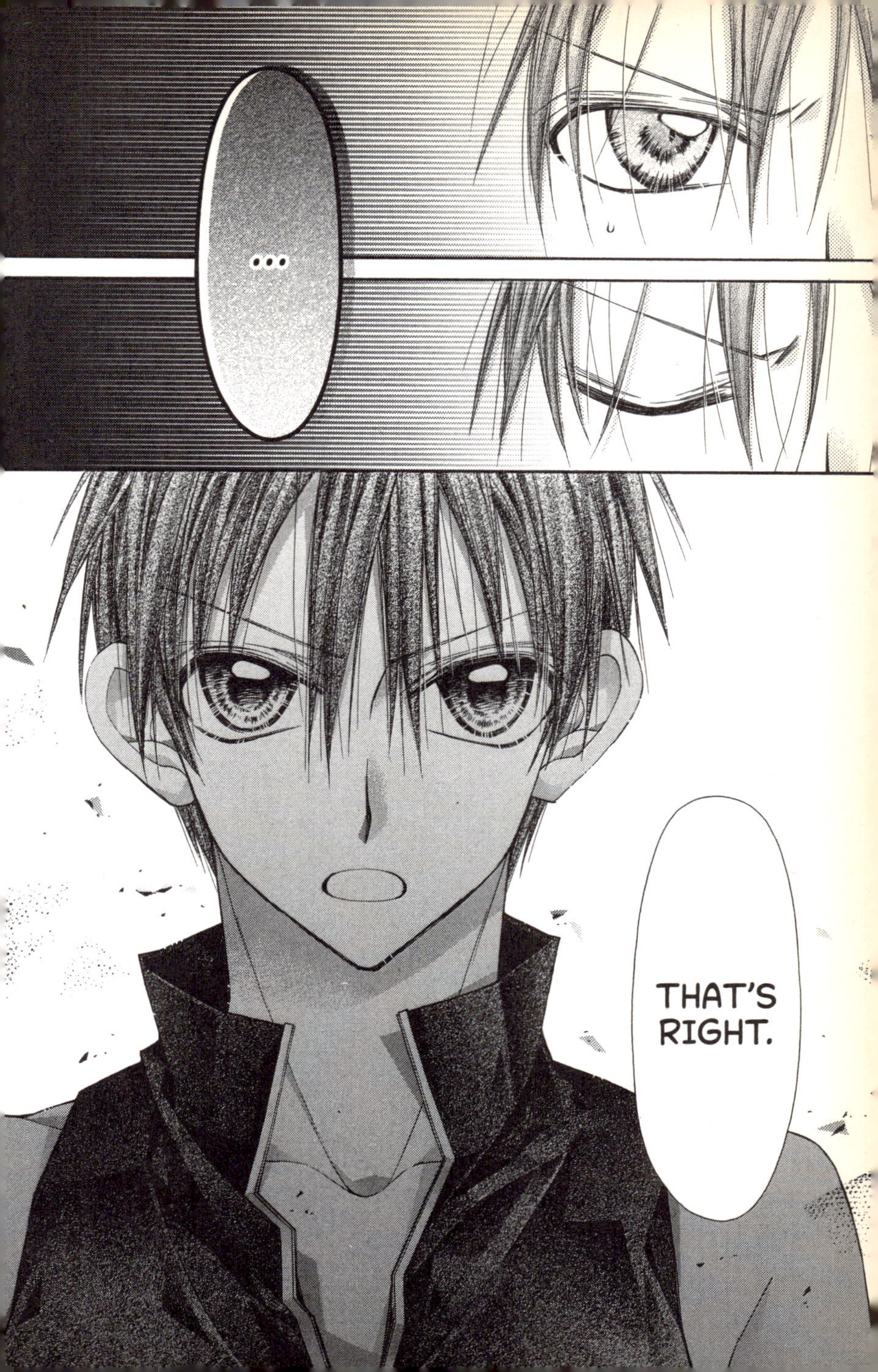
...
THAT'S RIGHT.

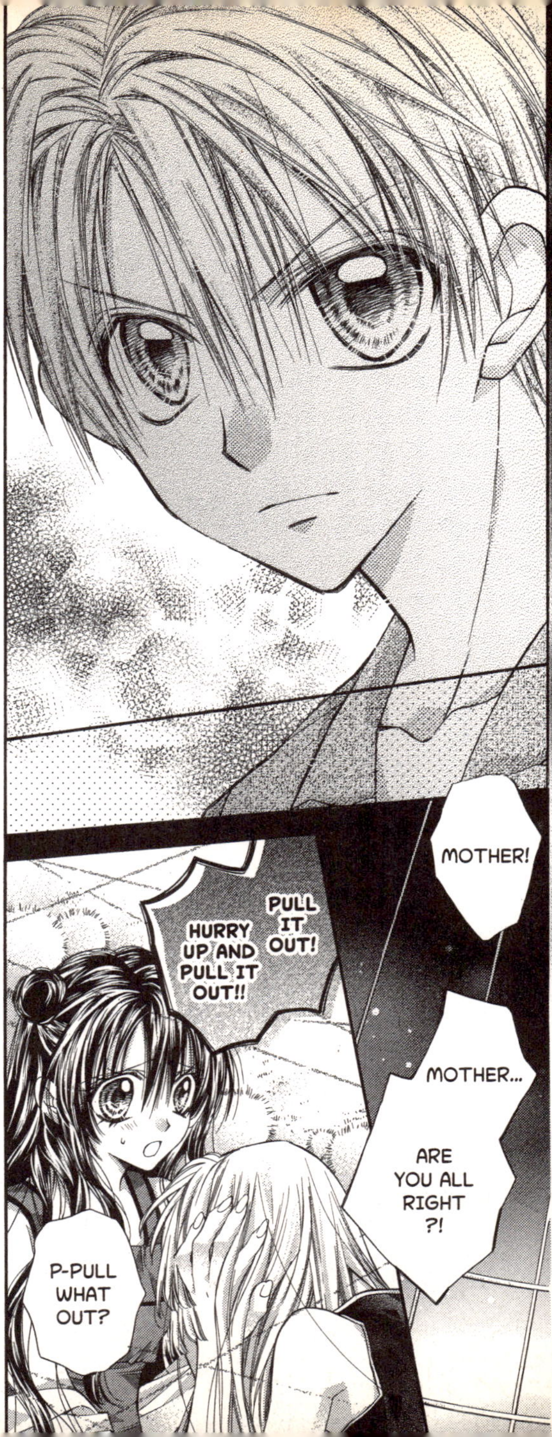
MOTHER!
PULL IT OUT!
HURRY UP AND PULL IT OUT!!
MOTHER...
ARE YOU ALL RIGHT ?!
P-PULL WHAT OUT?

Special Thanks

✿ Nakame
✿ Saori

✿ Yuko-chan ✿ Miwa-chan
✿ Chihiro-chan ✿ Hina-chan

✿ Ammonite Ltd.

✿ Supervisor S-san
Ex-supervisor Y-san
Designer Kawatani-san

✿ Shueisha Ribon Editorial Department

✿ Riku & Kai

Kazuhito and Maika will be on the cover of volume 9! Ooh... They've finally appeared...!! For those who are fans of the parents, please look forward to it!!

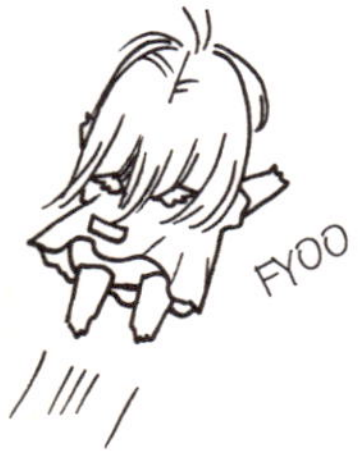
FYOO

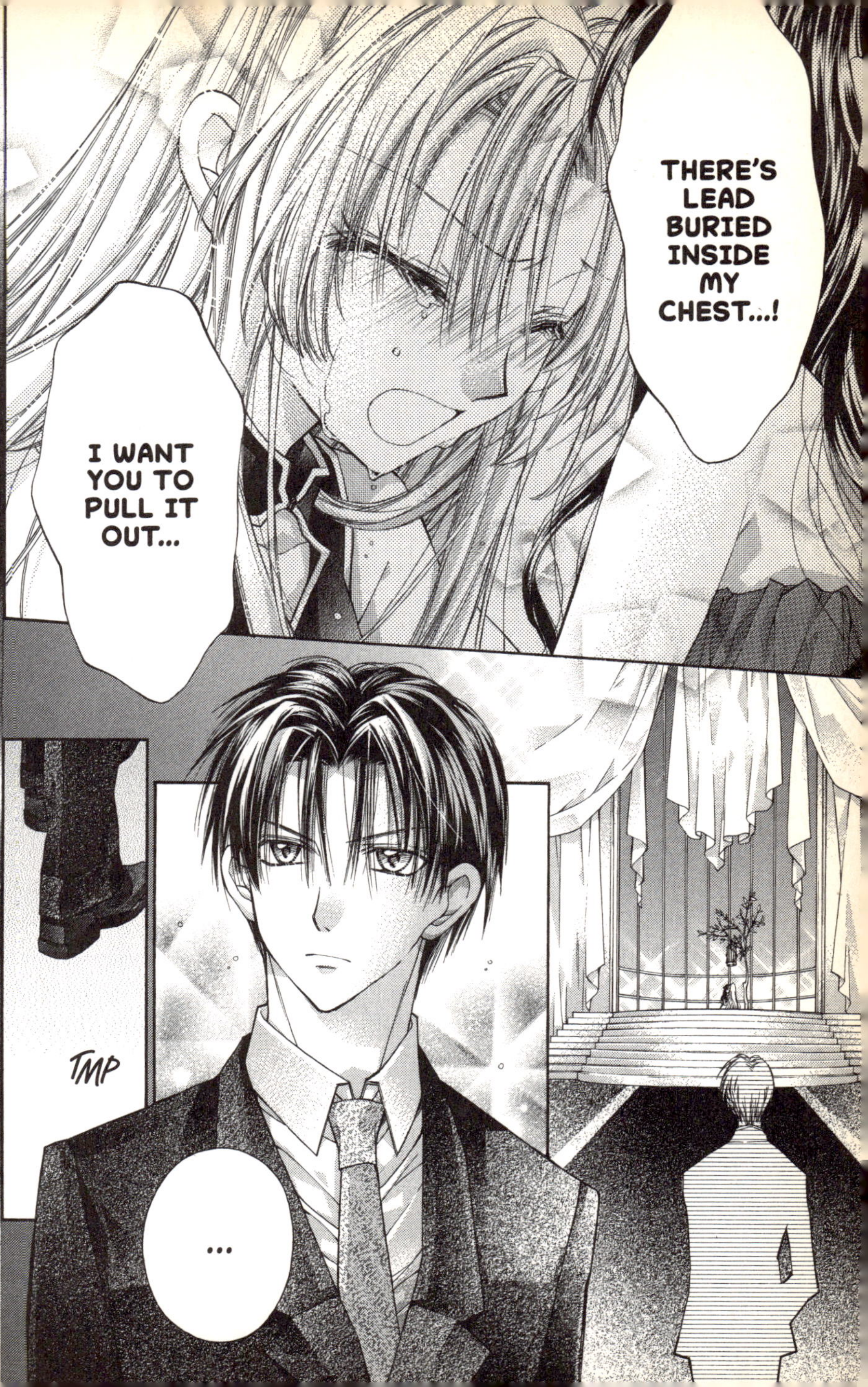
THERE'S LEAD BURIED INSIDE MY CHEST...!
I WANT YOU TO PULL IT OUT...
...
TMP

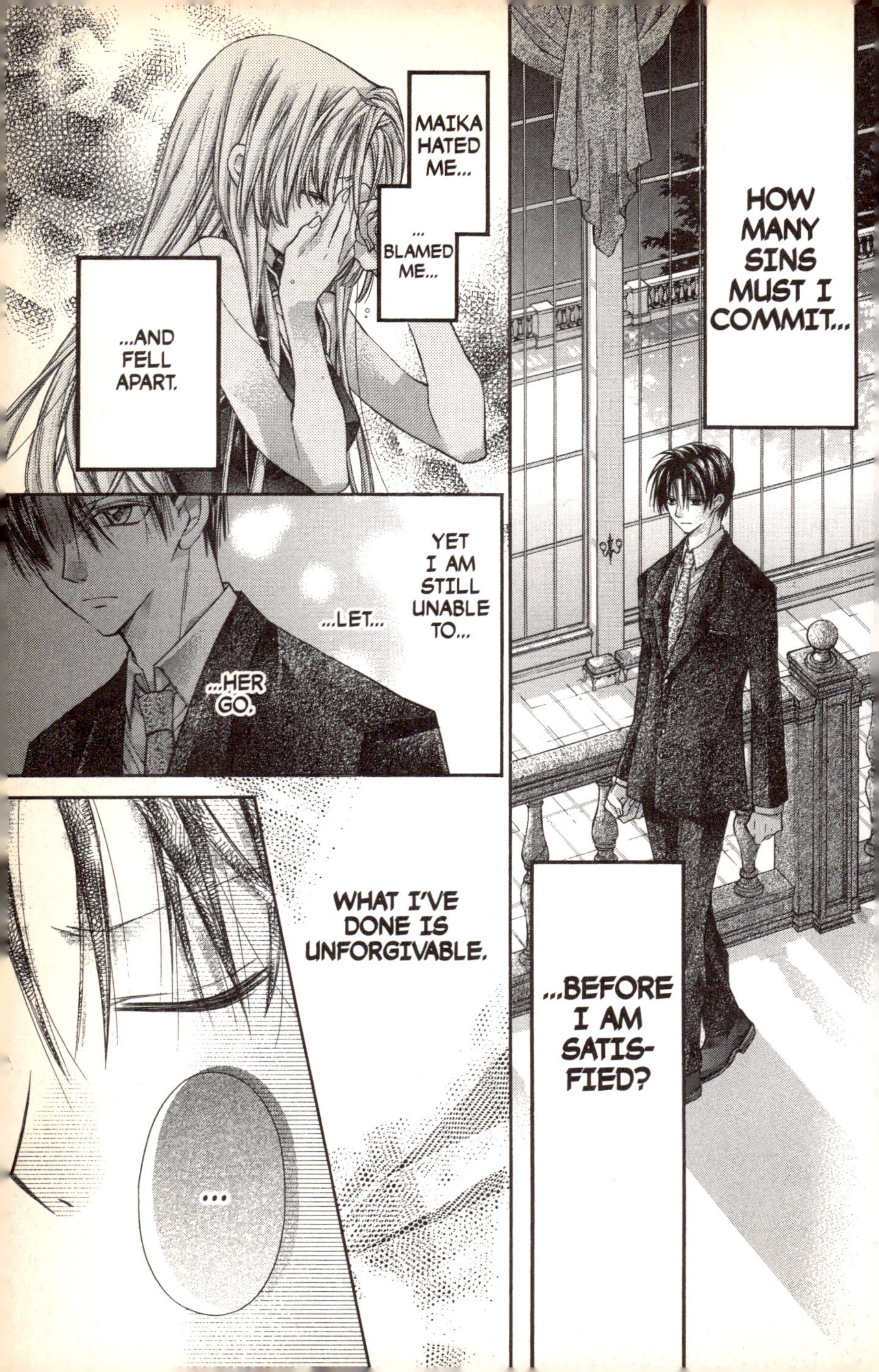
HOW MANY SINS MUST I COMMIT...
...BEFORE I AM SATISFIED?
MAIKA HATED ME...
... BLAMED ME...
...AND FELL APART.
YET I AM STILL UNABLE TO...
...LET...
...HER GO.
WHAT I'VE DONE IS UNFORGIVABLE.
...

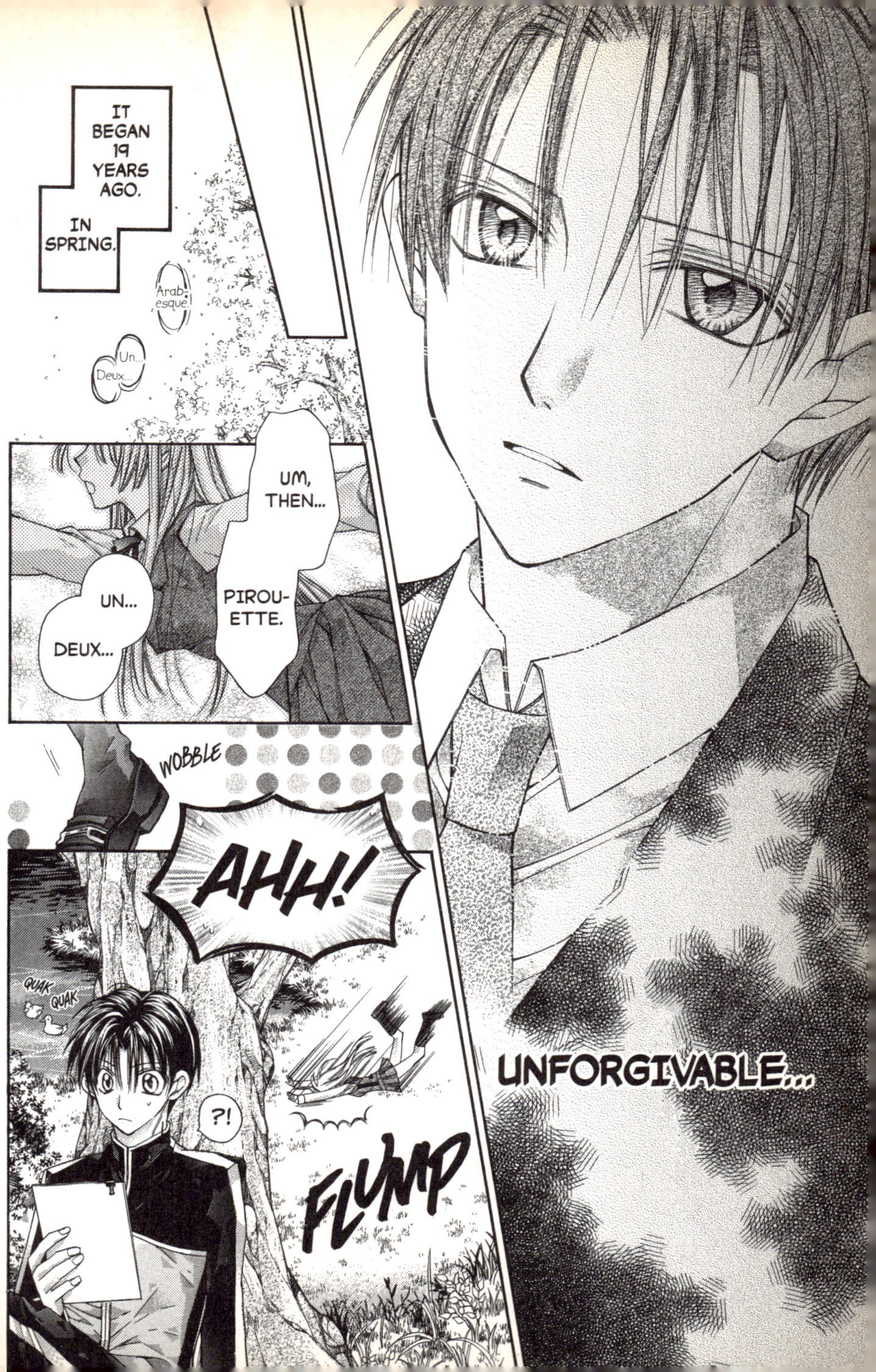
UNFORGIVABLE...
IT BEGAN 19 YEARS AGO.
IN SPRING.
Arabesque.
Un... Deux...
UM, THEN... PIROUETTE.
UN... DEUX...
WOBBLE
AHH!
FLUMP
?!
QUAK QUAK

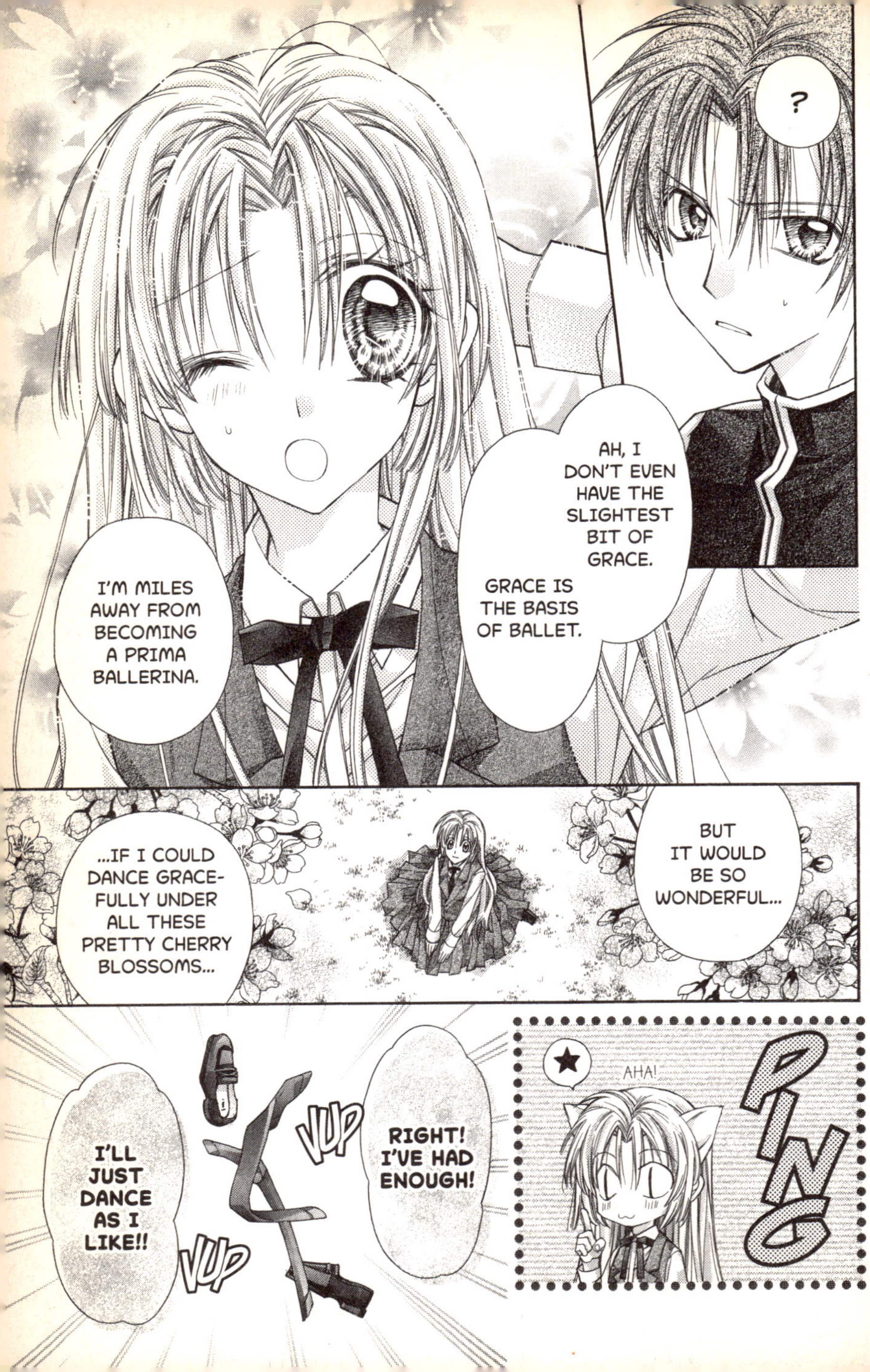
?
AH, I DON'T EVEN HAVE THE SLIGHTEST BIT OF GRACE.
GRACE IS THE BASIS OF BALLET.
I'M MILES AWAY FROM BECOMING A PRIMA BALLERINA.
BUT IT WOULD BE SO WONDERFUL...
...IF I COULD DANCE GRACE-FULLY UNDER ALL THESE PRETTY CHERRY BLOSSOMS...
PING
AHA!
RIGHT! I'VE HAD ENOUGH!
VUP
I'LL JUST DANCE AS I LIKE!!
VUP

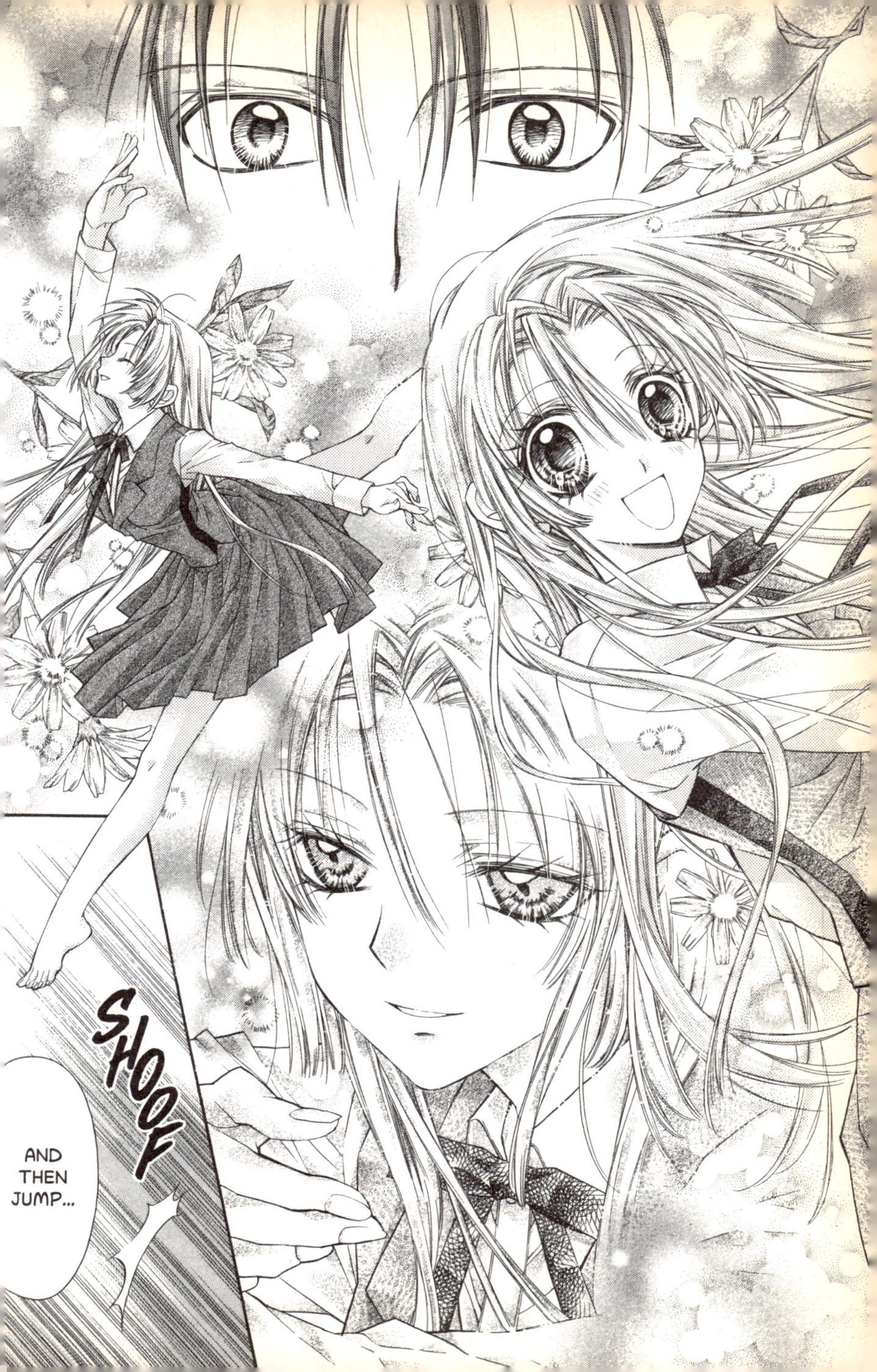
SHOOF
AND THEN JUMP...

Kazuhito Kamiya

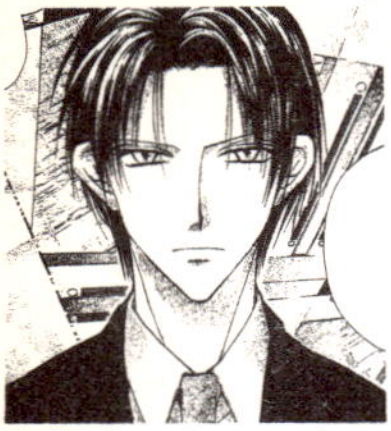

Birthday: December 21
Blood-Type: A

A hard-nosed perfectionist. He's Haine's father. He's in love with Maika and will do anything in his power to have her, but as a result he has the tendency to be indifferent toward other people. He holds an important post in the Emperor Association, as well as being the Chief Executive of a large company. He was the 39th Emperor.

Tachibana Kamiya

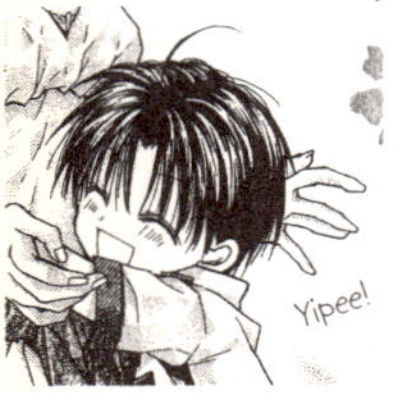
Yipee!

Birthday: October 18
Blood-Type: A

Haine and Komaki's little brother. He has a girlfriend. Like Komaki, he's got a strong affection for his elder sisters. Since his mother is in that state, I guess he wants somebody to depend on. He admires Shizumasa (Takanari, that is), and wants to become a fine Emperor too.

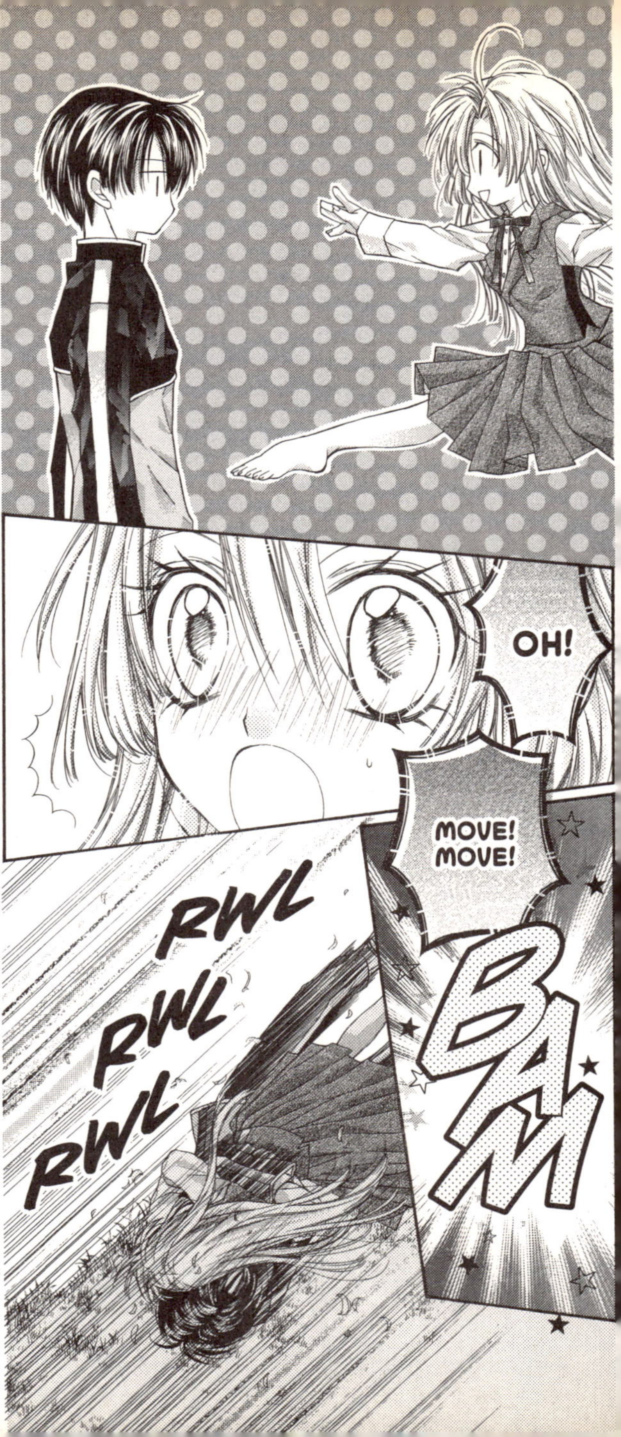
OH!
MOVE! MOVE!
BAM
RWL
RWL
RWL

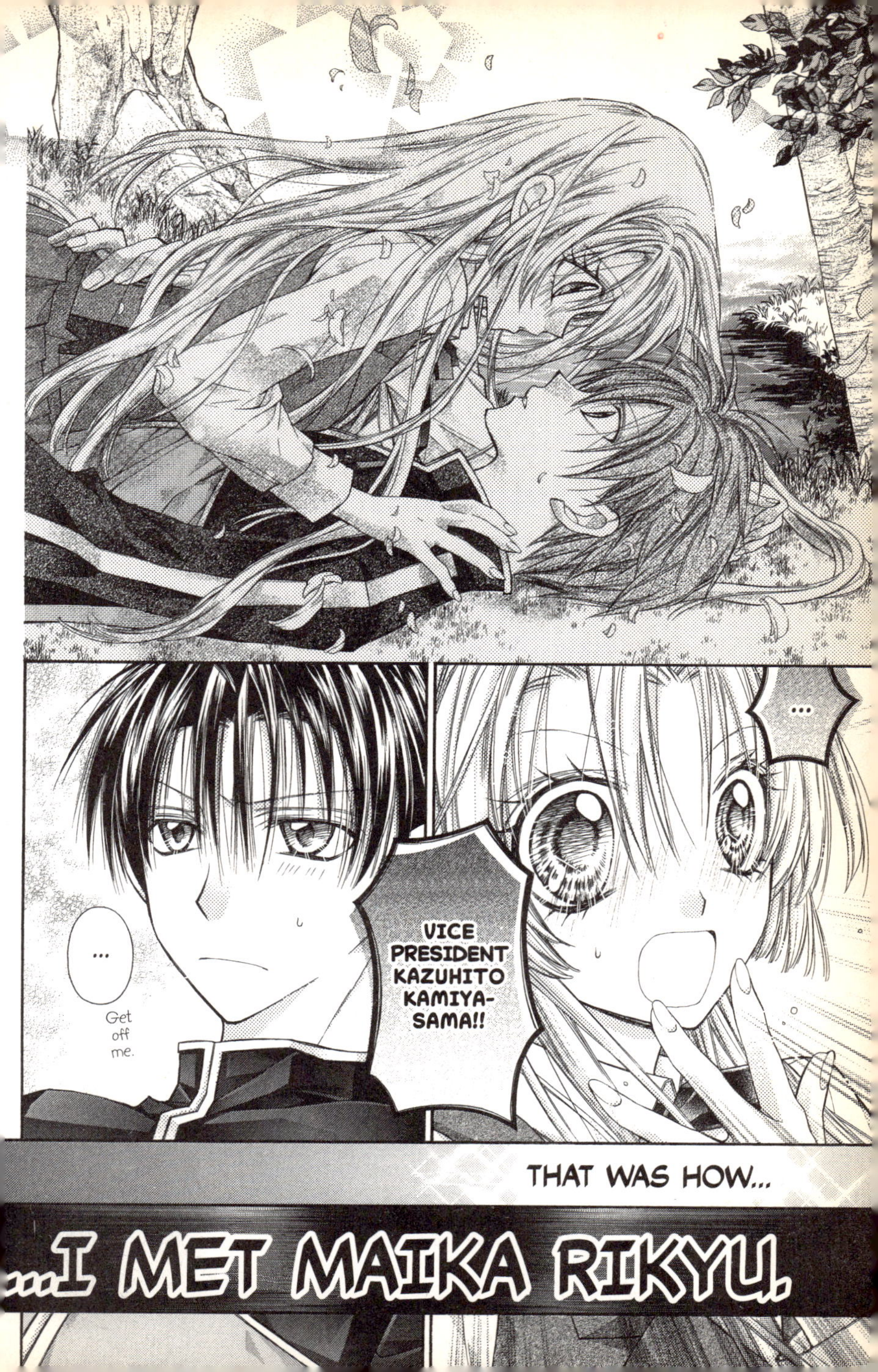
...
VICE PRESIDENT KAZUHITO KAMIYA-SAMA!!
...
Get off me.
THAT WAS HOW...
...I MET MAIKA RIKYU.

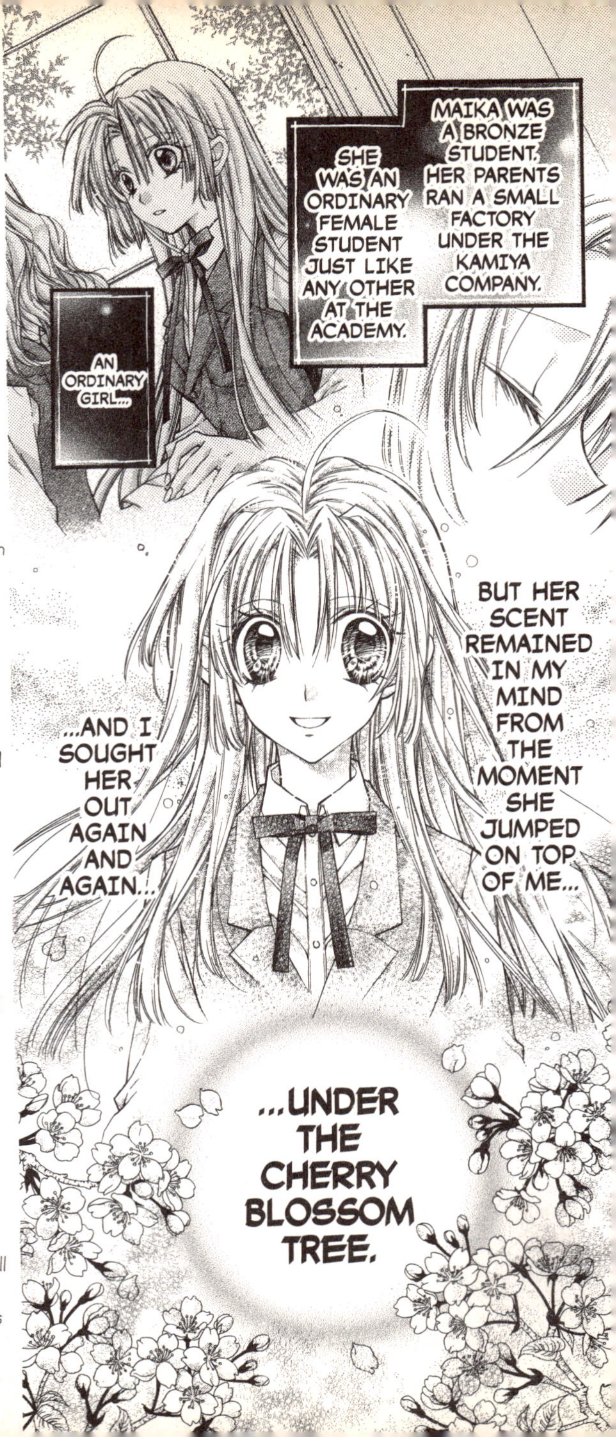
MAIKA WAS A BRONZE STUDENT. HER PARENTS RAN A SMALL FACTORY UNDER THE KAMIYA COMPANY.
SHE WAS AN ORDINARY FEMALE STUDENT JUST LIKE ANY OTHER AT THE ACADEMY.
AN ORDINARY GIRL...
BUT HER SCENT REMAINED IN MY MIND FROM THE MOMENT SHE JUMPED ON TOP OF ME...
...AND I SOUGHT HER OUT AGAIN AND AGAIN...
...UNDER THE CHERRY BLOSSOM TREE.

Kiriaki

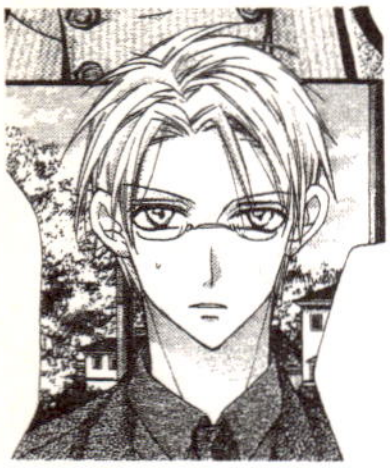

Birthday: April 12
Blood Type: A

Shizumasa's personal butler. He used to admire Senri when he was a student, but he dislikes him now after Senri changed after a certain incident. Deep inside, he knows he'll never be able to beat him, so he can't help asking Senri for help when in need. He supports Shizumasa's love for Haine.

Yukimitsu Tsujimiya

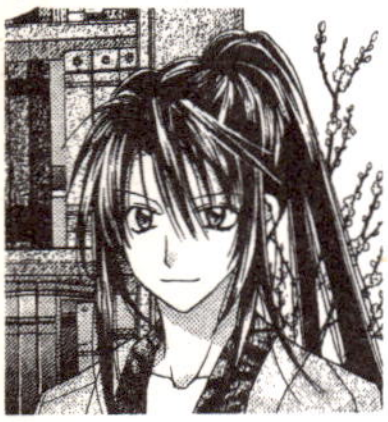

Birthday: November 11
Blood Type: B

The former Student Council President and leader of the Heretics. He's now the head of the School Discipline Committee. He's deeply in love with Ushio, but always gets rejected. His men are devoted to him, and they still wish for his return as Emperor. He's also Maguri's older brother. He cares deeply for his younger brother and dotes on him.

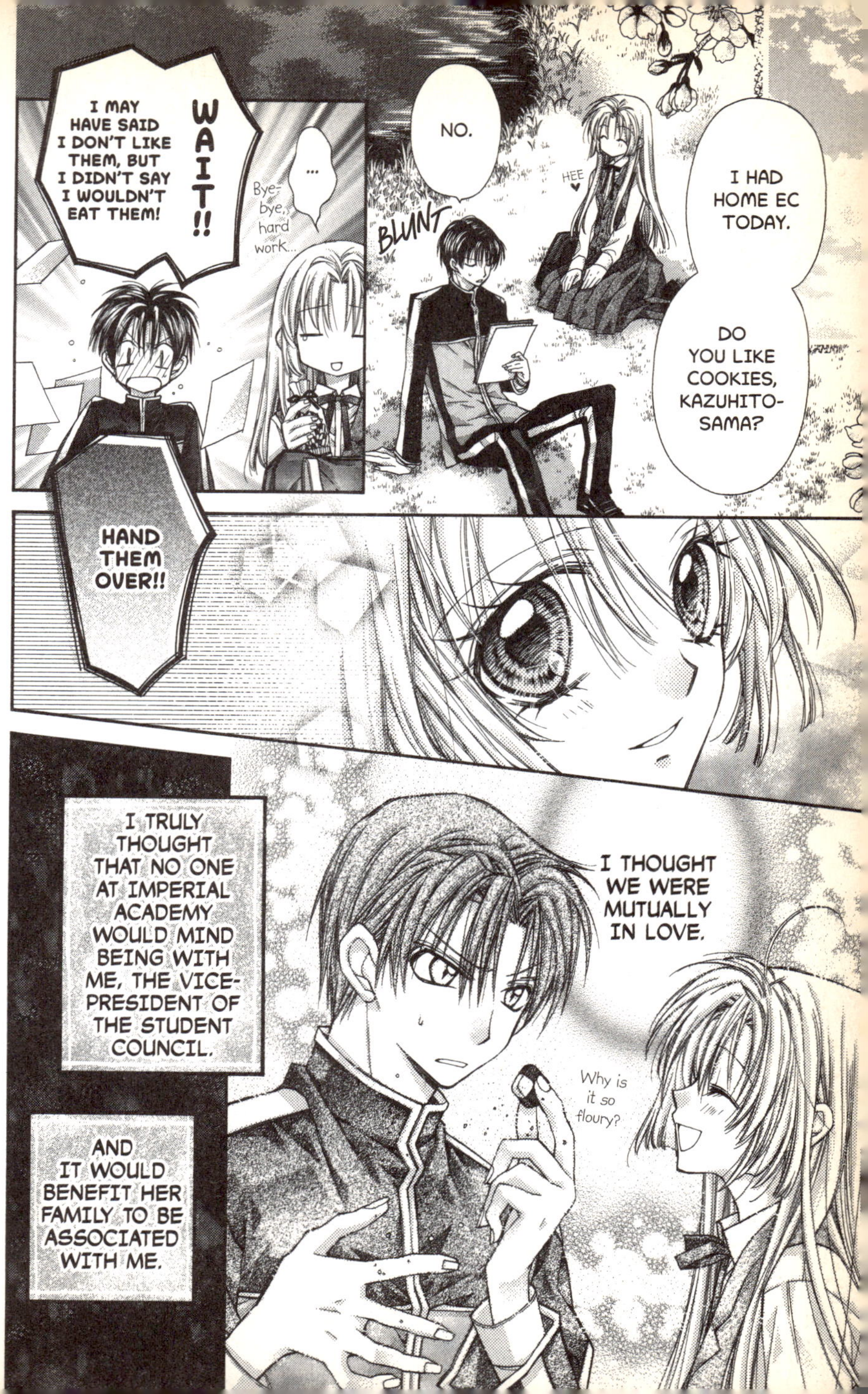

I HAD HOME EC TODAY.
DO YOU LIKE COOKIES, KAZUHITO-SAMA?
HEE ♥
NO.
BLUNT
...
Bye-bye, hard work...
WAIT!!
I MAY HAVE SAID I DON'T LIKE THEM, BUT I DIDN'T SAY I WOULDN'T EAT THEM!
HAND THEM OVER!!
I TRULY THOUGHT THAT NO ONE AT IMPERIAL ACADEMY WOULD MIND BEING WITH ME, THE VICE-PRESIDENT OF THE STUDENT COUNCIL.
AND IT WOULD BENEFIT HER FAMILY TO BE ASSOCIATED WITH ME.
I THOUGHT WE WERE MUTUALLY IN LOVE.
Why is it so floury?

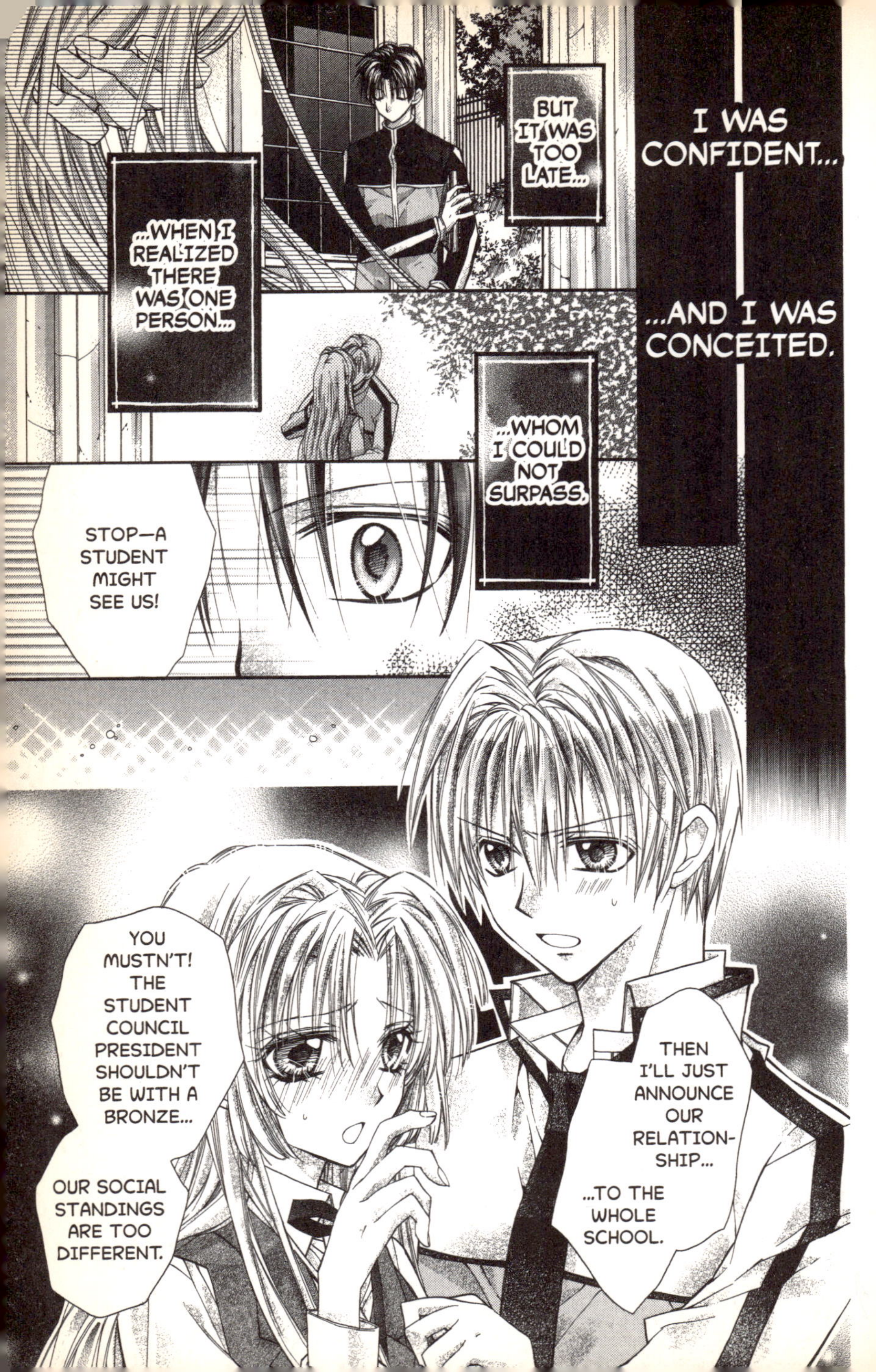
I WAS CONFIDENT...
...AND I WAS CONCEITED.
BUT IT WAS TOO LATE...
...WHEN I REALIZED THERE WAS ONE PERSON...
...WHOM I COULD NOT SURPASS.
STOP—A STUDENT MIGHT SEE US!
THEN I'LL JUST ANNOUNCE OUR RELATION-SHIP...
...TO THE WHOLE SCHOOL.
YOU MUSTN'T! THE STUDENT COUNCIL PRESIDENT SHOULDN'T BE WITH A BRONZE...
OUR SOCIAL STANDINGS ARE TOO DIFFERENT.

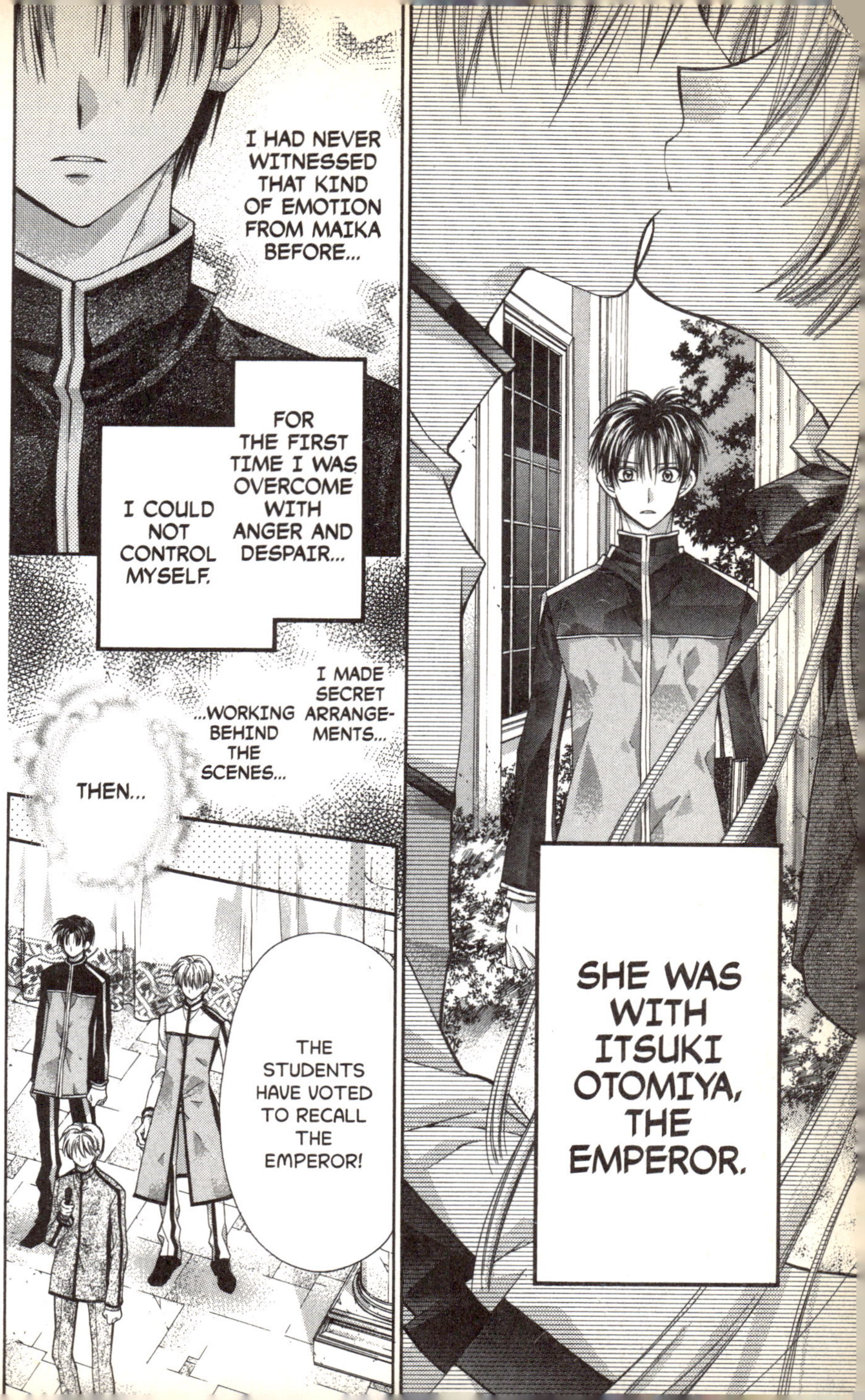
SHE WAS WITH ITSUKI OTOMIYA, THE EMPEROR.
I HAD NEVER WITNESSED THAT KIND OF EMOTION FROM MAIKA BEFORE...
FOR THE FIRST TIME I WAS OVERCOME WITH ANGER AND DESPAIR...
I COULD NOT CONTROL MYSELF.
I MADE SECRET ARRANGE-MENTS...
...WORKING BEHIND THE SCENES...
THEN...
THE STUDENTS HAVE VOTED TO RECALL THE EMPEROR!

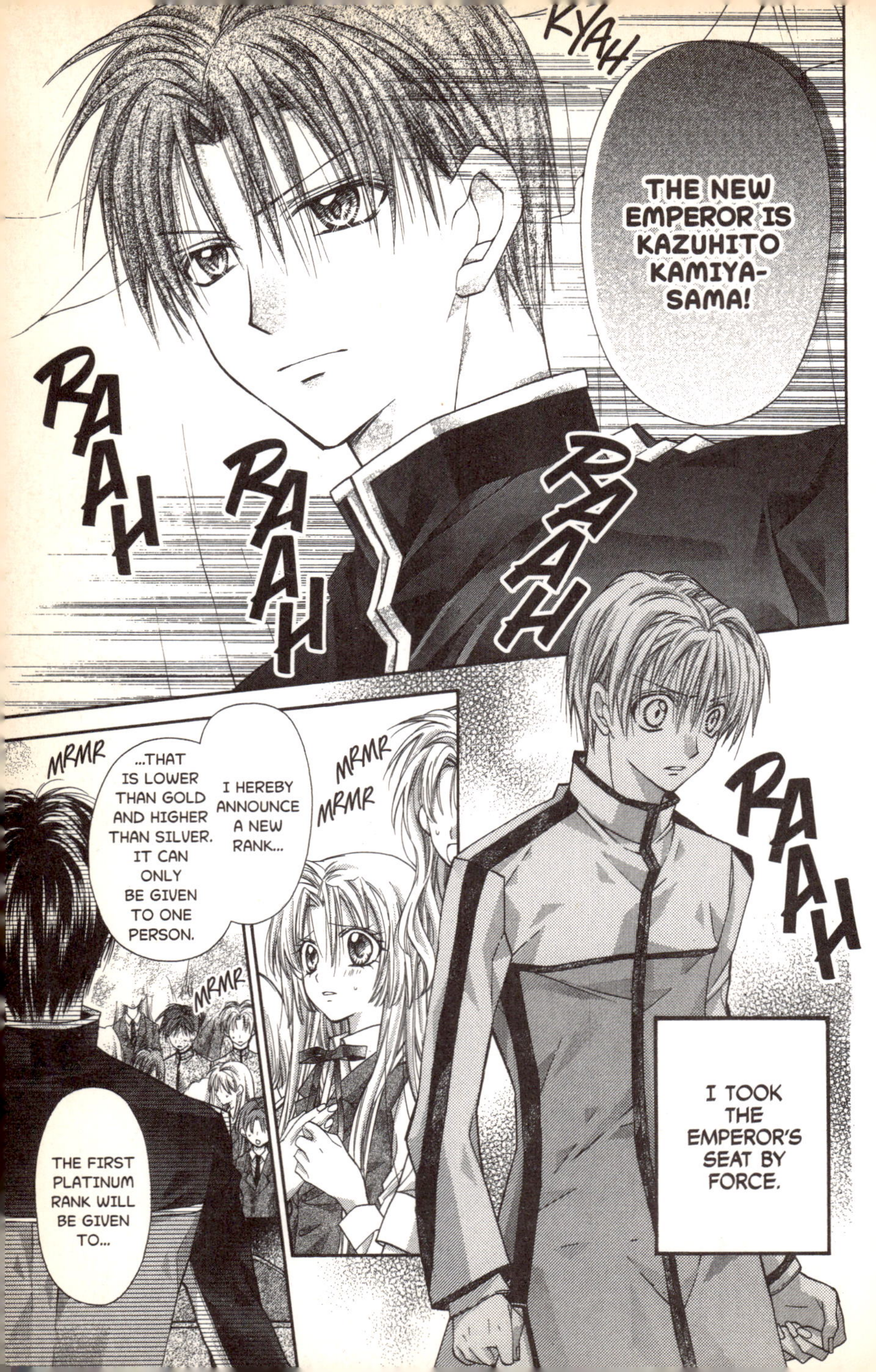
KYAH
THE NEW EMPEROR IS KAZUHITO KAMIYA-SAMA!
RAAH
RAAH
RAAH
RAAH
I TOOK THE EMPEROR'S SEAT BY FORCE.
MRMR MRMR
I HEREBY ANNOUNCE A NEW RANK...
...THAT IS LOWER THAN GOLD AND HIGHER THAN SILVER. IT CAN ONLY BE GIVEN TO ONE PERSON.
MRMR
MRMR
THE FIRST PLATINUM RANK WILL BE GIVEN TO...

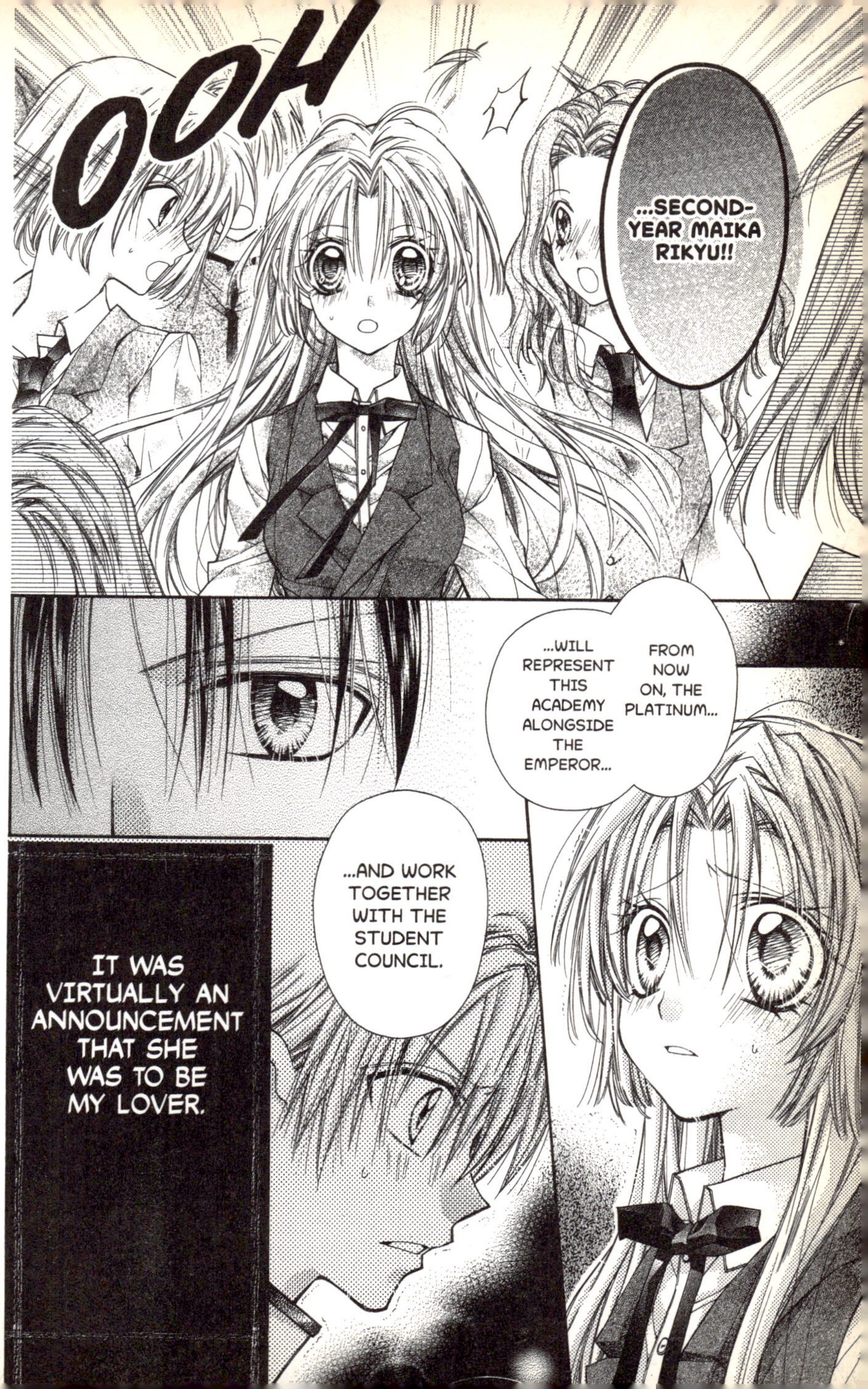
...SECOND-YEAR MAIKA RIKYU!!
OOH
FROM NOW ON, THE PLATINUM...
...WILL REPRESENT THIS ACADEMY ALONGSIDE THE EMPEROR...
...AND WORK TOGETHER WITH THE STUDENT COUNCIL.
IT WAS VIRTUALLY AN ANNOUNCEMENT THAT SHE WAS TO BE MY LOVER.

STUDENT COUNCIL
WHY...
NO!! WHY?! KAZUHITO-SAMA!!
...
WH...
HUFF
BECAUSE I LOVE YOU...
...MAIKA!

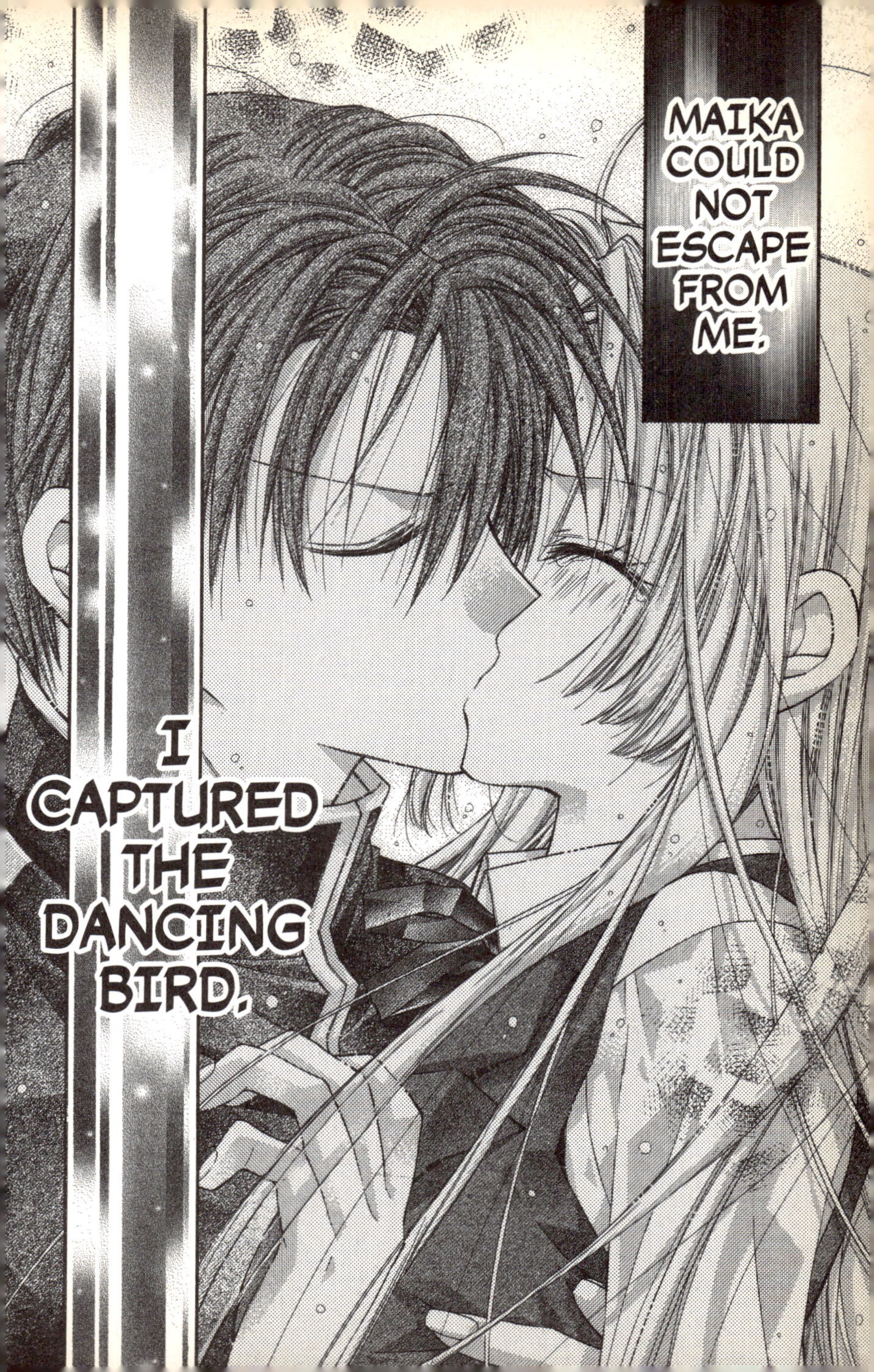
MAIKA COULD NOT ESCAPE FROM ME.
I CAPTURED THE DANCING BIRD.

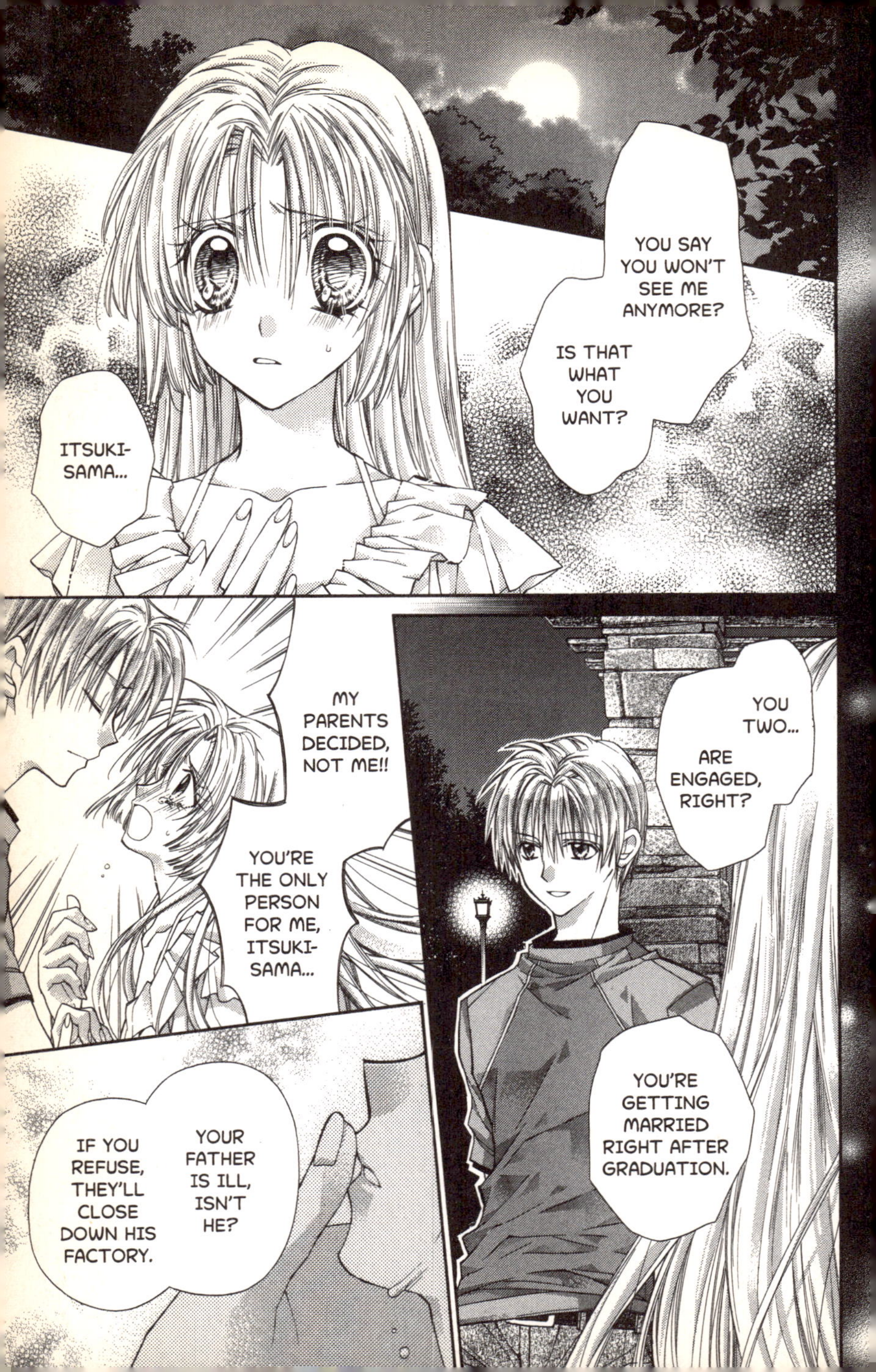
YOU SAY YOU WON'T SEE ME ANYMORE?
IS THAT WHAT YOU WANT?
ITSUKI-SAMA...
YOU TWO...
ARE ENGAGED, RIGHT?
YOU'RE GETTING MARRIED RIGHT AFTER GRADUATION.
MY PARENTS DECIDED, NOT ME!!
YOU'RE THE ONLY PERSON FOR ME, ITSUKI-SAMA...
YOUR FATHER IS ILL, ISN'T HE?
IF YOU REFUSE, THEY'LL CLOSE DOWN HIS FACTORY.

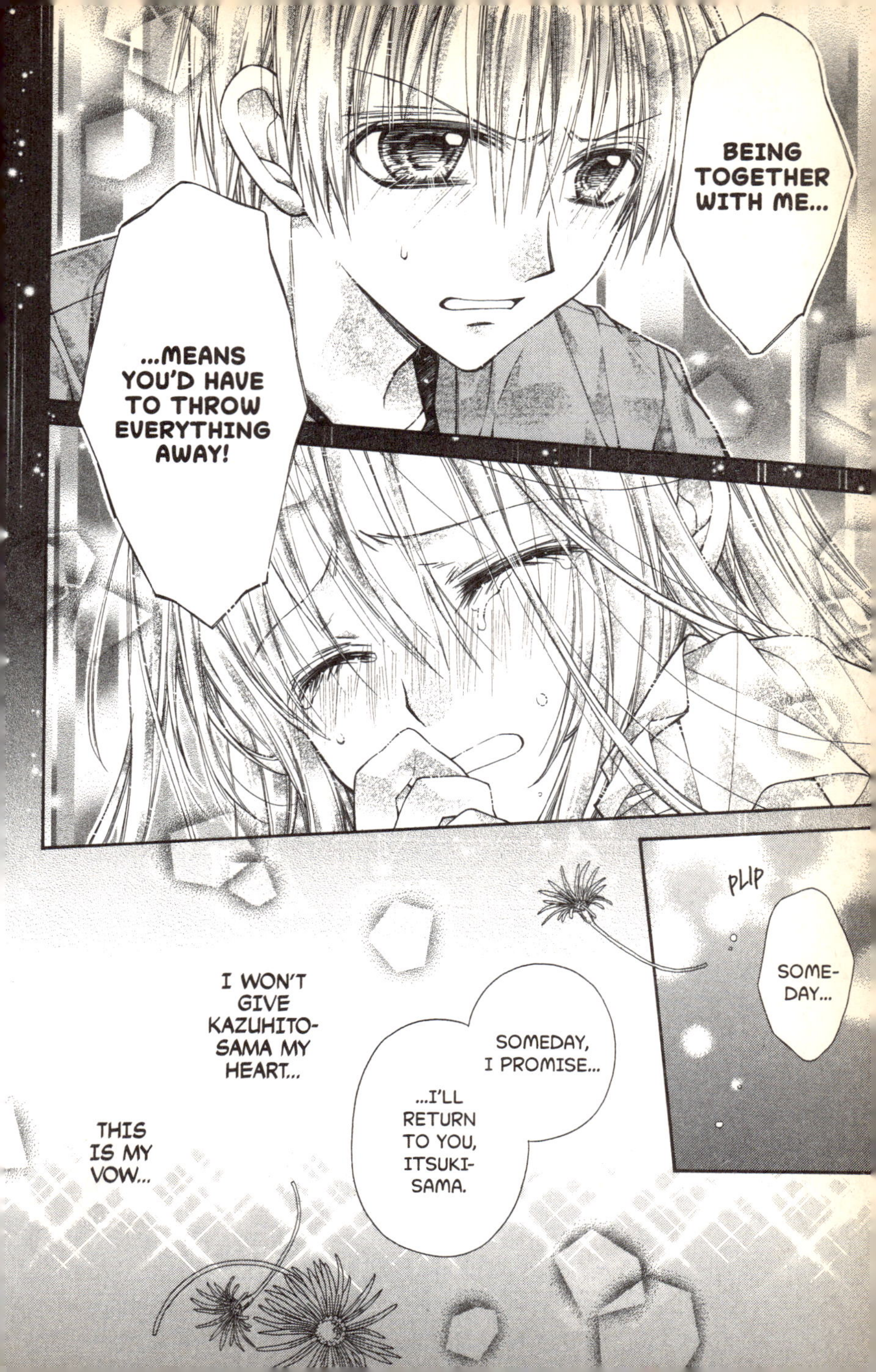
BEING TOGETHER WITH ME...
...MEANS YOU'D HAVE TO THROW EVERYTHING AWAY!
PLIP
SOME-DAY...
SOMEDAY, I PROMISE...
...I'LL RETURN TO YOU, ITSUKI-SAMA.
I WON'T GIVE KAZUHITO-SAMA MY HEART...
THIS IS MY VOW...

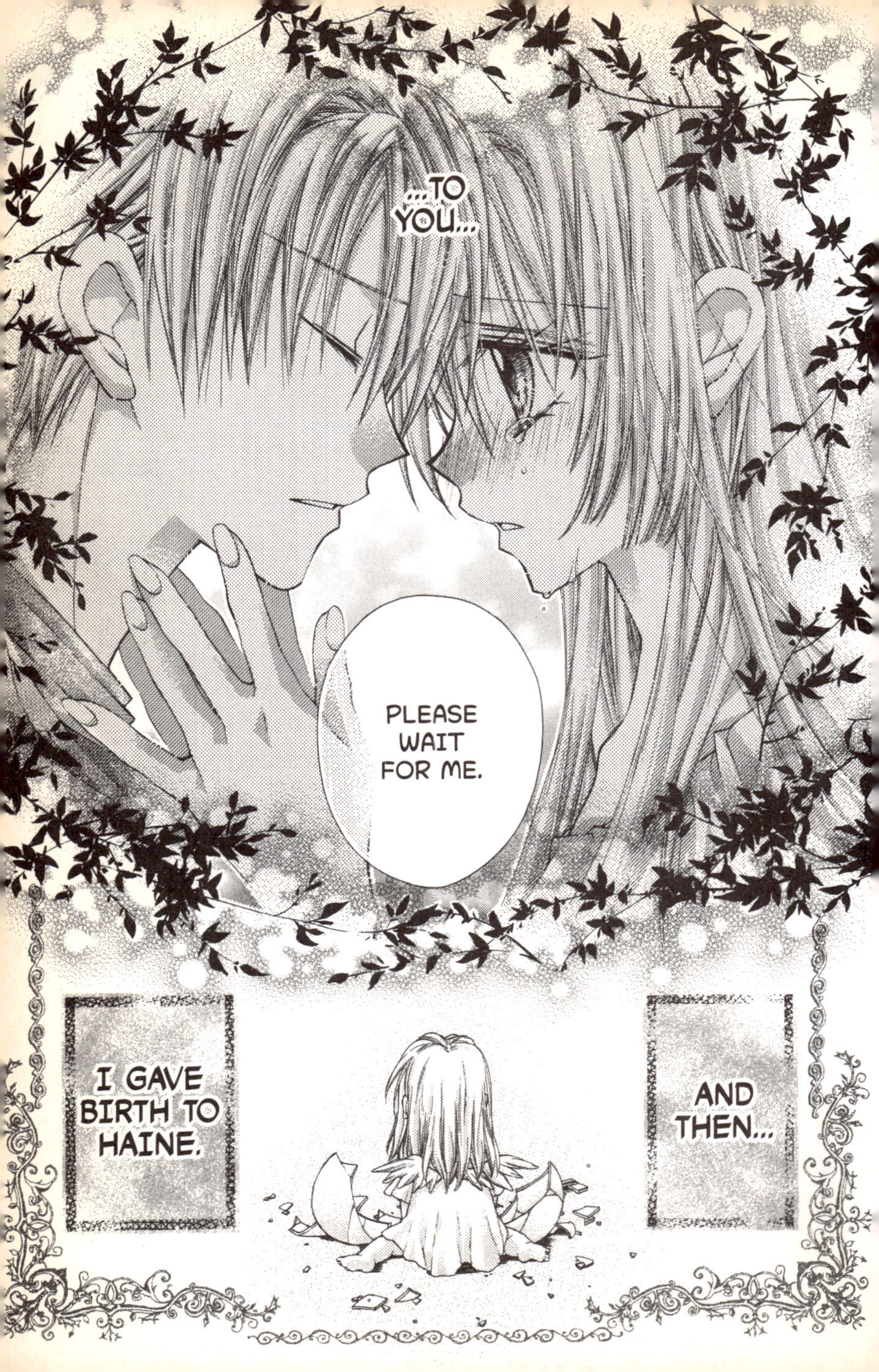
...TO YOU...
PLEASE WAIT FOR ME.
I GAVE BIRTH TO HAINE.
AND THEN...

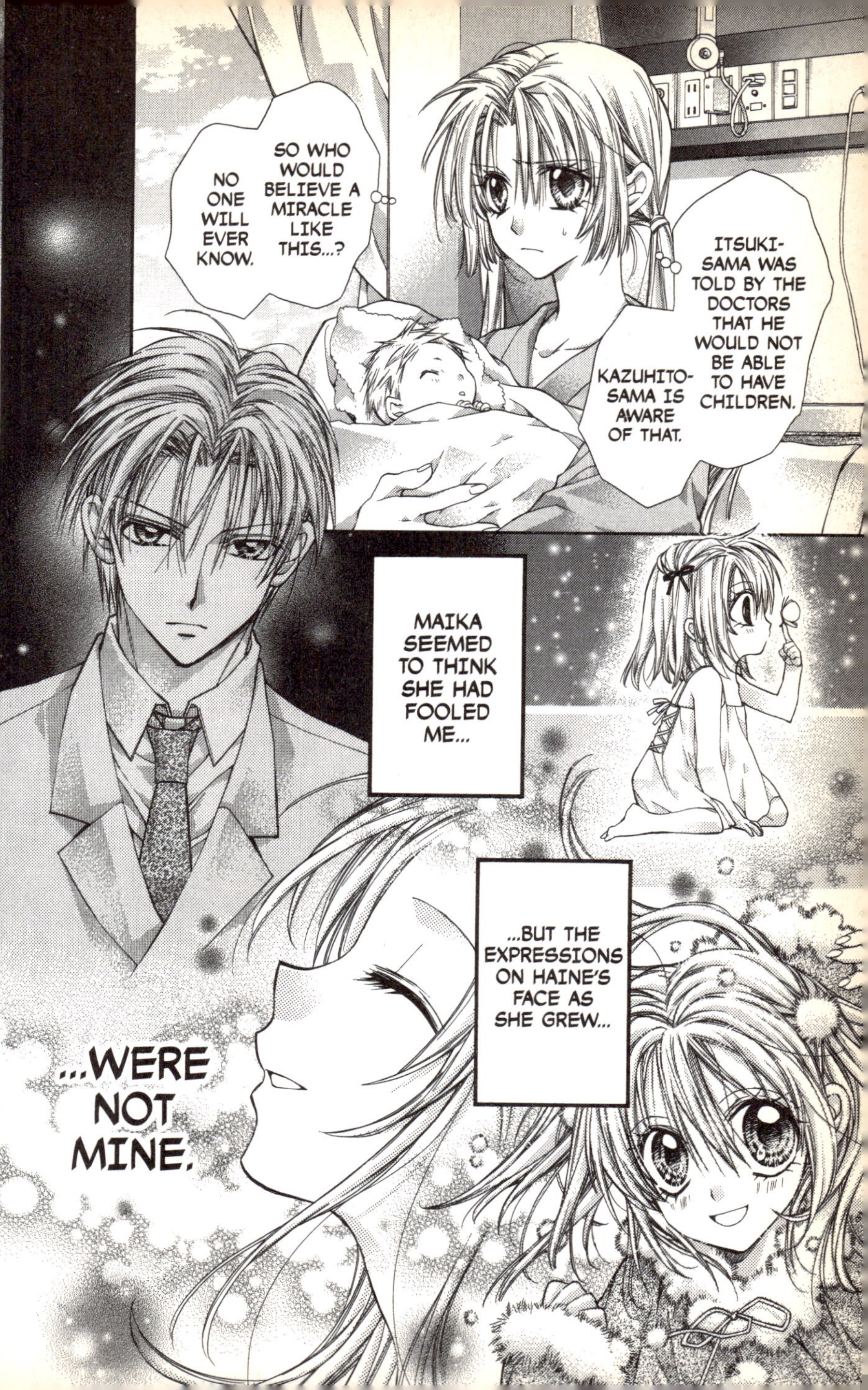
ITSUKI-SAMA WAS TOLD BY THE DOCTORS THAT HE WOULD NOT BE ABLE TO HAVE CHILDREN.
KAZUHITO-SAMA IS AWARE OF THAT.
SO WHO WOULD BELIEVE A MIRACLE LIKE THIS...?
NO ONE WILL EVER KNOW.
MAIKA SEEMED TO THINK SHE HAD FOOLED ME...
...BUT THE EXPRESSIONS ON HAINE'S FACE AS SHE GREW...
...WERE NOT MINE.

HAINE WAS PUT UP FOR ADOPTION ?!
YOU SENT HAINE OVER TO ITSUKI-SAMA'S PLACE?
IS IT TRUE?!
DID SHE DO SOME-THING WRONG ?!
KAZUHITO-SAMA!!
I MERELY RETURNED HER...
...TO HER RIGHTFUL FATHER.
HUH?

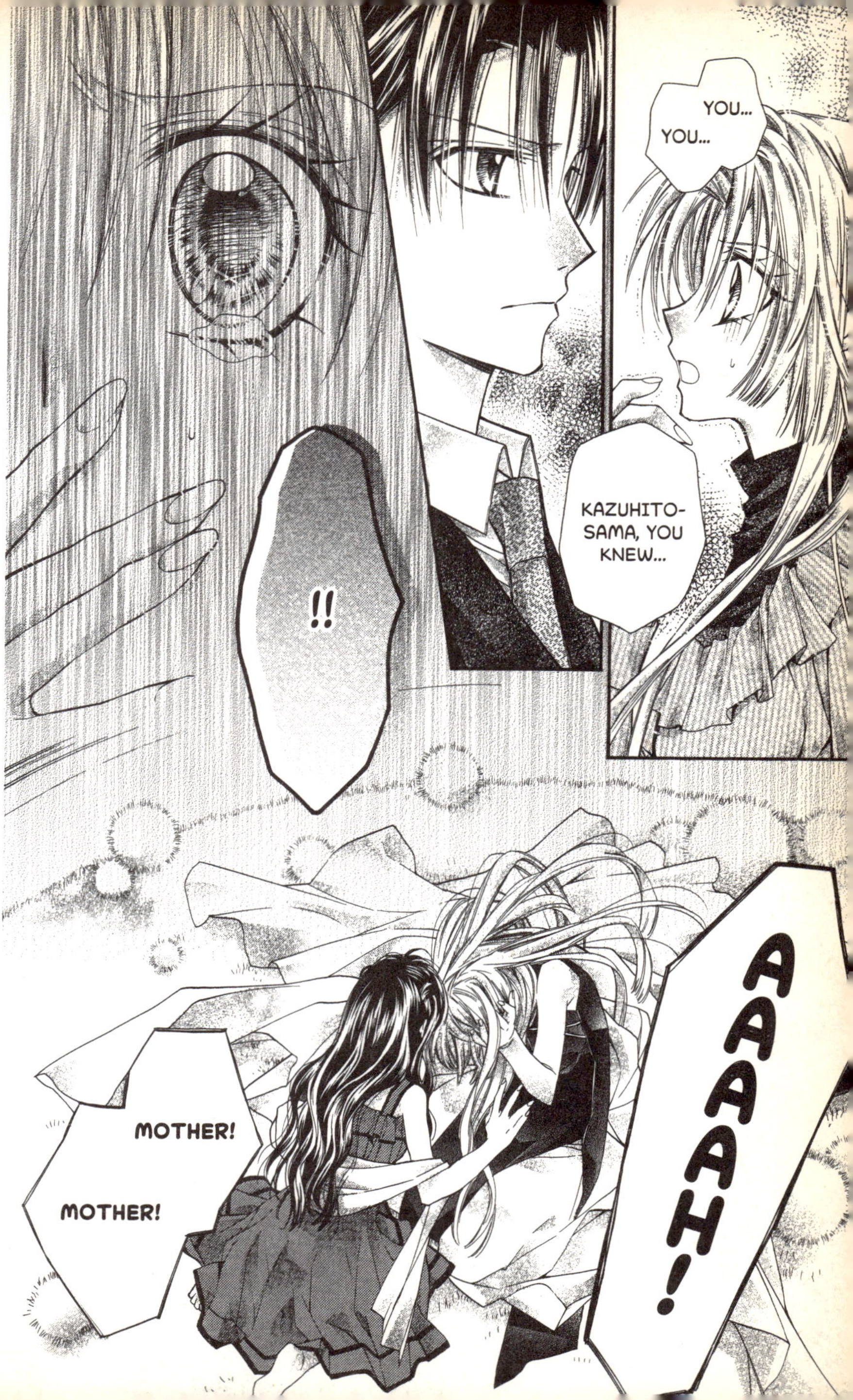
YOU... YOU...
KAZUHITO-SAMA, YOU KNEW...
!!
AAAAAH!
MOTHER! MOTHER!

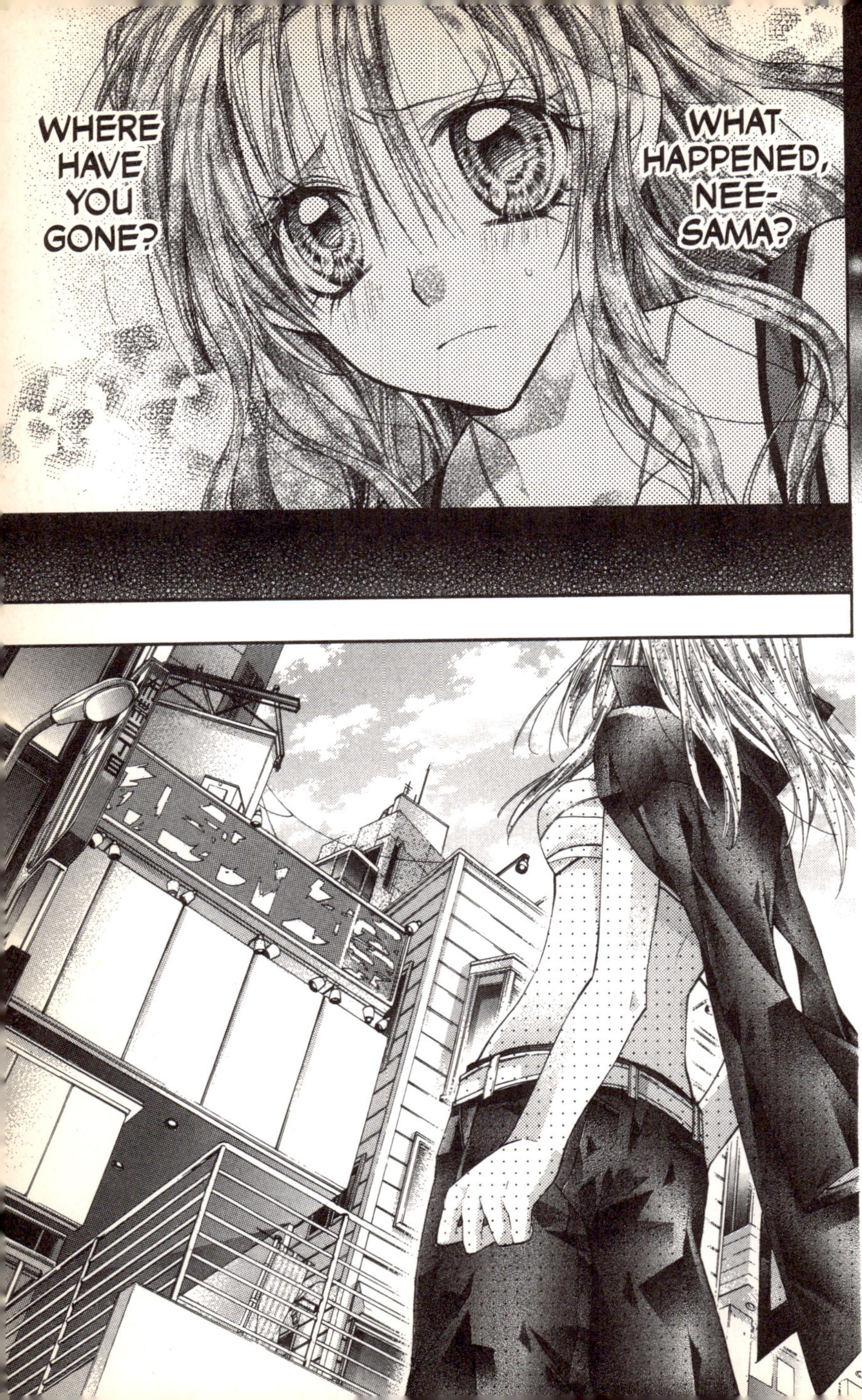
WHAT HAPPENED, NEE-SAMA?
WHERE HAVE YOU GONE?

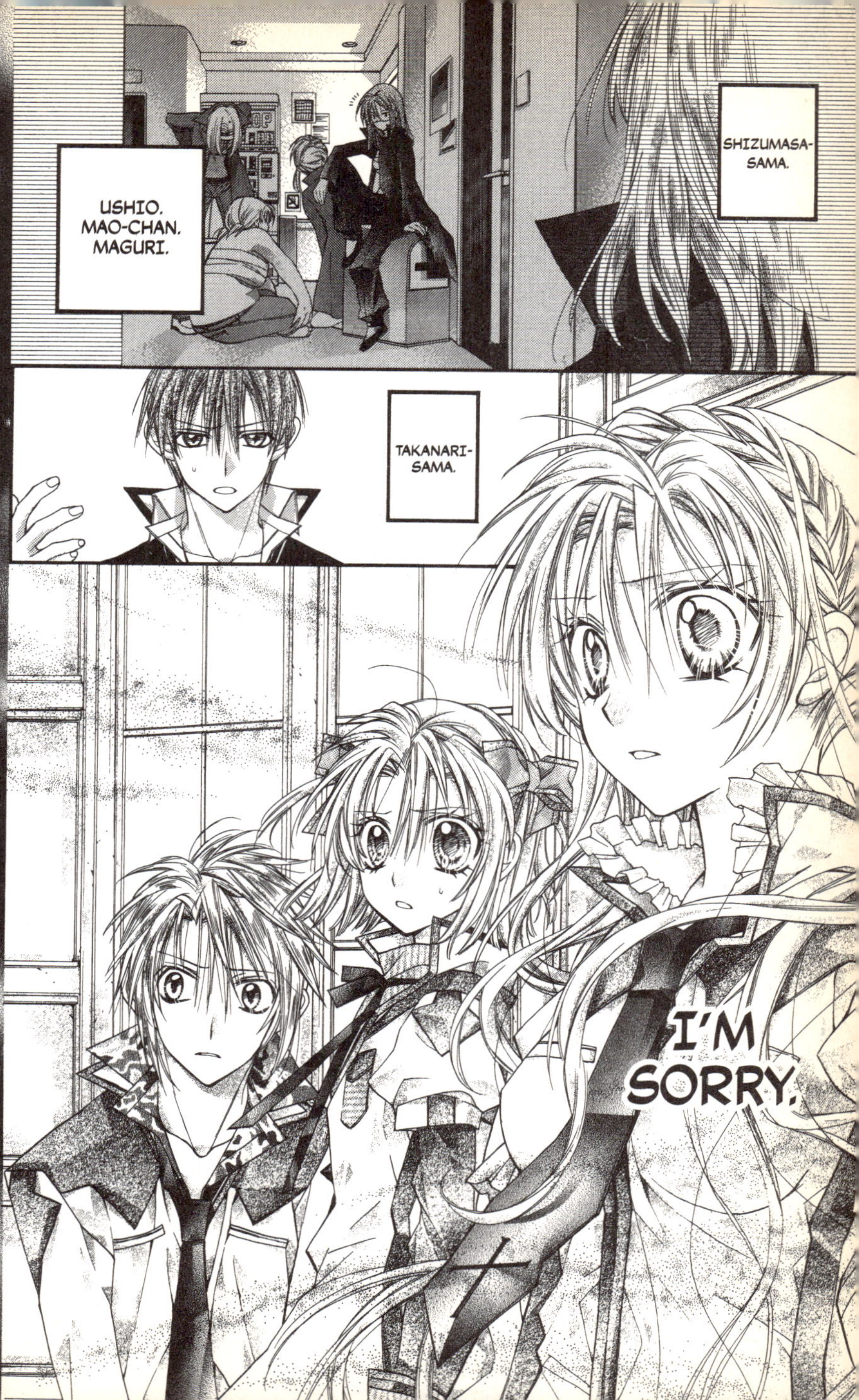
SHIZUMASA-SAMA.
USHIO. MAO-CHAN. MAGURI.
TAKANARI-SAMA.
I'M SORRY.

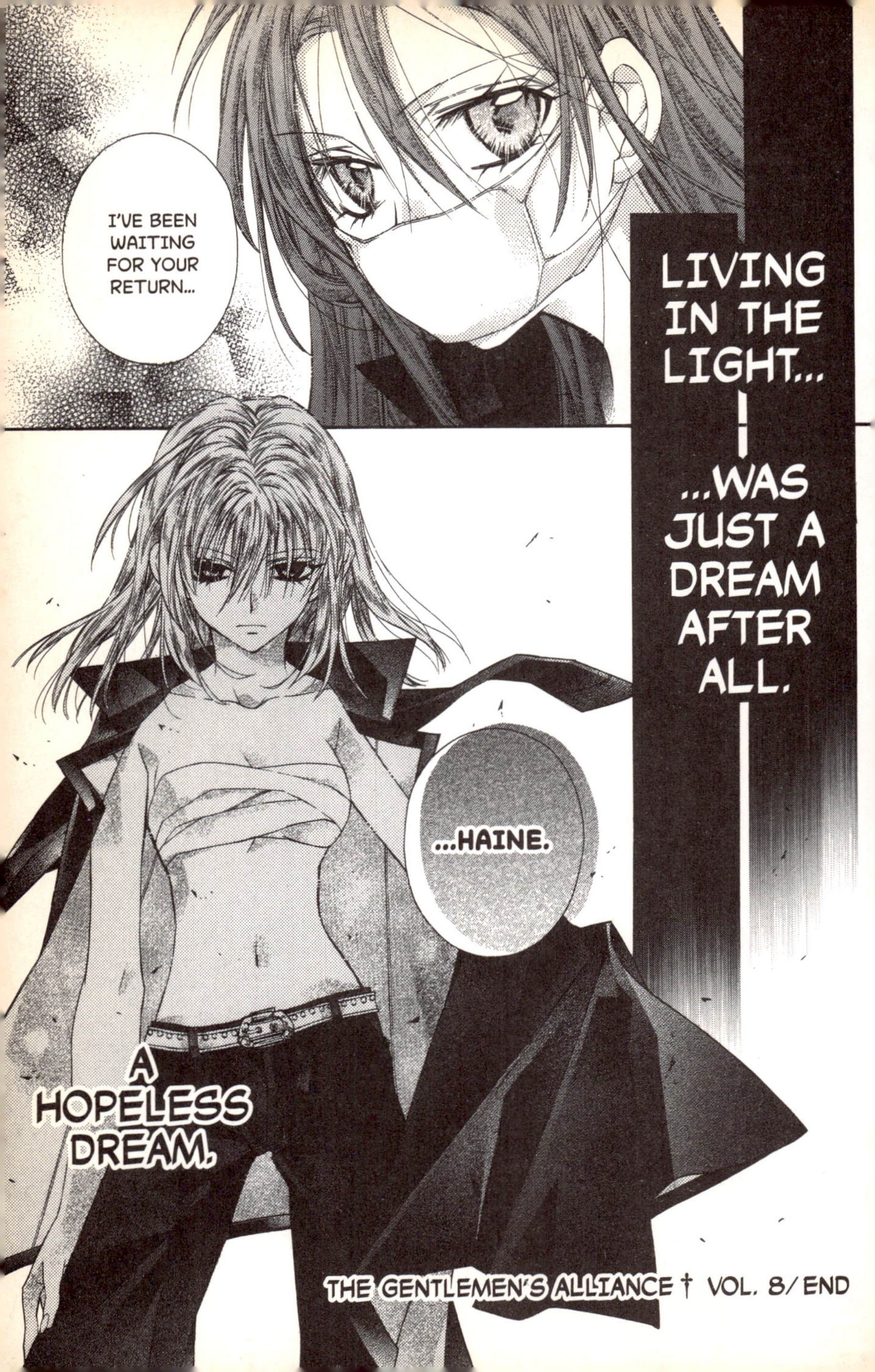
LIVING IN THE LIGHT...
...WAS JUST A DREAM AFTER ALL.
I'VE BEEN WAITING FOR YOUR RETURN...
...HAINE.
A HOPELESS DREAM.
THE GENTLEMEN'S ALLIANCE † VOL. 8/END

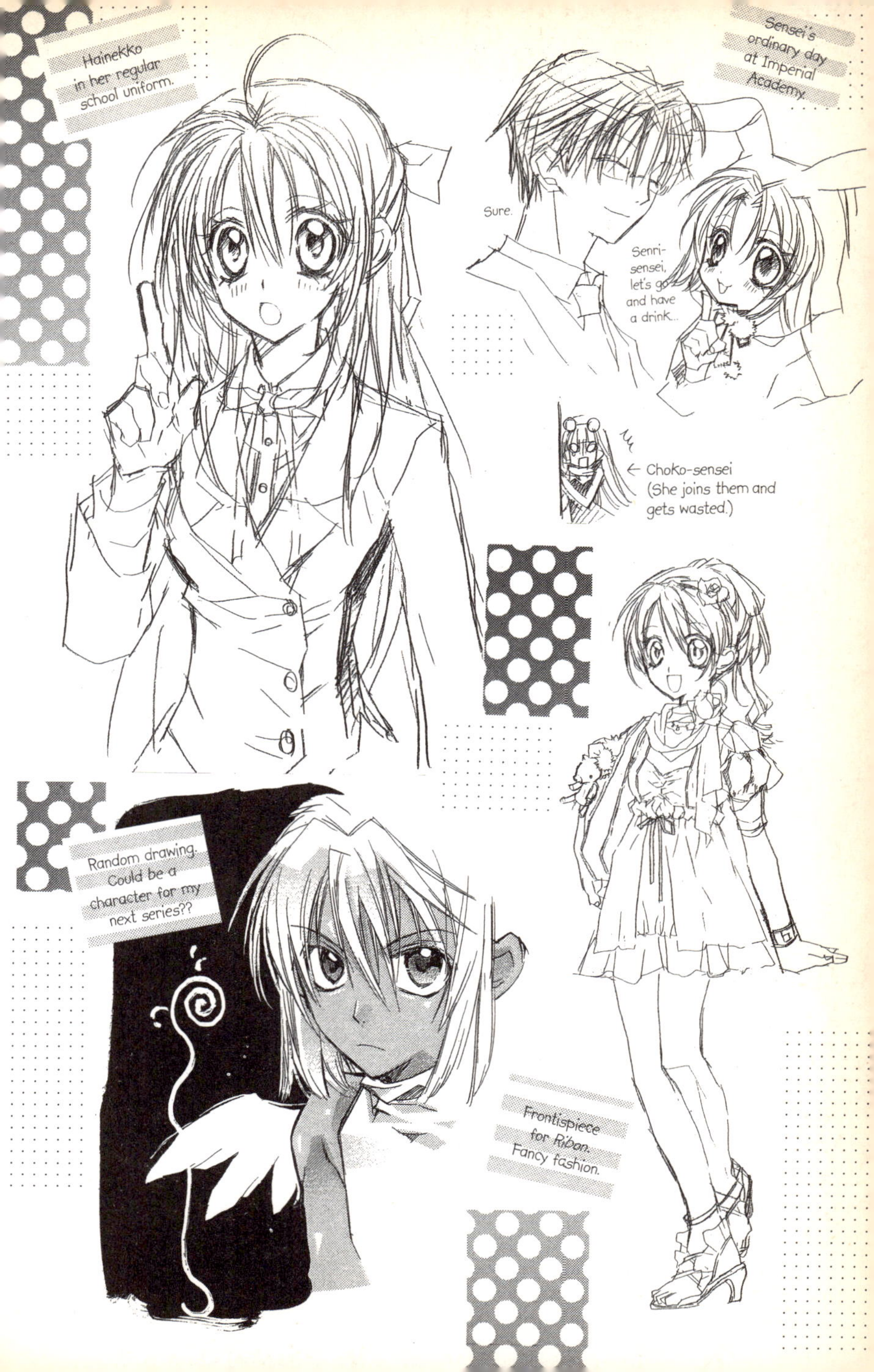
Sensei's ordinary day at Imperial Academy.
Senri-sensei, let's go and have a drink...
Sure.
← Choko-sensei (She joins them and gets wasted.)
Hainekko in her regular school uniform.
Frontispiece for Ribon. Fancy fashion.
Random drawing. Could be a character for my next series??

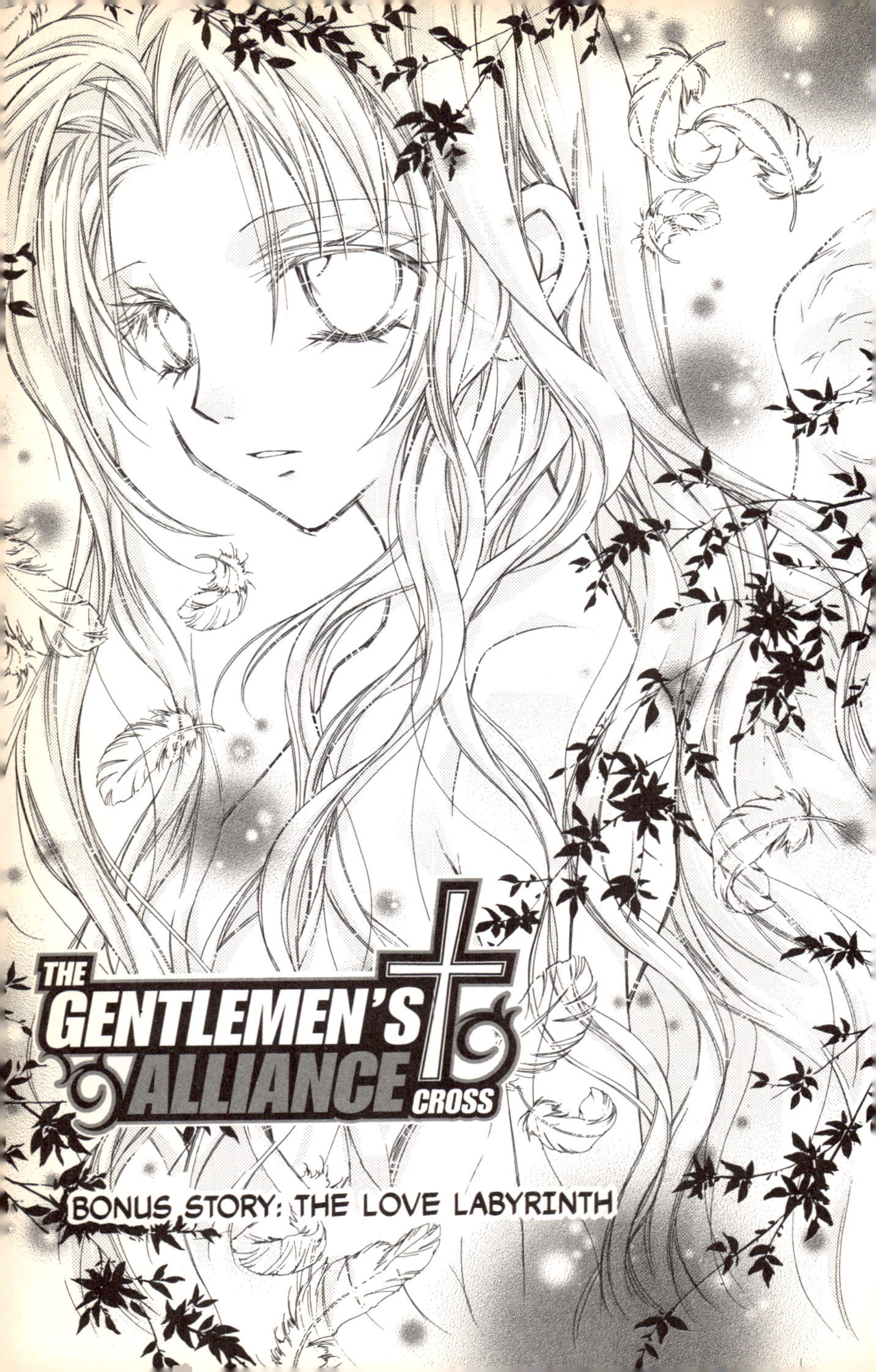
THE GENTLEMEN'S ALLIANCE CROSS
BONUS STORY: THE LOVE LABYRINTH

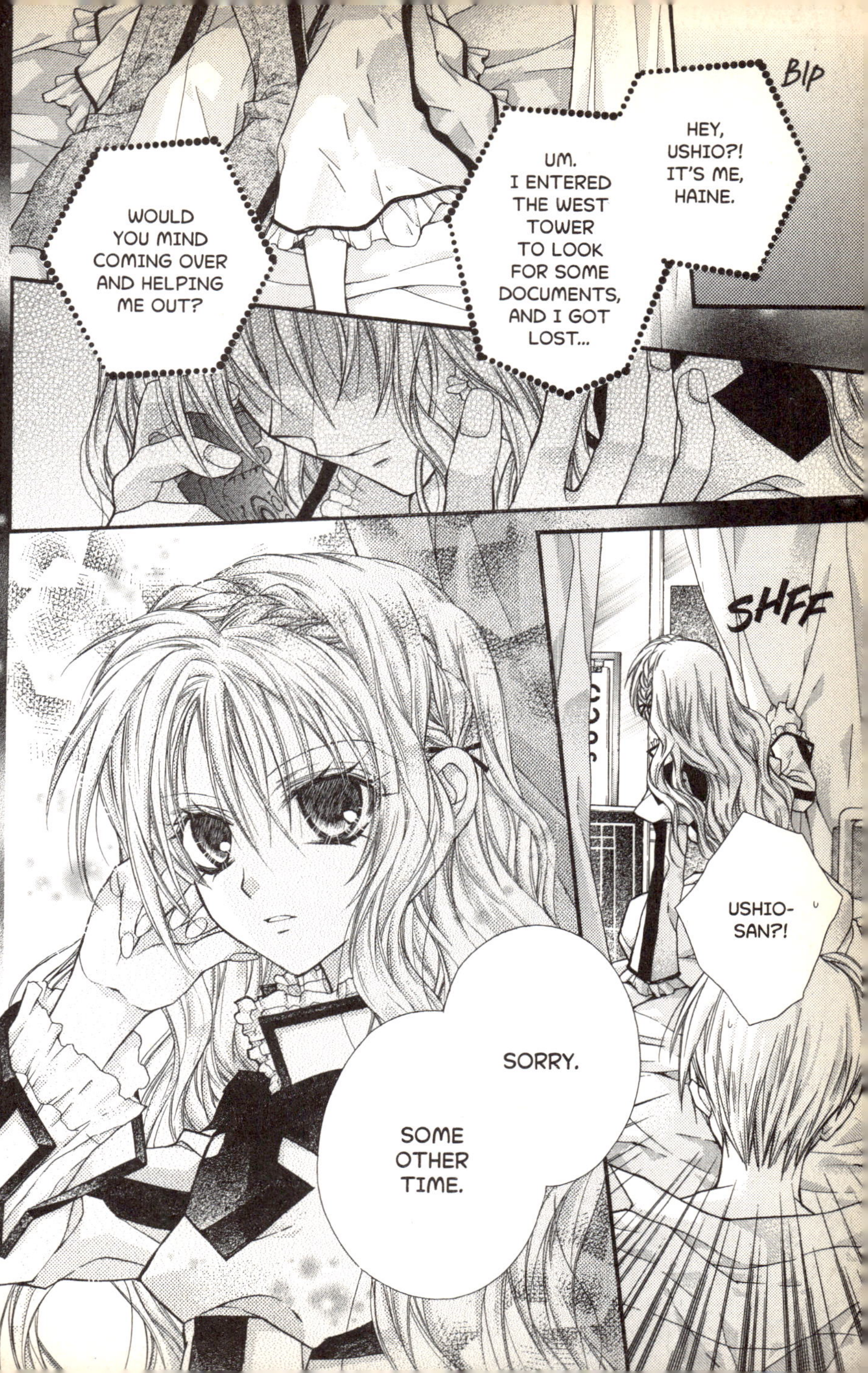
BIP
HEY, USHIO?! IT'S ME, HAINE.
UM. I ENTERED THE WEST TOWER TO LOOK FOR SOME DOCUMENTS, AND I GOT LOST...
WOULD YOU MIND COMING OVER AND HELPING ME OUT?
SHFF
USHIO-SAN?!
SORRY.
SOME OTHER TIME.

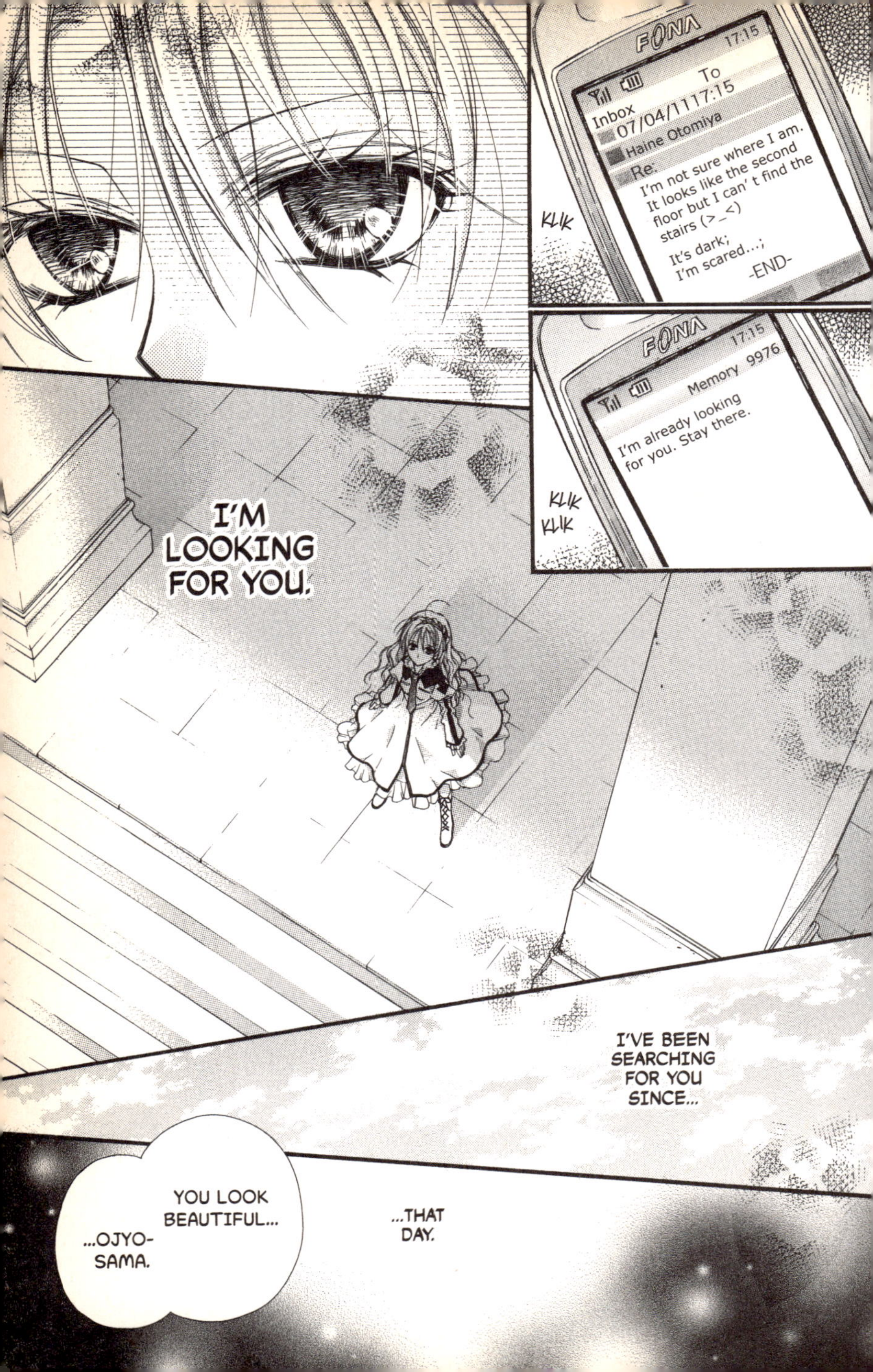
FONA
17:15
To
Inbox
07/04/11 17:15
Haine Otomiya
Re:
I'm not sure where I am. It looks like the second floor but I can' t find the stairs (>_<)
It's dark; I'm scared...;
-END-
KLIK
FONA
17:15
Memory 9976
I'm already looking for you. Stay there.
KLIK KLIK
I'M LOOKING FOR YOU.
I'VE BEEN SEARCHING FOR YOU SINCE...
...THAT DAY.
YOU LOOK BEAUTIFUL...
...OJYO-SAMA.

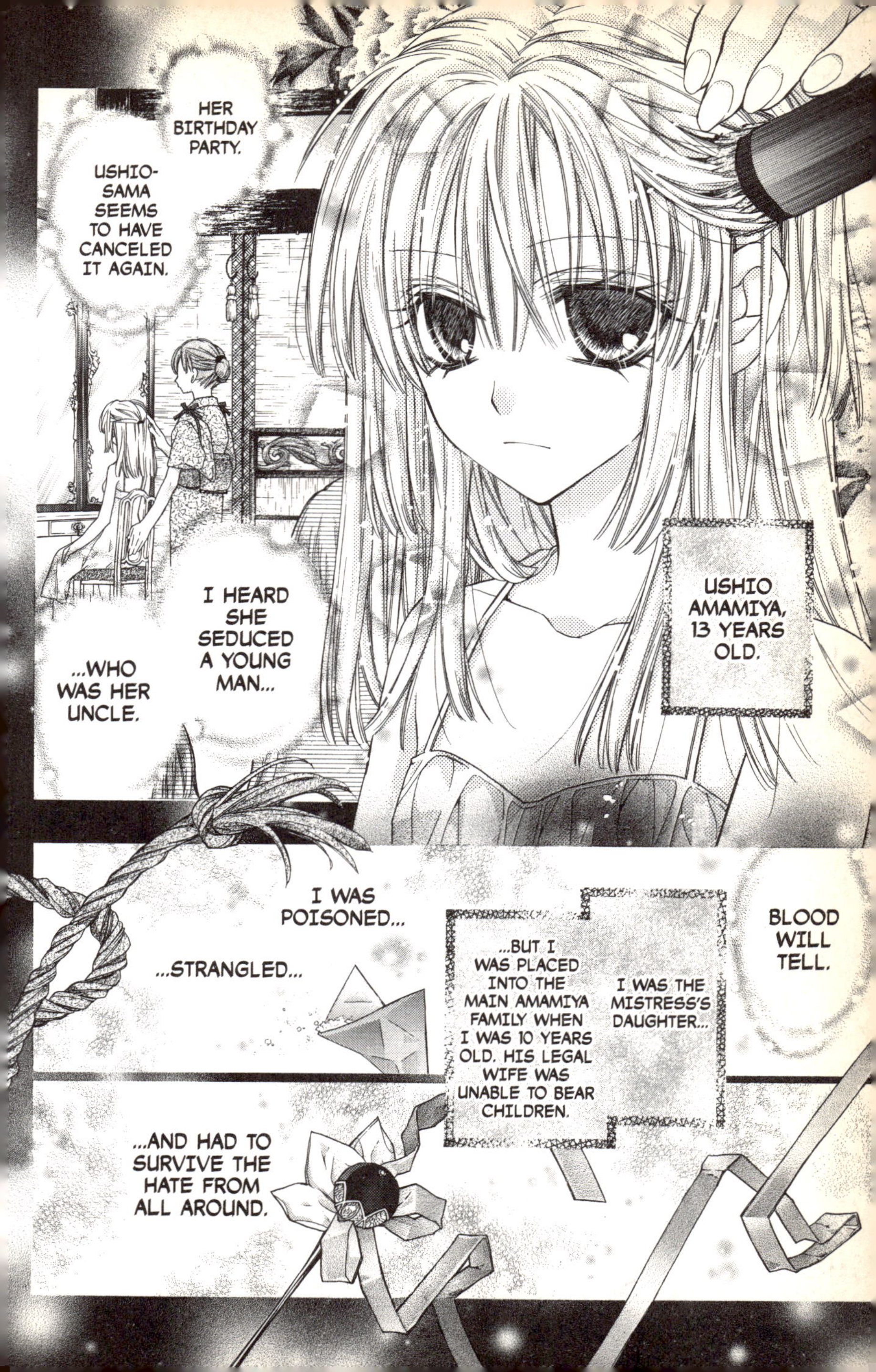
HER BIRTHDAY PARTY.
USHIO-SAMA SEEMS TO HAVE CANCELED IT AGAIN.
USHIO AMAMIYA, 13 YEARS OLD.
I HEARD SHE SEDUCED A YOUNG MAN...
...WHO WAS HER UNCLE.
BLOOD WILL TELL.
I WAS THE MISTRESS'S DAUGHTER...
...BUT I WAS PLACED INTO THE MAIN AMAMIYA FAMILY WHEN I WAS 10 YEARS OLD. HIS LEGAL WIFE WAS UNABLE TO BEAR CHILDREN.
I WAS POISONED...
...STRANGLED...
...AND HAD TO SURVIVE THE HATE FROM ALL AROUND.

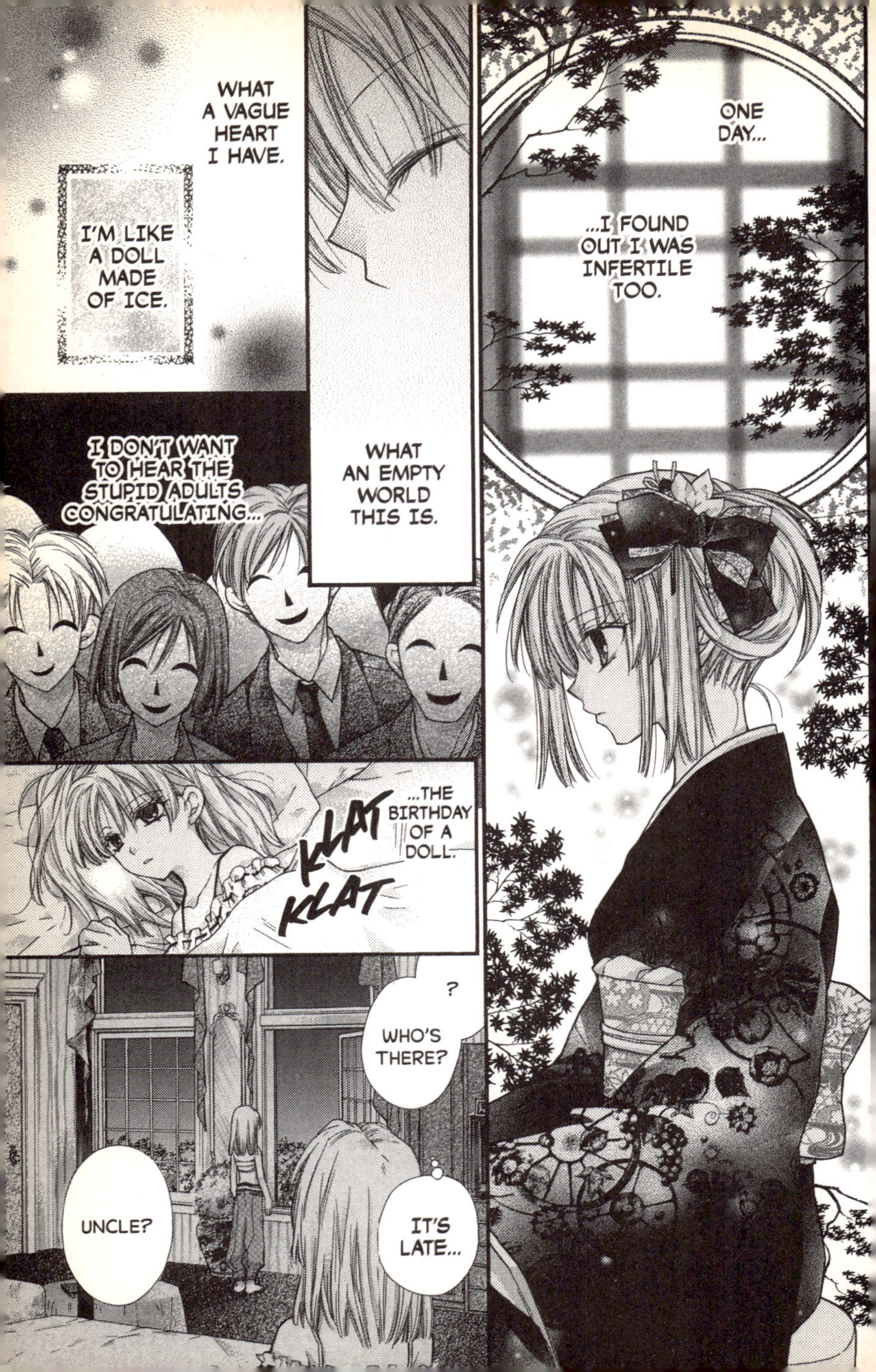
ONE DAY...
...I FOUND OUT I WAS INFERTILE TOO.
WHAT A VAGUE HEART I HAVE.
I'M LIKE A DOLL MADE OF ICE.
WHAT AN EMPTY WORLD THIS IS.
I DON'T WANT TO HEAR THE STUPID ADULTS CONGRATULATING...
...THE BIRTHDAY OF A DOLL.
KLAT
KLAT
?
WHO'S THERE?
IT'S LATE...
UNCLE?

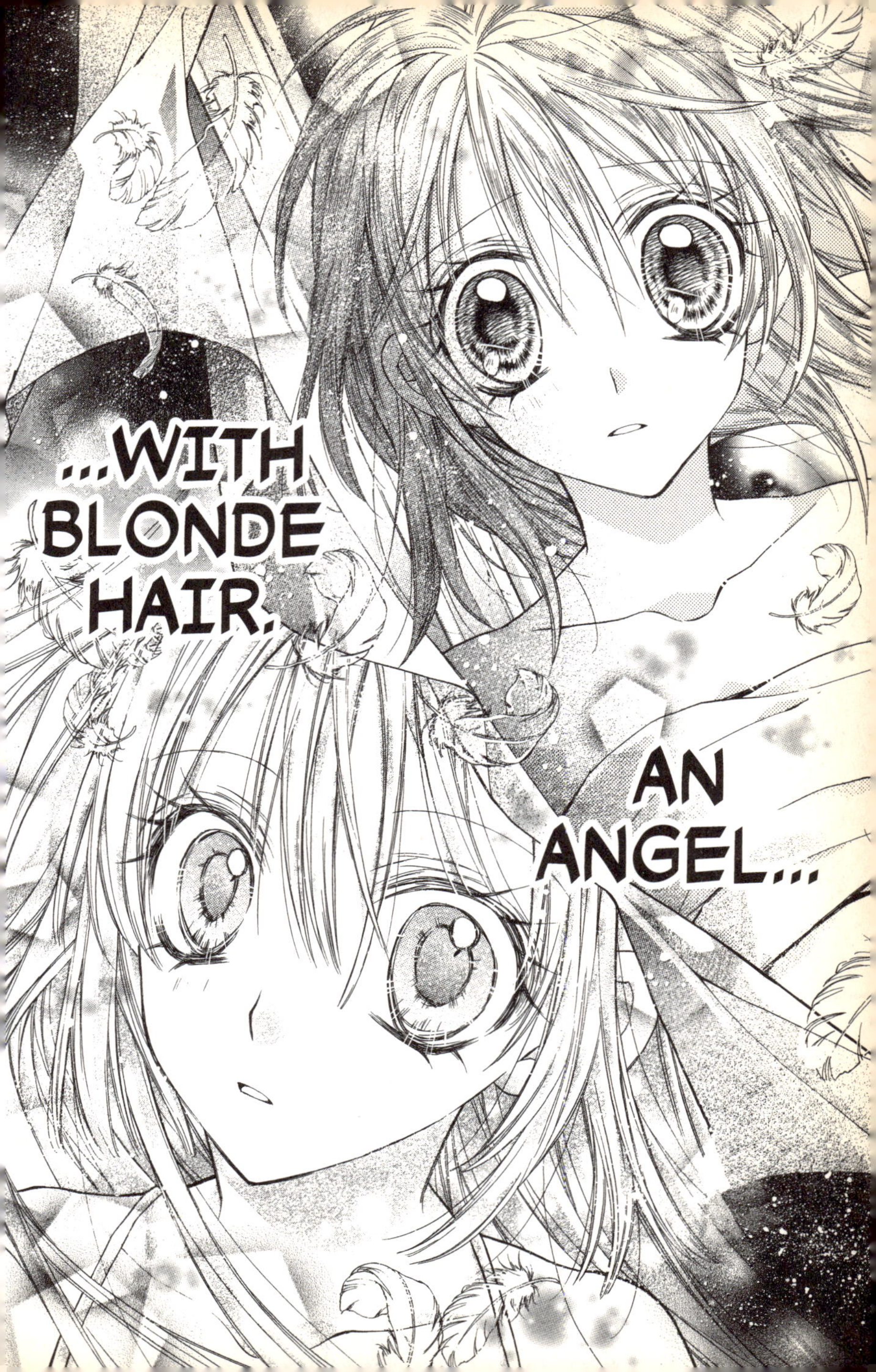
AN ANGEL...
...WITH BLONDE HAIR.

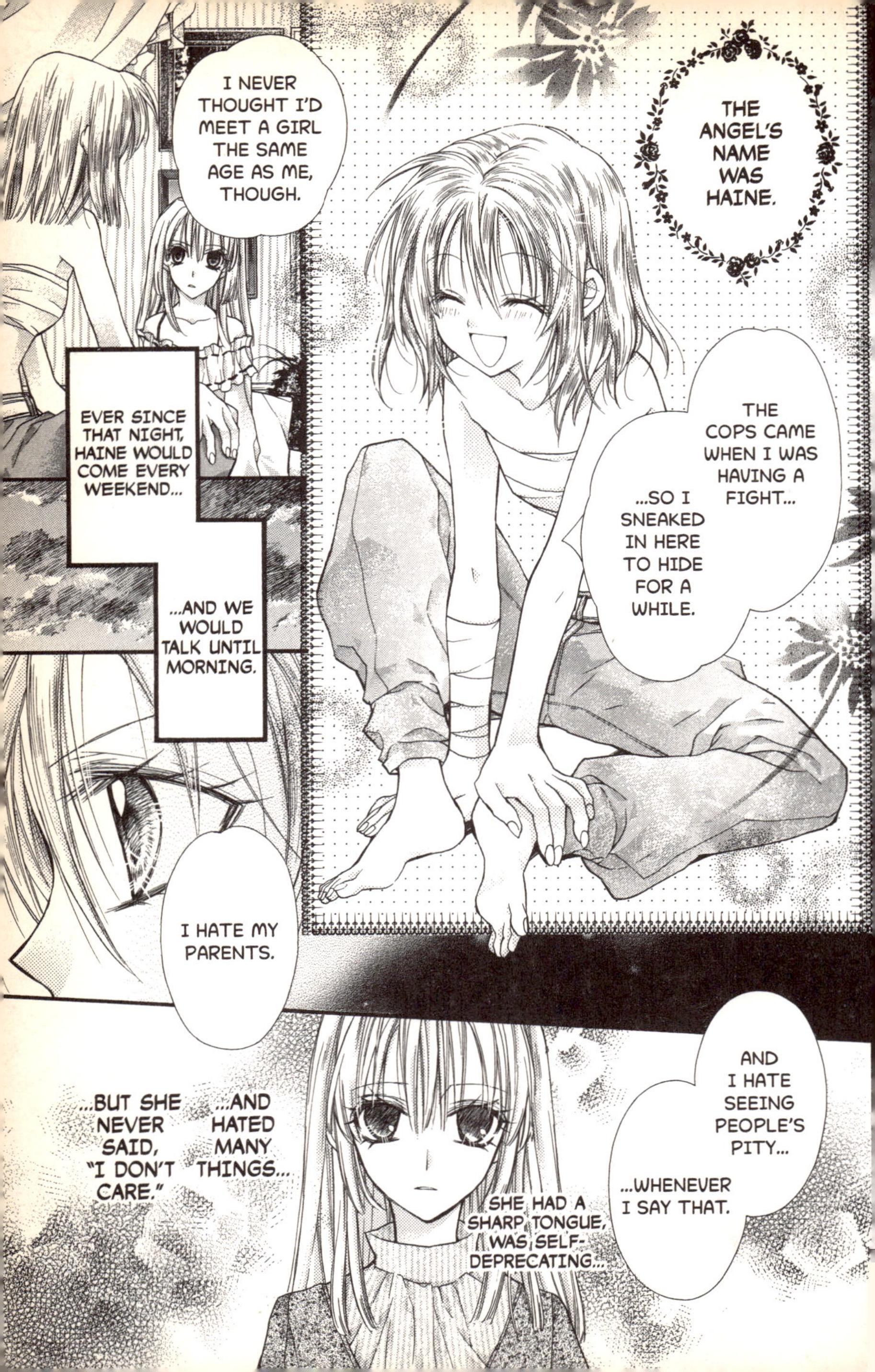
THE ANGEL'S NAME WAS HAINE.
THE COPS CAME WHEN I WAS HAVING A FIGHT...
...SO I SNEAKED IN HERE TO HIDE FOR A WHILE.
I NEVER THOUGHT I'D MEET A GIRL THE SAME AGE AS ME, THOUGH.
EVER SINCE THAT NIGHT, HAINE WOULD COME EVERY WEEKEND...
...AND WE WOULD TALK UNTIL MORNING.
I HATE MY PARENTS.
AND I HATE SEEING PEOPLE'S PITY...
...WHENEVER I SAY THAT.
SHE HAD A SHARP TONGUE, WAS SELF-DEPRECATING...
...AND HATED MANY THINGS...
...BUT SHE NEVER SAID, "I DON'T CARE."

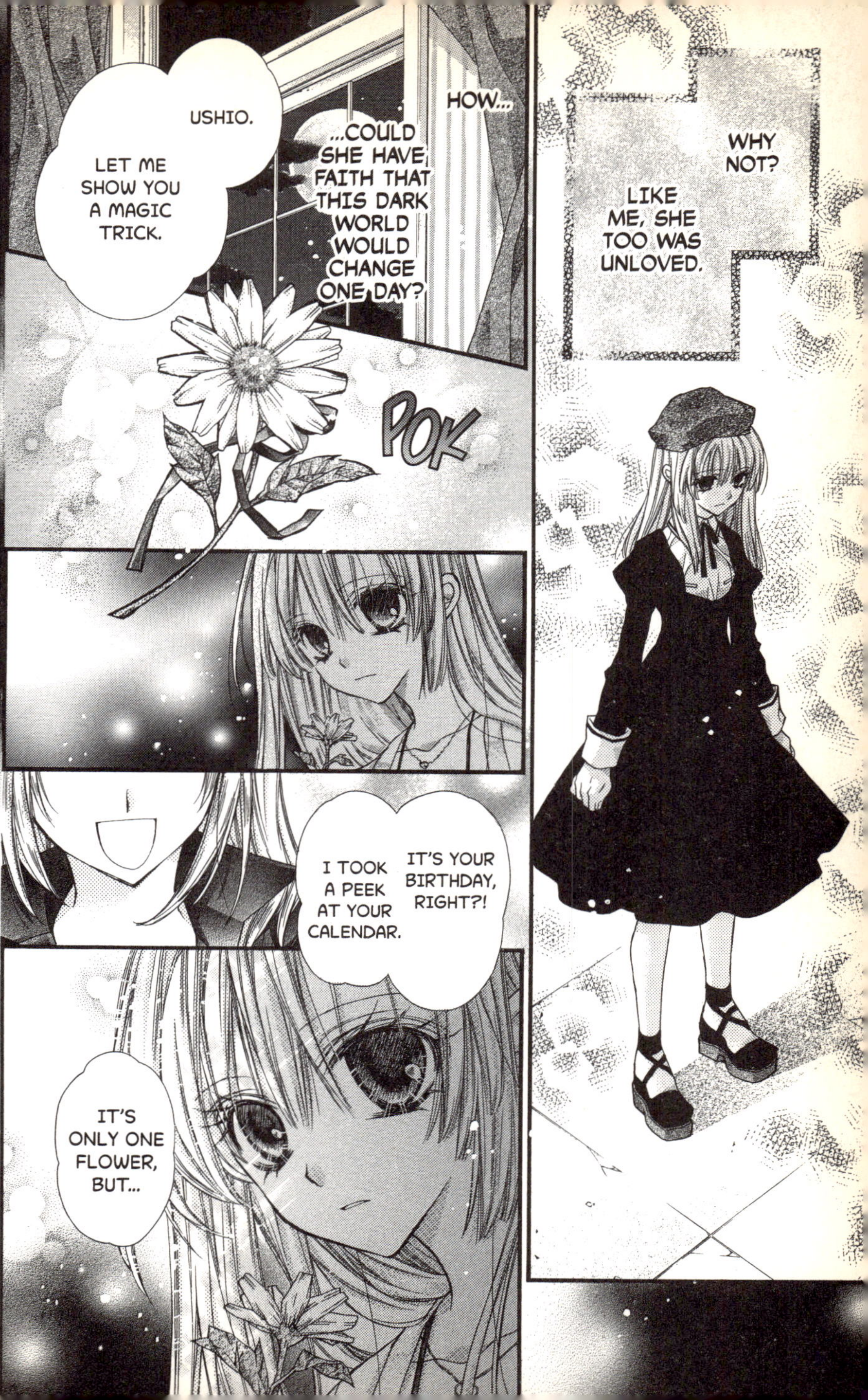
WHY NOT?
LIKE ME, SHE TOO WAS UNLOVED.
HOW...
...COULD SHE HAVE FAITH THAT THIS DARK WORLD WOULD CHANGE ONE DAY?
USHIO.
LET ME SHOW YOU A MAGIC TRICK.
POK
IT'S YOUR BIRTHDAY, RIGHT?!
I TOOK A PEEK AT YOUR CALENDAR.
IT'S ONLY ONE FLOWER, BUT...

IT'S A PRESENT FOR YOU.
HAPPY BIRTHDAY!
AH...
I KNOW WHY NOW.
THIS GIRL IS ABLE CREATE THINGS...
...OUT OF NOTHING.

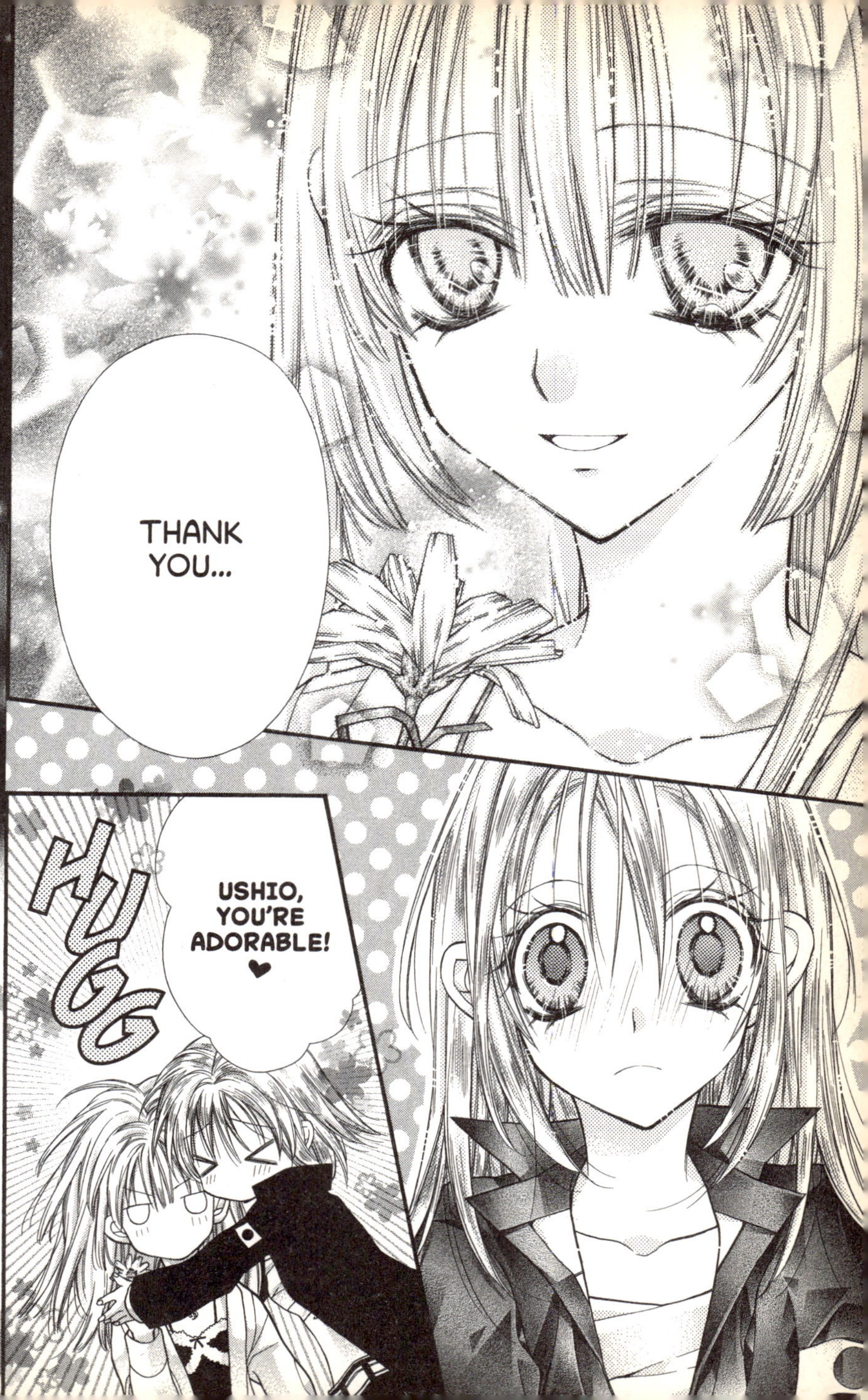
THANK YOU...
USHIO, YOU'RE ADORABLE! ♥
HUGG

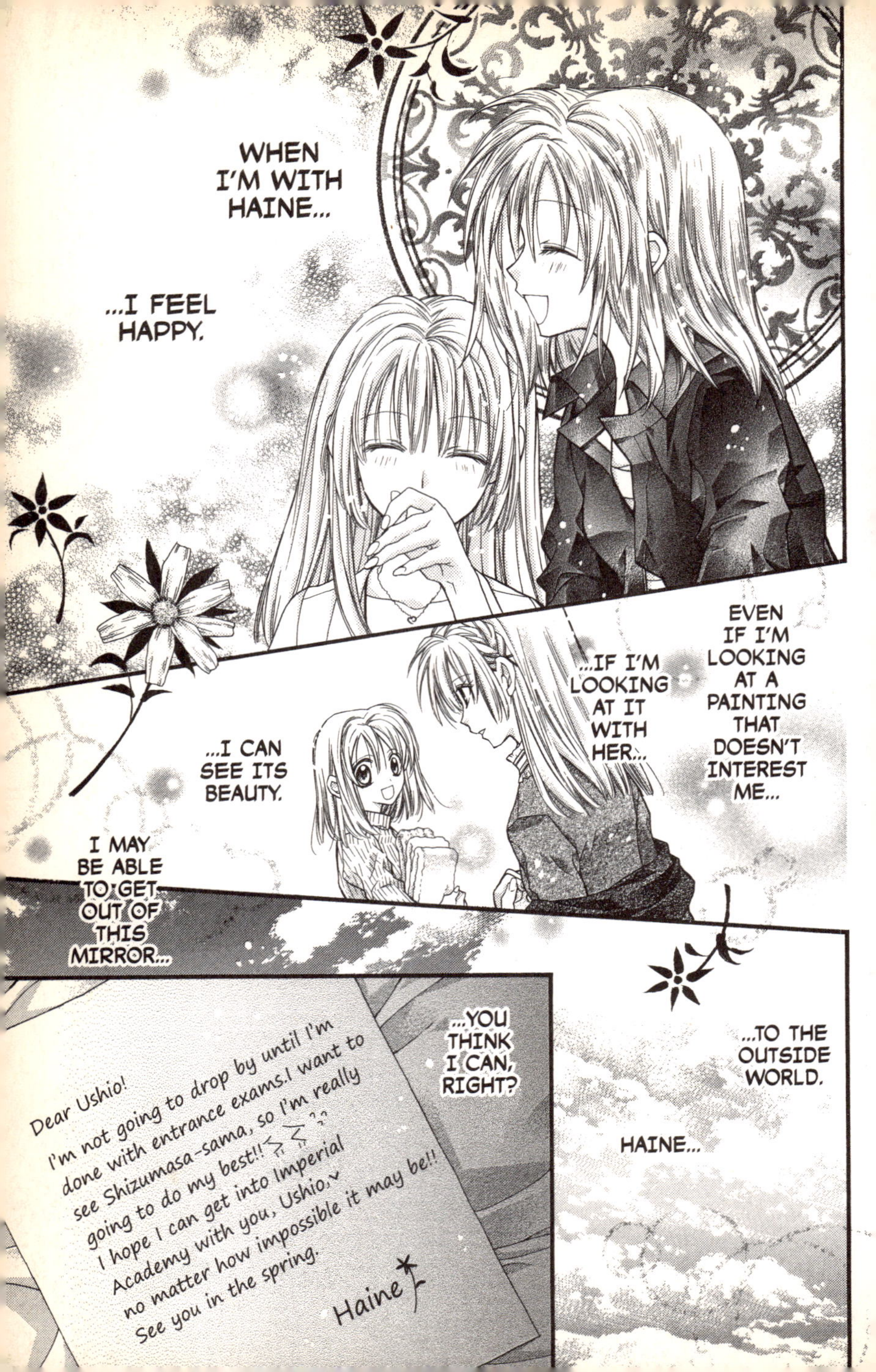
WHEN I'M WITH HAINE...
...I FEEL HAPPY.
EVEN IF I'M LOOKING AT A PAINTING THAT DOESN'T INTEREST ME...
...IF I'M LOOKING AT IT WITH HER...
...I CAN SEE ITS BEAUTY.
I MAY BE ABLE TO GET OUT OF THIS MIRROR...
...TO THE OUTSIDE WORLD.
HAINE...
...YOU THINK I CAN, RIGHT?
Dear Ushio!
I'm not going to drop by until I'm done with entrance exams. I want to see Shizumasa-sama, so I'm really going to do my best!!
I hope I can get into Imperial Academy with you, Ushio,
no matter how impossible it may be!!
See you in the spring.
Haine

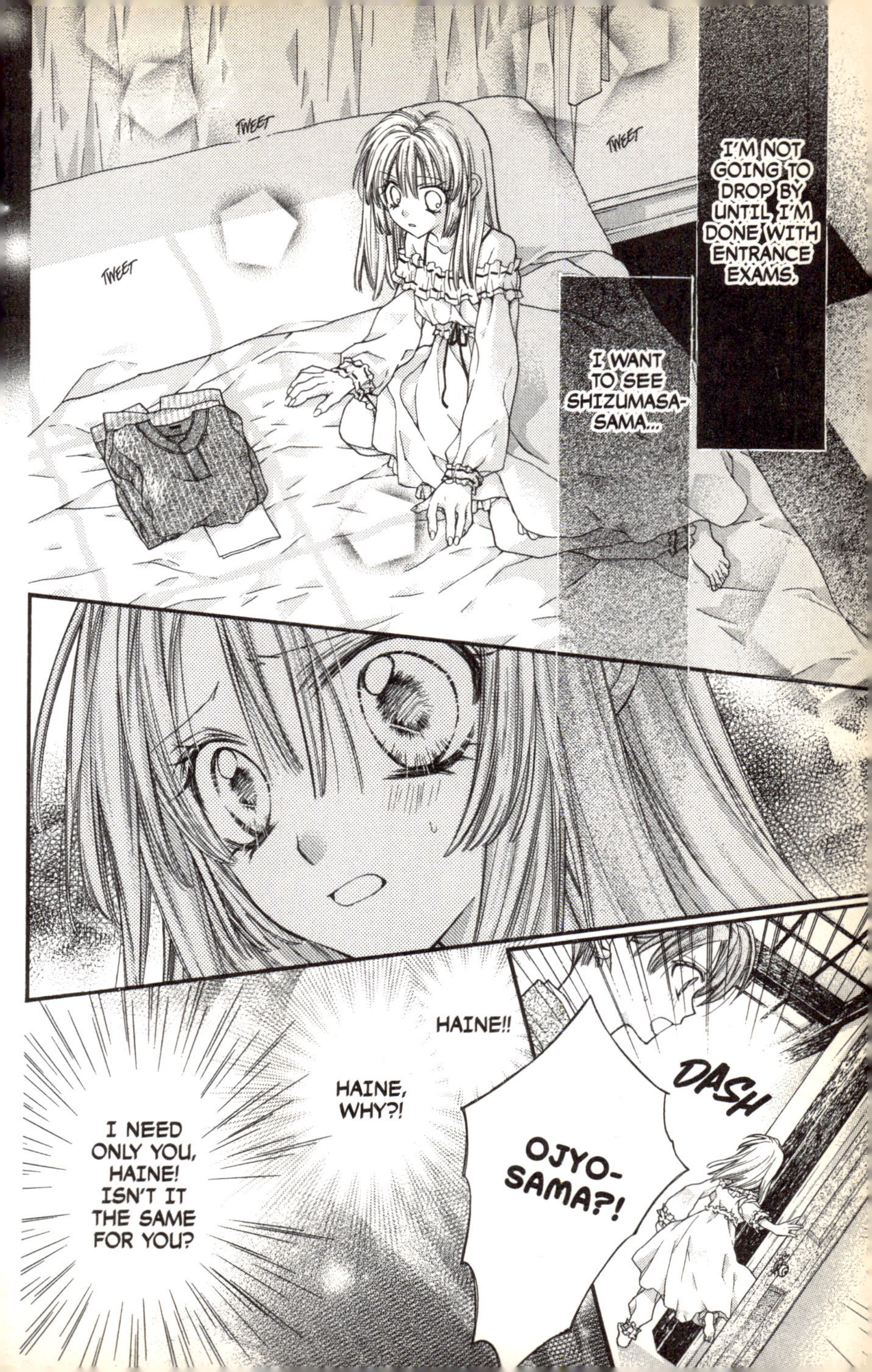
I'M NOT GOING TO DROP BY UNTIL I'M DONE WITH ENTRANCE EXAMS.
I WANT TO SEE SHIZUMASA-SAMA...
TWEET
TWEET
TWEET
DASH
OJYO-SAMA?!
HAINE!!
HAINE, WHY?!
I NEED ONLY YOU, HAINE! ISN'T IT THE SAME FOR YOU?

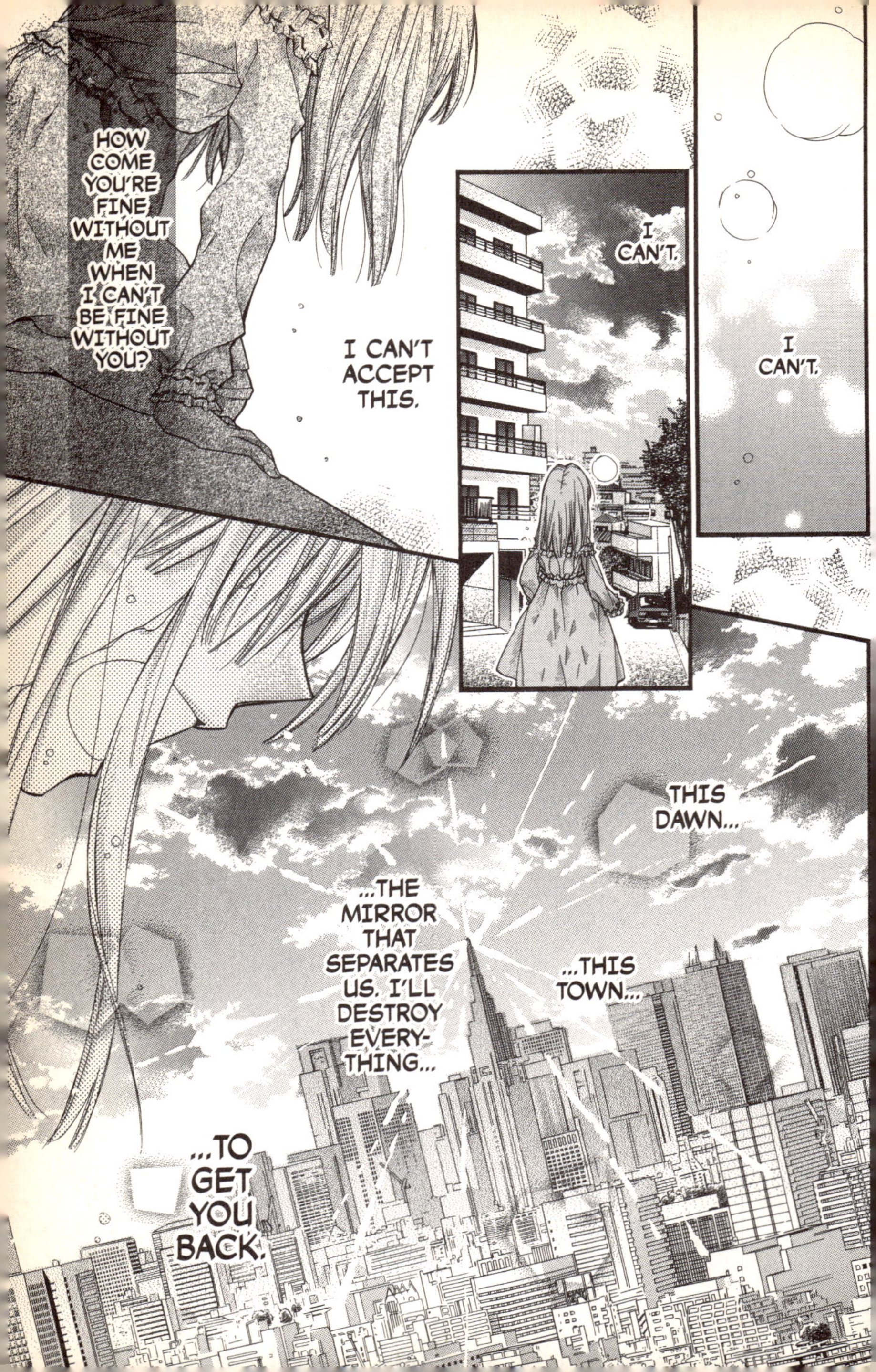
I CAN'T.
I CAN'T.
I CAN'T ACCEPT THIS.
HOW COME YOU'RE FINE WITHOUT ME WHEN I CAN'T BE FINE WITHOUT YOU?
THIS DAWN...
...THIS TOWN...
...THE MIRROR THAT SEPARATES US. I'LL DESTROY EVERY-THING...
...TO GET YOU BACK.

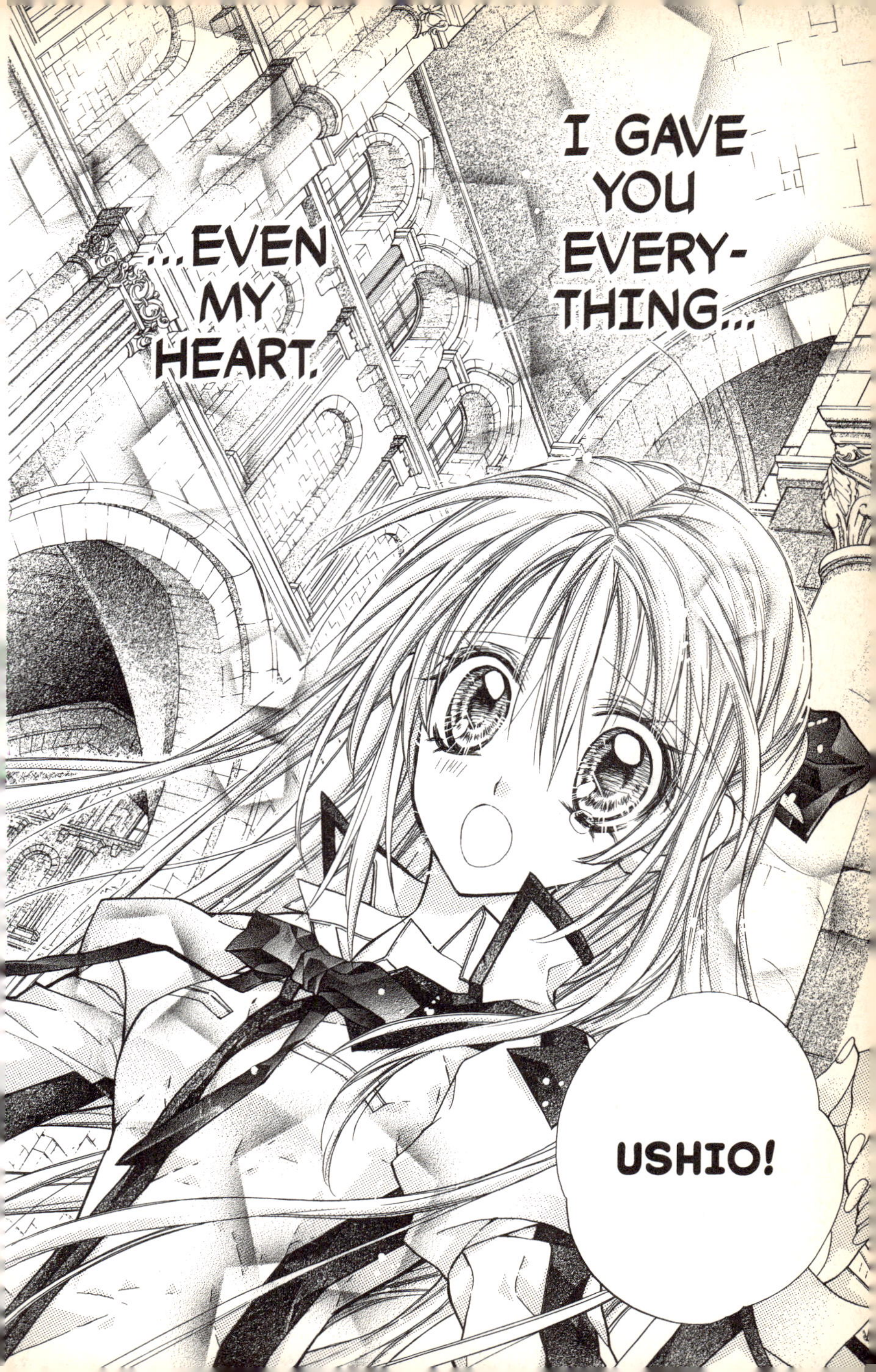
I GAVE YOU EVERY-THING...
...EVEN MY HEART.
USHIO!

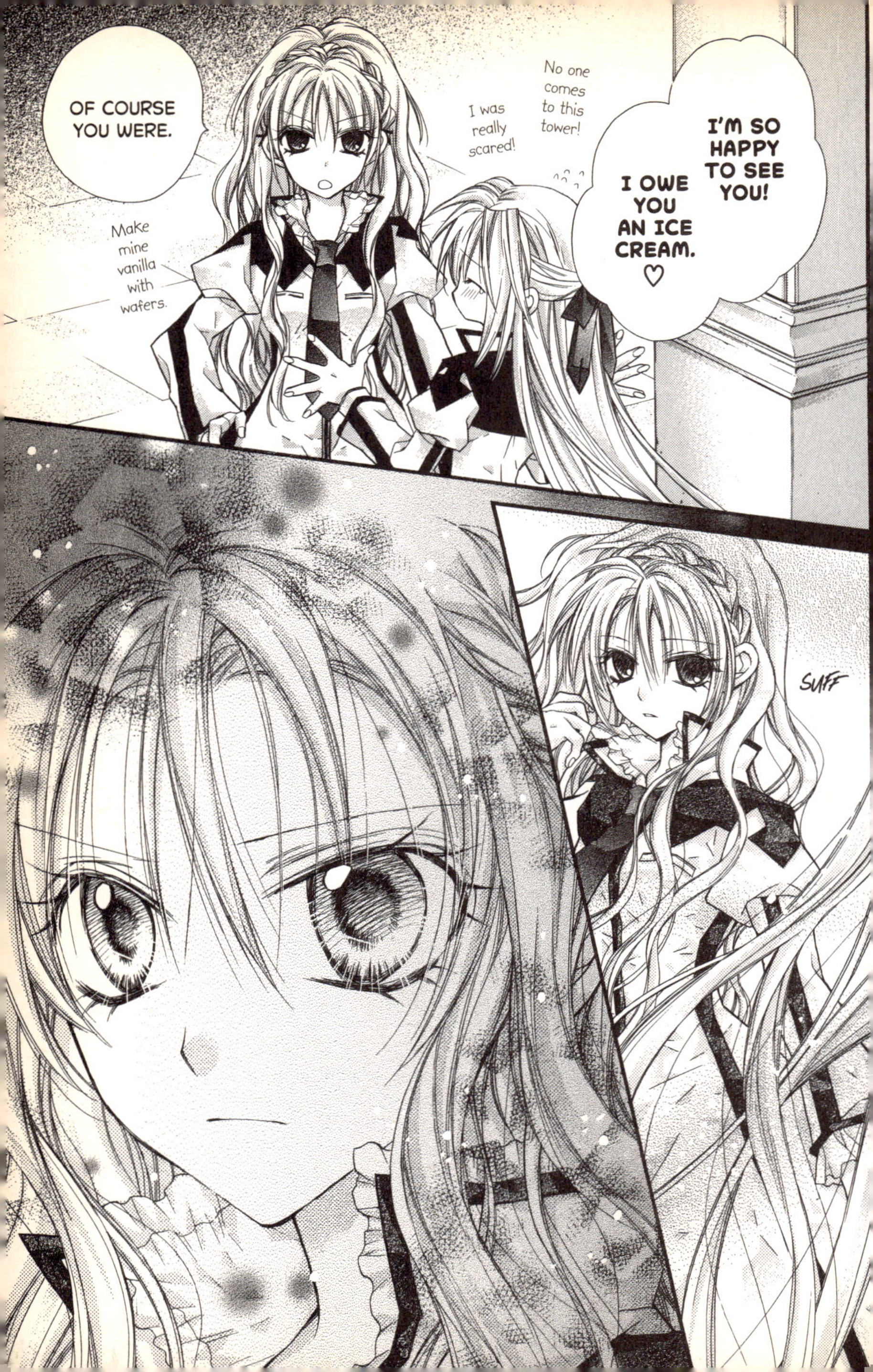
I'M SO HAPPY TO SEE YOU!
I OWE YOU AN ICE CREAM. ♡
No one comes to this tower!
I was really scared!
OF COURSE YOU WERE.
Make mine vanilla with wafers.
SUFF

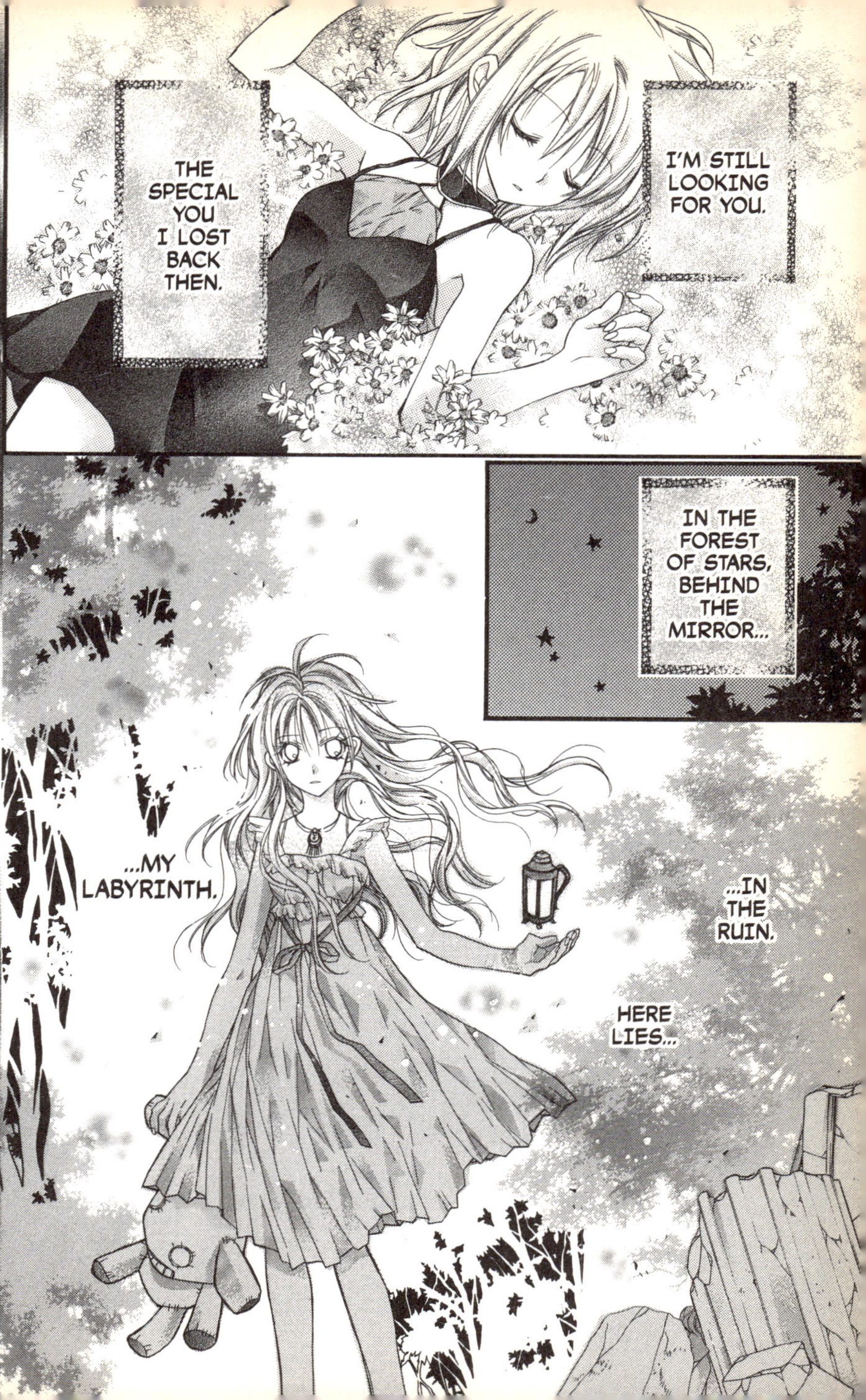
I'M STILL LOOKING FOR YOU.
THE SPECIAL YOU I LOST BACK THEN.
IN THE FOREST OF STARS, BEHIND THE MIRROR...
...IN THE RUIN.
HERE LIES...
...MY LABYRINTH.

Kissing scenes are hard to draw. I tend to be hyped-up when I'm doing the *name*, but I become depressed when I start the rough draft...

Rough Draft Collection

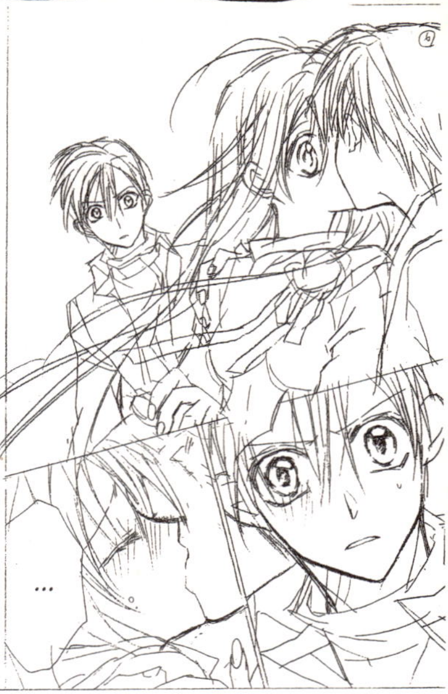
...

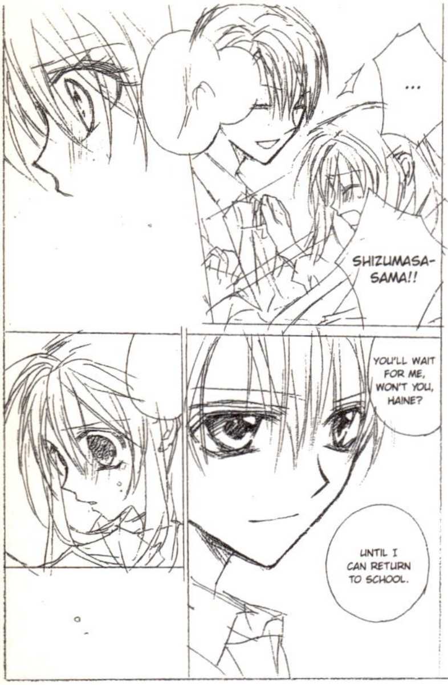
...
SHIZUMASA-SAMA!!
YOU'LL WAIT FOR ME, WON'T YOU, HAINE?
UNTIL I CAN RETURN TO SCHOOL.

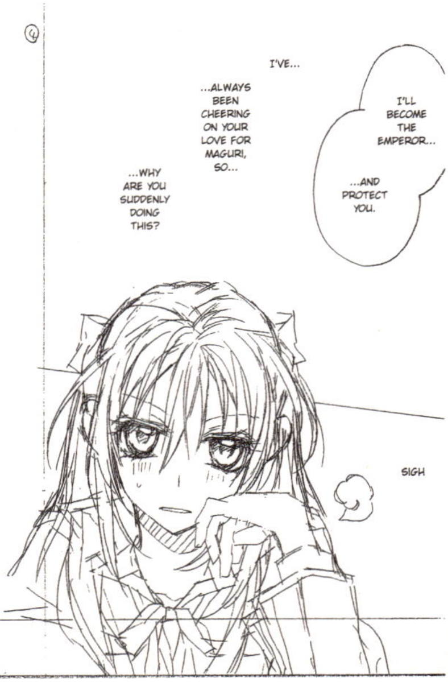
I'LL BECOME THE EMPEROR...
...AND PROTECT YOU.
I'VE...
...ALWAYS BEEN CHEERING ON YOUR LOVE FOR MAGURI, SO...
...WHY ARE YOU SUDDENLY DOING THIS?
SIGH

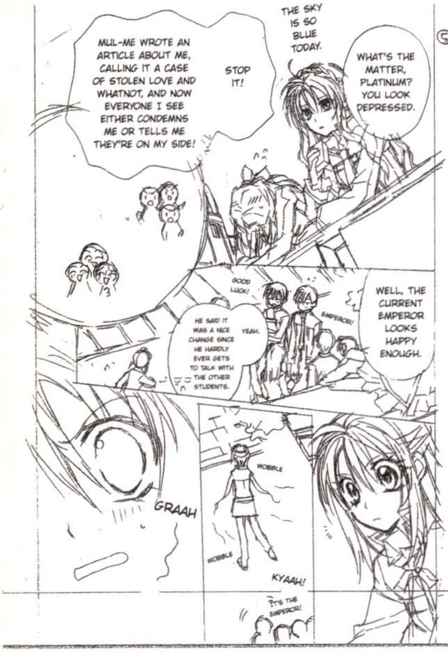
THE SKY IS SO BLUE TODAY.
WHAT'S THE MATTER, PLATINUM? YOU LOOK DEPRESSED.
STOP IT!
MUL-ME WROTE AN ARTICLE ABOUT ME, CALLING IT A CASE OF STOLEN LOVE AND WHATNOT, AND NOW EVERYONE I SEE EITHER CONDEMNS ME OR TELLS ME THEY'RE ON MY SIDE!
WELL, THE CURRENT EMPEROR LOOKS HAPPY ENOUGH.
EMPEROR!
GOOD LUCK!
YEAH.
HE SAID IT WAS A NICE CHANGE SINCE HE HARDLY EVER GETS TO TALK WITH THE OTHER STUDENTS.
WOBBLE
WOBBLE
KYAAH!
IT'S THE EMPEROR!
GRAAH

I love drawing an expression of shock like this.

TOGETHER WITH OKORIMAKURI-KUN! 1

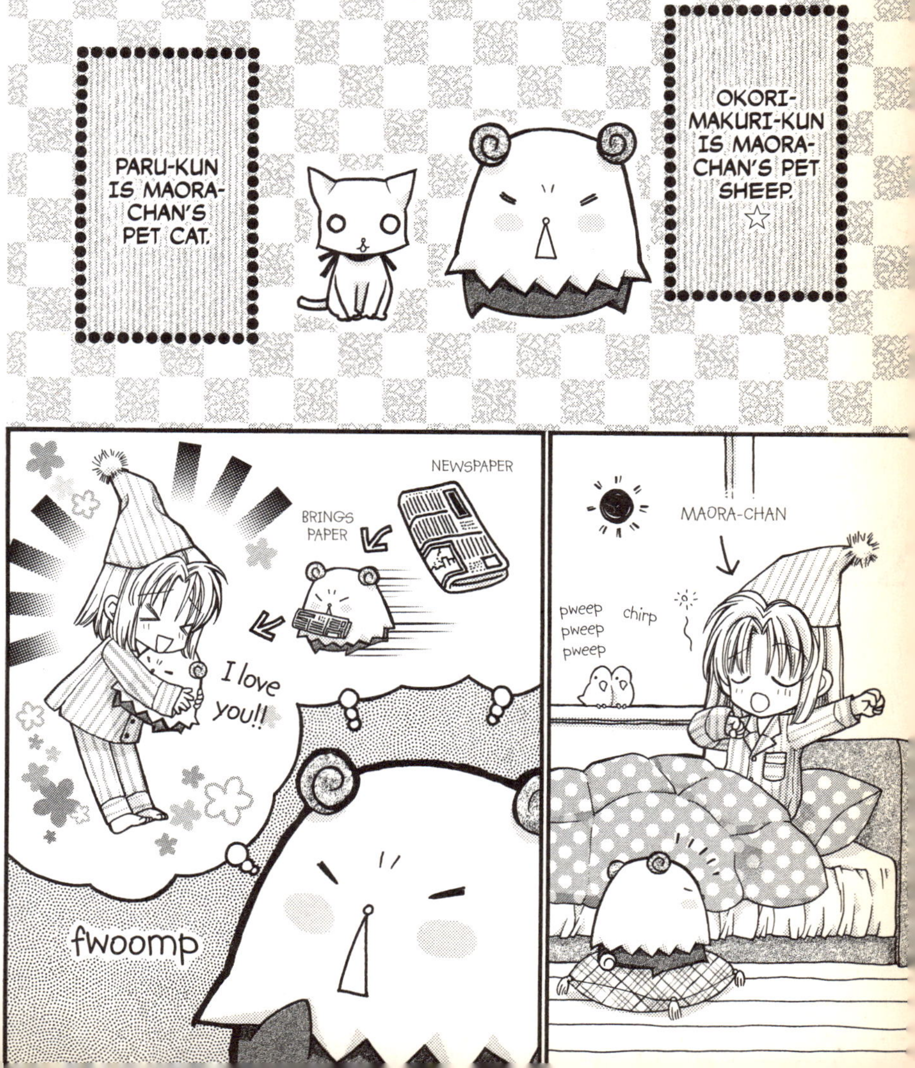
OKORI-MAKURI-KUN IS MAORA-CHAN'S PET SHEEP. ☆
PARU-KUN IS MAORA-CHAN'S PET CAT.
MAORA-CHAN
chirp
pweep pweep pweep
NEWSPAPER
BRINGS PAPER
I love you!!
fwoomp

I've never seen this before.
?
ORANGE
RWL
VUMP
KYAH! PARU-KUN, WHAT A GOOD BOY.
Thank you.
SHOCK
EH. SLIPPERS ...?
WHERE ARE MY SLIPPERS ?
TMP TMP TMP TMP
VUMP
Oh, this is...
RWL
Kyah!
You're so great, Paru-Kun!
SHOCK

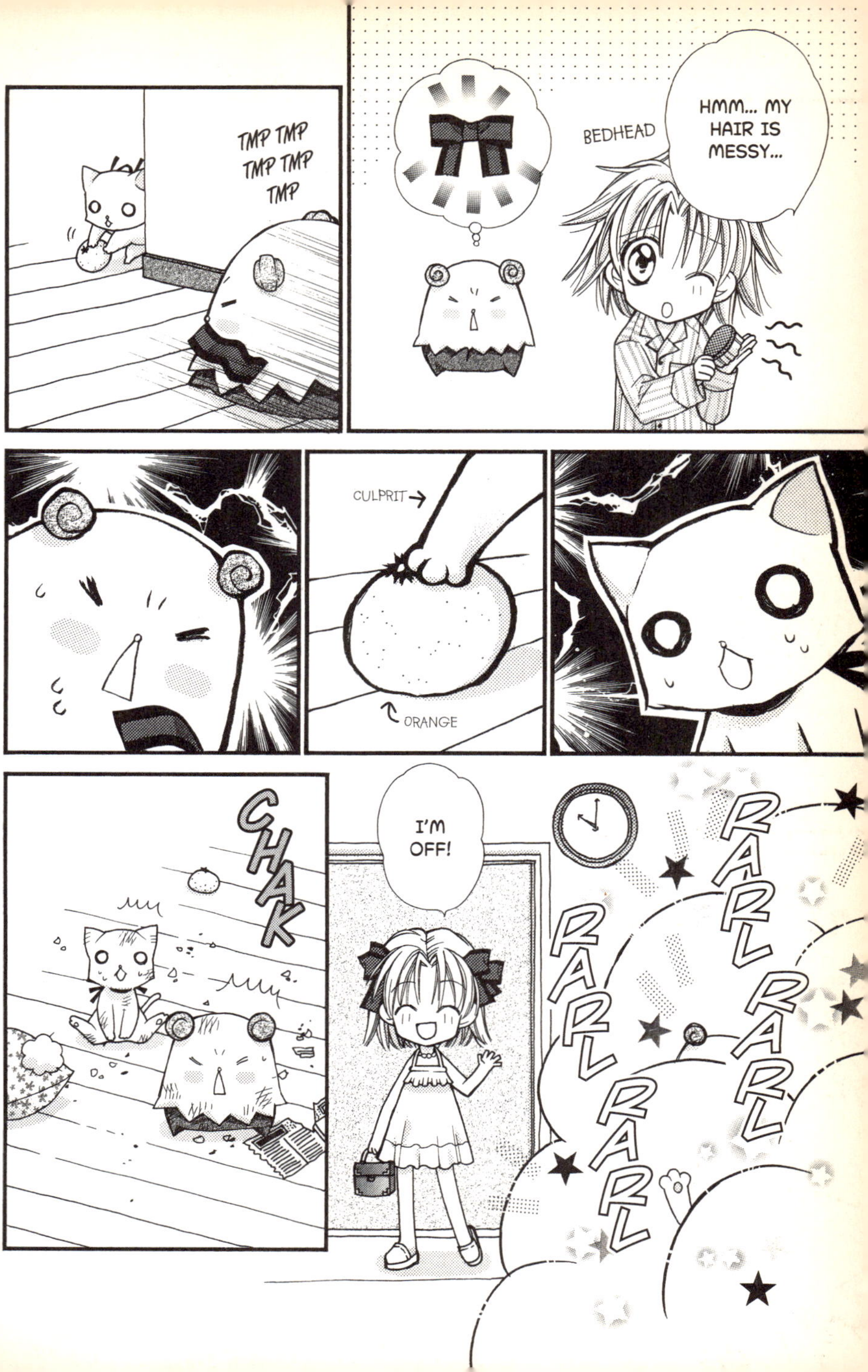
HMM... MY HAIR IS MESSY...
BEDHEAD
TMP TMP TMP TMP TMP
CULPRIT
ORANGE
RARL RARL RARL
RARL RARL
I'M OFF!
CHAK

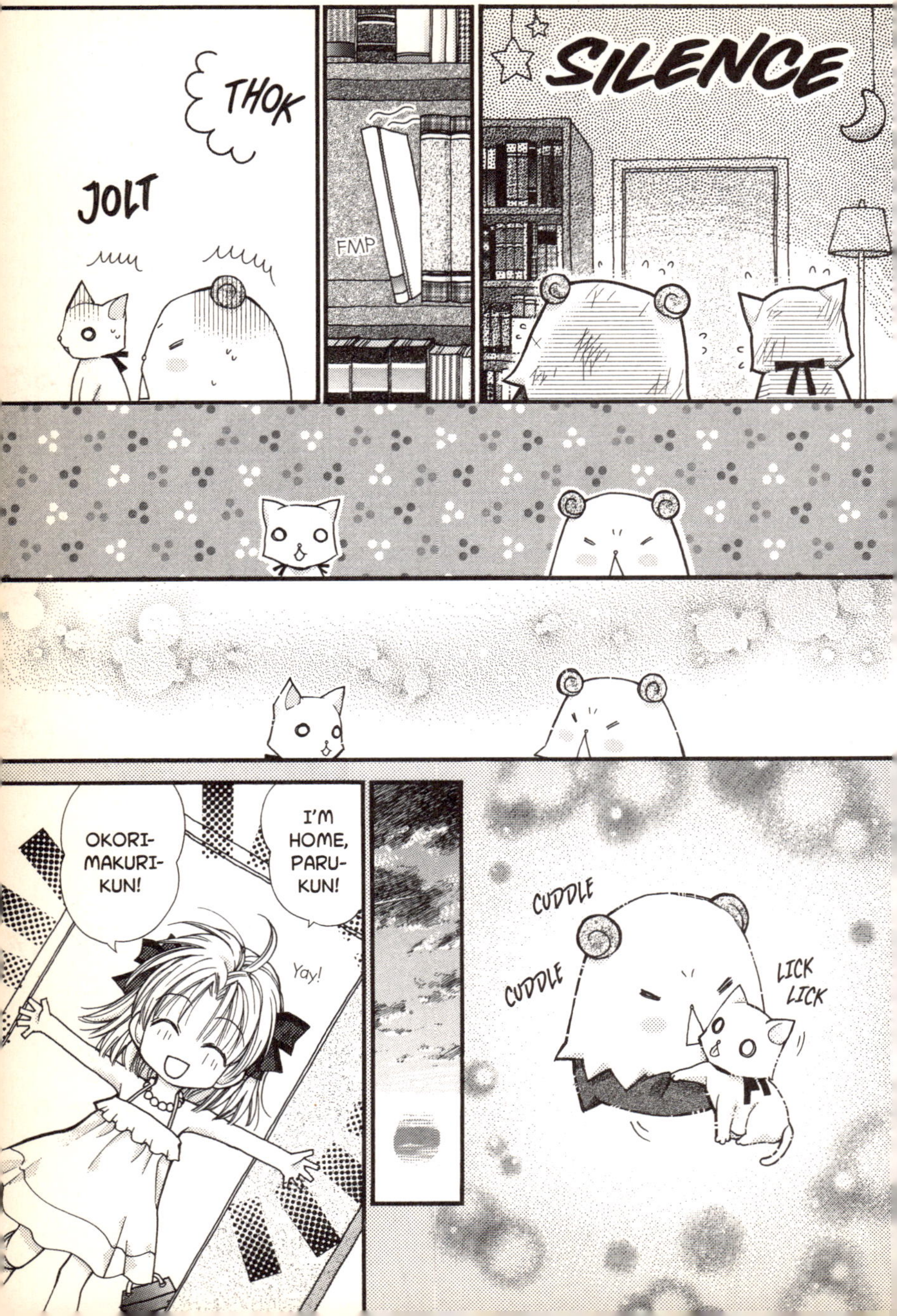
SILENCE
FMP
THOK
JOLT
CUDDLE
LICK LICK
CUDDLE
I'M HOME, PARU-KUN!
OKORI-MAKURI-KUN!
Yay!

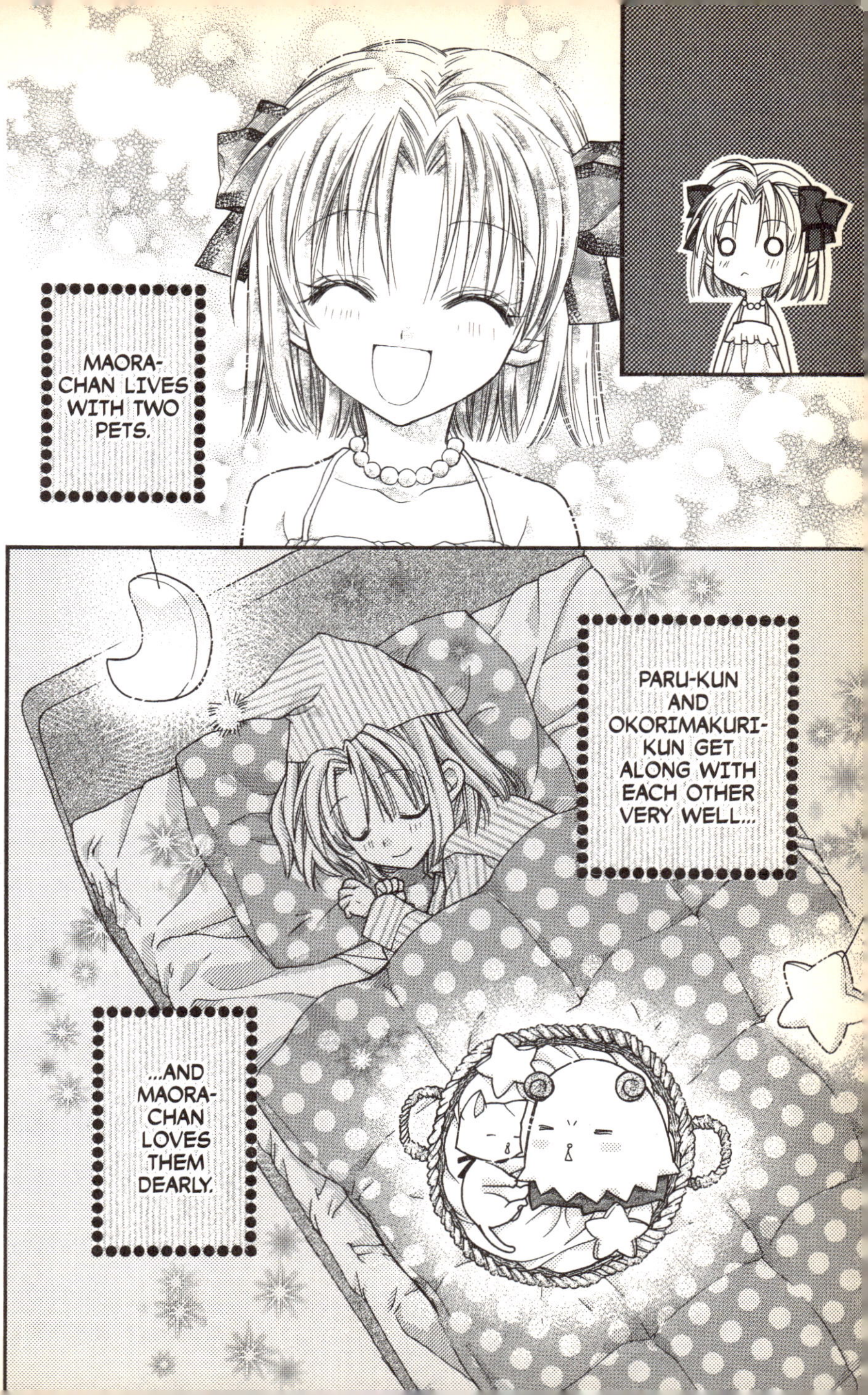
MAORA-CHAN LIVES WITH TWO PETS.
PARU-KUN AND OKORIMAKURI-KUN GET ALONG WITH EACH OTHER VERY WELL...
...AND MAORA-CHAN LOVES THEM DEARLY.

Rough Draft Collection

Remember this page?
I really like it.

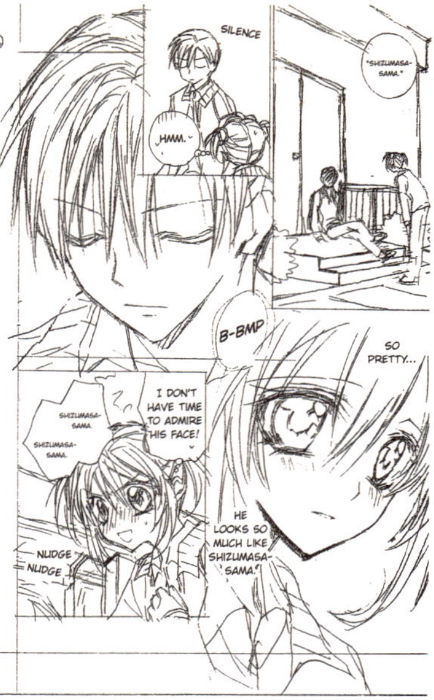
"SHIZUMASA-SAMA."
SILENCE
HMM.
B-BMP
SO PRETTY...
HE LOOKS SO MUCH LIKE SHIZUMASA-SAMA."
I DON'T HAVE TIME TO ADMIRE HIS FACE!
SHIZUMASA-SAMA.
SHIZUMASA-SAMA.
NUDGE
NUDGE

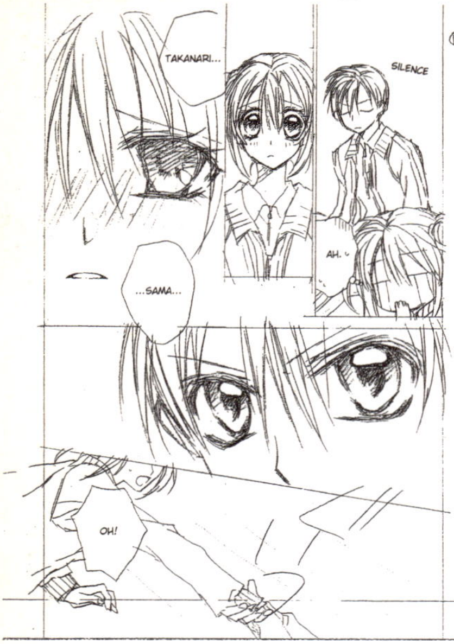
SILENCE
AH.
TAKANARI...
...SAMA...
OH!

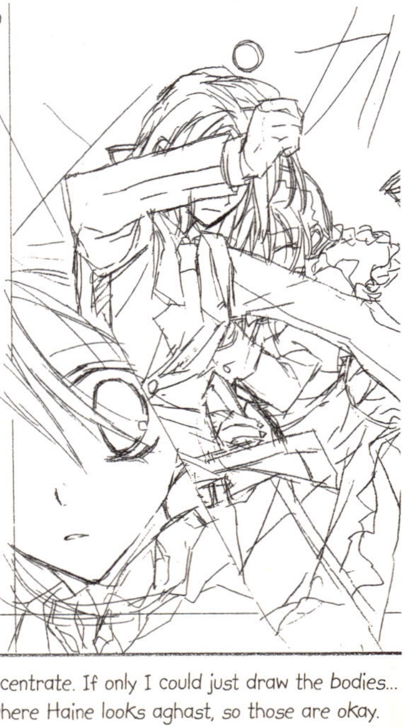

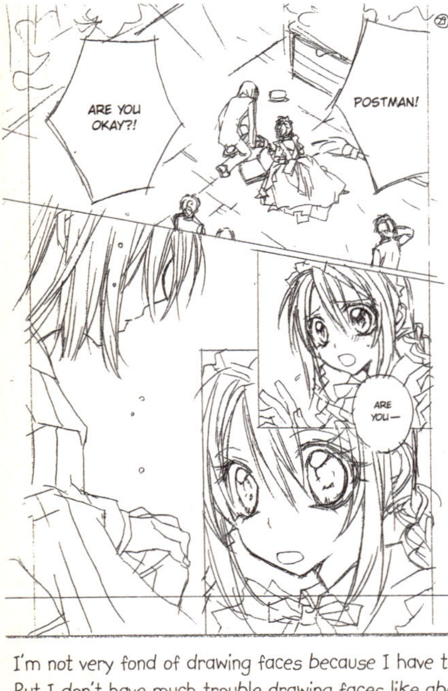
POSTMAN!
ARE YOU OKAY?!
ARE YOU—

I'm not very fond of drawing faces because I have to concentrate. If only I could just draw the bodies... But I don't have much trouble drawing faces like above where Haine looks aghast, so those are okay.

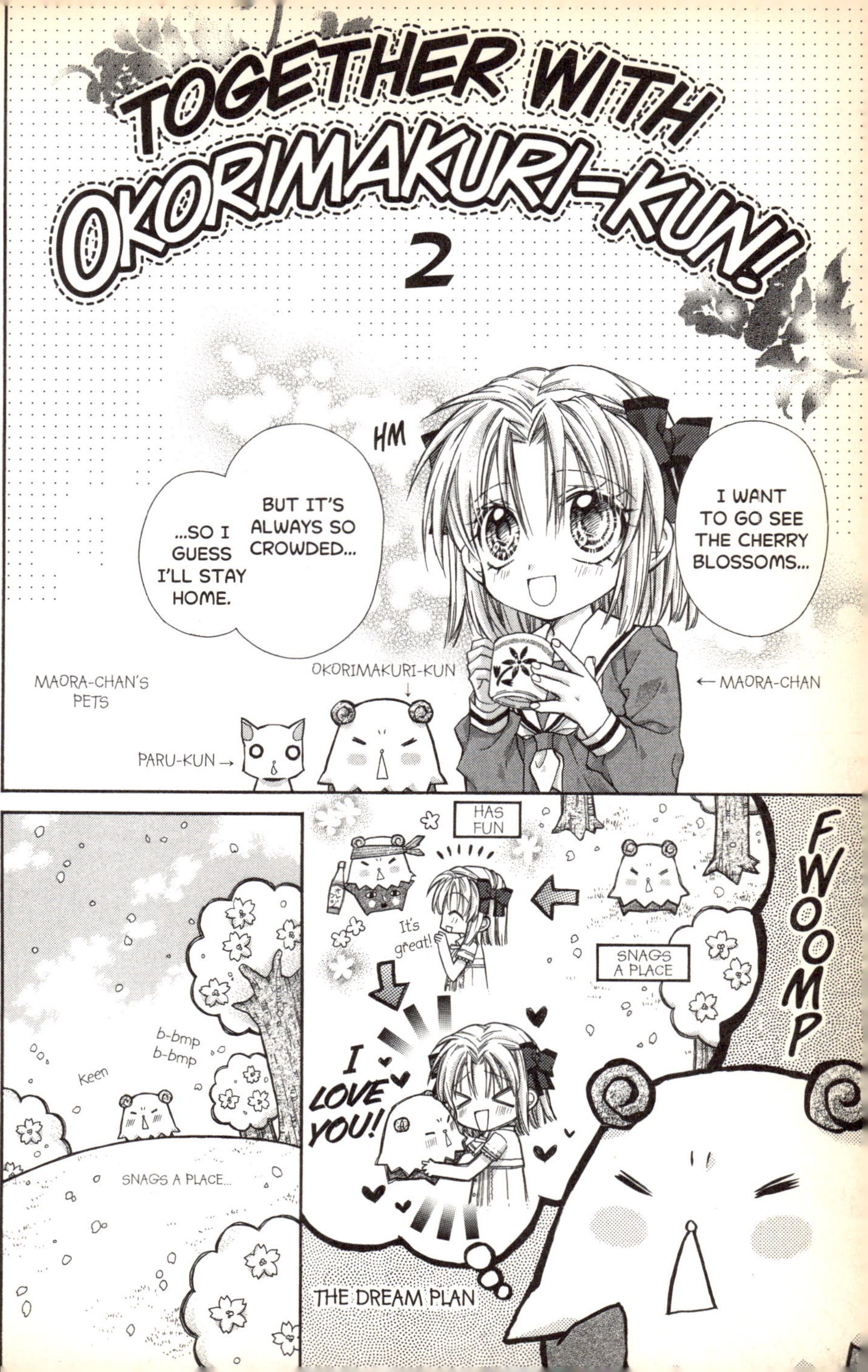
TOGETHER WITH OKORIMAKURI-KUN! 2
I WANT TO GO SEE THE CHERRY BLOSSOMS...
HM
BUT IT'S ALWAYS SO CROWDED...
...SO I GUESS I'LL STAY HOME.
← MAORA-CHAN
OKORIMAKURI-KUN ↓
MAORA-CHAN'S PETS
PARU-KUN →
FWOOMP
SNAGS A PLACE
HAS FUN
It's great!
I LOVE YOU!
THE DREAM PLAN
b-bmp b-bmp
Keen
SNAGS A PLACE...

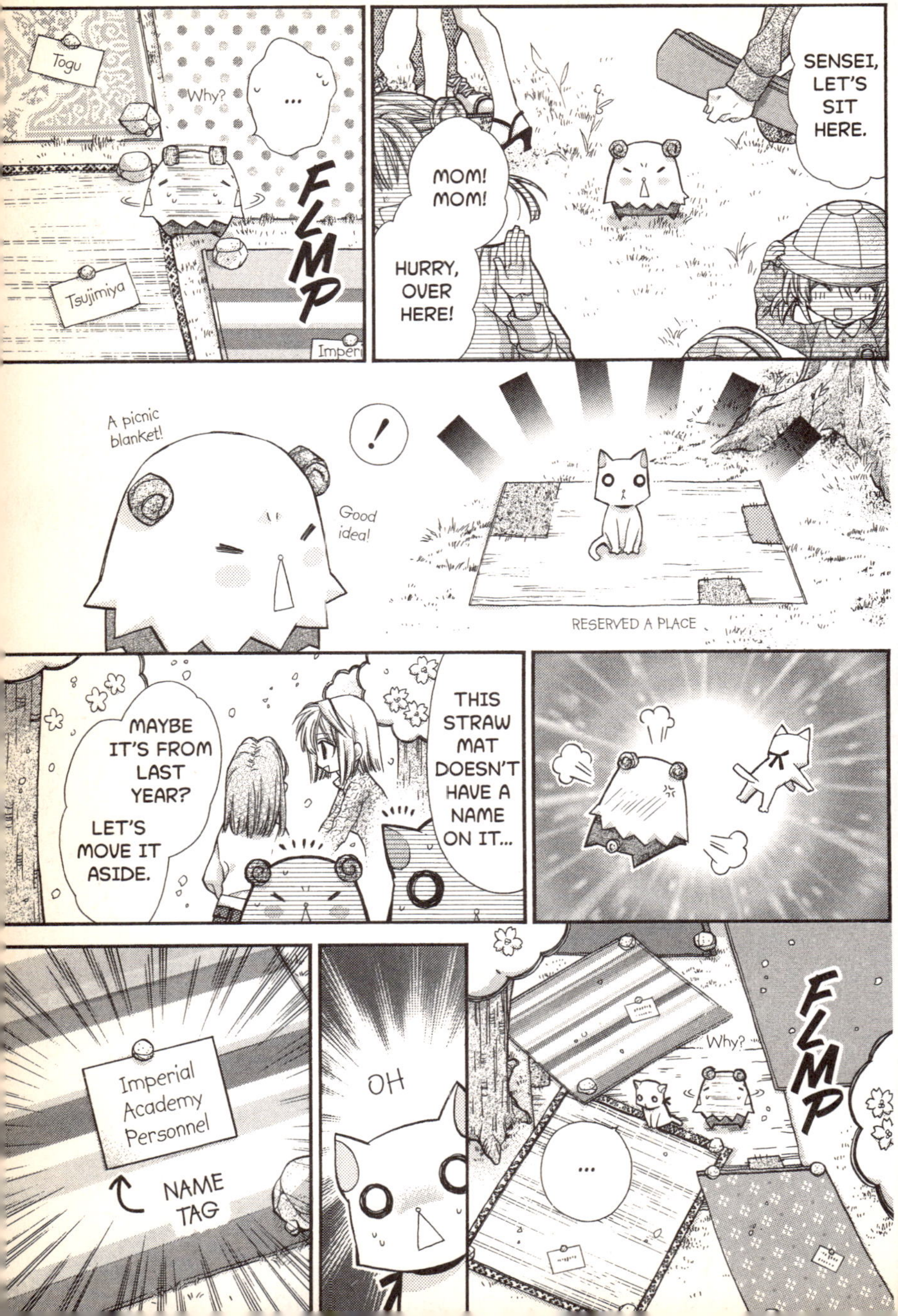
SENSEI, LET'S SIT HERE.
MOM! MOM!
HURRY, OVER HERE!
Togu
Why?
...
FLMP
Tsujimiya
!
A picnic blanket!
Good idea!
RESERVED A PLACE
THIS STRAW MAT DOESN'T HAVE A NAME ON IT...
MAYBE IT'S FROM LAST YEAR?
LET'S MOVE IT ASIDE.
FLMP
Why?
...
OH
Imperial Academy Personnel
NAME TAG

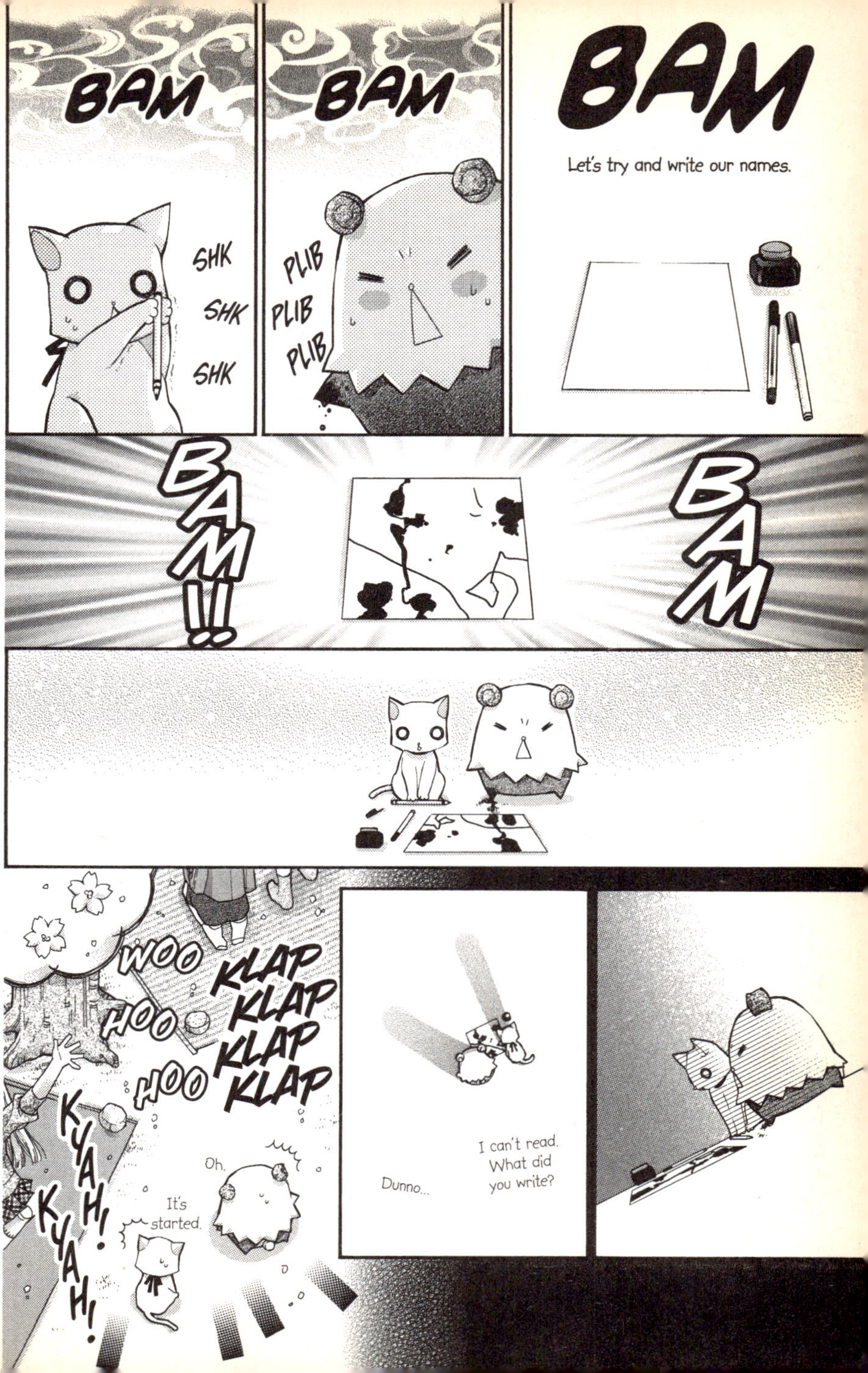
BAM
Let's try and write our names.
BAM
PLIB
PLIB
PLIB
BAM
SHK
SHK
SHK
BAM
BAM!!
I can't read. What did you write?
Dunno...
KLAP KLAP KLAP KLAP
WOO HOO HOO
Oh.
KYAH! KYAH!
It's started.

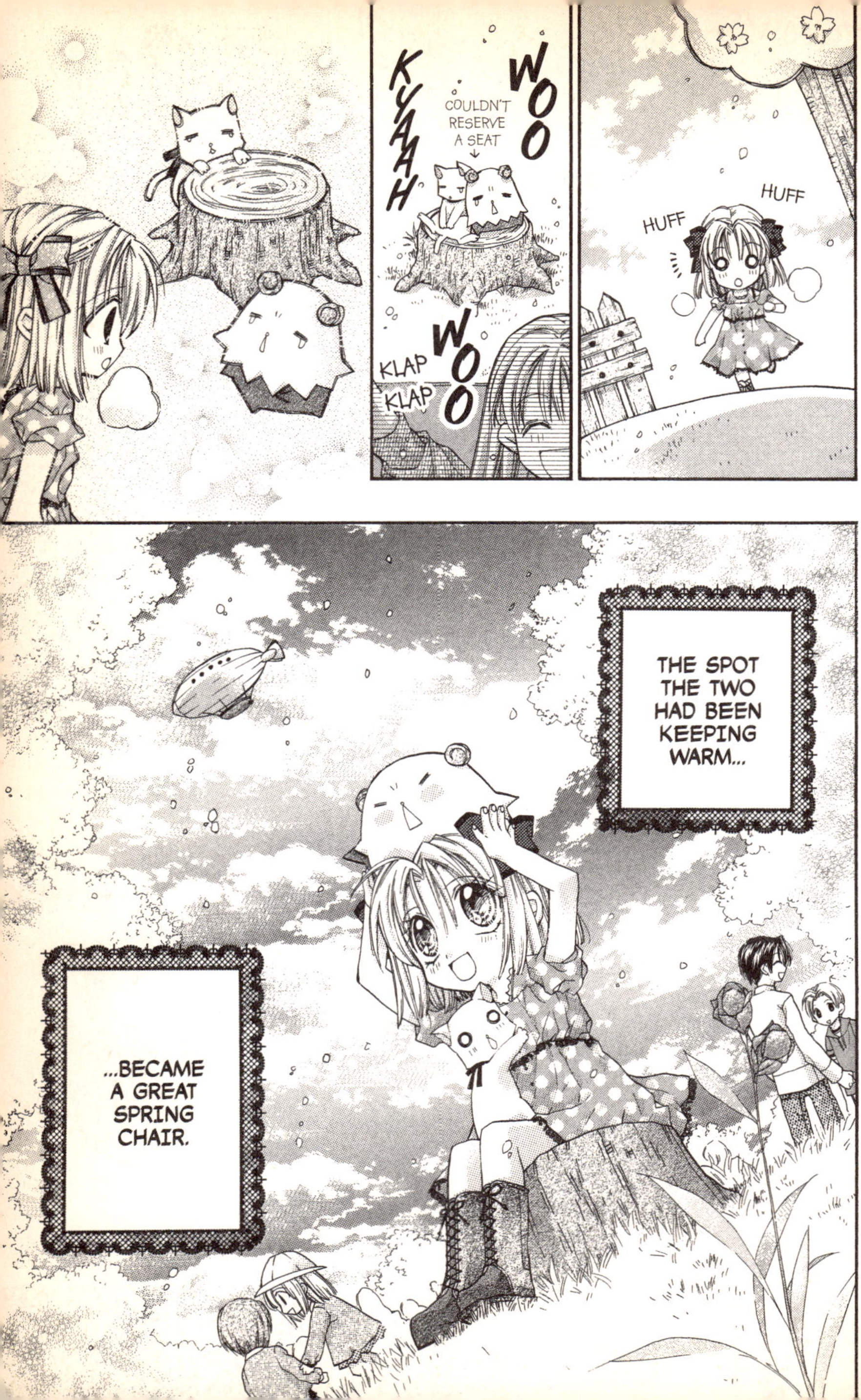
HUFF
HUFF
KYAAAH
WOO
COULDN'T RESERVE A SEAT
WOO
KLAP
KLAP
THE SPOT THE TWO HAD BEEN KEEPING WARM...
...BECAME A GREAT SPRING CHAIR.

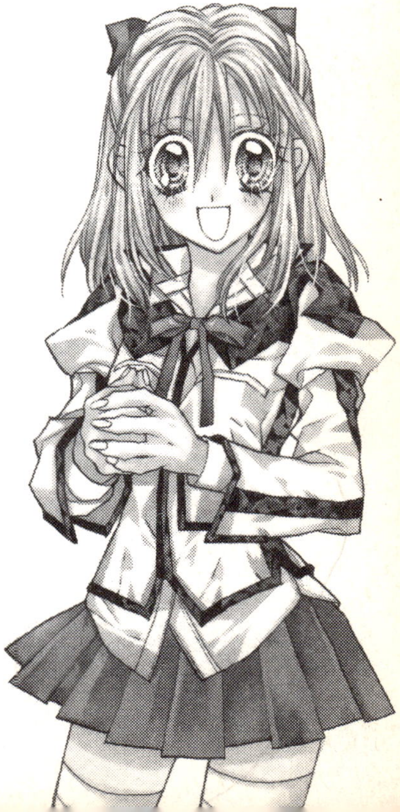

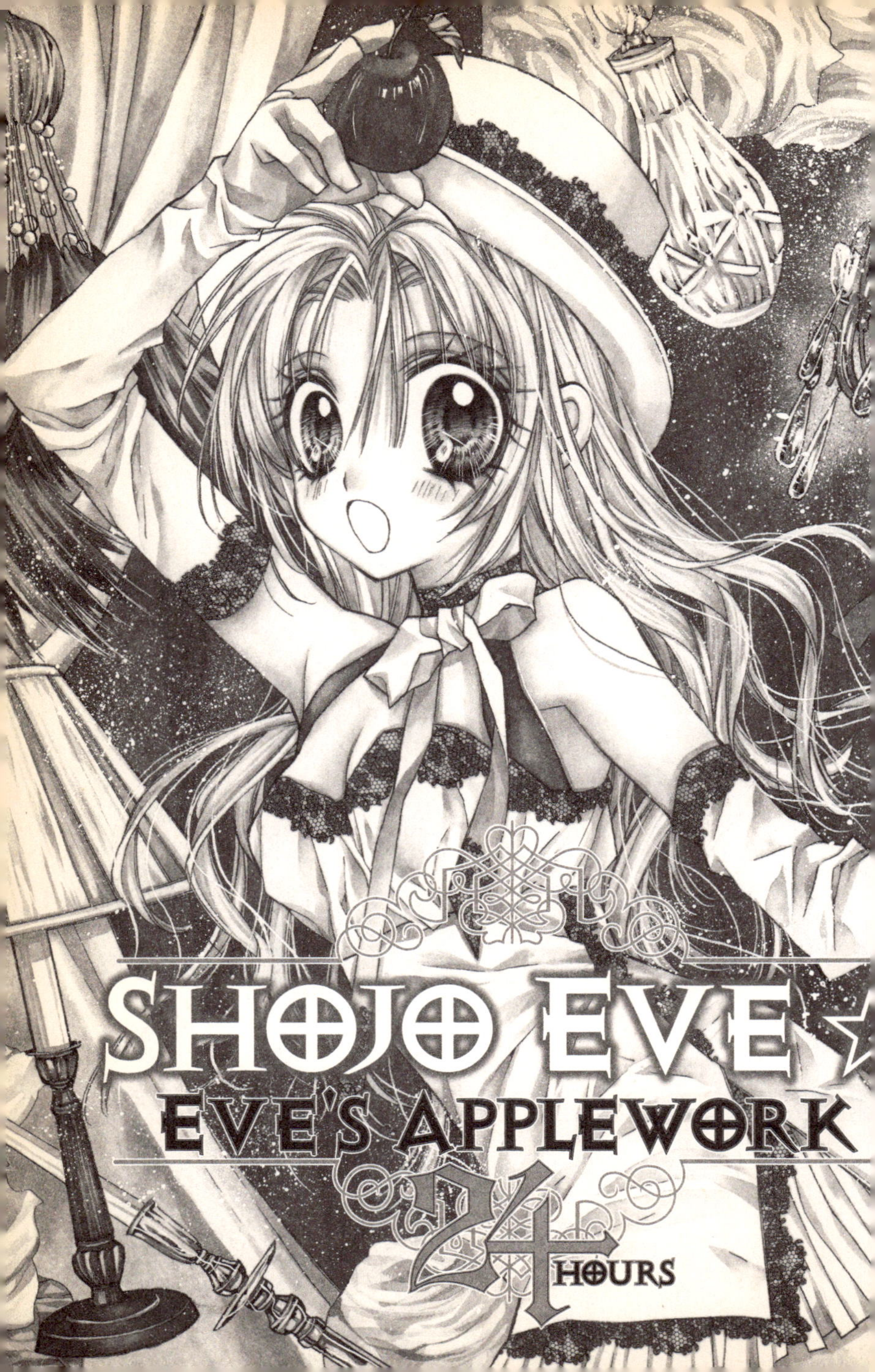
SHOJO EVE
EVE'S APPLEWORK
24 HOURS

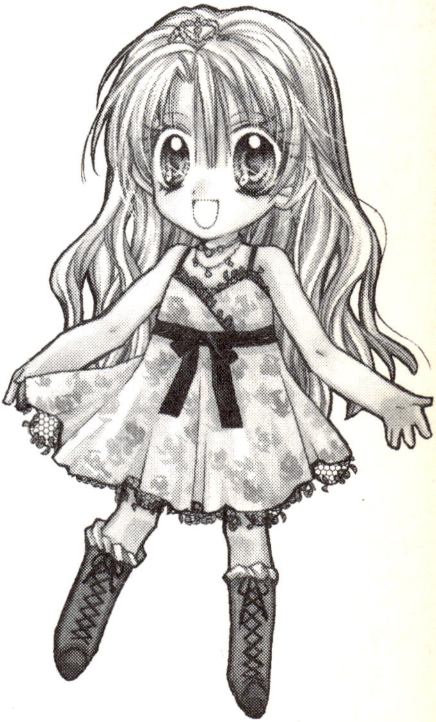

HMPH!
DON'T COME NEAR ME!!
RUMORS WILL START IF I'M SEEN TOGETHER WITH A POPULAR GUY LIKE YOU, KASHI-KUN!!
THEN LET'S START A RUMOR!
JUST GIVE UP AND GO OUT WITH ME!
RWAH
NO WAY!
DOOM
IT'S BEEN TWO MONTHS SINCE WE ENTERED SCHOOL AND YOU'RE ALREADY FAMOUS FOR BEING THE CUTEST GIRL HERE, EVE SHIRATORI..
RIGHT ?!
UGH
TWINKLE
AND THEN THERE'S ME, HISAKI KASHI, FAMOUS FOR BEING THE HANDSOMEST GUY IN SCHOOL...
RIGHT ?!
BAM!!

WE'D MAKE SUCH A ROMANTIC COUPLE, DON'T YOU THINK?!
STOP ASKING ME TO GO OUT WITH YOU FOR SUCH A STUPID REASON, YOU IDIOT!!
It's Shiratori-san.
Ooh!
I'M EVE SHIRATORI.
I'M 16 YEARS OLD.
Another person I don't know said hi to me...
EVER SINCE I WAS SMALL, I'VE BEEN TOLD TIME AND TIME AGAIN...
...THAT I WAS CUTE. I SHOULD BE HAPPY, BUT...
GRIP
...BEING CUTE...

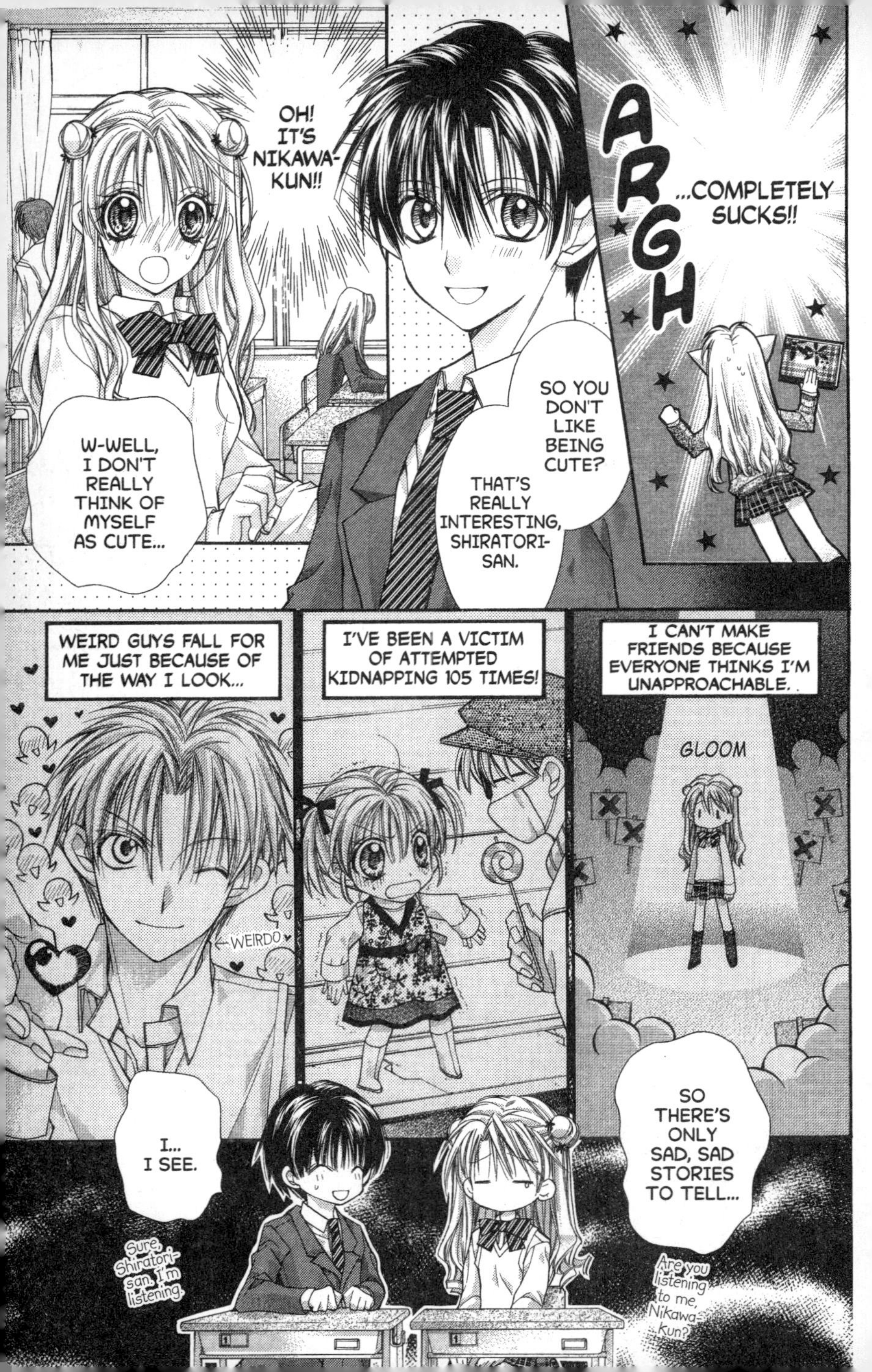
ARGH
...COMPLETELY SUCKS!!
OH! IT'S NIKAWA-KUN!!
SO YOU DON'T LIKE BEING CUTE?
THAT'S REALLY INTERESTING, SHIRATORI-SAN.
W-WELL, I DON'T REALLY THINK OF MYSELF AS CUTE...
I CAN'T MAKE FRIENDS BECAUSE EVERYONE THINKS I'M UNAPPROACHABLE.
GLOOM
I'VE BEEN A VICTIM OF ATTEMPTED KIDNAPPING 105 TIMES!
WEIRD GUYS FALL FOR ME JUST BECAUSE OF THE WAY I LOOK...
←WEIRDO
SO THERE'S ONLY SAD, SAD STORIES TO TELL...
Are you listening to me, Nikawa-Kun?
I... I SEE.
Sure, Shiratori-san, I'm listening.

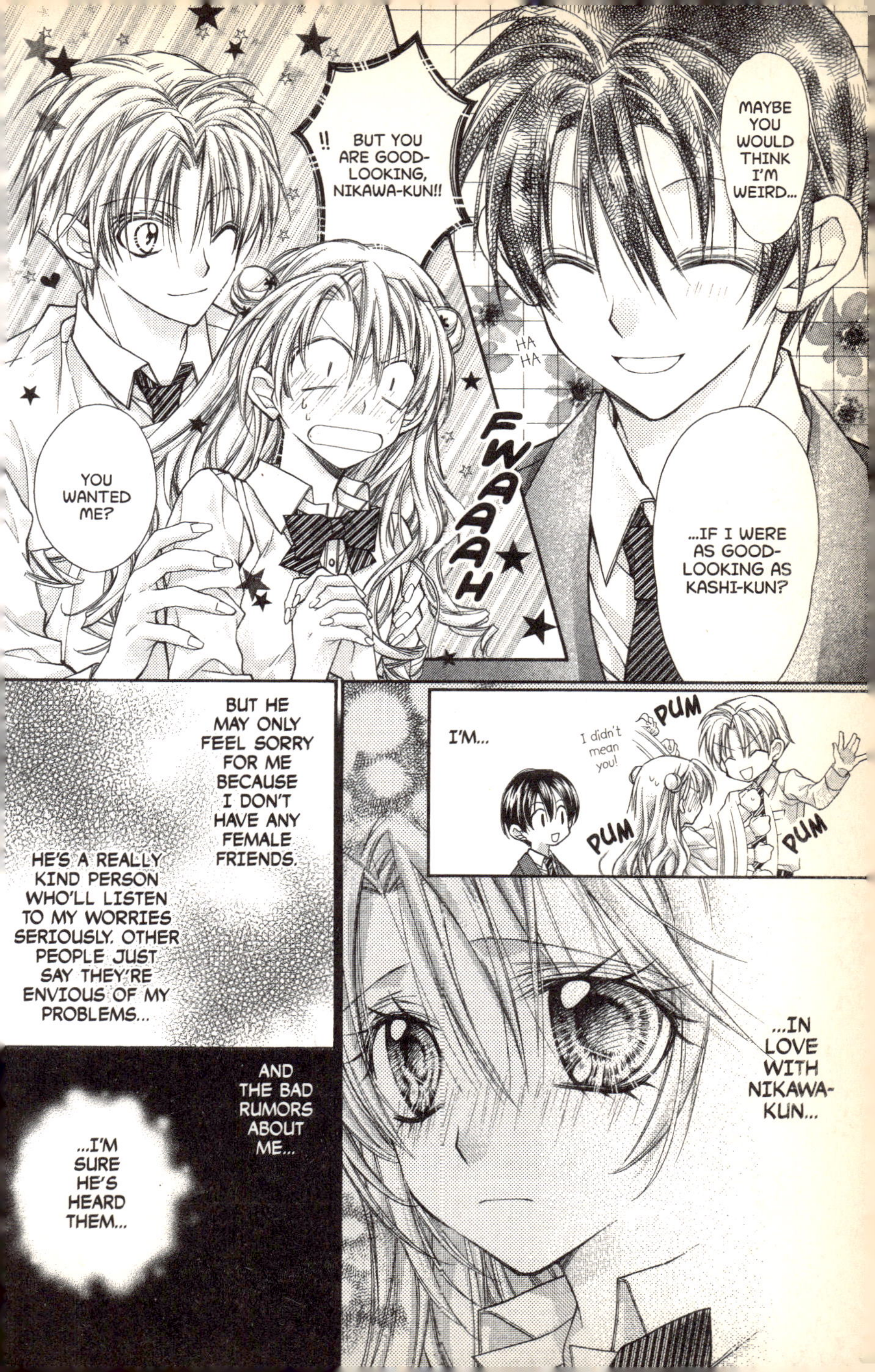
MAYBE YOU WOULD THINK I'M WEIRD...
...IF I WERE AS GOOD-LOOKING AS KASHI-KUN?
HA HA
!!
BUT YOU ARE GOOD-LOOKING, NIKAWA-KUN!!
FWAAAAH
YOU WANTED ME?
I'M...
I didn't mean you!
PUM
PUM
PUM
...IN LOVE WITH NIKAWA-KUN...
BUT HE MAY ONLY FEEL SORRY FOR ME BECAUSE I DON'T HAVE ANY FEMALE FRIENDS.
HE'S A REALLY KIND PERSON WHO'LL LISTEN TO MY WORRIES SERIOUSLY. OTHER PEOPLE JUST SAY THEY'RE ENVIOUS OF MY PROBLEMS...
AND THE BAD RUMORS ABOUT ME...
...I'M SURE HE'S HEARD THEM...

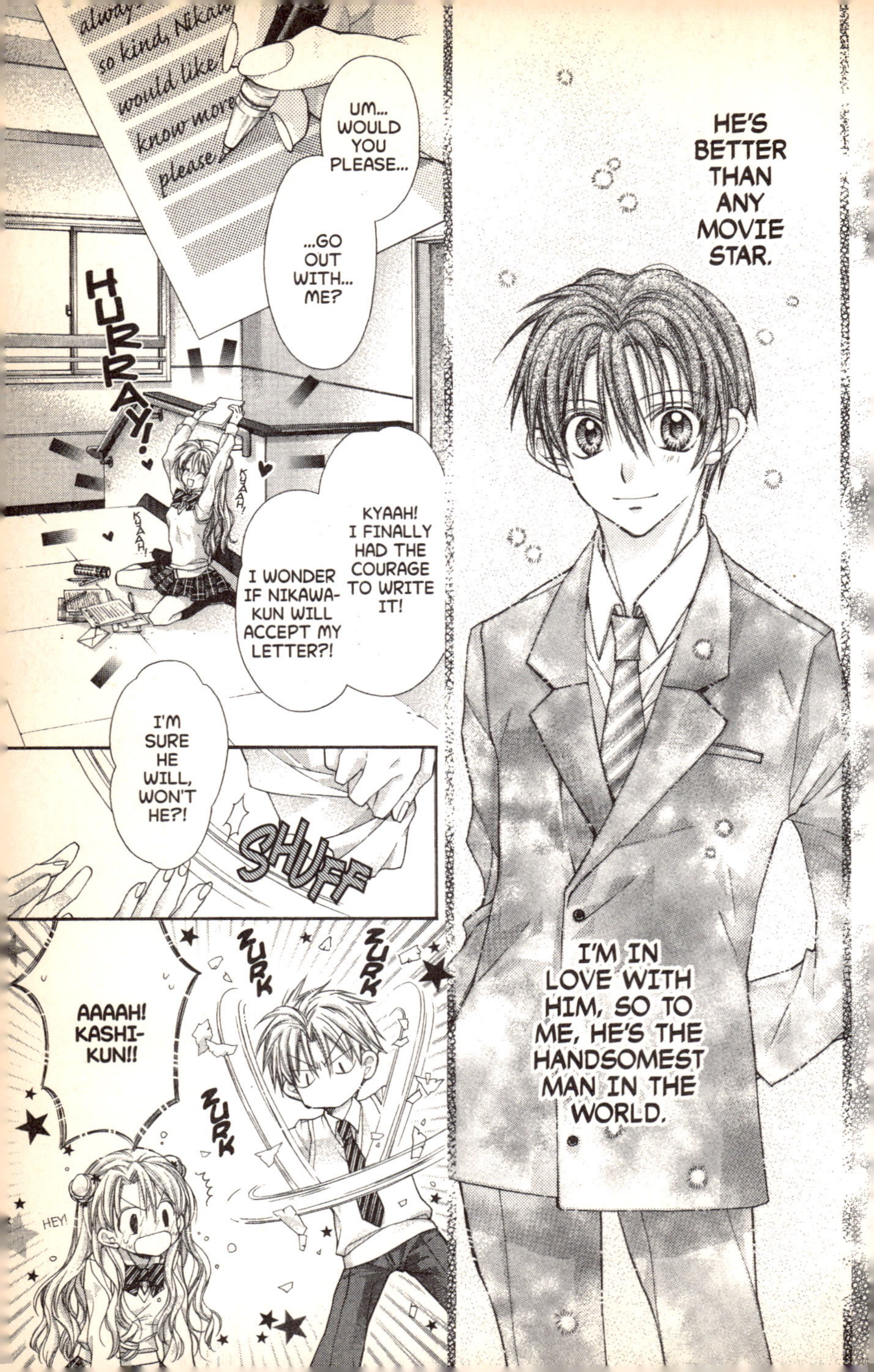
HE'S BETTER THAN ANY MOVIE STAR.
I'M IN LOVE WITH HIM, SO TO ME, HE'S THE HANDSOMEST MAN IN THE WORLD.
UM... WOULD YOU PLEASE...
...GO OUT WITH... ME?
HURRAY!
KYAAH!
KYAAH!
KYAAH! I FINALLY HAD THE COURAGE TO WRITE IT!
I WONDER IF NIKAWA-KUN WILL ACCEPT MY LETTER?!
I'M SURE HE WILL, WON'T HE?!
SHUFF
ZURK
ZURK
ZURK
AAAAH! KASHI-KUN!!
HEY!

IT WAS REALLY HARD FOR ME TO WRITE THAT, YOU KNOW!! YOU'RE SO STUPID!
LIKEWISE! YOU NEED TO ACCEPT THE FACT THAT CUTE GIRLS AND HANDSOME GUYS ARE SUPPOSED TO BE TOGETHER!!
BAM!
HOW MANY TIMES DO I HAVE TO TELL YOU THAT I LOVE YOU?
B-BMP
I'M NOT GOING TO LET...
...ANY OTHER GUY HAVE YOU!

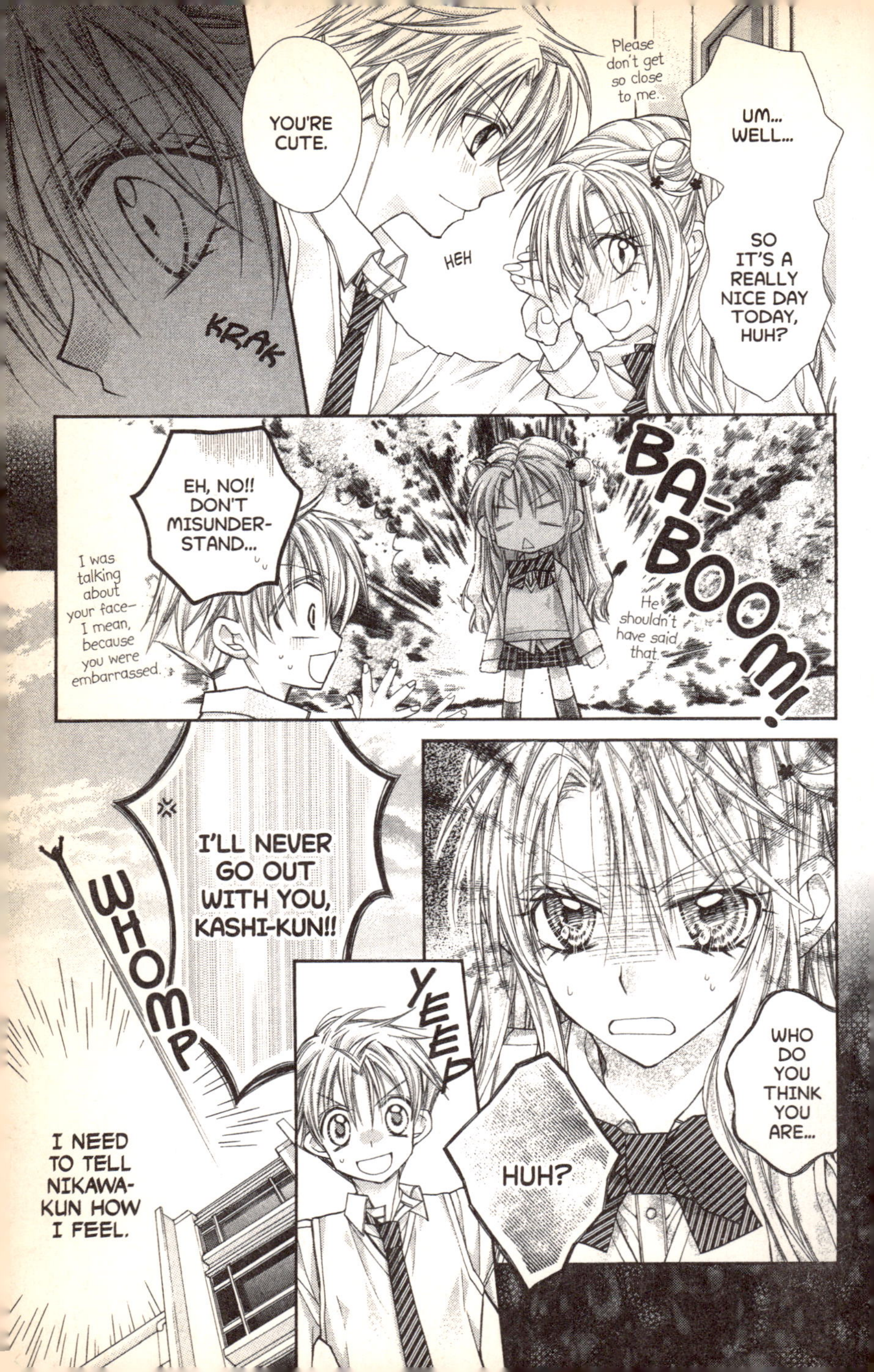
UM... WELL...
Please don't get so close to me...
SO IT'S A REALLY NICE DAY TODAY, HUH?
YOU'RE CUTE.
HEH
KRAK
BA-BOOM!!
He shouldn't have said that.
EH, NO!! DON'T MISUNDER-STAND...
I was talking about your face— I mean, because you were embarrassed.
WHO DO YOU THINK YOU ARE...
HUH?
YEEP
I'LL NEVER GO OUT WITH YOU, KASHI-KUN!!
WHOMP
I NEED TO TELL NIKAWA-KUN HOW I FEEL.

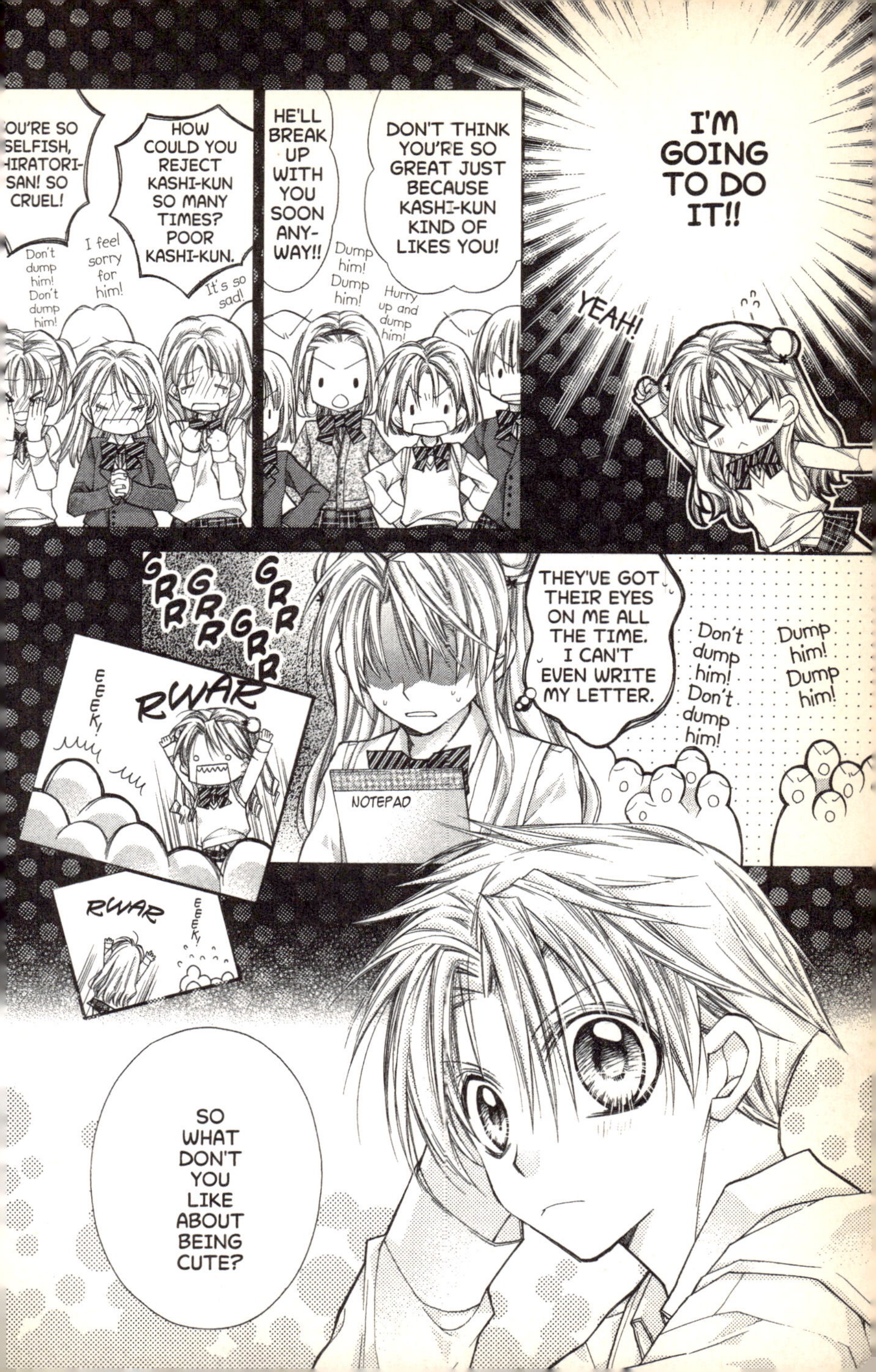

I'M GOING TO DO IT!!
YEAH!
DON'T THINK YOU'RE SO GREAT JUST BECAUSE KASHI-KUN KIND OF LIKES YOU!
Hurry up and dump him!
HE'LL BREAK UP WITH YOU SOON ANY-WAY!!
Dump him! Dump him!
HOW COULD YOU REJECT KASHI-KUN SO MANY TIMES? POOR KASHI-KUN.
It's so sad!
I feel sorry for him!
OU'RE SO SELFISH, HIRATORI-SAN! SO CRUEL!
Don't dump him! Don't dump him!
Dump him! Dump him!
Don't dump him! Don't dump him!
THEY'VE GOT THEIR EYES ON ME ALL THE TIME. I CAN'T EVEN WRITE MY LETTER.
NOTEPAD
GRR GRR GRR GRR
RWAR
EEEK!
RWAR
EEEK!
SO WHAT DON'T YOU LIKE ABOUT BEING CUTE?

I CAN'T MAKE ANY FRIENDS!
Not only do I not have any friends...
...but everyone dislikes me.
Kyaah! Kashi-kun!
Come over here!
?
?
DRAWING CONTEST
BUT BEING CUTE IS GENERALLY CONSIDERED TO BE A GOOD THING.
ALL THE GIRLS ARE ENVIOUS OF YOU.
YOU LOOK GOOD IN ANY KIND OF CLOTHES AND MAKEUP...
REPORT CARD
Japanese Literature English
D D D
BAM
BUT BEING CUTE DOESN'T MEAN YOU GET GOOD GRADES.
SIGH
SHE HAS A D AVERAGE?!
WH-WHY DON'T YOU STUDY?
A REASONABL QUESTION
I DON'T HAVE TIME. I HAVE TO ATTEND AN AESTHETIC CLINIC AND GO TO THE HAIRDRESSER. PLUS I HAVE TO WORK PART-TIME TO PAY FOR IT ALL...
HUMANS ARE STRANGE CREATURES. THEY ASSUME THAT A CUTE GIRL WHO ISN'T FASHIONABLE IS A SLOB...
I SEE...
I GUESS YOU'RE DOING YOUR BEST.
Yeah.
I DID HAVE A FRIEND BEFORE...
...IN MIDDLE SCHOOL.

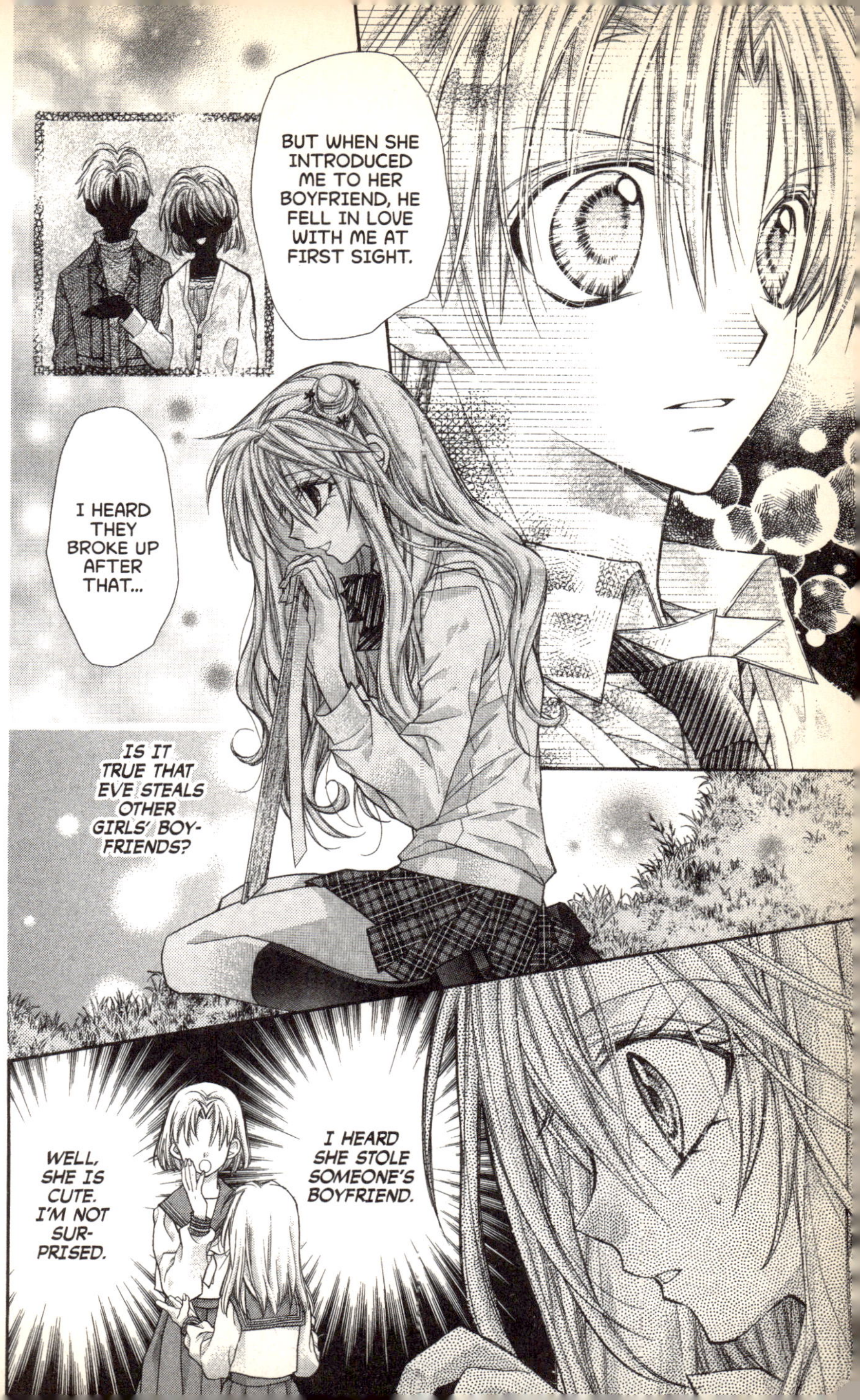
BUT WHEN SHE INTRODUCED ME TO HER BOYFRIEND, HE FELL IN LOVE WITH ME AT FIRST SIGHT.
I HEARD THEY BROKE UP AFTER THAT...
IS IT TRUE THAT EVE STEALS OTHER GIRLS' BOY-FRIENDS?
I HEARD SHE STOLE SOMEONE'S BOYFRIEND.
WELL, SHE IS CUTE. I'M NOT SUR-PRISED.

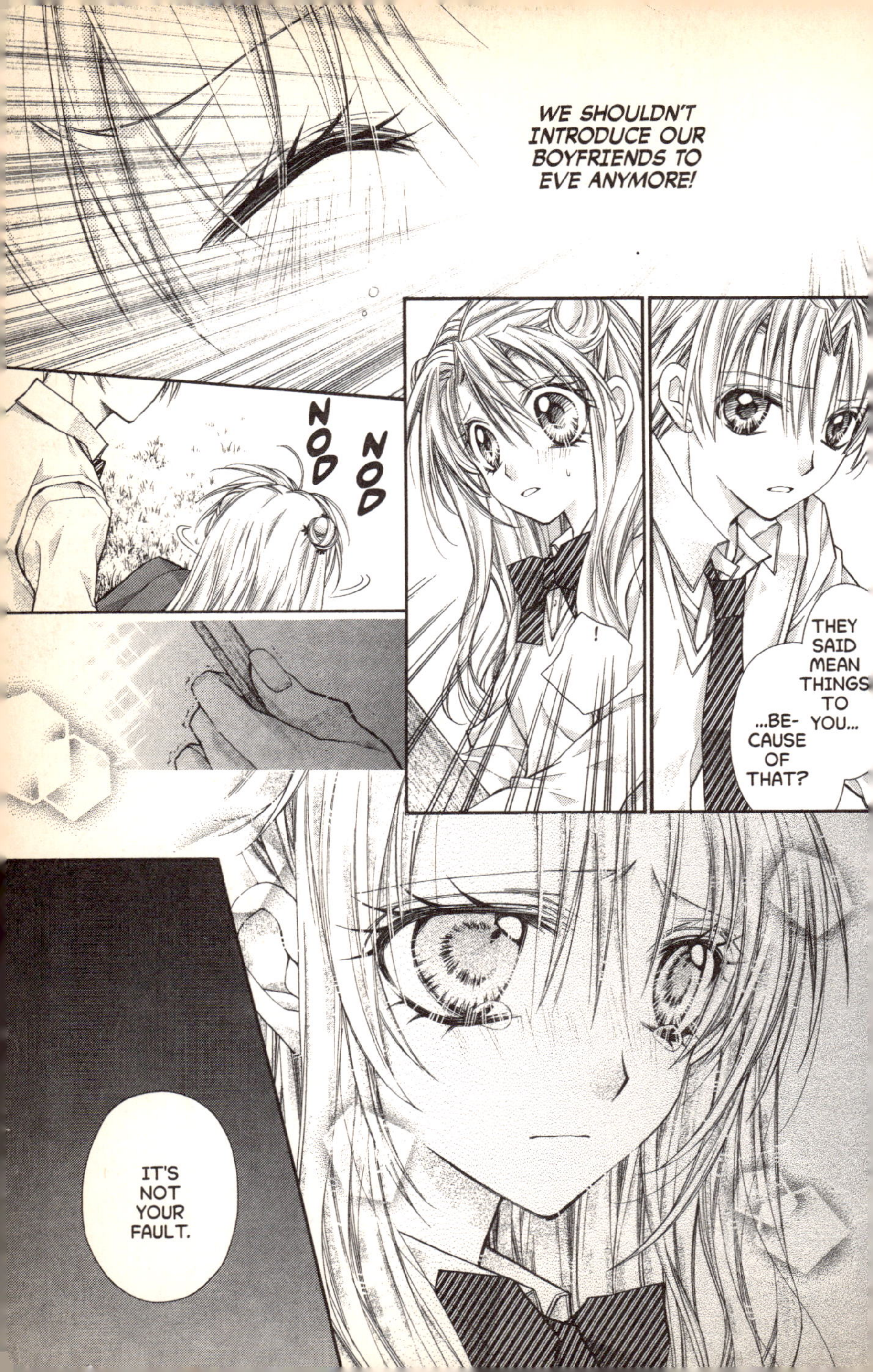
WE SHOULDN'T INTRODUCE OUR BOYFRIENDS TO EVE ANYMORE!
THEY SAID MEAN THINGS TO YOU... ...BE-CAUSE OF THAT?
!
NOD NOD
IT'S NOT YOUR FAULT.

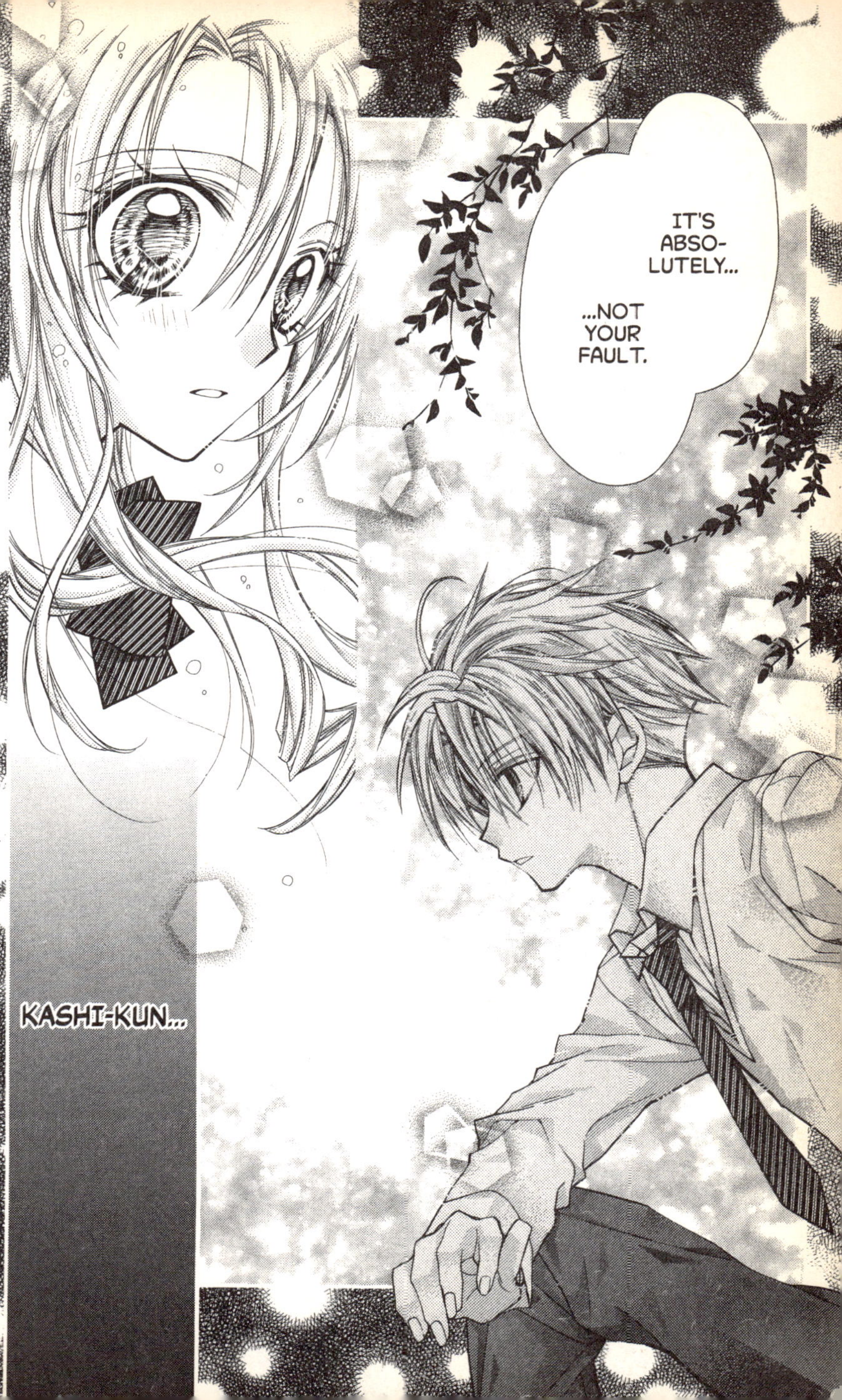
IT'S ABSO-LUTELY...
...NOT YOUR FAULT.
KASHI-KUN...

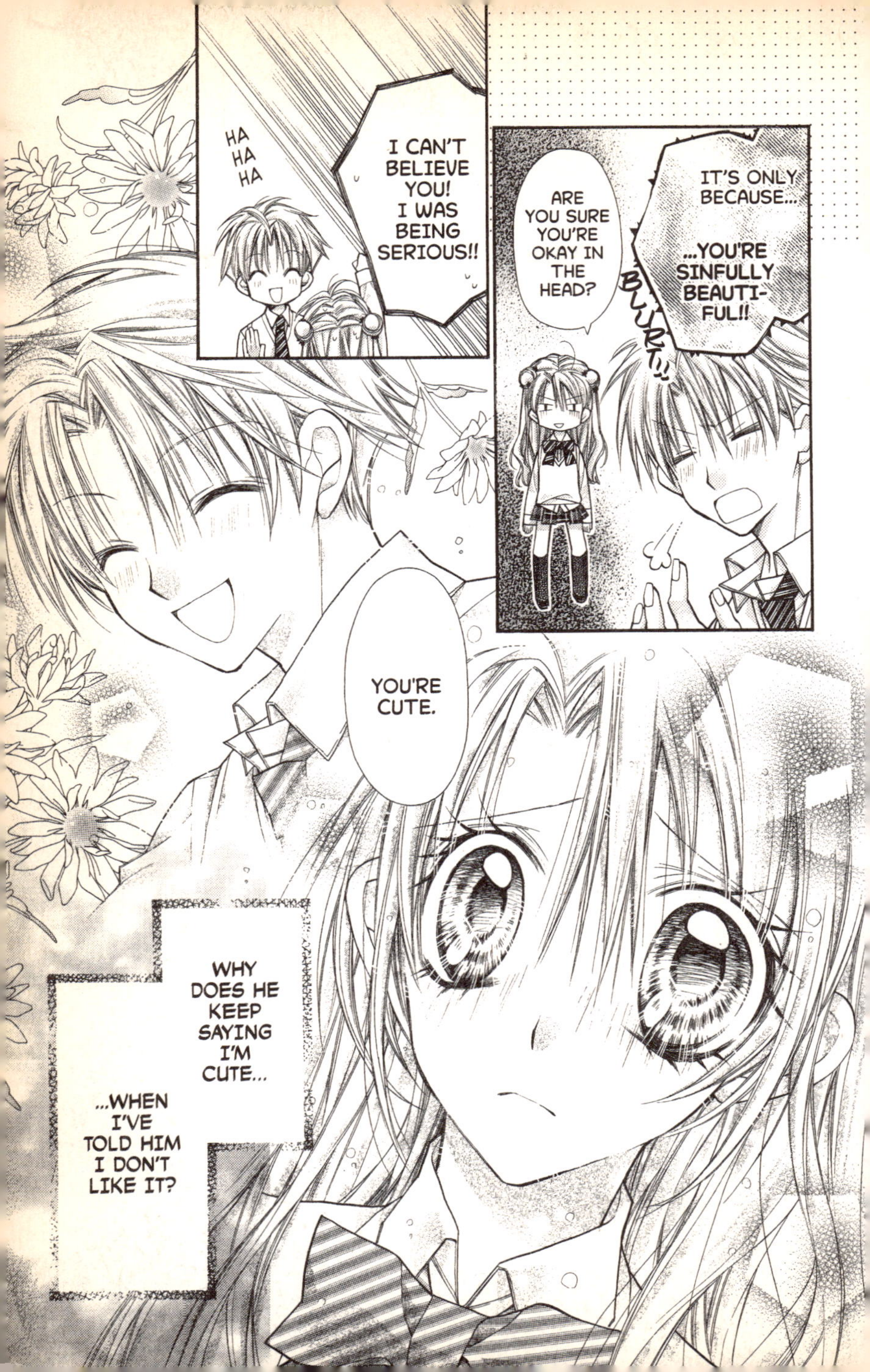

IT'S ONLY BECAUSE...
...YOU'RE SINFULLY BEAUTI-FUL!!
BLURT!!
ARE YOU SURE YOU'RE OKAY IN THE HEAD?
I CAN'T BELIEVE YOU! I WAS BEING SERIOUS!!
HA HA HA
YOU'RE CUTE.
WHY DOES HE KEEP SAYING I'M CUTE...
...WHEN I'VE TOLD HIM I DON'T LIKE IT?

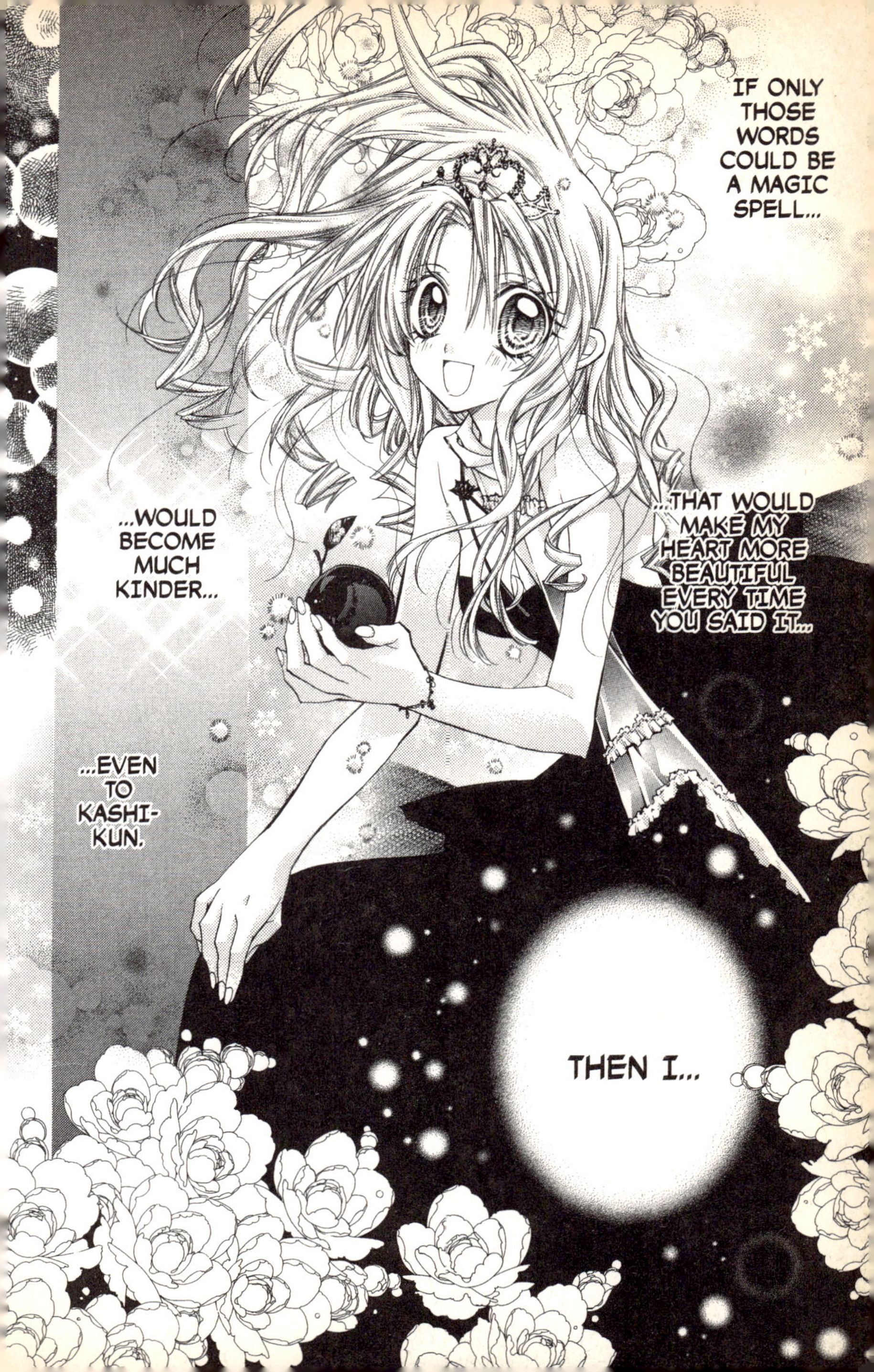
IF ONLY THOSE WORDS COULD BE A MAGIC SPELL...
...THAT WOULD MAKE MY HEART MORE BEAUTIFUL EVERY TIME YOU SAID IT...
...WOULD BECOME MUCH KINDER...
...EVEN TO KASHI-KUN.
THEN I...

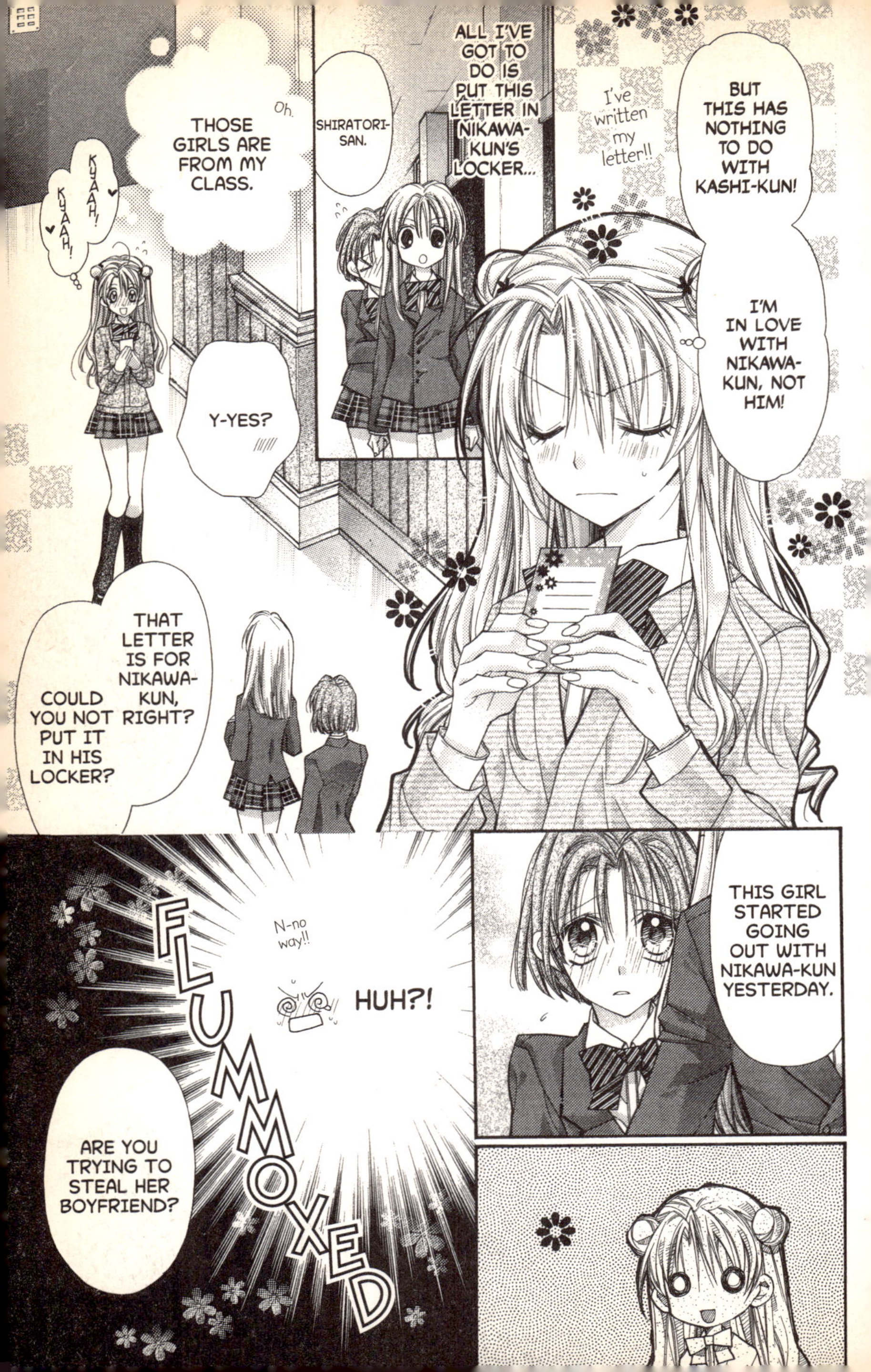
I've written my letter!!
BUT THIS HAS NOTHING TO DO WITH KASHI-KUN!
I'M IN LOVE WITH NIKAWA-KUN, NOT HIM!
ALL I'VE GOT TO DO IS PUT THIS LETTER IN NIKAWA-KUN'S LOCKER...
SHIRATORI-SAN.
Oh.
Y-YES?
THOSE GIRLS ARE FROM MY CLASS.
KYAAH!
KYAAH!
THAT LETTER IS FOR NIKAWA-KUN, RIGHT?
COULD YOU NOT PUT IT IN HIS LOCKER?
THIS GIRL STARTED GOING OUT WITH NIKAWA-KUN YESTERDAY.
HUH?!
N-no way!!
FLUMMOXED
ARE YOU TRYING TO STEAL HER BOYFRIEND?

I TOLD HIM ABOUT MY FEELINGS...
...AND HE ACCEPTED ME, BUT...
...HE'S GOOD FRIENDS WITH YOU TOO.
YOU'RE REALLY CUTE, SHIRATORI-SAN...
...SO HE MIGHT CHANGE HIS MIND AFTER HE READS YOUR LETTER!
BUT—
I'M IN LOVE WITH NIKAWA-KUN TOO.
YOU'RE A CUTE PERSON, SHIRATORI-SAN...
...YOU'VE GOT MANY OTHER BOYS TO CHOOSE FROM...

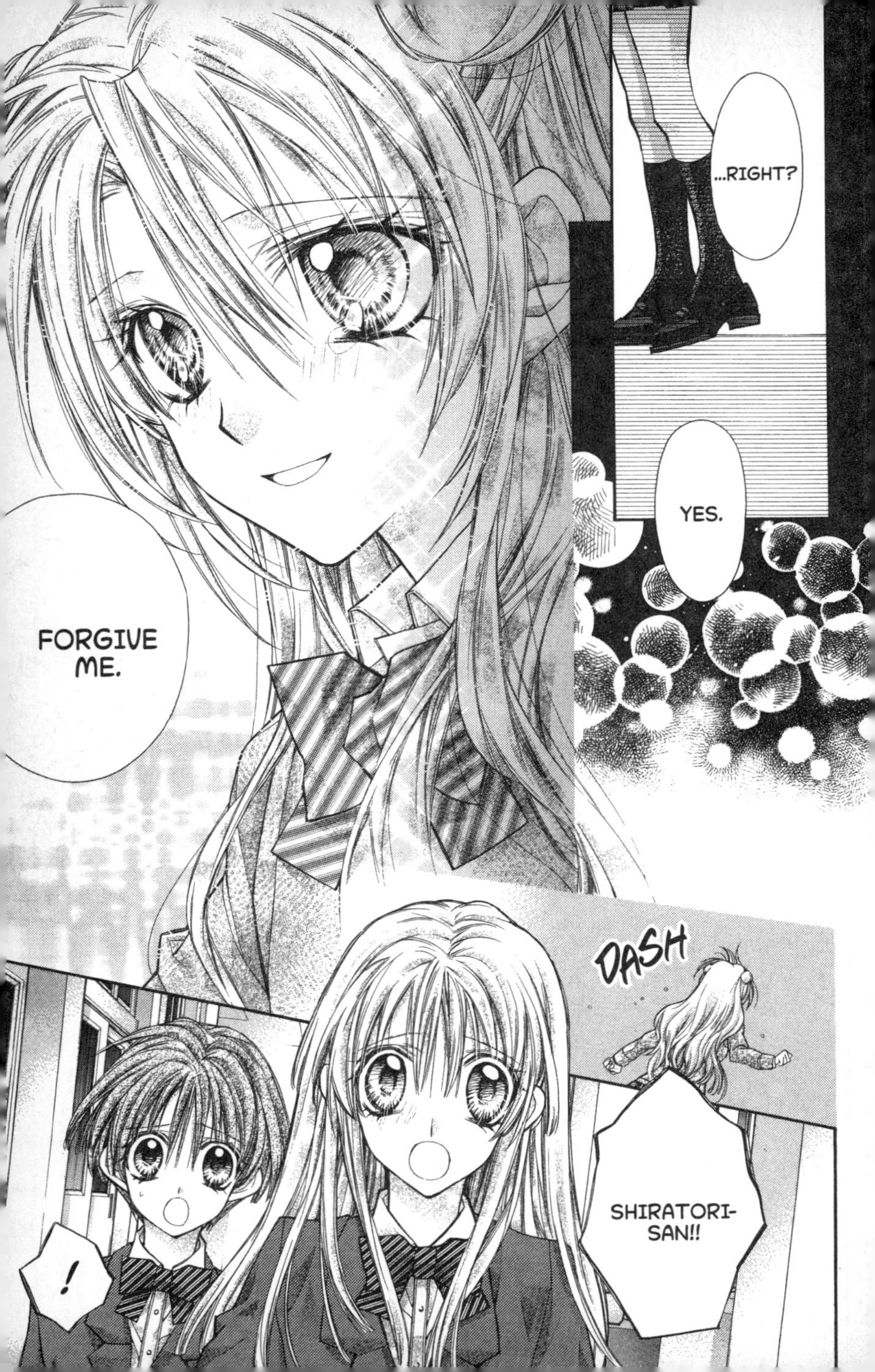
...RIGHT?
YES.
FORGIVE ME.
DASH
SHIRATORI-SAN!!
!

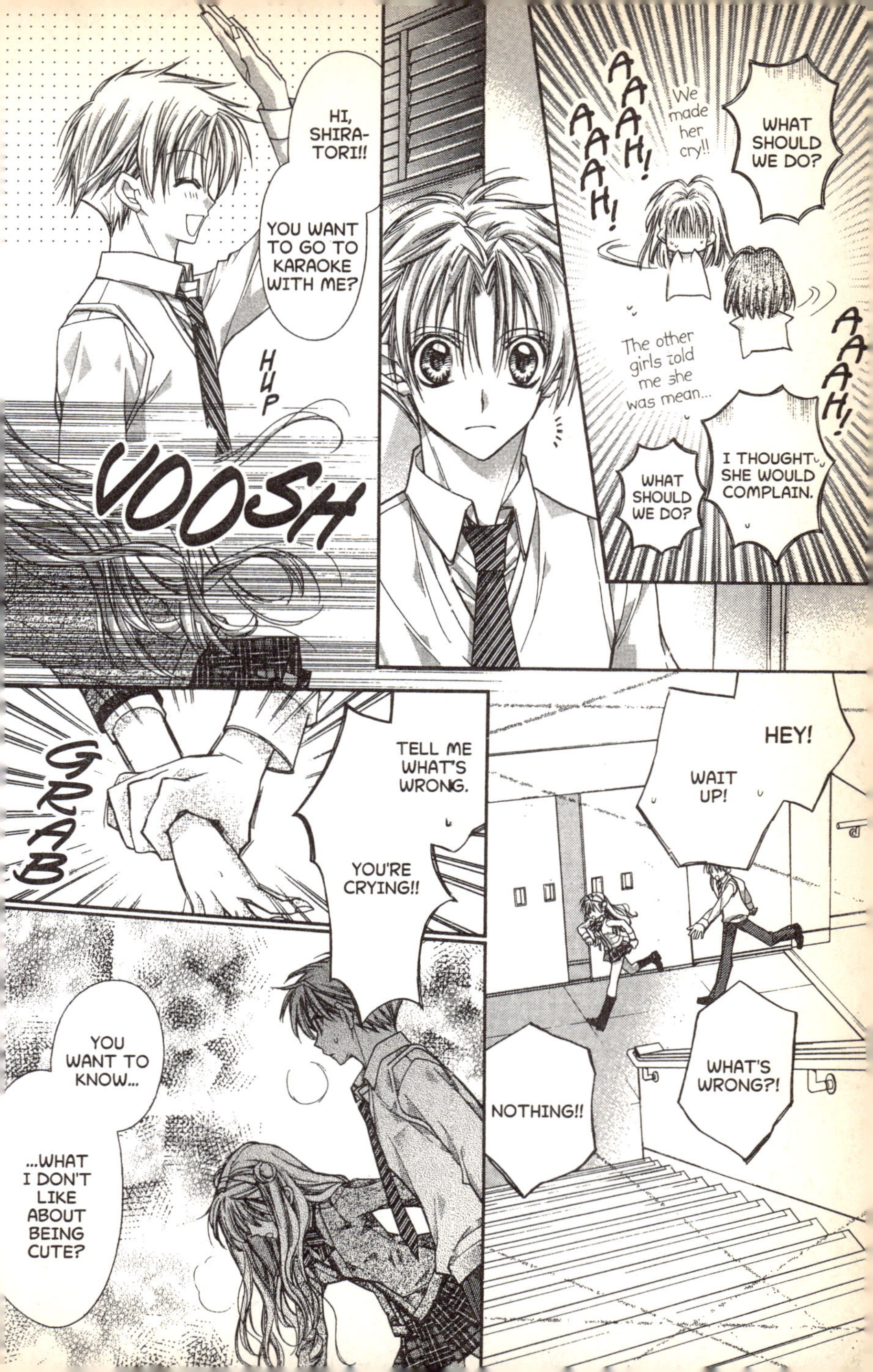

AAAAH!
AAAH!
We made her cry!!
WHAT SHOULD WE DO?
The other girls told me she was mean...
AAAAH!
I THOUGHT SHE WOULD COMPLAIN.
WHAT SHOULD WE DO?
HI, SHIRATORI!!
YOU WANT TO GO TO KARAOKE WITH ME?
HUP
VOOSH
HEY!
WAIT UP!
WHAT'S WRONG?!
NOTHING!!
TELL ME WHAT'S WRONG.
YOU'RE CRYING!!
GRAB
YOU WANT TO KNOW...
...WHAT I DON'T LIKE ABOUT BEING CUTE?

EVERY-THING!!
NO MATTER HOW CUTE I AM...
...IT'S MEANINGLESS UNLESS THE PERSON I'M IN LOVE WITH LOVES ME TOO!
I DON'T EVEN HAVE ANY FRIENDS...
I'M COMPLETELY ALONE!
THERE'S NO ONE–

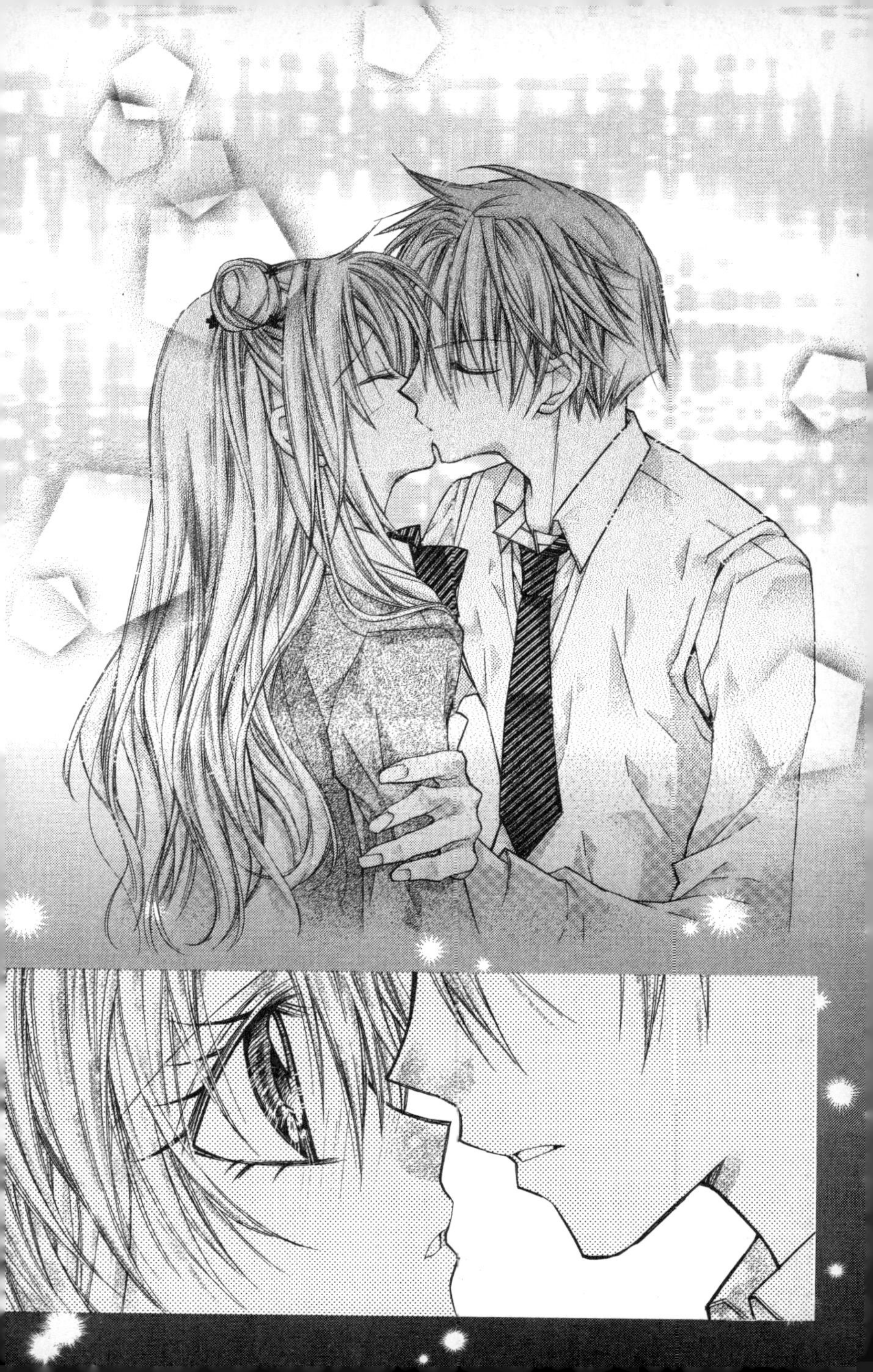

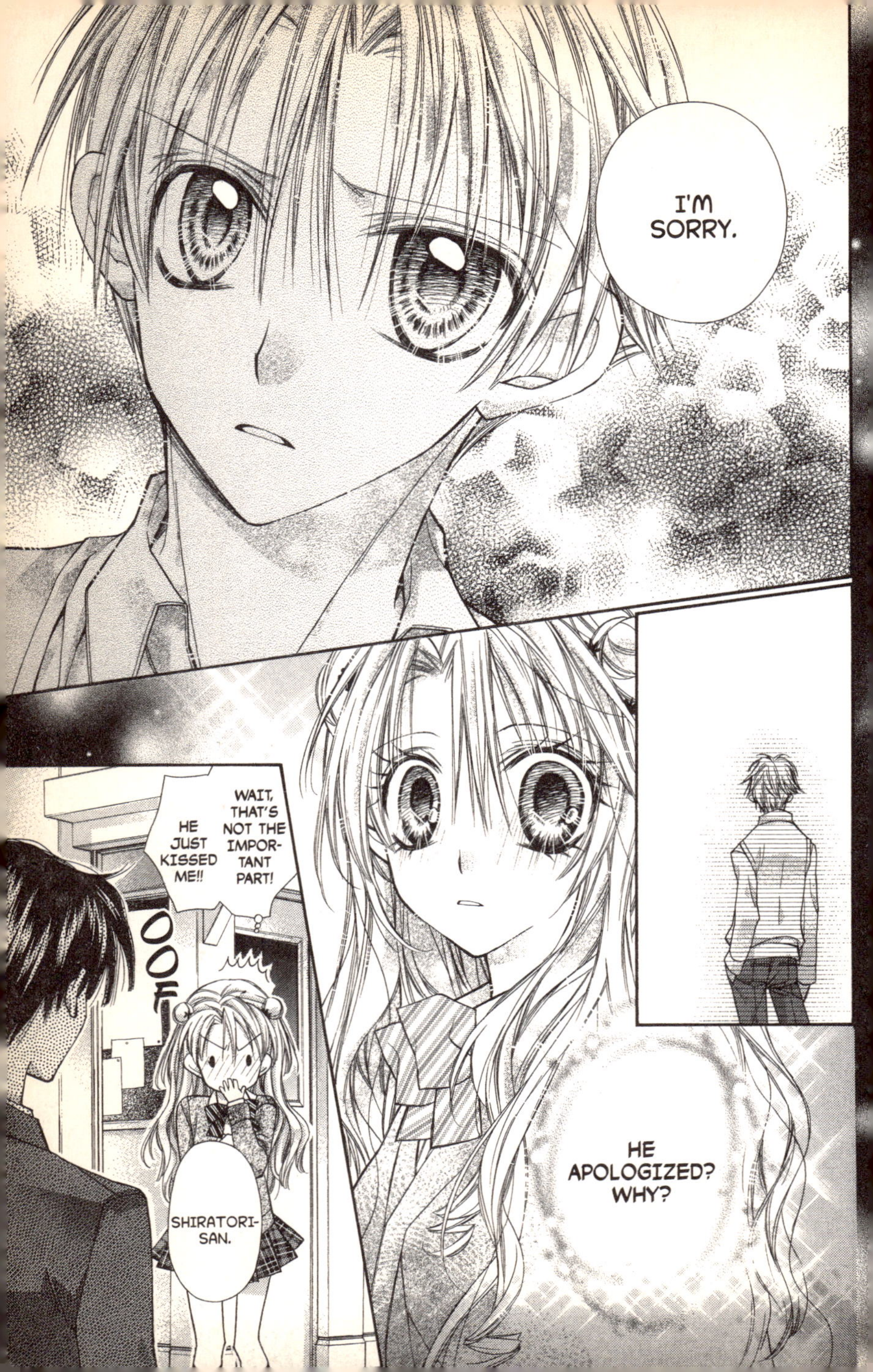
I'M SORRY.
HE APOLOGIZED? WHY?
WAIT, THAT'S NOT THE IMPORTANT PART!
HE JUST KISSED ME!!
OOF
SHIRATORI-SAN.

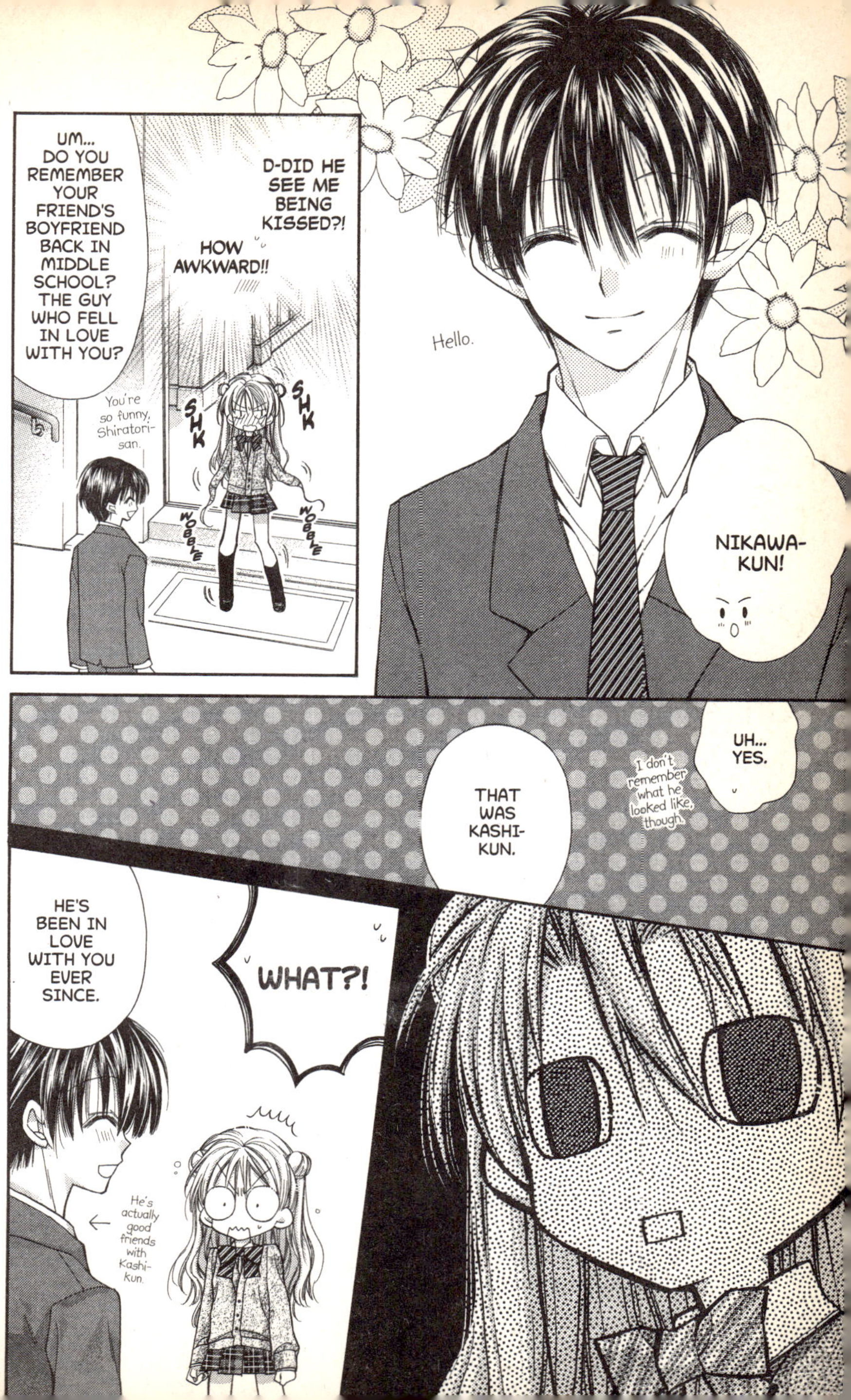
Hello.
NIKAWA-KUN!
D-DID HE SEE ME BEING KISSED?!
HOW AWKWARD!!
UM... DO YOU REMEMBER YOUR FRIEND'S BOYFRIEND BACK IN MIDDLE SCHOOL? THE GUY WHO FELL IN LOVE WITH YOU?
You're so funny, Shiratori-san.
SHK SHK
WOBBLE WOBBLE
UH... YES.
I don't remember what he looked like, though.
THAT WAS KASHI-KUN.
HE'S BEEN IN LOVE WITH YOU EVER SINCE.
WHAT?!
He's actually good friends with Kashi-kun.

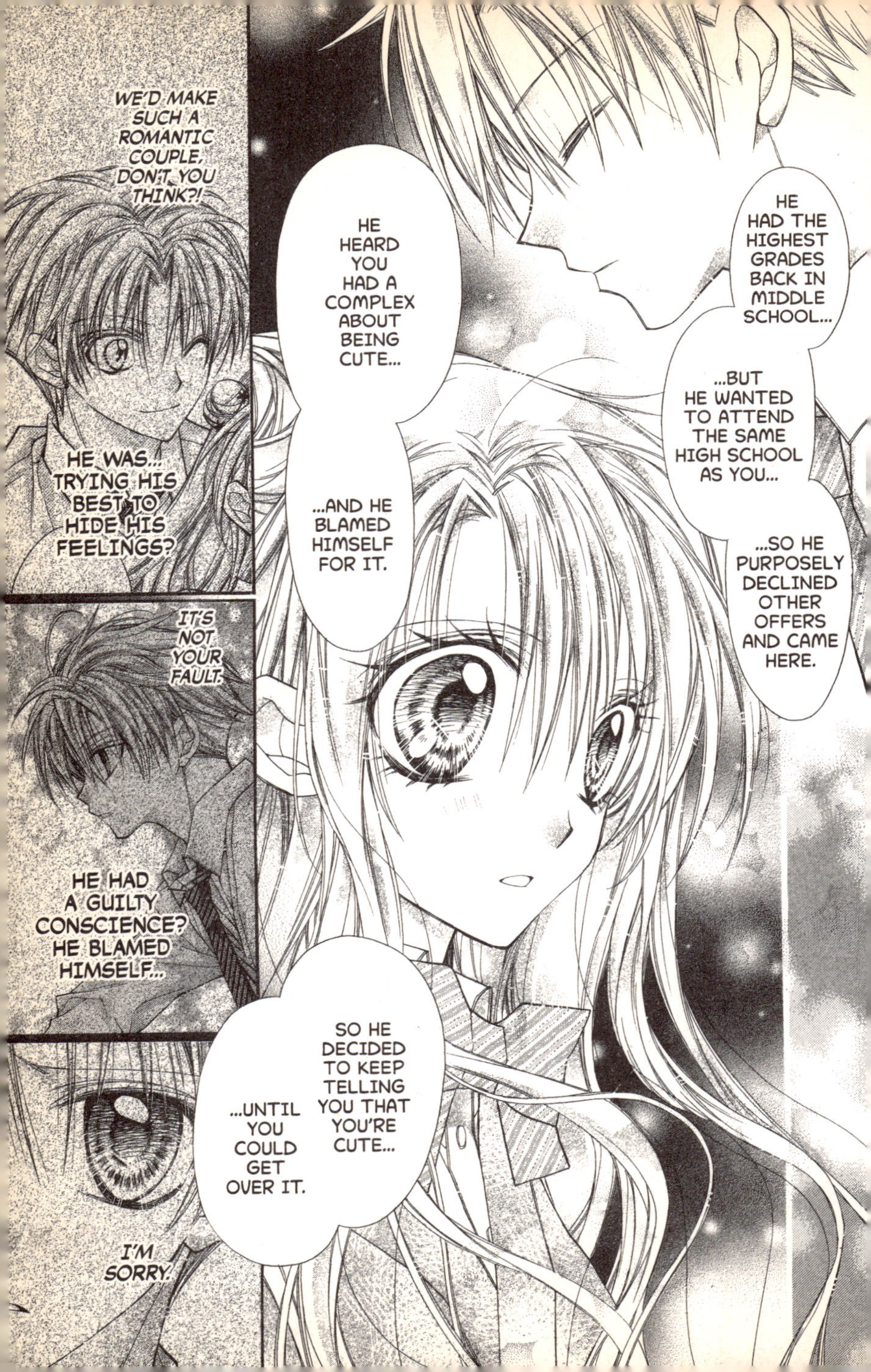
HE HAD THE HIGHEST GRADES BACK IN MIDDLE SCHOOL...
...BUT HE WANTED TO ATTEND THE SAME HIGH SCHOOL AS YOU...
...SO HE PURPOSELY DECLINED OTHER OFFERS AND CAME HERE.
HE HEARD YOU HAD A COMPLEX ABOUT BEING CUTE...
...AND HE BLAMED HIMSELF FOR IT.
SO HE DECIDED TO KEEP TELLING YOU THAT YOU'RE CUTE...
...UNTIL YOU COULD GET OVER IT.
WE'D MAKE SUCH A ROMANTIC COUPLE, DON'T YOU THINK?!
HE WAS... TRYING HIS BEST TO HIDE HIS FEELINGS?
IT'S NOT YOUR FAULT.
HE HAD A GUILTY CONSCIENCE? HE BLAMED HIMSELF...
I'M SORRY.

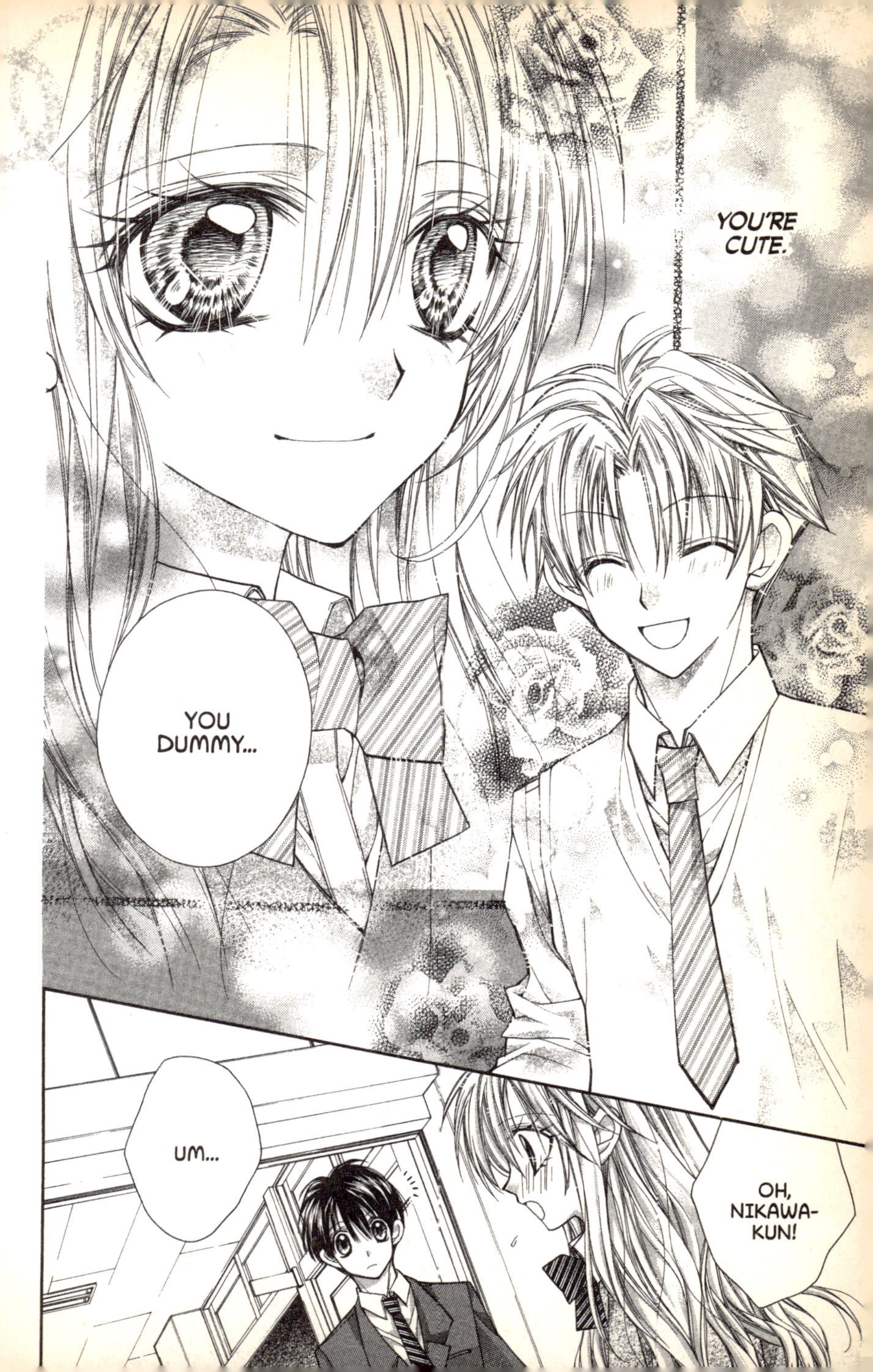
YOU'RE CUTE.
YOU DUMMY...
OH, NIKAWA-KUN!
UM...

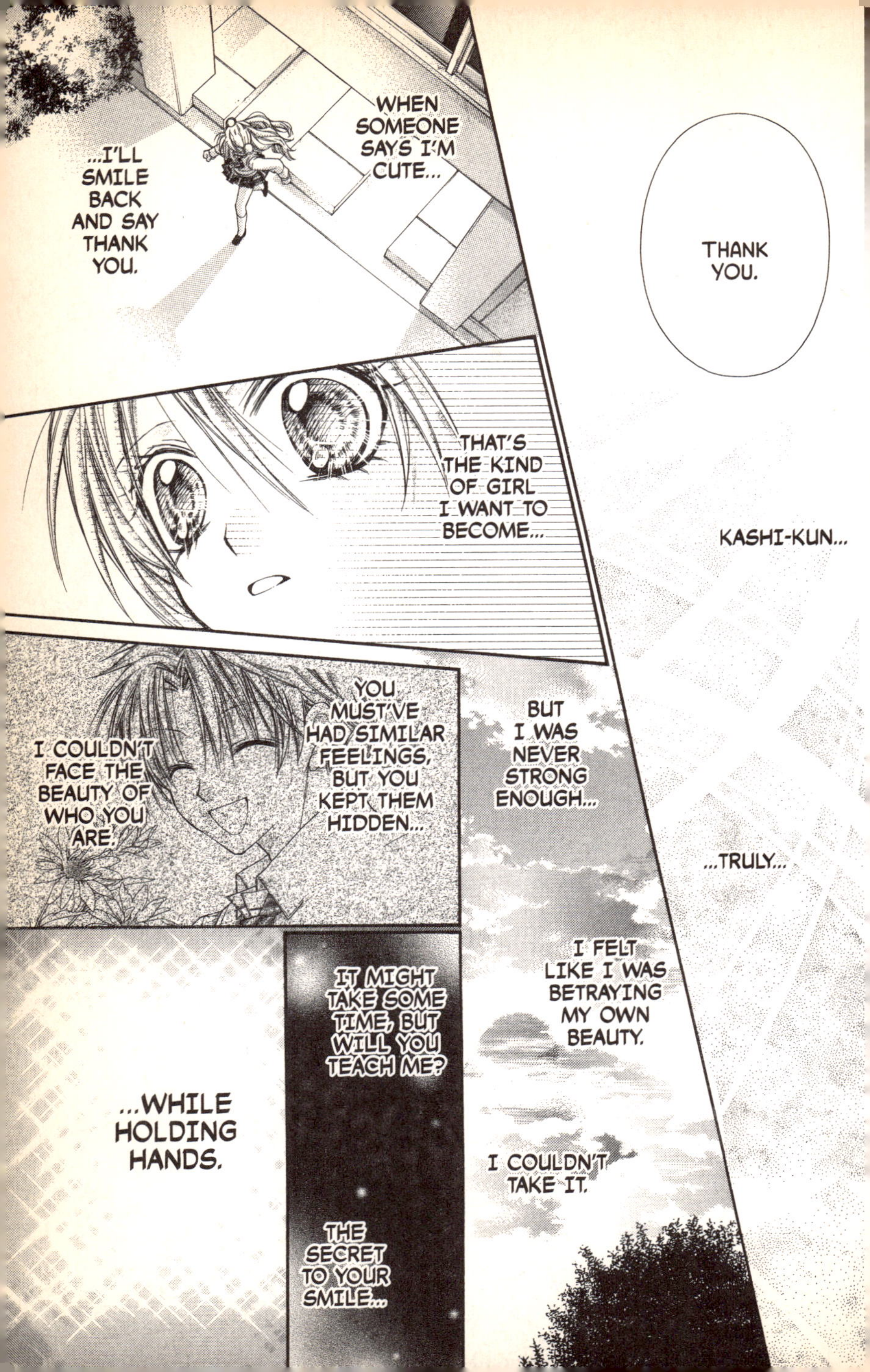
THANK YOU.
KASHI-KUN...
...TRULY...
WHEN SOMEONE SAYS I'M CUTE...
...I'LL SMILE BACK AND SAY THANK YOU.
THAT'S THE KIND OF GIRL I WANT TO BECOME...
BUT I WAS NEVER STRONG ENOUGH...
I FELT LIKE I WAS BETRAYING MY OWN BEAUTY.
I COULDN'T TAKE IT.
YOU MUST'VE HAD SIMILAR FEELINGS, BUT YOU KEPT THEM HIDDEN...
I COULDN'T FACE THE BEAUTY OF WHO YOU ARE.
IT MIGHT TAKE SOME TIME, BUT WILL YOU TEACH ME?
THE SECRET TO YOUR SMILE...
...WHILE HOLDING HANDS.

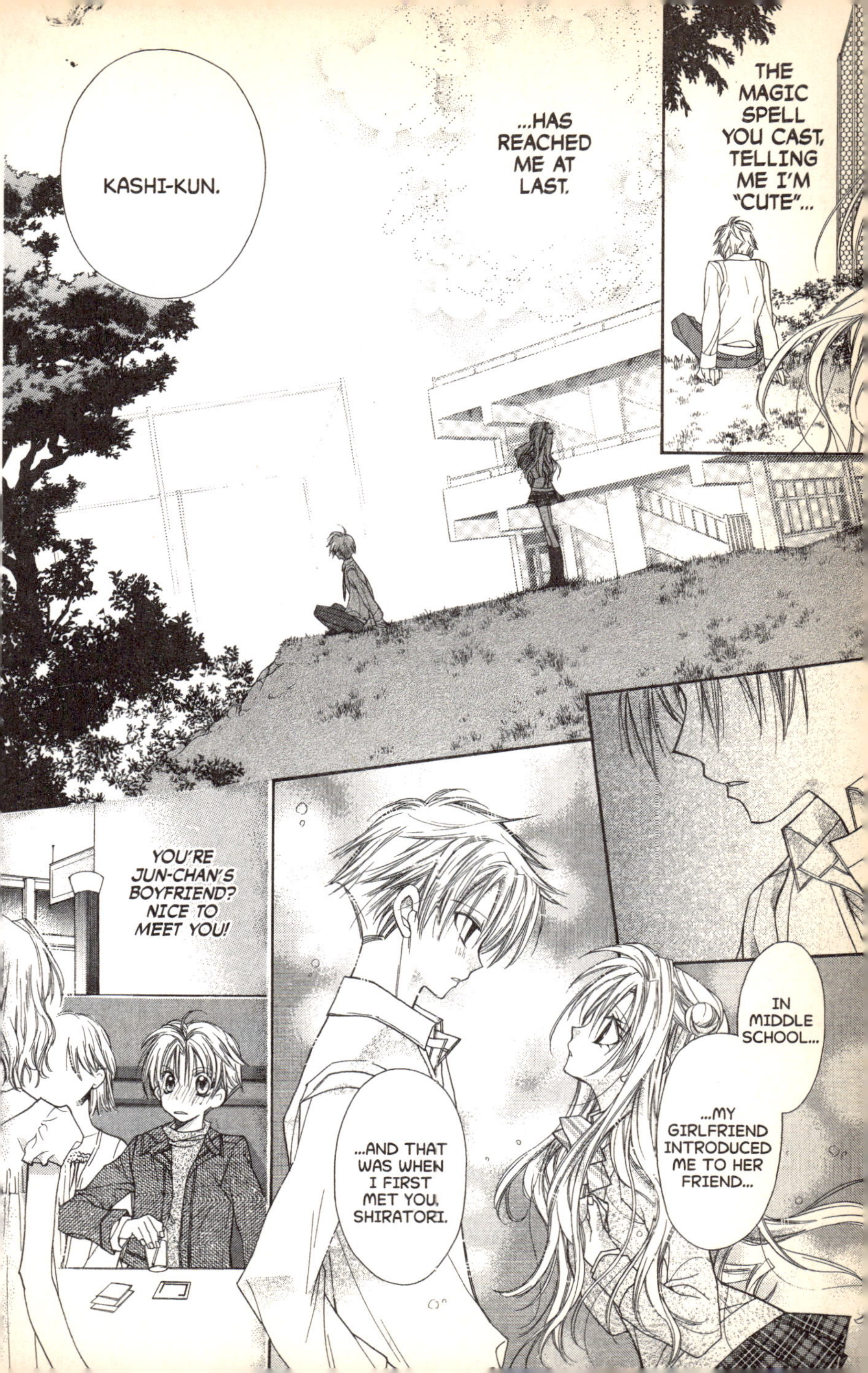
THE MAGIC SPELL YOU CAST, TELLING ME I'M "CUTE"...
...HAS REACHED ME AT LAST.
KASHI-KUN.
IN MIDDLE SCHOOL...
...MY GIRLFRIEND INTRODUCED ME TO HER FRIEND...
...AND THAT WAS WHEN I FIRST MET YOU, SHIRATORI.
YOU'RE JUN-CHAN'S BOYFRIEND? NICE TO MEET YOU!

Y-YOU
YOU'RE CUTE.
THANK YOU!
JUST ONCE MORE...
...I WANTED YOU TO SMILE LIKE THAT.

BLUSH
PBFFT
WH-WHAT?
IT'S NOTHING. I JUST REALIZED...
...I MADE A LONG DETOUR TO GET HERE.
HEY, SEE THIS?
?

IT'S MY NEW LIP BALM.
WHAT DO YOU THINK?
Wh-wh-wh-what?
APPLE
CUTE.
THE NEXT TIME...
...YOU TELL ME YOU LOVE ME...

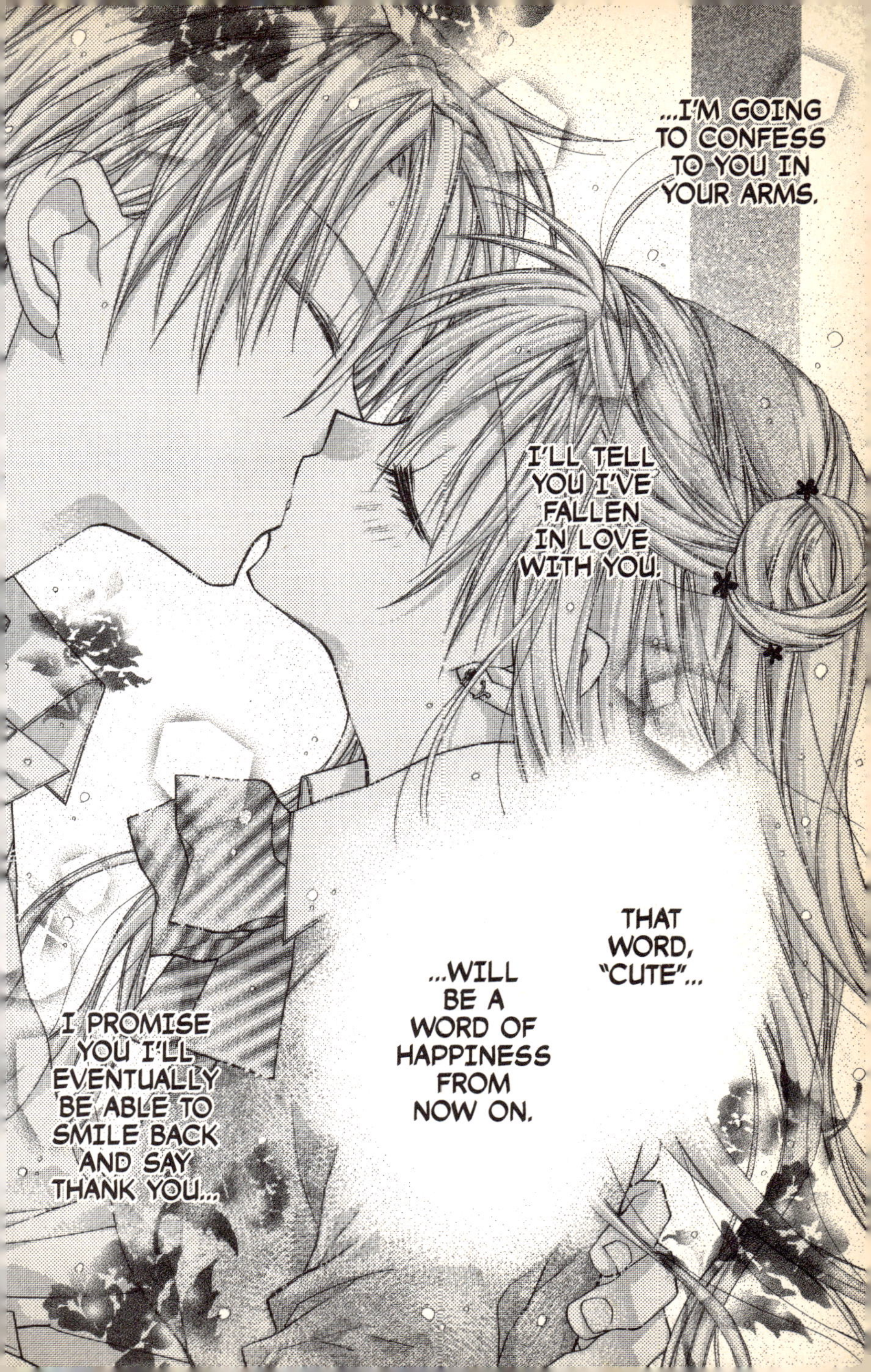
...I'M GOING TO CONFESS TO YOU IN YOUR ARMS.
I'LL TELL YOU I'VE FALLEN IN LOVE WITH YOU.
THAT WORD, "CUTE"...
...WILL BE A WORD OF HAPPINESS FROM NOW ON.
I PROMISE YOU I'LL EVENTUALLY BE ABLE TO SMILE BACK AND SAY THANK YOU...

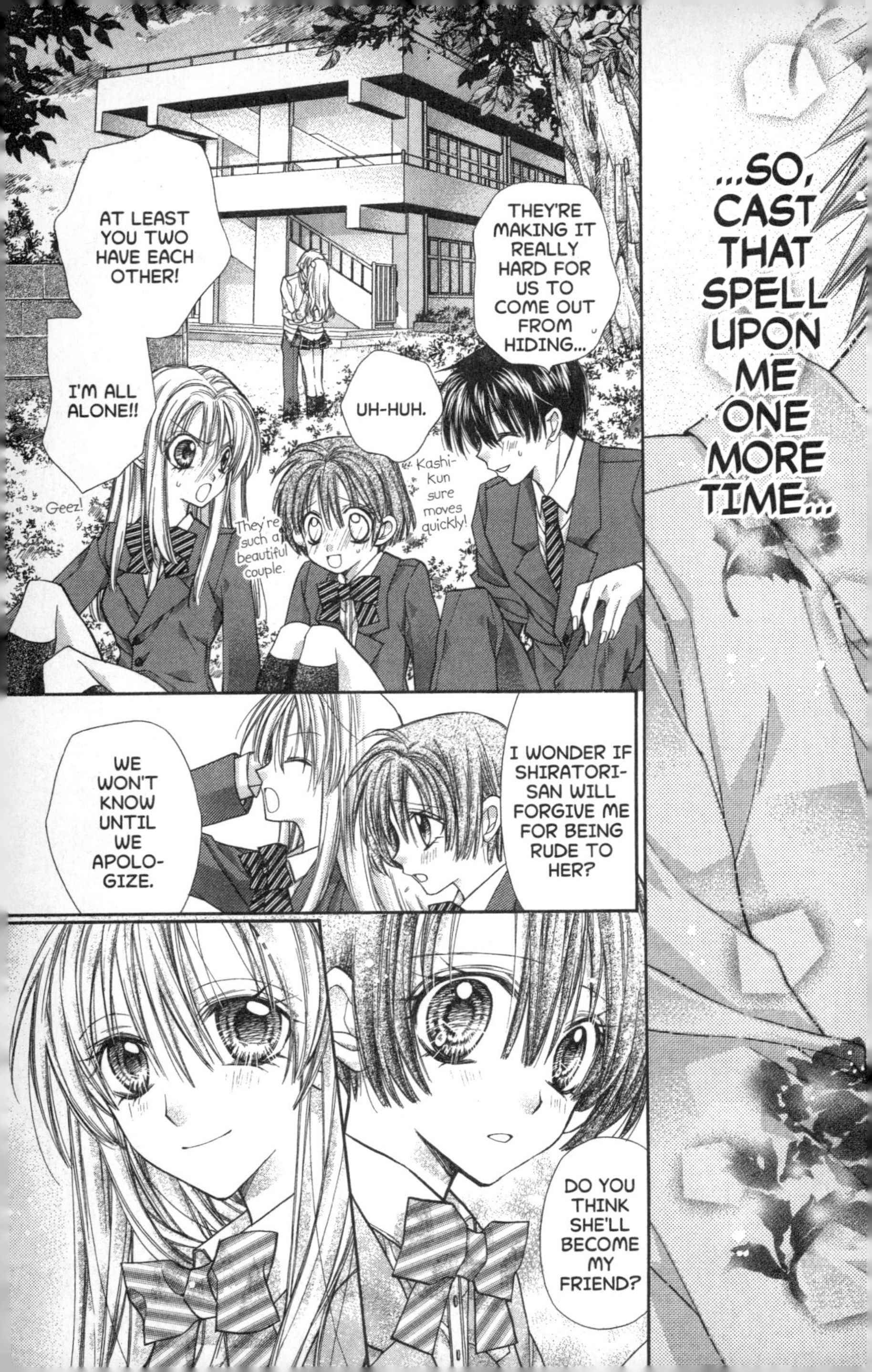
...SO, CAST THAT SPELL UPON ME ONE MORE TIME...
THEY'RE MAKING IT REALLY HARD FOR US TO COME OUT FROM HIDING...
UH-HUH.
Kashi-Kun sure moves quickly!
They're such a beautiful couple.
AT LEAST YOU TWO HAVE EACH OTHER!
I'M ALL ALONE!!
Geez!
I WONDER IF SHIRATORI-SAN WILL FORGIVE ME FOR BEING RUDE TO HER?
WE WON'T KNOW UNTIL WE APOLOGIZE.
DO YOU THINK SHE'LL BECOME MY FRIEND?

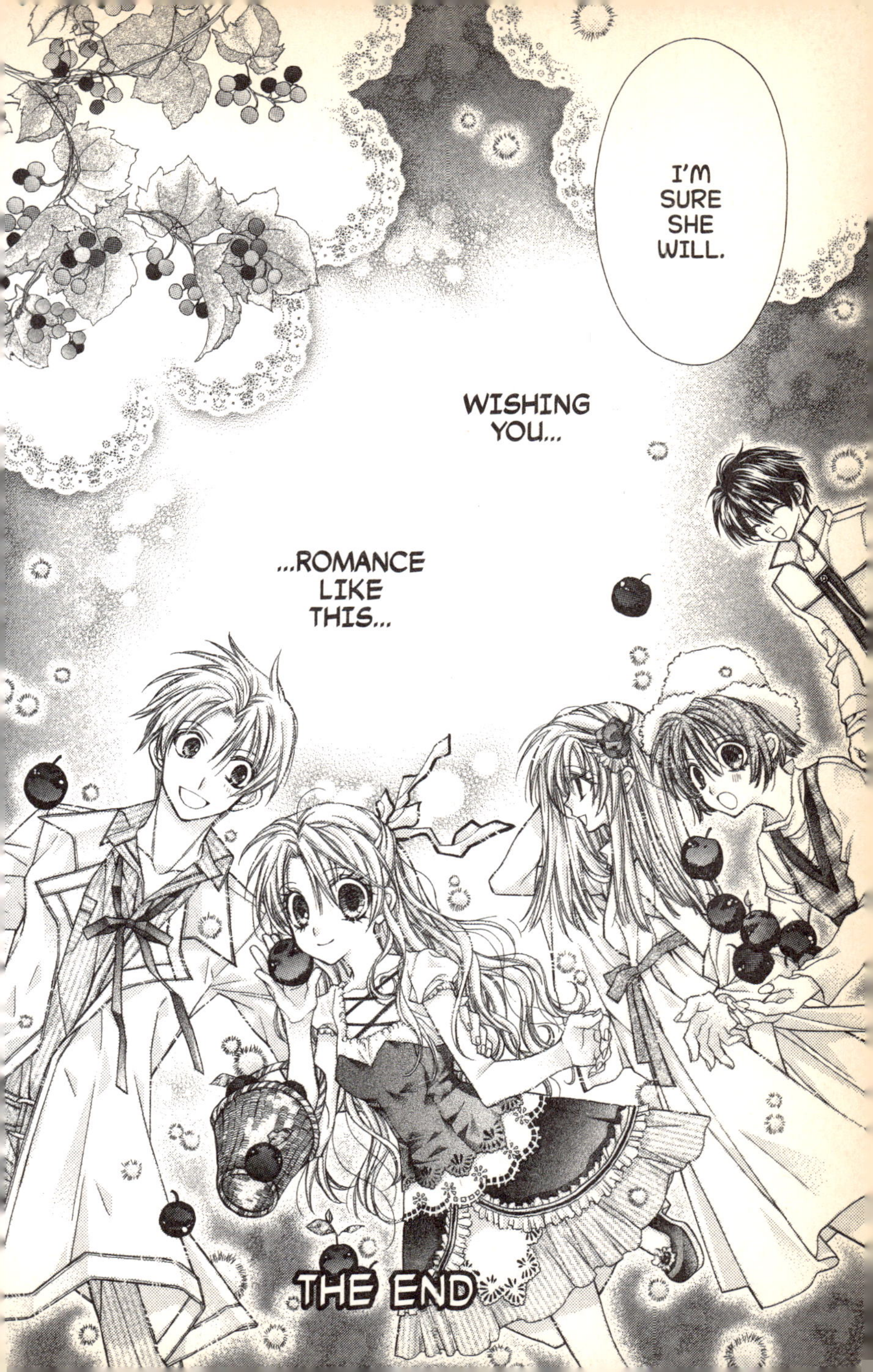
I'M SURE SHE WILL.
WISHING YOU...
...ROMANCE LIKE THIS...
THE END

NOTES ON THE TEXT

PAGE 17:

Fish Scoop
This is a popular Japanese festival game. The full name is *kingyo sukui*, or "goldfish scoop." The aim is to use the scoop to catch a goldfish from the pool without having the scoop break before the fish can be brought up out of the water. The scoops are usually made out of something flimsy like tissue paper.

PAGE 28:

Annoying?
The term here used is *uzai*. It's slang for being irritating or annoying.

PAGE 52:

Name
Name ("ne-mu") is what we would call a storyboard. It's the first rough draft of the manga.

PAGE 54:

Sensei
Sensei is an honorific used to address professionals, such as teachers, doctors, and mangaka.

PAGE 69:

-shi
The honorific *-shi* is like a more formal *-san*. It is used in formal writing and address, and it can refer to either a man or a woman.

PAGE 81:

Haine
In Haine's name, the kanji for *hai* means "ash" and *ne* means "music" or "sound."

PAGE 121:

(>_<)
This is a face mark. It means shock, surprise, or worry.

;
The semicolons on the phone screen are an abbreviation for this: (^^;)
The face mark with a sweat drop is used to show discomfort.

Ojyo-sama
Ojyo-sama means "young miss." Servants would use this term to refer to the young lady of the household.

PAGE 129:

Mirror
Ushio sees herself as being separated from the actual world by her reflection that she sees in the water. This is a *mizu kagami*, or "water mirror."

PAGE 133:

Make mine vanilla with wafers.
Ushio is actually asking for a *monaka*, which is ice cream inside a light wafer. There is also a red-bean filling version of the dessert.

Ushio's chapters have finished, and Haine's chapters have finally begun. I've been longing to draw these chapters, so I'm really giving it everything I've got. There are some stories that pertain to what went on earlier in the story, so this may be a good time to reread the series from volume 1. ☆

—Arina Tanemura

Arina Tanemura was born in Aichi, Japan. She got her start in 1996, publishing *Nibanme no Koi no Katachi* (The Style of the Second Love) in *Ribon Original* magazine. Her early work includes a collection of short stories called *Kanshaku Dama no Yuutsu* (Short-Tempered Melancholic). Two of her titles, *Kamikaze Kaito Jeanne* and *Full Moon*, were made into popular TV series. Tanemura enjoys karaoke and is a huge *Lord of the Rings* fan.

THE GENTLEMEN'S ALLIANCE † vol.8
The Shojo Beat Manga Edition

STORY & ART BY
ARINA TANEMURA

English Translation & Adaptation/Tetsuichiro Miyaki
Touch-up Art & Lettering/George Caltsoudas
Design/Amy Martin
Editor/Nancy Thistlethwaite

Editor in Chief, Books/Alvin Lu
Editor in Chief, Magazines/Marc Weidenbaum
VP, Publishing Licensing/Rika Inouye
VP, Sales & Product Marketing/Gonzalo Ferreyra
VP, Creative/Linda Espinosa
Publisher/Hyoe Narita

THE GENTLEMEN ALLIANCE -CROSS- © 2004 by Arina Tanemura. All rights reserved. First published in Japan in 2004 by SHUEISHA Inc., Tokyo. English translation rights arranged by SHUEISHA Inc. The stories, characters and incidents mentioned in this publication are entirely fictional.

No portion of this book may be reproduced or transmitted in any form or by any means without written permission from the copyright holders.

The rights of the author(s) of the work(s) in this publication to be so identified have been asserted in accordance with the Copyright, Designs and Patents Act 1988. A CIP catalogue record for this book is available from the British Library.

Printed in Canada

Published by VIZ Media, LLC
P.O. Box 77010
San Francisco, CA 94107

Shojo Beat Manga Edition
10 9 8 7 6 5 4 3 2 1
First printing, December 2008

PARENTAL ADVISORY
THE GENTLEMEN'S ALLIANCE † is rated T+ for Older Teen and is recommended for ages 16 and up. This volume contains suggestive themes.
ratings.viz.com

Arina Tanemura Series

The Gentlemen's Alliance †
Haine Otomiya joins Imperial Academy in pursuit of the boy she's loved since she was a child, unaware that he has many secrets of his own.

I•O•N
Chanting the letters of her first name has always brought Ion Tsuburagi good luck—but her good-luck charm is really the result of psychic powers!

Full Moon
Mitsuki Koyama dreams of becoming a pop star, but she is dying of throat cancer. Can she live out a lifetime of dreams in just one year?

Short-Tempered Melancholic
A collection of short stories including Arina Tanemura's debut manga, "In the Style of the Second Love"!

Time Stranger Kyoko
Kyoko Suomi must find 12 holy stones and 12 telepaths to awaken her sister who has been trapped in time since birth.

THE GENTLEMEN ALLIANCE -CROSS- © 2004 by Arina Tanemura/SHUEISHA Inc. I·O·N © 1997 by Arina Tanemura/SHUEISHA Inc. FULLMOON-WO SAGASHITE © 2001 by Arina Tanemura/SHUEISHA Inc. KANSHAKUDAMA NO YUUTSU © 1998 by Arina Tanemura/SHUEISHA Inc. TIME STRANGER KYOKO © 2000 by Arina Tanemura/SHUEISHA Inc.

Short-Tempered Melancholic and Other Stories
by Arina Tanemura

A Collection of Shorts by One of Shojo's Biggest Names

[A] one-volume manga featuring early short stories from the [cre]ator of *Full Moon*, *The Gentlemen's Alliance †*, *I•O•N* and [*Ti]me Stranger Kyoko*.

[Fin]d out what makes Arina Tanemura a fan favorite—buy [Sho]rt-Tempered Melancholic and Other Stories today!

Shojo Beat

On sale at **www.shojobeat.com**
Also available at your local bookstore and comic store.

KANSHAKUDAMA NO YUUTSU © 1996 by Arina Tanemura/SHUEISHA Inc.

RATED T FOR TEEN — ratings.viz.com

VIZ MEDIA — www.viz.com

Turn Back the Clock

In the 30th century, Kyoko Suomi is the princess of Earth—but she wants absolutely nothing to do with the throne! In order to get out of her royal responsibilities, she'll have to travel through time to find her long-lost twin. Will Kyoko locate her missing sister, or will she end up as Earth's reluctant ruler?

Find out in *Time Stranger Kyoko*— manga on sale now!

Time Stranger Kyoko

By Arina Tanemura, creator of *Full Moon*, *The Gentlemen's Alliance†* and *I•O•N*

On sale at:
www.shojobeat.com
Also available at your local bookstore and comic store

TIME STRANGER KYOKO © 2000 by Arina Tanemura/SHUEISHA Inc.

Art book featuring 216 pages of beautiful color images personally selected by Tanemura

Read where Mitsuki's pop dreams began in the manga—all 7 volumes now available

Complete your collection with the anime, now on DVD

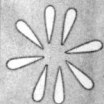

ON-WO SAGASHITE © 2001 by Arina Tanemura/SHUEISHA Inc.
© 2004 by Arina Tanemura/SHUEISHA Inc.
FULL MOON © 2001 Arina Tanemura

www.viz.com

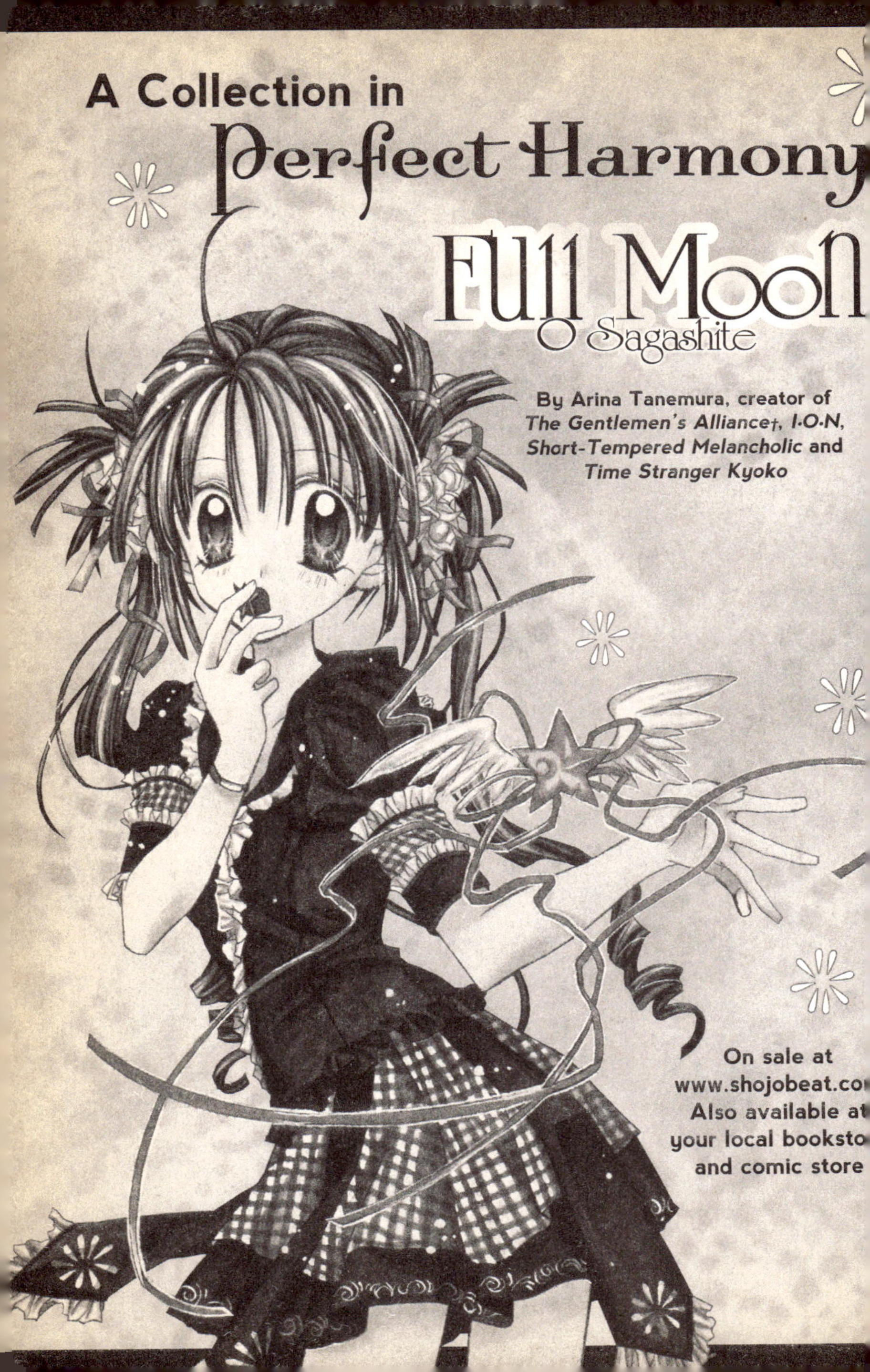
A Collection in
Perfect Harmony
Full Moon
O Sagashite
By Arina Tanemura, creator of
The Gentlemen's Alliance†, I·O·N,
Short-Tempered Melancholic and
Time Stranger Kyoko
On sale at
www.shojobeat.co
Also available at
your local booksto
and comic store

Tell us what you think about Shojo Beat Manga!

Our survey is now available online. Go to:

shojobeat.com/mangasurvey

Help us make our product offerings better!

THE REAL DRAMA BEGINS IN...

FULL MOON WO SAGASHITE © 2001 by Arina Tanemura/SHUEISHA Inc.
Fushigi Yûgi: Genbu Kaiden © 2004 Yuu WATASE/Shogakukan Inc.
Ouran Koko Host Club © Bisco Hatori 2002/HAKUSENSHA, Inc.

Shojo Beat
VAMPIRE KNIGHT
LIVE BEAUTIFUL
Exclusive Story by Superstar Arina Tanemura!
SPECIAL MUSIC ISSUE
JAPAN'S FASHION ICON
OVER 340 PAGES

Save OVER 50% off the cover price!

Shojo Beat
MANGA from the HEART

The Shojo Manga Authority

This monthly magazine is injected with the most **ADDICTIVE** shojo manga stories from Japan. PLUS, unique editorial coverage on the arts, music, culture, fashion, and much more!

☑ **YES!** Please enter my one-year subscription (12 GIANT issues) to **Shojo Beat** at the LOW SUBSCRIPTION RATE of **$34.99!**

Over **300 pages** per issue!

NAME

ADDRESS

CITY   STATE   ZIP

E-MAIL ADDRESS   P7GNC1

☐ MY CHECK IS ENCLOSED (PAYABLE TO *Shojo Beat*)   ☐ BILL ME LATER

CREDIT CARD: ☐ VISA   ☐ MASTERCARD

ACCOUNT #   EXP. DATE

SIGNATURE

CLIP AND MAIL TO → SHOJO BEAT
Subscriptions Service Dept.
P.O. Box 438
Mount Morris, IL 61054-0438

Canada price for 12 issues: $46.99 USD, including GST, HST and QST. US/CAN orders only. Allow 6-8 weeks for delivery. Must be 16 or older to redeem offer By redeeming this offer I represent that I am 16 or older.

Vampire Knight © Matsuri Hino 2004/HAKUSENSHA, Inc. Nana Kitade © Sony Music Entertainment (Japan), Inc.
CRIMSON HERO © 2002 by Mitsuba Takanashi/SHUEISHA Inc.

RATED T+ FOR OLDER TEEN
ratings.viz.com